The New Food Activism

The New Food Activism

OPPOSITION, COOPERATION, AND
COLLECTIVE ACTION

EDITED BY

Alison Hope Alkon and
Julie Guthman

UNIVERSITY OF CALIFORNIA PRESS

University of California Press, one of the most distinguished university presses in the United States, enriches lives around the world by advancing scholarship in the humanities, social sciences, and natural sciences. Its activities are supported by the UC Press Foundation and by philanthropic contributions from individuals and institutions. For more information, visit www.ucpress.edu.

University of California Press
Oakland, California

Library of Congress Cataloging-in-Publication Data

Names: Alkon, Alison Hope, editor. | Guthman, Julie, editor.
Title: The new food activism : opposition, cooperation, and collective action /
    Edited by Alison Hope Alkon and Julie Guthman.
Description: Oakland, California : University of California Press, [2017] |
    Includes bibliographical references and index.
Identifiers: LCCN 2016053880 (print) | LCCN 2016057072 (ebook) |
    ISBN 9780520292130 (cloth : alk. paper) | ISBN 9780520292147 (pbk.) |
    ISBN 9780520965652 (ebook)
Subjects: LCSH: Food security—United States. | Sustainable agriculture—
    Social aspects—United States. | Organic farming—United States. | Food—
    Political aspects. | Food consumption—United States. | Social justice—
    United States.
Classification: LCC TX360.U6 N486 2017 (print) | LCC TX360.U6 (ebook) |
    DDC 338.1/973—dc23
LC record available at https://lccn.loc.gov/2016053880

Manufactured in the United States of America

26 25 24 23 22 21 20 19 18 17
10 9 8 7 6 5 4 3 2 1

CONTENTS

PREFACE

This book is, in many ways, an attempt to address some of the debates and themes we have been writing about for nearly a decade, namely the ways that whiteness and neoliberalism constrain contemporary food politics and hamper the emergence of a multiracial, class-inflected movement that can transform both food systems and broader socio-environmental inequalities. While our previous work has drawn on social theory and ethnographic data to formulate these critiques, this book examines the ways that various food activists confront and move beyond them.

Many times, scholars write only for one another. We are proud to be part of a discourse where this is most certainly not the case. We have had the pleasure of dialoguing about our work with those we've studied, and with those who are doing similar work across the country and around the world. Not only have our critiques been shaped by their perspectives and lived experiences, but we've been pleased to watch as they thoughtfully evaluate and discuss our writings. It's an honor to now be able to write about their efforts to move beyond critiques and debates that, while happening at least in part within academia, are certainly not merely academic.

For that reason, our first and most heartfelt thanks go to those who are doing this work on the ground, both those who are depicted in this book and those who are not. Secondly, we want to acknowledge the scholars with whom we've been discussing and debating these issues. Some are authors of the various chapters in this volume, while others have been our coauthors, conference panelists, students, and reviewers for this and other work on these themes. While we can't name everyone, we want to especially acknowledge Patricia Allen and Rachel Slocum, whose under-acknowledged writings were ahead of their time and helped shape the critique that animates this book. To these multiple and intersecting communities, thank you for helping us to sharpen our insights, to push us beyond easy and obvious answers, and to make us responsive both to those we study and to broader political questions. This book is stronger because of our ongoing dialogues, and we look forward to continuing them into the future.

Further, it's been a pleasure to work with such a dedicated group of authors. Each of you took both our comments and our deadlines to heart and produced work that we think makes a real contribution. We also want to thank our reviewers for offering thoughtful responses that became integral to the manuscript.

Lastly, we'd like to dedicate this book to Cedar and Sierra. The birth of Alison's son Cedar provided the real deadline for manuscript submission while Julie's daughter Sierra was away at college becoming her own kind of antiracist warrior.

ONE

Introduction

Alison Hope Alkon and Julie Guthman

> Making good food fair and affordable cannot be achieved with-
> out affecting the whole system. These are not just food questions;
> they are questions of justice and equality and rights, of enhanc-
> ing rather than restricting democracy, of making a more rational,
> legitimate economy.
>
> MARK BITTMAN

IN A 2014 *NEW YORK TIMES* OP-ED, noted food writer Mark Bittman described having a negative visceral reaction to the word *foodie*. Foodies, he argued, are too often "new-style epicures" who enjoy "watching competitive cooking shows, doing 'anything' to get a table at the trendy restaurant, scour-ing the web for single-estate farro, or devoting oneself to finding the best food truck." If and when these foodies go beyond the pursuit of gastronomic pleasure, they tend to put their energies into consumer support for sustain-able food systems, for example by spending money on organic and local foods, community-supported agriculture, and farmers' markets.

Bittman's column drew on and amplified a critique that scholars writing under the loosely defined label "critical food studies," including the editors and authors featured in this volume, have been making for over a decade. We've argued that many foodies and food activists focus on a politics of con-sumption, and that this has limited even the most sustainability-minded among them to relatively apolitical strategies such as patronizing and creating alternative food businesses (Alkon 2012, Guthman 2011). Moreover, these strategies are accessible largely to those with wealth and white skin, both because a politics of consumption is a "pay to play" approach and because the imaginaries put forward by advocates of the sustainable agriculture movement tend to romanticize the histories of whites, while eliding the contributions of people of color who have labored in past and present agricultural systems (Alkon 2012, Allen et al. 2004, Guthman 2008a, 2008b, Slocum 2007).

Moreover, attempts by foodies and food activists to shift the public's eating habits toward their notion of "good food" have too often been encased in a politics of conversion that attempts to change individuals' eating habits without understanding the multiple circumstances, pressures, and desires that inform food choices (Johnston and Baumann 2010). This approach is particularly troublesome when it is engaged by white, class-privileged actors who target low-income communities and communities of color (Alkon 2012, Guthman 2008c). Even more problematically, such efforts scrutinize individuals' and communities' everyday food choices while taking for granted the harmful practices of food producers and processors, including the spreading of toxic chemicals and abysmal wages and working conditions (Guthman 2011).

This, however, is beginning to shift. Increasingly, food activists such as those described in this book are looking beyond their plates and taking aim at a variety of injustices throughout the food system. Some, like those profiled by Jill Lindsey Harrison in chapter 2, are members of front-line communities working to restrict the toxic chemicals and pesticides that poison their bodies, families, and communities. Others, like the Dudley Street Neighborhood Initiative described by Penn Loh and Julian Agyeman in chapter 11, are the product of alliances between activists, policymakers, and planners and work to ensure that the benefits of urban agriculture can be enjoyed by low-income communities. By describing and analyzing the work of activists like these, we hope to inspire foodies and sustainable agriculture advocates to develop more capacious notions of equity and justice, and to build collaborations that are both strategic and political in their efforts to effect changes in the food system and beyond.

When supporters of sustainable agriculture pursue this path, they encounter long-standing struggles for equity. These struggles are often led by farm and other food workers, by marginalized farmers, and by communities lacking geographic and economic access to healthy food. Though at times they make use of the foodies' politics of consumption, these struggles often seek to hold the state accountable for the regulation of industrial food in the interest of health and social justice or to push corporations and other businesses to cease harmful practices. These struggles tend to be rooted in communities that experience the toxic effects of industrial agriculture, though more privileged groups also play significant roles. What is common to all of them is that they work to change not only the way we eat, but the ways we live, work, and govern ourselves.

The goal of this book is to inspire food scholars, students, and activists to engage with projects and campaigns that move beyond the provision of market-based alternatives and toward a fight for just and sustainable food. In these pages, readers will meet farmers, food service workers, and, yes, foodies, all engaged in campaigns and projects that seek to limit the power of the industrial food system to harm bodies, senses of identity, and everyday lives. As the various chapters in this volume will demonstrate, by working with and within these struggles, activists have begun to forge alliances that have the potential to affect the whole food system, from the seed to the restaurant worker who brings food to the table.

CHALLENGING INDUSTRIAL FOOD

It is no secret that corporate involvement in food production and consumption has resulted in an array of problems. Environmentally, agribusiness companies have convinced farmers to use an increasing array of chemical pesticides, herbicides, and fertilizers, which, over the long term, deplete the soil (requiring even more the next year) and pollute waterways as well as the bodies of the workers and nearby communities (Altieri 2000, Harrison 2011). Economically, corporate processors and distributors have the power to set standards and prices that farmers must accept in order to sell their products, and these prices are often so low as to leave farmers in tremendous debt and, eventually, force them out of business. In the case of fruit and vegetable farmers, those who remain often operate on narrow margins, surviving off what agricultural economists call the "immigrant subsidy"—that is, the ability to pay undocumented migrant workers far less than citizens receive (and far less than the value of their work), let alone a living wage (Taylor and Martin 1997). Large-scale commodity farmers, on the other hand, rely more on mechanization than exploited labor. To stay in business, the remaining farms must eschew biodiversity, instead growing genetically identical monocultures of single crops. This farming strategy guarantees that they remain dependent on chemical pesticides, fertilizers, and the like, as it is only with these kinds of inputs that farms can, to paraphrase former Secretary of Agriculture Earl Butts, "get big" rather than "get out." From the standpoint of consumers, activists point to the lack of fresh produce in low-income areas, the high price of fresh foods compared to processed ones, and the health consequences associated with diets high in salt, sugar, and fat as reasons why this industrial, corporate food system is not just unethical but dangerous. Exposés uncovering how food is grown and processed have become commonplace in newspapers, magazines, and TV news, ranging from massive coverage of a meat product called "pink slime" to Michael Moss's (2014) whistle-blowing description of the ways that processed foods are designed to ensnare the taste buds of young users with massive amounts of salt, sugar, and fat.

Toward a Sustainable Food System

Those critical of these circumstances have done more than just document them. Together they have worked to create alternatives to the industrial agriculture system that can provide foods produced in more ecologically friendly ways and ensure more stable livelihoods for farmers. Agroecological farming, of course, predates the invention of chemical inputs and has been employed by poor and peasant farmers worldwide. Still, in the United States, the 1960s countercultural movement and the 1970s birth of the environmental movement created a renewed interest, especially among white, young urbanites, in these techniques as a means for human and environmental health (Belasco 1993). Organic production and local and regional sales became the cornerstones of the alternative foods movement, and the movement began to catch on.

Organic foods are now commonplace at health food stores, restaurants, and even supermarkets across the country, at least in affluent areas. Retail sales of organic products in the United States were only $3.6 billion in 1997 but reached $21.1 billion in 2008, and organic acreage more than doubled between 1997 and 2005 (Dimitri and Oberholtzer 2009). Earthbound Farms, a large producer of organic salad mix and other packaged produce, boasted a revenue of roughly $460 million in 2012 (Oran and Kim 2013). As of 1997, natural food stores were the primary distributor of organic foods, but by 2008 nearly half of this food was purchased in chain supermarkets (Dimitri and Oberholtzer 2009). Big-box stores like Walmart and Safeway, which the counterculture once labeled as inherently contrary to organic philosophies, are now major retailers of organic products. Local, decentralized distribution has grown as well. For example, the number of farmers' markets in the United States quadrupled from less than two thousand in 1994 to more than eight thousand in 2013 (U.S. Department of Agriculture 2013).

But All Is Not Well . . .

Despite the undeniable accomplishments of many producing and advocating for local organic food, and the astounding economic success of the organic food industry, the movement for environmentally sustainable and socially just food systems has quite a ways to go. While sales of organic and local food are on the rise, organic farms were still less than 1 percent of U.S. farm acreage in 2008, and organic sales slowed markedly during the economic recession of 2008–09 (Guthman 2014). Nor has the rise in organics diminished the amount of pesticides used or the sales of highly processed foods. Indeed, the production and sale of organic and local foods does not challenge the corporate food system but merely creates an alternative to it, an alternative that industrial food increasingly incorporates into its supply chains (Guthman 2014, 2011). The farms, factories, and restaurants that produce, package, and serve these foods are often as likely as conventional food purveyors to treat workers poorly, oppose unionization, and fight against progressive legislation (Brown and Getz 2008, Gray 2014, Guthman 2014, Jayaraman 2013).

In an attempt to strengthen food activism, scholars and activists have offered two important and generative critiques of alternative food systems. The first focuses on the importance of food justice—the ways that race, class, gender, and other forms of inequality affect both conventional and alternative food systems. The authors in this volume, as well as many others, have called for a food system that is not only ecologically sustainable, but also responds to racial and economic disparities, and for a food movement that highlights the contributions that low-income communities and communities of color have made to agriculture (Alkon and Agyeman 2011). In this way, food becomes a tool toward broader social justice and antiracist organizing.

The second critique revolves around the complex concept of neoliberalism. Neoliberalism is, in the first instance, a political economic philosophy that asserts that human well-being can best be achieved if the so-called "free" market is allowed to function with little or no intervention from the state (Harvey 2005, 2). In practice, much of what goes under the name of "letting markets work" entails developing new regulatory mechanisms and bending the rules so as to shore up corporate profitability (Harvey 2010, Mann 2013). In relation to food activism, prominent social scientists have argued that current modes of food activism may explicitly oppose what market orthodoxy has wrought but have nevertheless tended to embrace neoliberal forms of governance, including voluntary regulation and the reliance on markets rather than the state to pursue change (Allen 2008, Allen et al. 2003, Brown and Getz 2008, Guthman 2008c, Harrison 2008). These food justice and neoliberalism critiques are interrelated, because strategies pursued through the market, such as starting a business or buying particular kinds of goods, are by definition less accessible to low-income people, notwithstanding the often economically tenuous efforts within food activism to encourage food entrepreneurialism among low-income people (Alkon 2012, Allen 1999, Guthman 2008b).

In response to both of these lines of inquiry, scholars have called for food activists to intensify their critique of production agriculture, particularly around issues of labor, as well as their attention to inequalities throughout the food system (Alkon and Agyeman 2011, Allen 2008, Brown and Getz 2008, Guthman 2011, 2008c, Harrison 2011, 2008, Levkoe 2011). The remainder of this introduction will lay out these critiques in order to frame the struggles of the activists profiled in this volume, who are both attending to food justice and pushing back against neoliberalism. Their work exists at a cultural moment in which neoliberalism is a dominant feature of our political economy and ecology, and rather than ignore or work around market-based approaches, the activists depicted in this book often make use of them in creative and interesting ways. Thus, these strategies hold the potential to become harbingers of a new shift in food and agricultural movements, one that uses market-based strategies to build toward collective action on inequalities, labor, sustainability, and social justice. They have much to teach, not only to activists, but also to the scholars who have been critical of neoliberal food activism.

THE FOOD JUSTICE CRITIQUE

Perhaps the most thorough definition of *food justice* comes from Rasheed Hislop (2014, 19), who describes it as "the struggle against racism, exploitation, and oppression taking place within the food system that addresses inequality's root causes both within and beyond the food chain." The term was commonly used among activists prior to any scholarly writing on it, particularly by grassroots groups consisting of and working in communities of color to develop sustainable local food systems. This concept, however, has been broadened and refined through engagement and debate among activists and within the academic literature, which has drawn upon critical race theory to better understand how and to what effect exploitation in the food system has taken and continues to take place. Although the goals of this scholarship are transnational, to date it has focused mainly on U.S.-based projects and sectors and has examined the effects of specific local, state, and national policies while the related concept of *food sovereignty* is more often associated with the Global South (for an overview, see La Vía Campesina 2007, Wittman et al. 2010).

In some ways, food justice activism grows out of the environmental justice movement through which low-income communities and communities of color documented their disproportionate proximity to environmental toxins and argued that access to a safe, healthy, and clean environment was an issue of racial and economic justice (Bullard 1990, Gottlieb 2001, Schlosberg 2007, Taylor 1998). Later activists added that marginalized communities were not only more likely to be exposed to environmental bads, but also less likely to have access to environmental benefits such as neighborhood green spaces and healthy food (Agyeman 2005, Park and Pellow 2011, Pellow and Brulle 2005). As it gained momentum, those focused on creating a food system that was both environmentally sustainable and socially equitable came to call their movement *food justice* (Alkon 2012, Gottlieb and Joshi 2010). In the critical tensions between food justice activists and the broader food movement, this movement mirrors its environmental-justice predecessor and highlights the polyvocality of approaches to food and environmental issues.

Food justice is a necessary corrective to a food activism that largely ignored the needs and desires of low-income consumers, producers, and workers. In the 1990s, activists working under the banner of community food security began to rectify this by combining economic support for local farmers with increased access to their products among low-income residents (Allen 2004, Gottlieb and Fisher 1996, Winne 2008). In practice, however, support for farmers, often in the form of demands for premium prices, tended to trump consumer needs (Allen 2004, Guthman et al. 2006). Moreover, the Community Food Security Coalition, the primary organization advocating this goal, was predominantly composed of privileged white activists who, despite a general desire to "do good," were often unwilling to confront issues of racism both within their organization and in the food system at large (Bradley and Herrera 2016, Slocum 2007). Food justice, with its focus on food access in low-income communities of color, arose in response to both the whiteness of community food security and its privileging of producers' needs.

Often working closely with activists, scholars have highlighted many of the barriers that make it more difficult for those with low incomes and people of color to access local and organic food as both producers and consumers. For example, academic work has illustrated the processes whereby farmers of color have been disenfranchised, ranging from discrimination by the U.S. Department of Agriculture to forced relocation to immigration laws that bar land ownership by particular ethnic groups, all of which have made it difficult for communities of color to produce food for themselves (Gilbert et al. 2002, Minkoff-Zern et al. 2011, Norgaard et al. 2011). Despite these obstacles, agriculture has remained a proud tradition in many communities of color, as highlighted through projects like Natasha Bowens's (2015) *The Color of Food,* a photo documentary book and interactive website created to "amplify, preserve and celebrate the stories of Black, Latino, Asian and Indigenous farmers and food activists working to revolutionize the food system in our communities." But perhaps the harshest struggles have been those of farmworkers, who are among the lowest-paid workers in the United States and, ironically, often suffer from hunger and diet-related diseases (Brown and Getz 2011, Gray 2014, Holmes 2013). And yet, as we will see in chapter 7, farmworkers are at the forefront of efforts to create a broader and more confrontational food politics.

Marginalized communities also face difficulties in purchasing local, organic, and fresh foods, and academic researchers have measured this disparity and chronicled efforts to address it (Beaulac et al. 2009). These foods tend to be more expensive than conventional alternatives, especially with regard to canned and packaged items. It is, of course, quite difficult for low-income people to afford these foods, particularly in the context of escalating housing and health-care costs (Alkon et al. 2013, Lea and Worsley 2005). The sustainable agriculture movement has largely privileged the economic needs of producers—small organic farmers—and has therefore argued that the price of their goods should be high. This helps ensure stable livelihoods for sustainable farmers, but it is contrary to the needs of low-income people (Allen 2008, 2004, 1999, Guthman et al. 2006).

A second barrier to marginalized communities' lack of consumption of fresh food is the relative lack of available produce—let alone locally grown and organic options—in low-income communities and communities of color (Kato 2013, Kato et al. 2014, Morland et al. 2002, Wrigley et al. 2002). These areas are often referred to as "food deserts," though activists are critical that the desert imagery naturalizes the political and economic processes that create them. Moreover, too much emphasis on the presence or absence of supermarkets results in the offering of incentives to chain supermarkets rather than addressing root causes such as racism and poverty (Holt-Giménez and Shattuck 2011, Short et al. 2007). Nonetheless, there is a fair amount of agreement that the lack of available fresh produce is one obstacle to its consumption. This lack of availability is the result of long-standing processes of disinvestment in communities of color, including redlining and urban renewal (McClintock 2011, Meyer forthcoming). As we will see with the food hubs depicted in chapter 9, in low-income communities and communities of color, a space to procure high-quality food can become a way to push back against these long-standing processes (see also Bradley and Galt 2013, Cohen and Reynolds 2016, White 2010).

A third barrier can be found in the language of the sustainable agriculture movement itself. Scholars have argued that farmers' markets and other spaces where sustainable agriculture is practiced are culturally coded as white, not only because they are primarily and disproportionately frequented by whites, but because of the discourses that circulate through them (Alkon and McCullen 2010, Guthman 2008a, Slocum 2007, 2006). For example, Guthman (2008b, 394) argues that phrases common to the sustainable agriculture movement, such as "getting your hands dirty in the soil" and "looking the farmer in the eye," all point to "an agrarian past that is far more easily romanticized by whites than others." Given the disenfranchisement of so many African American, Native American, Latino/a, and Asian American farmers (Romm 2001), Guthman suggests that it is likely these phrases do not resonate with communities of color in the ways intended by their primarily white speakers. This cultural barrier can suggest to low-income communities and communities of color that sustainable agriculture is not for them, especially when combined with the lack of available organic and local produce in their neighborhoods (Alkon 2012). Activist chefs and writers such as Bryant Terry (2009), Breeze Harper (2010), and Luz Calvo and Catriona Esquibel (2015) have responded by attempting to recast sustainable food systems in ways they feel are more culturally resonant.

As a whole, food justice scholarship contributes to a vibrant debate among food activists and other movement participants about how sustainable agriculture should best be pursued. Some argue that local and sustainable food systems are inherently more just, and more accessible and democratic, than global agribusiness (Fairfax et al. 2012). Others have focused on the need to overcome the barriers faced by low-income communities and communities of color. Scholars have profiled organizations that create farmers' markets, community-supported-agriculture programs, and community gardens in these neighborhoods and have worked to make this food more affordable through subsidies, work exchanges, and a variety of other strategies (Broad 2016, Gottlieb and Joshi 2010). Food banks and other emergency food projects have moved toward offering local and organic food, sometimes creating partnerships with local farmers or nonprofit organizations to do so (Friedman 2007, Kato 2013). Other activists have planned conferences and events to discuss the ways that race and racism are produced and reproduced in both conventional and sustainable food systems, and they have worked to create local food systems that are led by people of color and that function as a form of resistance to racism (Alkon and Agyeman 2011, Cohen and Reynolds 2016, Morales 2011, Sbicca 2012). For example, the Black Land and Liberation Initiative, launched just as this book was going into publication, will train young people in political education in Black[1] liberation, land reform, and ecology as well as agroecological skills and direct action.

More reformist visions of food justice, such as those aiming to ameliorate food deserts and health disparities, have seen support from major foundations such as Kellogg and Robert Wood Johnson, and policymakers in various cities have adjusted zoning ordinances in order to encourage new stores, though white-led organizations continue to receive more funding than those led by people of color (Cohen and Reynolds 2016). There are now thousands of nonprofit organizations and activists across the country working toward "food justice," and many of them are in direct conversation with scholars who document and analyze their work.

THE NEOLIBERALISM CRITIQUE

Neoliberalism is most widely known as the principle behind free trade and austerity. Some of its most important components include deregulation (the removal of laws restricting the ways that businesses can function, such as environmental or occupational health and safety requirements), trade liberalization (the removal of protectionist tariffs designed to support domestic businesses), and the privatization of state enterprises and public services (Harvey 2005, Peck and Tickell 2002). Each of these practices is designed to ensure business profitability, with the expectation that any social benefits will somehow trickle down. The term *neoliberalism* is often associated with the World Bank and the International Monetary Fund (IMF), which have spent decades encouraging the free flow of capital and pressuring governments to eliminate taxes and tariffs and remove supports for domestic farmers, workers, and those in need of assistance.

Neoliberal approaches to food and public health are generally framed within a "corporate-driven food enterprise discourse," rooted in the idea that free-market solutions are superior to those traditionally found in the public sector and civil society (Holt-Giménez and Shattuck 2011, 119). Food crises such as low-income communities' difficulties accessing fresh produce thus provide an opportunity for increased investment from corporations and/or philanthropists. In the United States, this approach has given rise to incentives encouraging corporate supermarkets like Walmart to establish locations in so-called food deserts (ibid.).

While food activists' emphasis on local and ecologically sustainable production is quite a departure from solutions reliant on corporate agribusiness, scholars have argued that much of contemporary food and agricultural activism is often quite removed from a politics that names and addresses other existing neoliberalizations in the food system. To the contrary, in their focus on creating alternatives—farmers' markets, community-supported agriculture, urban farms, and the like—rather than contesting state and corporate power, many food organizations may produce and reproduce neoliberal forms and spaces of governance (Guthman 2008c).

Social movement scholars have noted that this is to be expected. Cox and Nilsen (2014) write that "significant elements of almost all movements in the neoliberal period have been constrained within logics of identity politics, branding, and the politics of opinion, which fit well with the wider world of neoliberalism. It would be strange if matters had been otherwise." For example, efforts by women and communities of color to highlight economic success stories from their communities, and to create additional ones, can be seen as neoliberal in that they uphold individual wealth as an indicator, if not a method, of social change. The United Nations Collaborative Programme on Reducing Emissions from Deforestation and Development attempts to increase the carbon stored in forests by assigning it economic value as a means to incentivize sustainable development and replanting. And the fight against breast cancer has become a commercial enterprise in and of itself, as pink products become both symbol and strategy toward combatting the disease.

Additionally, though it is not a social movement per se, the rise in social enterprise and social entrepreneurship evidences the degree to which market solutions to social problems have become normalized. It is worth noting, though, that substantial critiques of these strategies have come from more radical feminists, antiracist activists, environmentalists, and scholars, much in the same way that this volume seeks to address neoliberal tendencies in food movements. The central premise of this book is that a more vibrant, diverse food activism depends on understanding the ways that neoliberalism constrains political possibilities, and that this theoretical undertaking can help create space for other forms of food politics to develop.

Neoliberalism and Food Movements

Neoliberalism is, first and foremost, an argument for the primacy of the so-called free market, unconstrained by government intervention. Even social goods, the thinking goes, can best be achieved when informed consumers are willing to pay for them. When food activists argue that the best way to create a sustainable food system is to become a producer or consumer of local and organic food, they are working within this neoliberal worldview. Indeed, food activism has become so predominantly market-based that Michael Pollan (2006) refers to it as a "market-as-movement," in which supporters "vote with our forks" for the kind of food system we want to see. While Pollan believes this to be a positive development, this ideal elides and eclipses long-standing social-movement strategies pursuing state-mandated protections for labor, the environment, and the poor, leaving individual entrepreneurialism and consumer choice as the primary pathways to social change (Lavin 2009). Activists encourage one another to build and support alternative food businesses, and they believe that change will come through shifting market demand (Alkon 2012, Allen et al. 2003, Guthman 2011). Even the few prescient food activists who were raising issues of worker justice as early as the mid-2000s pursued their goals through third-party labeling certification, encouraging consumers to choose products based on this standard as well (Brown and Getz 2008). These strategies articulate with neoliberalism's claim that state intervention in markets should be minimized in order to allow the latter to allocate goods and services.

Another way that food activists reproduce neoliberalism is through what Peck and Tickell (2002) call "roll-out neoliberalism." In their widely cited article, these scholars noted that neoliberalism consisted of two phases: a rolling back of state provisioning, including the social safety net and some regulatory functions, and then a rolling out of non-governmental organizations (NGOs) and other third-sector actors attempting to take the state's place, usually with significantly less funding and a reliance on volunteerism (see also Agyeman and McEntee 2014, Milligan et al. 2008, Pudup 2008, Wolch 1990). In terms of food activism, one way in which roll-out neoliberalism takes place is the development of nonbinding forms of regulation in which farmers or other employers agree to abide by a set of standards, best practices, or other codes of conduct (Brown and Getz 2008, Guthman 2008c, 2008d). The limitations of this approach are most evident when these standards ought to be legally binding, or already are so but not enforced: for example, paying minimum wage, not working in heat, supplying protective equipment for pesticide use (Besky and Brown 2015, Gray 2014). Closely related and even overlapping are regulatory mechanisms in which consumers can choose foods produced with higher standards (e.g, fair trade, organics). Here, voting with your fork is significant not only because it is a market-based mechanism, but because it devolves regulatory responsibility from publicly accountable experts to consumers who can decide for themselves whether certain practices should be condoned or condemned (Guthman 2003, 2007).

Roll-out neoliberalism is also seen in the increasing array of community groups that have cropped up in attempts to fill the holes in services left by a shrinking state (Guthman 2008c). For instance, food justice organizations have taken responsibility for the provisioning of food in low-income communities and communities of color, inadvertently helping justify the dismantling of food assistance programs. While these groups have often effectively served their communities, when they trumpet their abilities to do so they implicitly argue that it is their role, and not the state's, to provide such services. It is to this dynamic that author and social critic Arundhati Roy (2004) refers when she writes, "It's almost as though the greater the devastation caused by neoliberalism, the greater the outbreak of NGOs."

Not only do food activists attempt to do the work abandoned by the neoliberal state, but, in their efforts to secure adherents and funding, they trumpet their own abilities to do it better. For example, supporters of sustainable agriculture highlight the federal government's inability to protect the public and the environment from pesticides, toxic-though-legal ingredients, and even contamination. They argue that the best and indeed the only way to protect oneself and one's family is through the purchase of organic food from local farmers one can trust (Szasz 2007). Similarly, food justice advocates call attention to the decades of institutionally racist development patterns that ensured that urban Black neighborhoods would not prosper (McClintock 2011). But rather than seeking government investment in these areas, they argue that local residents and supporters can create green economic development through farmers' markets, health food stores, and urban farms. These examples suggest that everyday people can work together to solve social problems through the buying and selling of goods. While this certainly can be empowering, the lack of a role for government policy, and its replacement with NGOs and markets, helps relieve the state of its responsibility to provide environmental protection and a social safety net, a responsibility that is particularly important in light of the state's role in pursuing or permitting the destruction of communities and environments in the first place. In contrast to the market-based strategies most commonly advocated by food justice activists, the examples provided in part 1 of this volume depict activists attempting to hold the state accountable for the provision of environmental and human health through the regulation of pesticides and genetically modified organisms.

In addition to their overt political work, social movements help shape subjectivities—senses of proper selfhood and citizenship—whether explicitly in trainings or implicitly through modeling particular languages and behaviors. Many food activists unreflexively espouse and perpetuate ideas compatible with neoliberal notions of good citizenship through their emphases on self-responsibility, individualism, and entrepreneurialism (Bondi and Laurie 2005, Dean 1999, Larner and Craig 2005, Rose 1999). For example, many U.S. food justice organizations focus on alleviating food insecurity through the development of support for local food entrepreneurs, such as chef-training programs and small-business incubators. Such an approach, however, while perhaps generative of individual success, concedes decreasing political support for entitlement programs, designed in part to make the food-insecure independent of the charity of others (Allen 1999). Moreover, they neglect that small businesses are competitive and often fail, making them a poor substitute for direct assistance.

Many food organizations also emphasize citizen empowerment in a more generic sense, often in the form of efforts to instill particular values and ways of being. For instance, farm-to-school programs are promoted with the idea of giving children the ability to make right choices, to improve standardized test scores, and to conform to normative body sizes (Allen and Guthman 2006). Garden-oriented projects (in prisons, in schools, and among "at-risk" populations) are viewed as mechanisms to produce "empowered," self-sufficient subjects and encourage "citizenship" more broadly (Pudup 2008). While community empowerment is, of course, beneficial in many ways, it also reinforces the notion that individuals and community groups are responsible for addressing problems that were not of their own making. Moreover, in focusing on food and nutritional education—and obesity prevention in particular—many food justice organizations participate in the reconfiguring of health care as an individual rather than a public responsibility and reinforce ideas about normative body sizes (Guthman 2014, 2011).

Finally, in treating the consumption of local and organic food as somewhat of a cure-all, these movements can be depoliticizing. Food justice organizations often proclaim food as an organizing tool to address institutional racism, environmental injustices, and economic inequalities, though in practice there seems to be more emphasis on food than on organizing (Guthman 2011). Indeed, social movement logics become imbued into commodities as these struggles become frames to foster the buying and selling of local and organic foods (Alkon 2012). Together, all these tendencies constrain what Guthman (2008a) refers to as the "politics of the possible," or our collective imaginaries of what kinds of social changes can be brought about and through what means. In contrast, the projects described in this volume are more politicized, strategic, and confrontational. For example, the pesticide reform activists profiled in chapter 2 make demands that the state protect workers' bodies, wages, and working conditions, while the food workers' organizations described in chapter 6 embarrass employers into changing their practices. In addition, the cooperative markets in chapters 8 and 9 and the urban farms in chapters 11 and 12 challenge neoliberal notions of individualism and private ownership. As a whole, the activists we have profiled focus less on training people to be entrepreneurial or more informed consumers and instead work collectively for good jobs, healthy workplaces, affordable healthy food, land, and collective ownership of the means of production. By highlighting examples of politicized struggles for more sustainable and equitable food systems, this volume aims to expand the possibilities of food activism.

Critiques and Counter-Critiques

Within scholarly circles, some have objected to the use of *neoliberalism* to describe both the problems and the solutions that food activists attempt.

One counter-critique is primarily theoretical, arguing that if neoliberalism is simultaneously seen as a political economic project, a mode of citizenship, IMF-imposed austerity, a philosophy, and an era, then the term has become so loose as to mean both everything and nothing, much like what happened to *globalization* (Castree 2008, Weller and O'Neill 2014). Even in championing the continued use of the term, Brenner et al. (2010, 184) write that *neoliberalism* has become "a rascal concept—promiscuously pervasive, yet inconsistently defined, empirically imprecise and frequently contested." While it is too large and tangential a debate to take up here, we will simply note that in writing about food politics, we often see the conflation of neoliberalism with capitalism more generally, as anything that involves markets, consumer choice, or profit making is dismissed (or defended) as neoliberal. We believe that the framing of neoliberalism offered above, as well as in the chapters that follow, is more precise and demonstrates the continued, if more limited, usefulness of this admittedly complex concept.

A second, and more pointed, counter-critique comes from those who share the concern of J. K. Gibson-Graham (2008, 2006, 1996) that seeing neoliberalism everywhere can "dampen and discourage" emergent alternatives and initiatives (2008, 3). Analyses such as those we describe above, they argue, make it more difficult to imagine and cultivate alternative ways of being.

> These [strategies include] the tendency to represent economy as a space of invariant logics and automatic unfolding that [offers] no field for intervention; the tendency to theorize economy as a stable and self-reproducing structure . . . these tendencies [contribute] to an affect and attitude of entrenched opposition . . . a habit of thinking and feeling that [offers] little emotional space for alternatives. (Gibson-Graham 2006, xxii)

Barnett similarly argues that theories of neoliberalism "have great difficulty accounting for, or indeed even in recognizing, new forms of 'individualized collective-action' (Marchetti 2003) that have emerged in tandem with the apparent ascendancy of neoliberal hegemony" (Barnett 2005, 10).

With regard to food movement activism and alternative food systems, Harris (2009) paints the critique of alternative food as neoliberal as constituting what Hart (2002) refers to as a "disabling discourse," totalizing and self-fulfilling, discursively foreclosing possibilities of transforming food systems. Harris argues instead that scholars should adopt the directive of Gibson-Graham to "read for difference" in order to develop "an alternative stance in which place-based activism is not seen as already 'sold-out' to neoliberalism." This representational strategy, he continues, "might better acknowledge attempts to imagine and enact a food politics that achieves different socio-environmental justice outcomes to those of conventional food systems, and offer a more constructive academic critique" (Harris 2009, 60).

In response, we argue that the diverse and alternative economies that Gibson-Graham seek to highlight, while potentially generative, exist at the margins of the neoliberal political economy. Moreover, they are all-too-often vulnerable to the food justice critique, failing to include or resonate with those who are most harmed by neoliberalism, namely low-income communities, communities of color, and low-wage and increasingly precarious workers. We also believe that too much emphasis on the merits of these alternatives, and too little focus on the circumstances of those who are not served by them, works to convince a generation of activists that it is impossible to confront the state or corporations in the interest of human and environmental health, fostering the very neoliberal subjectivities we described above.

This volume offers a variety of cases in which critiques of alternative food systems as neoliberal have helped to broaden, rather than limit, food movement activists' notions of the kinds of socio-environmental activism and change that are possible. Analytically, we argue that in order to fundamentally shift the food system into one that is environmentally sustainable and socially just, activists will need to identify the threads of neoliberalism that inform their own discourses and, even more so, their practices, working within them when appropriate and abandoning them when it serves their larger strategic aims.

While the provision of alternatives remains food activists' primary strategy, some of the most prominent among them have embraced, at least in part, the broader, more politicized forms of activism described in this volume. Mark Bittman, whose words begin this chapter, is a noteworthy example, and a look back through his *New York Times* column reveals an increasing awareness of workers' rights, racial justice, and the need for a politicized food movement. At the same time, however, his recent departure from the *Times* in order to work for a start-up that will "make it easier for people to eat more plants" demonstrates that the creation of alternatives remains the dominant mode of food politics (though he has since left that position as well). Michael Pollan has been similarly equivocal. Despite a complete ignorance of workers' issues in his earlier writing, he has more recently called on his readers to support both the Coalition of Immokalee Workers and striking fast-food workers (Dean 2014). While this shift in the writings of movement luminaries is both noteworthy and influential, the groundwork that makes it possible comes from the farmworkers, food workers, and other activists whose stories populate the pages that follow.

For the authors of this volume, critiques of neoliberalism have not been a disabling discourse, but rather an invitation to highlight collective campaigns for health and justice throughout the food system, as well as projects that push back against the neoliberal primacy of concepts like individual responsibility and private-sector ownership. Indeed, the kinds of alliances between food activists, antipoverty groups, and labor unions described by Joshua Sbicca in chapter 5 only become possible when the former look beyond the provision of alternatives and work strategically and collaboratively to effect social change. In other words, critiques of neoliberalism in food movements have pushed food activists to craft new strategies, subjectivities, and alliances.

The chapters that follow are examples of projects and campaigns that address both the neoliberal and food justice critiques described above. The activist projects documented in these chapters are conscious of the ways that race, class, and gender pervade both industrial agriculture and its alternatives, and they work to increase social equity within the food system. Moreover, each of them recognizes and moves within a political economy dominated by neoliberalism while attempting to push beyond it. While they are imperfect in their abilities to address both hierarchies of oppression and neoliberal modes of thought and action, these campaigns may help strengthen and inspire activists and supporters from many parts of the food movement to see the progressive possibilities beyond neoliberalism, and to create bridges to other forms of social justice activism.

OVERVIEW OF THIS BOOK

Part 1, "Regulatory Campaigns," explores efforts to constrain the power of industrial agriculture in the interest of the physical and economic health of producers and workers. First, Jill Lindsey Harrison showcases the work of California's pesticide drift activists who aim to hold the state accountable for its responsibility to reduce environmental problems by advocating for regulatory restrictions on the use of the most toxic and unruly pesticides. Emily Eaton's chapter describes another important, successful campaign, this one of Canadian producers against genetically modified wheat. She argues that a focus on production, rather than consumer health, made this victory possible. In the final chapter in this section, Julie Guthman and Sandy Brown analyze the campaign to ban the use of the soil fumigant methyl iodide in California's strawberry production, highlighting how activists played on the strategic weaknesses of the industry they confronted.

Part 2, "Working for Workers," examines the ways that workers' rights campaigns across the food system have built alliances with and strengthened alternative food movements. In this section's opening chapter, Joshua Sbicca argues that emphasizing economic inequalities and working conditions and engaging in confrontational politics have been essential to the creation of alliances between food justice activists and food workers in Los Angeles. Next, Joann Lo and Biko Koenig of the Food Chain Workers Alliance describe the rise in campaigns for good jobs, good wages, and good food across the food system, highlighting examples from a New York bakery, a farm in California's Central Valley, and national worker-organizing at Walmart. Finally, in her analysis of campaigns by the Coalition of Immokalee Workers and United Farm Workers, Laura-Anne Minkoff-Zern argues that consumer support for farmworker advocacy can push food activists beyond romantic imaginaries of alternative food systems and into multiracial, multiclass, movement-based work.

Part 3, "Collective Practices," examines the kinds of alternative institutions that, despite their status as alternatives, challenge forms of ownership associated with individual entrepreneurship. First, two chapters on cooperative markets, one by Andrew Zitcer and the other by Meleiza Figueroa and Alison Alkon, highlight examples from Philadelphia, Chicago, and Oakland. While Zitcer's described organizations are predominantly white and Figueroa and Alkon's are predominantly Black, both chapters argue that democratic ownership and collective buying practices resist the individualizing tendency of neoliberal subjectivities and promote interest in broader movement activities. Next, Michelle Glowa examines various ways that Bay Area urban gardeners have pursued land sovereignty in a competitive real estate market, recreating and challenging the institutional landscape of land rights and community development and pushing back against the trend toward neoliberal urbanization that has so dominated Bay Area real estate. Loh and Agyeman offer a similar case study of the Dudley Street Neighborhood Initiative in Boston, a land trust that has developed both low-income housing and urban agriculture. Lastly, Tanya Kerssen and Zoe Brent describe the ways that rural and urban farmers, marginalized populations, and people of color in particular are affected by changes in land tenure and mechanisms of land access and control. They also discuss forms of land-based resistance and alliances that might enhance the effectiveness of struggles for food justice as well as for food and land sovereignty.

There are two important limitations to these chapters that we believe need to be explicitly discussed at the beginning. First, despite the national and even global nature of food activism, our chapters are disproportionately sited in California. This reflects our own locations and the networks of scholars with whom we work, as well as California's leading role in alternative food activism and critical food studies. While there are talented scholars doing critical work throughout the United States, those who are explicitly addressing issues of food justice and neoliberalism are disproportionately found in California. A second and more troubling limitation is the lack of attention to gender and sexuality. There have been wonderful studies examining the ways that inequalities of gender and sexuality are reproduced by food and agriculture, as well as the ways that food work contributes to gender identity, family, and community (for an excellent overview, see Allen 2004). However, this scholarship is all-too-rarely in dialogue with work on food justice, neoliberalism, or food movements. We look forward to future studies that correct these imbalances.

Taken together, these chapters highlight a new direction in food activism, or, more accurately, a return to a more collective, social justice–oriented tradition of food activism that never went away but has been overshadowed by the emphasis on the creation of market-oriented alternatives. We hope that by highlighting these examples, we can help foodies and food activists expand our collective vision of what we are fighting for far beyond our own tables. We believe that collective campaigns rooted in the realities of those most harmed by the industrial food system and alternatives that push back against neoliberal strategies and subjectivities can nourish new political possibilities within the world of food activism.

NOTES

1. Although it seems inconsistent, we think it's important to capitalize *Black* but not *white*. The argument in favor of capitalizing *Black* has a long history, tracing back to W. E. B. Du Bois's petitioning of the *New York Times* to capitalize the *N* in *Negro*. When they eventually agreed, the editorial staff wrote that "It is not merely a typographical change, it is an act in recognition of racial respect for those who have been generations in the 'lower case'" (quoted in Tharps 2014). We want to convey

this same respect. *Black*—like *Latino/a, Asian,* or *Arab*—refers to a culture, a community, and an ethnicity, and thus the word should be capitalized. In this sense, *white* is different, because most whites identify with more specific origins like Irish or Jewish (Waters 1996). Thus, we do not believe that *white* deserves the same treatment.

REFERENCES

Agyeman, Julian. 2005. *Sustainable Communities and the Challenge of Environmental Justice.* New York: NYU Press.

Agyeman, Julian, and Jesse McEntee. 2014. "Moving the Field of Food Justice Forward through the Lens of Urban Political Ecology." *Geography Compass* 8: 211–220.

Alkon, Alison Hope. 2012. *Black, White, and Green: Farmers Markets, Race, and the Green Economy.* Athens: University of Georgia Press.

Alkon, Alison Hope, and Julian Agyeman, Eds. 2011. *Cultivating Food Justice: Race, Class, and Sustainability.* Cambridge, MA: MIT Press.

Alkon, Alison Hope, Daniel Block, Kelly Moore, Katherine Gillis, Nicole DiNuccio, and Noele Chavez. 2013. "Foodways of the Urban Poor." *Geoforum* 48: 126–135.

Alkon, Alison Hope, and Christine McCullen. 2010. "Whiteness and Farmers Markets: Performances, Perpetuations ... Contestations?" *Antipode* 43: 937–959.

Allen, Patricia. 1999. "Reweaving the Food Security Safety Net: Mediating Entitlement and Entrepreneurship." *Agriculture and Human Values* 16: 117–129.

———. 2004. *Together at the Table: Sustainability and Sustenance in the American Agrifood System,* new edition. University Park, PA: Penn State University Press.

———. 2008. "Mining for Justice in the Food System: Perceptions, Practices, and Possibilities." *Agriculture and Human Values* 25: 157–161.

Allen, Patricia, Margaret Fitzsimmons, Michael Goodman, and Keith Warner. 2003. "Shifting Plates in the Agrifood Landscape: The Tectonics of Alternative Food Initiatives in California." *Journal of Rural Studies* 19: 61–75.

Allen, Patricia, and Julie Guthman. 2006. From "Old School" to "Farm-to-School": Neoliberalization from the Ground Up." *Agriculture and Human Values* 23: 401–415.

Altieri, Miguel A. 2000. "Ecological Impacts of Industrial Agriculture and the Possibilities for Truly Sustainable Farming." In *Hungry for Profit: The Agribusiness Threat to Farmers, Food, and the Environment,* ed. Fred Magdoff, John Bellamy Foster, and Frederick H. Buttel, 77–92. New York: Monthly Review Press.

Barnett, Clive. 2005. "The Consolations of 'Neoliberalism.'" *Geoforum* 36: 7–12.

Beaulac, Julie, Elizabeth Kristjansson, and Steven Cummins. 2009. "A Systematic Review of Food Deserts, 1966–2007." *Preventing Chronic Disease* 6(3): A105.

Belasco, Warren. 1993. *Appetite for Change: How the Counterculture Took On the Food Industry.* Ithaca, NY: Cornell University Press.

Besky, Sarah, and Sandy Brown. 2015. "Looking for Work: Placing Labor in Food Studies." *Labor* 12: 19–43.

Bittman, Mark. 2014. "Rethinking the Word 'Foodie.'" *The New York Times,* June 24. www.nytimes.com/2014/06/25/opinion/mark-bittman-rethinking-the-word-foodie.html.

Bondi, Liz, and Nina Laurie. 2005. "Working the Spaces of Neoliberalism: Activism, Professionalisation, and Incorporation: Introduction." *Antipode* 37: 393–401.

Bowens, Natasha. 2015. *The Color of Food: Stories of Race, Resilience and Farming.* New York: New Society.

Bradley, Karen. 1995. "Agrarian Ideology: California Grangers and the Post–World War II Farm Policy Debate." *Agriculture History* 69: 240–256.

Bradley, Katharine, and Ryan E. Galt. 2013. "Practicing Food Justice at Dig Deep Farms & Produce, East Bay Area, California: Self-Determination as a Guiding Value and Intersections with Foodie Logics." *Local Environment: The International Journal of Justice and Sustainability* 19: 172–186.

Bradley, Katherine, and Hank Herrera. 2016. "Decolonizing Food Justice: Naming, Resisting, and Researching Colonizing Forces in the Movement." *Antipode* 48: 97–114.

Brenner, Neil, Jamie Peck, and Nik Theodore. 2010. "Variegated Neoliberalization: Geographies, Modalities, Pathways." *Global Networks* 10: 182–222.

Broad, Garrett. 2016. *More Than Just Food.* Berkeley: University of California Press.

Brown, Sandy, and Christy Getz. 2008. "Privatizing Farm Worker Justice: Regulating Labor through Voluntary Certification and Labeling." *Geoforum* 39: 1184–1196.

———. 2011. "Farmworker Food Insecurity and the Production of Hunger in California." In *Cultivating Food Justice: Race, Class, and Sustainability,* ed. Alison Hope Alkon and Julian Agyeman, 121–146. Cambridge, MA: MIT Press.

Bullard, Robert. 1990. *Dumping in Dixie.* Boulder, CO: Westview Press.

Calvo, Luz, and Catriona Rueda Esquibel. 2015. *Decolonize Your Diet.* Vancouver, BC: Arsenal Pulp Press.

Castree, Noel. 2008. "Neoliberalising Nature: The Logics of Deregulation and Reregulation." *Environment and Planning A* 40: 131–152.

Cohen, Nevin, and Kristin Reynolds. 2016. *Beyond the Kale.* Athens: University of Georgia Press.

Cox, Laurence, and Alf Gunvald Nilsen. 2014. "Neoliberalism and Social Movements." *E-International Relations.* www.e-ir.info/author/laurence-cox-and-alf-gunvald-nilsen/.

Dean, Amy B. 2014. "Michael Pollan: 'Our Food Is Dishonestly Priced.'" Moyers and Company. http://billmoyers.com/2014/02/03/michael-pollan-our-food-is-dishonestly-priced/. Accessed May 22, 2014.

Dean, Mitchell. 1999. *Governmentality: Power and Rule in Modern Society.* London: Sage.

Dimitri, Carolyn and Lydia Oberholtzer. 2009. "Marketing U.S. Organic Foods: Recent Trends from Farms to Consumers."Economic Information Bulletin 58. U.S. Department of Agriculture, Economic Rearch Service. www.ers.usda.gov /webdocs/publications/eib58/11009_eib58_1_.pdf. Accessed January 10, 2014.

Fairfax, Sally, Louise N. Dyble, Grieg T. Guthey, Lauren Gwin, Monica Moore, and Jennifer Sokolove. 2012. *California Cuisine and Just Food.* Cambridge, MA: MIT Press.

Friedman, Harriet. 2007. "Scaling Up: Bringing Public Institutions and Food Service Corporations into the Project for a Local Sustainable Food System in Ontario." *Agriculture and Human Values* 24: 389–393.

Gibson-Graham, J.K. 1996. *The End of Capitalism (As We Knew It): A Feminist Critique of Political Economy.* Minneapolis: University of Minnesota Press.

———. 2006. *A Postcapitalist Politics.* Minneapolis: University of Minnesota Press.

———. 2008. "Diverse Economies: Performative Practices for 'Other Worlds.'" *Progress in Human Geography* 32: 613–632.

Gilbert, Jess, Gwen Sharp, and M. Sindy Felin. 2002. "The Loss and Persistence of Black-Owned Farms and Farmland: A Review of the Research Literature and Its Implications." *Southern Rural Sociology* 18(2): 1–30.

Gilmore, Ruth W. 2007. *Golden Gulag: Prisons, Surplus, Crisis and Opposition in Globalizing California.* Los Angeles: University of California Press.

Gottlieb, Robert. 2001. *Environmentalism Unbound: Exploring New Pathways for Change.* Cambridge, MA: MIT Press.

Gottlieb, Robert, and Andrew Fisher. 1996. "'First Feed the Face': Environmental Justice and Community Food Security." *Antipode* 28: 193–203.

Gottlieb, Robert, and Anupama Joshi. 2010. *Food Justice.* Cambridge, MA: MIT Press.

Gray, Margaret. 2014. *Labor and the Locavore: The Making of a Comprehensive Food Ethic.* Berkeley: University of California Press.

Guthman, Julie. 2003. "Eating Risk: The Politics of Labeling Transgenic Foods." In *Remaking the World: Genetic Engineering and Its Discontents,* ed. Rachel Schurman and Dennis Takahashi-Kelso, 130–151. Berkeley: University of California Press.

———. 2007. "The Polanyian Way? Voluntary Food Labels as Neoliberal Governance." *Antipode* 39: 456–478.

———. 2008a. "Bringing Good Food to Others: Investigating the Subjects of Alternative Food Practice." *Cultural Geographies* 15: 431–447.

———. 2008b. "'If They Only Knew': Color Blindness and Universalism in California Alternative Food Institutions." *The Professional Geographer* 60: 387–397.

———. 2008c. "Neoliberalism and the Making of Food Politics in California." *Geoforum* 39: 1171–1183.

———. 2008d. "Thinking inside the Neoliberal Box: The Micro-politics of Agrofood Philanthropy." *Geoforum* 39: 1241–1253.

———. 2011. *Weighing In: Obesity, Food Justice, and the Limits of Capitalism.* Berkeley: University of California Press.

———. 2014. *Agrarian Dreams: The Paradox of Organic Farming in California,* second edition. Berkeley: University of California Press.

Guthman, Julie, and Melanie DuPuis. 2006. "Embodying Neoliberalism: Economy, Culture and the Politics of Fat." *Environment and Planning D: Society and Space* 24: 427–448.

Guthman, Julie, Amy Morris, and Patricia Allen. 2006. "Squaring Farm Security and Food Security in Two Types of Alternative Food Institutions." *Rural Sociology* 71: 662–684.

Harper, A. Breeze. 2010. *Sistah Vegan: Food, Identity, Health, and Society: Black Female Vegans Speak.* Herndon, VA: Lantern Books.

Harris, Edmund. 2009. "Neoliberal Subjectivities or a Politics of the Possible? Reading for Difference in Alternative Food Networks." *Area* 41: 55–63.

Harrison, Jill Lindsey. 2008. "Lessons Learned from Pesticide Drift: A Call to Bring Production Agriculture, Farm Labor, and Social Justice Back into Agrifood Research and Activism." *Agriculture and Human Values* 25: 163–167.

———. 2011. *Pesticide Drift and the Pursuit of Environmental Justice.* Cambridge, MA: MIT Press.

Hart, Gillian. 2002. "Development/s beyond Neoliberalism? Power, Culture, Political Economy." *Progress in Human Geography* 26: 812–822.

Harvey, David. 2005. *A Brief History of Neoliberalism.* New York: Oxford University Press.

———. 2010. *The Enigma of Capital and the Crisis This Time.* Paper prepared for the American Sociological Association Meetings in Atlanta. http://davidharvey .org/2010/08/the-enigma-of-capital-and-the-crisis-this-time/. Accessed May 22, 2015.

Hislop, Rasheed. 2014. "Reaping Equity across the USA: FJ Organizations Observed at the National Scale." Master's thesis, University of California–Davis.

Holmes, Seth. 2013. *Fresh Fruit, Broken Bodies: Migrant Farmworkers in the United States.* Berkeley: University of California Press.

Holt-Giménez, Eric, and Annie Shattuck. 2011. "Food Crises, Food Regimes and Food Movements: Rumblings of Reform or Tides of Transformation?" *Journal of Peasant Studies* 38: 109–144.

Jayaraman, Saru. 2013. *Behind the Kitchen Door.* Ithaca, NY: Cornell University Press.

Johnston, Josee, and Shyon Baumann. 2009. *Foodies: Democracy and Distinction in the Gourmet Foodscape.* New York: Routledge.

Kato, Yuki. 2013. "Not Just the Price of Food: Challenges of an Urban Agriculture Organization in Engaging Local Residents." *Sociological Inquiry* 83: 369–391.

Kato, Yuki, Catarina Passidomo, and Daina Harvey. 2014. "Political Gardening in a Post-disaster City: Lessons from New Orleans." *Urban Studies* 51:1833–1849.

Krahmann, Elke. 2010. *States, Citizens and the Privatization of Security.* Cambridge, UK: Cambridge University Press.

Larner, Wendy, and David Craig. 2005. "After Neoliberalism? Community Action and Local Partnerships in Aotearoa New Zealand." *Antipode* 37: 402–424.

La Vía Campesina. 2007. "Declaration of Nyéléni." February 27. http://viacampesina.org/en/index.php/main-issues-mainmenu-27/food-sovereignty-and-trade-mainmenu-38/262-declaration-of-nyi.

Lavin, Chad. 2009. "Pollanated Politics, or, the Neoliberal's Dilemma." *Politics and Culture* 2: 57–67.

Lea, Emma, and Anthony Worsley. 2005. "Australians' Organic Food Beliefs, Demographics and Values." *British Food Journal* 107: 855–869.

Levkoe, Charles. 2011. "Towards a Transformative Food Politics." *Local Environment* 16: 687–705.

Mann, Michael. 2013. "Globalizations." In *The Sources of Social Power, vol. 4: Globalizations, 1945–2011* (e-book, pp. 1–12). Cambridge, UK: Cambridge University Press.

Marchetti, Michelle. 2003. *Shopping and the Politics of Virtue.* London: Palgrave.

Mares, Teresa, and Devon Peña. 2011. "Environmental and Food Justice: Toward Local, Slow, and Deep Food Systems." In *Cultivating Food Justice: Race, Class, and Sustainability,* ed. Alison Hope Alkon and Julian Agyeman, 197–220. Cambridge, MA: MIT Press.

McClintock, Nathan. 2011. "From Industrial Garden to Food Desert: Unearthing the Root Structure of Urban Agriculture in Oakland, California." In *Cultivating Food Justice: Race, Class, and Sustainability,* ed. Alison Hope Alkon and Julian Agyeman, 89–120. Cambridge, MA: MIT Press.

Meyers, Justin. Forthcoming. *Beyond Access.* New Brunswick, NJ: Rutgers University Press.

Milligan, Christine, Liz Bondi, Nicholas R. Fyfe, and Wendy Larner. 2008. "Placing Voluntary Activism in Neo-liberal Welfare States: A Comparative Study." ESRC End of Award Report, RES-000-23-1104. Swindon, UK: Economic and Social Research Council.

Minkoff-Zern, Laura-Anne. 2014. "Knowing 'Good Food': Immigrant Knowledge and the Racial Politics of Farmworker Food Insecurity." *Antipode* 46: 1190–1204.

Minkoff-Zern, Laura-Anne, Nancy Peluso, Jenny Sowerwine, and Christy Getz. 2011. "Race and Regulation: Asian Immigrants in California Agriculture." In *Cultivating Food Justice: Race, Class, and Sustainability,* ed. Alison Hope Alkon and Julian Agyeman, 65–86. Cambridge, MA: MIT Press.

Morales, Alfonso. 2011. "Growing Food *and* Justice." In *Cultivating Food Justice: Race, Class, and Sustainability,* ed. Alison Hope Alkon and Julian Agyeman, 149–176. Cambridge, MA: MIT Press.

Morland, Kimberly, Steve Wing, Ana Deiz Roux, and Charles Poole. 2002. "Neighborhood Characteristics Associated with the Location of Food Stores and Food Service Places." *American Journal of Preventive Medicine* 22: 23–29.

Moss, Michael. 2014. *Salt Sugar Fat: How the Food Giants Hooked Us.* New York: Random House.

Norgaard, Kari, Ron Reed, and Carolina Van Horn. 2011. "A Continuing Legacy: Institutional Racism, Hunger, and Nutritional Justice on the Klamath." In

Cultivating Food Justice: Race, Class, and Sustainability, ed. Alison Hope Alkon and Julian Agyeman, 23–46. Cambridge, MA: MIT Press.

Oran, Olivia, and Soyoung Kim. 2013. "Organic Salad Producer Earthbound Farm Prepped for Sale." *Reuters,* May 6. www.reuters.com/article/earthbound-sale-idUSL2N0DK1JX20130506. Accessed January 9, 2015.

Park, Lisa Sun-Hee, and David Naguib Pellow. 2011. *The Slums of Aspen: Immigrants vs. the Environment in America's Eden.* New York: NYU Press.

Peck, Jamie, and Adam Tickell. 2002. "Neoliberalizing Space." In *Spaces of Neoliberalism: Urban Restructuring in North America and Western Europe,* ed. Neil Brenner and Nik Theodore. Malden, MA: Oxford's Blackwell Press.

Pellow, David N., and Robert J. Brulle. 2005. *Power, Justice, and the Environment: A Critical Appraisal of the Environmental Justice Movement.* Cambridge, MA: MIT Press.

Pollan, Michael. 2006. "Voting with Your Fork." *The New York Times,* May 7. http://pollan.blogs.nytimes.com/2006/05/07/voting-with-your-fork/.

Pudup, Mary Beth. 2008. "It Takes a Garden: Cultivating Citizen-Subjects in Organized Garden Projects." *Geoforum* 39: 1228–1240.

Romm, Jeff. 2001. "The Coincidental Order of Environmental Justice." In *Justice and Natural Resources,* ed. Kathryn Mutz, Gary Bryner, and Douglas Kenney. Washington, DC: Island Press.

Rose, Nikolas. 1999. *Powers of Freedom: Reframing Political Thought.* Cambridge, UK: Cambridge University Press.

Roy, Arundhati. 2004. "Public Power in the Age of Empire." *Socialist Worker.* http://socialistworker.org/2004-2/510/510_06_Roy.shtml. Accessed August 6, 2013.

Sbicca, Joshua. 2012. "Growing Food Justice by Planting an Anti-oppression Foundation: Opportunities and Obstacles for a Budding Social Movement." *Agriculture and Human Values* 29: 455–466.

Schlosberg, David. 2007. *Defining Environmental Justice: Theories, Movements, and Nature.* New York: Oxford University Press.

Short, Anne, Julie Guthman, and Samuel Raskin. 2007. "Food Deserts, Oases, or Mirages? Small Markets and Community Food Security in the San Francisco Bay Area." *Journal of Planning Education and Research* 26: 352–364.

Slocum, Rachel. 2006. "Anti-racist Practice and the Work of Community Food Organizations." Antipode 38: 327–349.

———. 2007. "Whiteness, Space, and Alternative Food Practice." *Geoforum* 38: 520–533.

Szasz, Andrew. 2007. *Shopping Our Way to Safety: How We Changed from Protecting the Environment to Protecting Ourselves.* Minneapolis: University of Minnesota Press.

Taylor, Dorceta. 1998. "Race, Class, Gender and American Environmentalism." USDA. www.fs.fed.us/pnw/pubs/gtr534.pdf. Accessed January 9, 2015.

Taylor, Edwin J., and Paul L. Martin. 1997. "The Immigrant Subsidy in US Agriculture: Farm Employment, Poverty, and Welfare." *Population and Development Review* 23: 855–874.

Terry, Bryant. 2009. *Vegan Soul Kitchen: Fresh, Healthy, and Creative African-American Cuisine.* New York: Da Capo Press.

Tharps, Lori L. 2014. "The Case for Black with a Capital B." *The New York Times,* November 18. www.nytimes.com/2014/11/19/opinion/the-case-for-black-with-a-capital-b.html. Accessed January 22, 2017.

U.S. Department of Agriculture. 2013. "Farmers Markets and Local Food Marketing." www.ams.usda.gov/AMSv1.0/ams.fetchTemplateData.do?template. TemplateS&leftNav.WholesaleandFarmersMarkets&page.WFMFarmersMarket Growth&description.Farmers Market Growth. Accessed March 17, 2014.

Waters, Mary C. 1996. "Optional Ethnicities: For Whites Only?" In *Origins and Destinies: Immigration, Race and Ethnicity in America,* ed. Sylvia Pedraza and Ruben Rumbaut, 444–454. Belmont, CA: Wadsworth Press.

Weller, Sally, and Phillip O'Neill. 2014. "An Argument with Neoliberalism: Australia's Place in a Global Imaginary." *Dialogues in Human Geography* 4: 105–130.

White, Monica M. 2010. "Shouldering Responsibility for the Delivery of Human Rights: A Case Study of the D-Town Farmers of Detroit." *Race/Ethnicity: Multidisciplinary Global Perspectives* 3: 189–211.

———. Manuscript. *Freedom Farms: Agricultural Resistance and the Black Freedom Movement.*

Wittman, Hannah, Annette Desmarais, and Nettie Wiebe. 2010. *Food Sovereignty: Reconnecting Food, Nature and Community.* Oakland, CA: Food First Books.

Winne, Mark. 2008. *Closing the Food Gap: Resetting the Table in the Land of Plenty.* Boston: Beacon Press.

Wolch, Jennifer. 1990. *The Shadow State: Government and Voluntary Sector in Transition.* New York: Foundation Center.

Wrigley, Neil, Daniel Warm, Barrie Margetts, and Amanda Whelan. 2002. "Assessing the Impact of Improved Retail Access on Diet in a 'Food Desert': A Preliminary Report." *Urban Studies* 39: 2061–2082.

PART ONE

Regulatory Campaigns

Taking a Different Tack

PESTICIDE REGULATORY-REFORM
ACTIVISM IN CALIFORNIA

Jill Lindsey Harrison

INTRODUCTION TO PESTICIDE DRIFT

Pesticide drift—the offsite, airborne movement of pesticides away from their target location—has become an increasingly controversial issue at the urban–agricultural interface, particularly in the wake of the large-scale drift incidents that have occurred every year or two since 1999 in California's southern San Joaquin Valley (Harrison 2011). In each of these large-scale incidents, up to several hundred workers and residents of farmworker communities have been exposed to highly toxic airborne soil fumigants and/or aerially applied insecticides. These events produce serious acute illness (nausea, vomiting, eye and skin irritation, difficulty breathing) and contribute to the many chronic diseases these pesticides are known to cause, including asthma and other lung diseases, cancer, birth defects, immune-system suppression, behavioral disorders, and neurological disorders (Kegley et al. 2003, O'Malley 2004).

Pesticide drift incidents unfold on a regular basis in the context of considerable social marginalization. The ability of California's one million farmworkers to politically engage pesticide drift and other problems is deeply constrained by the fact that this population is largely politically disenfranchised and socially subordinated. Over 90 percent are immigrants from Mexico; their average income falls between $7,500 and $12,500 per year; they experience job insecurity because of the seasonal nature of agricultural work and competition for jobs; few are covered by union contracts; and at least 50 percent are unauthorized and, thus, subject to the surveillance and other consequences of heightened immigration enforcement (Coleman 2009, Rosas 2006, U.S. Department of Labor 2005). To a large extent, this vulnerability has been actively constructed. Since the late nineteenth century, California's growers and the state have worked together to deliberately recruit different racially marked groups of workers. Those workers are kept cheap and vulnerable through physical repression, racist disparagement, the denial of particular rights, and racist immigration and labor laws that help growers replace one group with another, more "compliant" one in times of labor organizing (often mischaracterized as a "labor shortage"; McWilliams 1999, Wells 1996). Because of these factors, farmworkers and their kin and peers are disproportionately exposed to pesticide drift, their exposures are not usually reported, and they have disproportionately less ability to seek medical care or compensation when they are exposed.

Official data and statements portray pesticide drift as an unfortunate but ultimately small and technical problem, and the social context described above plays no role in regulatory analysis or narratives (California Department of Pesticide Regulation [CDPR] 2012). The CDPR has addressed the issue by discussing the need for improved emergency response protocol, increasing the minimum fines for pesticide violations that cause harm or damage, and issuing fines in some cases where errors have been documented. Regulatory officials justify this response by framing the issue as a series of isolated, localized accidents occurring within an otherwise protective system (Harrison 2011). However, a wide range of toxicological, epidemiological, sociological, and other data indicate that agricultural pesticide drift is pervasive, that it often exceeds regulatory agencies' health benchmarks, and that those benchmarks underrepresent the extent and risks of exposure (Harrison 2011, Kegley et al. 2003).

A nascent social movement has formed in recent years around concern about pesticide drift in California's agricultural communities. The core participants are low-income, Latino farmworkers, their kin, and a racially and class-diverse mix of other agricultural community residents who are supported by lawyers, scientists, students, and a few sympathetic government agency staff. Directing their critiques at the regulatory arena, these pesticide drift activists allege that officials drastically underestimate the scope of the issue and do not adequately regulate pesticides. This nascent social movement emphasizes the "everyday" nature of pesticide drift and the social inequalities and relations of oppression that make it largely invisible, and it pursues state- and federal-level regulatory restrictions on pesticide use as rights-based protections from pesticide exposure for all residents. Pesticide drift activists are best understood as part of the environmental justice movement, which critically highlights the ways that oppression and inequality exacerbate environmental inequalities like pesticide drift while also rendering them invisible (Harrison 2014, 2011).

In contrast, California's sustainable agriculture movement has taken a market-based approach to addressing environmental problems like pesticide drift: pursuing change by developing alternative markets, creating private certification standards, encouraging people to vote with their forks and dollars, and otherwise framing politics in terms of consumer choice. As detailed in chapter 1, scholars have argued that this turn accommodates rather than confronts the neoliberalization of environmental governance, thereby limiting the transformative potential of activists' work (Allen 1999, Allen and Guthman 2006, Allen and Kovach 2000, Allen et al. 2003, Brown and Getz 2008, DuPuis and Goodman 2005, Guthman 2011, 2008, Harrison 2014, 2011). Such work suggests the need for alternatives to market-based agrifood politics—and thus the importance of health-protective environmental regulatory reform.

In this chapter, I argue that pesticide drift activists' push for stronger pesticide regulations is essential for addressing pesticide drift in a socially just way. To make this case, I describe the changes in pesticide politics in California over the past fifty years. I first show that neoliberal reforms weakened the state and federal pesticide regulatory apparatuses. I then show that California's sustainable agriculture movement responded by developing alternative technologies and offering market-based incentives to encourage more sustainable farming practices. I argue that these tactical shifts in the state and the sustainable agriculture movement effectively sideline the problem of pesticide exposure as experienced by people living and working within the spaces of conventional agricultural production. I illustrate, however, that recent pesticide drift incidents illuminate and problematize these abandoned bodies and geographical spaces of sacrifice and, thus, the inability of market-based strategies to secure a basic level of protection for all—especially the most marginalized—members of the agrifood system. Next, I argue that pesticide drift activists' unwavering pursuit of health-protective pesticide regulatory reform is a valuable way to address these problems. Responding to the deadly fallout of neoliberal regulatory reforms and market-based sustainable agriculture activism, pesticide drift activists show that stronger pesticide regulations are possible and why they are necessary.

I draw on a variety of primary and secondary data that I have collected since 2002. I conducted ethnographic observation at regulatory and activist events; more than 120 in-depth, qualitative interviews with pesticide regulators, activists, scientists, and industry representatives; and countless shorter, informal interviews with those same actors. I also reviewed documents from pesticide regulatory agencies, activist organizations, and other research institutions. All unreferenced quotes are excerpts from my own interviews and observations.

NEOLIBERALIZATION WITHIN THE U.S. PESTICIDE REGULATORY COMPLEX

It is not entirely surprising that pesticide drift incidents occur regularly in California. With less than 3 percent of all U.S. cropland but 25 percent of the nation's agricultural pesticide use, California agriculture is notoriously pesticide intensive (CDPR 2006b; U.S. Department of Agriculture 2002; U.S. Environmental Protection Agency 2004, tables 3.5 and 4.2). Moreover, a large percentage of the pesticides used within the state are highly toxic and prone to drifting off site (Kegley et al. 2003). The majority of California's massive public-university research and extension resources have consistently served to develop productionist, pesticide-intensive agriculture (Warner 2007). Furthermore, the particular geographic and atmospheric conditions (e.g., basin shape, inversion layer, heat) of the San Joaquin Valley trap pesticides and other air pollutants and make them volatilize very quickly, thus confounding the state's ability to safely regulate pesticide use in a way that would prevent pesticide drift.

Scholars have shown that many aspects of pesticide regulation serve the economic interests of the agricultural industry rather than the health needs of the public (Baker 1988, Lake and Disch 1992). Risk assessments typically do not account for the effects of chemical mixtures, so-called inert ingredients, or a given pesticide's breakdown ingredients, and the burden of proof for challenging a registered pesticide rests with the public. Agencies' preoccupation with nozzle sizes and wind speeds as drift-control measures shifts attention away from the actual variations of toxicity posed by different chemicals. Also, the Federal Insecticide, Fungicide, and Rodenticide Act, the basis for federal regulatory authority, requires that all pesticide regulatory decisions be based on a cost-benefit analysis—that is, the benefits of a restriction must outweigh its costs. However, benefits of restrictive regulations are typically conceived of very narrowly because most impacts of pesticide use are uncertain, long-term, diffuse, and thus nearly impossible to quantify.

By order of the California State Legislature in 1972, considerable pesticide regulatory responsibility and discretion rests in the hands of county agriculture commissioners (CACs; CDPR 2001, 8). They are politically appointed by local elites, charged with the contradictory task of both promoting the local agricultural industry and regulating its chemical use, and operate under extraordinary social and political pressure to keep all pest management tools available to growers. I have shown elsewhere that CACs demonstrate a systemic reluctance to take regulatory actions against growers or pesticide applicators, that industry control over state regulatory leadership weakens the available oversight mechanism, and that some of California's most "progressive" and seemingly health-protective regulatory requirements (e.g., its pesticide-use reporting system and the restricted-materials permit system) do not actually provide CACs with the technical grounds for restricting pesticide use in a health-protective manner (see Harrison 2011, 2006).

Additionally, some restrictions actually exacerbate pesticide exposures in agricultural communities. Some of the strongest regulatory restrictions on pesticides—including those that addressed environmentally persistent pesticides such as DDT and the more recent Food Quality Protection Act—were focused on reducing the risks posed to consumers by pesticide residues on food. Such restrictions prompted growers to shift to less persistent but more acutely toxic pesticides that pose a greater risk to workers and people living near the site of production (Wright 2005). Pesticide regulations for workers tend to focus on personal protective equipment and reentry intervals, neither of which addresses the hazards posed to nearby residents.

These points notwithstanding, U.S. and California pesticide regulatory apparatuses are massive and present considerable potential for health-protective regulation of agricultural pesticide use. The Keynesian-era U.S. Environmental Protection Agency (U.S. EPA) employs 16,000 people and in 2013 operated with a budget of $8 billion; as of 2007, its Office of Pesticide Programs had a staff of 850 and a budget of $140 million (U.S. EPA 2014b, 2014c). The noteworthy regulatory interventions of the 1970s, including the establishment of the U.S. EPA and the passage of the Clean Air Act and the Clean Water Act, are occasionally augmented by health-protective policies (notably the 1996 Food Quality Protection Act) and restrictions on the use of chemical pesticides (notably DDT and Alar).

The CDPR, given departmental status within the California Environmental Protection Agency in 1991, is widely regarded as the nation's largest state-level pesticide regulatory program, and CDPR decisions often drive U.S. EPA pesticide regulatory actions. This relatively strong commitment to environmental regulation and CDPR's reputation for setting the bar for federal pesticide regulations suggest a tremendous capacity to protect public health from hazardous industry practices.

However, relatively big budgets and moments of legislative and regulatory muscle-flexing mask the broader processes of agri-environmental regulatory neoliberalization. The U.S. EPA's budget was cut sharply throughout the late 1970s after the agency's inception and has not increased since that time (see Harrison 2011, 101–102; Slesinger 2014). Those early cuts and the continued inadequate levels of funding for EPA activities limit regulators' abilities to reevaluate the safety of old pesticides in light of new evidence. Indeed, the EPA was unable to complete its first round of pesticide reevaluations—initially mandated in 1972—until 2008. Recently, state scientists and other staff vociferously opposed cutbacks in funding for EPA libraries and databases that provided information about toxic chemicals to the public (PEER 2006). In 2008, the U.S. Department of Agriculture (USDA) downsized its pesticide-use data collection and reporting, further constraining scientists' abilities to conduct pesticide risk assessments that are already compromised by data gaps (Sass 2008). In California's budget crisis of 2001–02, CDPR's pesticide risk-assessment capacity was cut by one-third, and its already starved funding for air sampling and analysis—essential for identifying where pesticide regulations need to be strengthened—were cut by 60 percent (CDPR 2003).

In addition to budget cuts, regulatory agency personnel have been increasingly pressured not to regulate during the neoliberal era. Procedural changes made during the George W. Bush administration shifted decision-making power away from U.S. EPA scientists and increasingly into the hands of politically appointed officials (New York Times 2006). During that time, many regulatory scientists publicly announced that their work was actively constrained by the political interests of top agency officials in ways that directly led to shoddy risk assessments and inadequate pesticide regulation (Harris and Pear 2007, Welch et al. 2006). In confidential interviews with me, some regulatory scientists have admitted that regulatory decision-making processes are conducted under extraordinary and increasing pressure from industry, that managers often disregard scientific information, and that activist groups have disproportionately low influence over decisions compared to industry groups.

Furthermore, agencies increasingly rely on market-based measures and voluntary programs in lieu of pesticide regulations—positioning the marketplace and the local community, rather than the state, as the new sites of governance in the wake of "roll-back neoliberalization." Agencies promote programs like California's voluntary educational program Spray Safe, with officials declaring, "It's far more effective if growers can kind of in a sense police themselves" (Khokha 2009). In October 2014, U.S. EPA announced its new Drift Reduction Technology (DRT) program—a voluntary program through which manufacturers can get their products verified and labeled as having reduced drift potential and that encourages applicators to use those products. During program design, EPA explained that the "ultimate goal" of the program is "to achieve risk reduction by promoting sales and use of lower-drift application equipment" (U.S. EPA 2005, 19), and EPA now confidently claims that "the program will move the agricultural sector toward the widespread use of low-drift technologies" (U.S. EPA 2014a). CDPR and U.S. EPA fast-track the evaluation and registration of new, "greener" pesticides and defend the success of regulatory programs by gauging regulatory improvement in terms of the number of less toxic pesticides they register for use. As a typical example, CDPR officials in 2006 boasted that the latest pesticide-use data indicate that a "dramatic increase occurred in the use of some newer, reduced-risk pesticides," and recently the new director exuberantly proclaimed that such data indicate that "This is just another indication that we are moving in the right direction" (CDPR 2006a).

However, CDPR's stated support for "reduced-risk" pest management has not translated into less use of many of the most drift-prone and highly toxic pesticides—those that pose the greatest risk to public health. According to CDPR's latest pesticide-use data (CDPR 2014), the use of carcinogenic pesticides increased by 3 percent from 2011 to 2012 and by 9 percent from 2004 to 2012. The department applauds the decline in use of the soil fumigant methyl bromide, yet this drop should be unsurprising, given the product's scheduled phaseout in accordance with the international Montreal Protocol's restrictions on ozone-depleting substances. Moreover, methyl bromide continues to be widely used because the federal government continues to grant "critical use exemptions" to commodity groups that claim to have no viable alternatives (Gareau 2013). More importantly, several other highly toxic and volatile chemical fumigants are increasingly (and quietly) being used as replacements for methyl bromide; these include 1,3-dicholoropropene, a carcinogen (34 percent increase in use since 2004); metam sodium, a carcinogen and reproductive and developmental toxin (in decreased use since 2004 but still used in greater quantities in California than most other pesticides); metam potassium, a carcinogen (*ninefold* increase since 2004, now rivaling metam sodium); and chloropicrin, an exceptionally acutely toxic pesticide (24 percent increase from 2011 to 2012, nearly doubled since 2004). Moreover, U.S. EPA has approved new toxic pesticides—including a new herbicide, containing 2,4-D, that accompanies the USDA-approved crops that have been genetically engineered to withstand applications of that herbicide, despite appeals from scientists, more than sixty members of the U.S. Congress, and activists (Center for Food Safety 2014). In glossing over the increased reliance on the most highly toxic and drift-prone chemicals, CDPR's emphasis on "nature-friendly alternatives" disingenuously disguises a regulatory system that has proved much more capable of ushering new products to market than of restricting the use of others that are known to be exceptionally dangerous—even those for which viable and less toxic alternatives exist.

In sum, California and U.S. pesticide regulatory apparatuses are potentially powerful opportunities for regulating pesticide use in a health-protective fashion. However, relatively massive regulatory budgets mask structures and practices that have often served the interests of industry better than those of public health, and this set of imbalances has been deepened by recent neoliberal roll-backs of agency funding and disablements of regulatory intervention into industry affairs. Moreover, sanctioned solutions to pesticide conflicts that rely on voluntary and incentive-based measures both obfuscate the deleterious impacts of these regulatory reforms and serve to "roll out" neoliberal ideology.

PESTICIDE ACTIVISM

It is against this backdrop of regulatory change that pesticide activism developed in California. Here, I relate key moments in the history of California's pesticide activism, showing that agrifood politics in California have taken a neoliberal turn in recent decades. Examining this historical development will help elucidate why pesticide drift activists have instead pursued health-protective pesticide regulatory reforms.

The UFW Campaign: Focus on Farmworker Exposure

Rachel Carson's *Silent Spring* (1962) catalyzed public concern about the environmental and public health impacts of chemical use and helped propel the development of the new national environmental institutions and environmental policies. During the same period, farm-labor organizing in California played an important role in the development of early worker protections from agricultural pesticide exposure. Pulido (1996) describes how Cesar Chavez and the United Farm Workers Organizing Committee (UFWOC) capitalized on the favorable unionizing conditions created by the cessation of the Bracero program in the early 1960s, pursuing pesticide protections as a key component of the overall project to address the exploitation and vulnerability of California farmworkers through union contracts. With little pesticide regulatory apparatus to rely on and few possibilities for traction in the legislative arena at that time, the union focused most of its attention on consumers, workers, and growers. The union adamantly argued that UFWOC union contracts (with their pesticide reduction provisions) were *the* critical tool necessary for securing pesticide protections. To secure contracts, the UFWOC engaged in a series of well-publicized lawsuits and broad-scale consumer boycotts—the success of the latter due largely to their demonstration of the overlapping health problems that some widely used pesticides posed to both consumers and workers.

Demands for pesticide protections were a useful tool for the United Farm Workers (UFW) in their overall project to "remedy the great power imbalance between growers and field workers" as they "served to attract the support of those who otherwise may not have supported the UFWOC" (Pulido 1996, 71, 84), including several sustainable agriculture organizations. Ultimately, the UFWOC's organizing, boycotts, and lawsuits led to a court ruling that pesticide reports are public documents, helped lead to a national ban on DDT, helped illustrate the inextricable relationships between environmental problems and social inequalities, and secured union contracts containing relatively elaborate pesticide-protection clauses for tens of thousands of California's farmworkers.

However, UFW representation declined precipitously in the 1980s, as the union was plagued by its own internal problems, competition from other labor unions, the shift of political power in California's leadership to the Republican Party, growers' increased reliance on farm-labor contractors and unauthorized immigrant workers, and the growing power of agribusiness and its antiunion politics (Brown and Getz 2008, Majka and Majka 2000, Pulido 1996, Wells 1996). This decline in union power highlights one of the primary weaknesses of the UFW's pesticide campaign: Its insistence on securing pesticide protections through individual union contracts rendered those protections temporary, vulnerable, and spatially uneven. Nonetheless, the UFW pesticide campaign of the 1960s (and its less coherent reemergence in the 1980s) left behind the important legacies of coalition-building and of conceptualizing economic inequalities as the root of environmental problems—a practice and a perspective, respectively, that would come to influence pesticide drift activism after 2000.

The dissipation of broad-scale attention to farmworker pesticide exposure after the 1970s can be attributed to multiple interrelated factors, including farmworkers' decreasing political power and the rise of neoliberal ideology and practice throughout the 1980s. The porous nature of the farm-labor market that contributed to the downfall of the UFW similarly served to increase farmworker vulnerability and the invisibility of farmworkers' problems throughout California. Throughout the 1980s and '90s, brutal authoritarian regimes in Central America, neoliberal economic restructuring within Mexico, and neoliberal U.S.–Mexican trade agreements created widespread insecurity in the Latin American countryside and thus compelled increased immigration into the United States from those regions, thus saturating the labor market, further suppressing farm wages, and thwarting unionization efforts (Barry 1995, Majka and Majka 2000, Wright 2005). At the same time, contemporary U.S. border policies deepen immigrants' vulnerabilities by further militarizing the border zone (pushing people to cross in increasingly dangerous and remote deserts and mountains and to rely on smugglers), policing those racially marked as Mexican within the interior of the United States, as well as detaining, deporting, and criminally prosecuting immigrants on an unprecedented scale (Andreas 2001, Coleman 2009, Cornelius 2001, Golash-Boza 2012, Nevins 2002, Rosas 2006).

The Sustainable Agriculture Movement: Market-Based Change

Within this context of deepening farmworker vulnerability, the shrinking power of farmworker unions, the decline of the broader civil rights movement, and the rise in neoliberal regulatory reform and ideology throughout the 1980s, most California activists concerned about pesticides have, over time, come to drop their involvement in oppositional, justice-based, and agricultural workplace-oriented work. Today, agrifood activists concerned about pesticides focus largely on building alternatives to conventional farming and food systems: developing less-toxic farming practices, disseminating those practices through voluntary educational programs, developing alternative marketing systems that link participating farmers with consumers willing to pay more for sustainably grown food, and boosting information to facilitate consumer choice (Allen et al. 2003, Guthman 2008). Organizations leading the sustainable agriculture movement in California include California Certified Organic Farmers (CCOF), Community Alliance with Family Farmers, the Ecological Farming Association, and the Organic Farming Research Foundation, all members of the National Sustainable Agriculture Coalition (NSAC). Their work is supported by many others, including academics, popular food writers, celebrity chefs, and a legion of enthusiastic shoppers.

That is, during the same period that neoliberal reforms were undermining the pesticide regulatory apparatus, sustainable agriculture activists' favored practices have taken a decidedly market-based turn, much like those of the mainstream environmental movement (Faber 2008, Park and Pellow 2011). Organic farming constitutes the primary way activists have addressed agricultural pesticide problems, relying on consumer demand and organic price premiums to entice farmers to reduce pesticide use (Guthman 2008, 2004). Those organizations that approach pesticide issues through policy reform do so by advocating for Farm Bill reforms that help incentivize farmers' (voluntary) transitions to organic agriculture (e.g., NSAC 2013). Consumers' increasing demand for organic food rewards environmental stewardship, has enabled more acres to be devoted to organic production, demonstrates the practicability and economic viability of less toxic pest management, compels further research and development of organic production methods, and provides an avenue through which many consumers start thinking critically about food-system ecology and politics. "Fair trade," "beyond organic," and "sustainably grown" efforts similarly seek to reduce pesticide problems by differentiating food in the marketplace with labels touting environmentally sustainable production practices. Advocates also widely promote local-food marketing arrangements such as farmers' markets, community-supported agriculture, urban farms, and direct contracts between farms and local restaurants, schools, and other institutions, arguing that buying locally eliminates "pesticide induced illness suffered by farmers or consumers," among many other benefits (Locavores 2013).

The market-based turn in sustainable agriculture activists' practice is also reflected in their discourse. As one politically active and well-known organic farmer declared in his presentation at a pesticide activist conference in 2010, "I don't have the patience for policy reform. . . . How do you capture health?

You eat better. You grow a garden. We don't have to wait for Washington." At the same conference, an activist leader stated in her presentation that to address environmental problems in agriculture, "We need to turn vacant lots into local gardens instead of going to Washington." Frustrated with the state, sustainable agriculture organizations stridently eschew the possibility of reducing pesticide pollution through regulatory reform and instead encourage changes in individual behaviors to reduce pesticide exposure. CCOF bumper stickers urge consumers to "Save Yourself—Eat Organic," and organic advocates widely urge us to express our food politics by "voting with our dollars." A CCOF newsletter advocates market-based measures as the only reasonable way to solve pesticide problems: "The only easy solution that seems to work is for consumers to ... vote for the future of farming and vitality of our environment with their dollars and sense, shifting the market toward organic foods and sustainable products" (Bednarz 2007, 18).

Popular food writers like Michael Pollan fuel this fire, urging readers to address their concerns by changing the ways they shop, cook, and eat (Bobrow-Strain 2012, DuPuis 2007, Guthman 2007). A recent op-ed by *New York Times* food writer Mark Bittman exemplifies this discourse. In the essay, originally posted online with the teaser "A powerful personal food policy doesn't have to rely on corporate benevolence or the government getting things right—thank goodness," Bittman claims that "real change doesn't come from ... government" and that readers can give up on regulatory change precisely because we can shop and eat differently (Bittman 2014).

Pesticide politics has thus largely undergone a significant set of transitions since the 1960s: from an interrogation of social injustices at the site of production to a focus on the final product; from collective action that crossed class divides to individualized consumer politics; from a prioritization of farmworker unionizing to a reliance on food labeling; from aiming to combat pesticide use in conventional agriculture to targeting support for alternative spaces of production; and from a broad conceptualization of pesticides' environmental and public health risks to a focus on food safety.

Allen et al. (2003) show that numerous factors compelled sustainable agriculture advocates to shift to market-based practices in recent years. With the decline of the civil rights movement, neoliberal evisceration of regulatory agencies, and decline of foundation funding for policy work, activists found the oppositional and confrontational work of regulatory and policy change to be slow, outgunned, unfunded, and emotionally taxing. At the same time, advocates found that collaborative work on alternative farming systems was more pleasurable, effectively helped many farmers transition to less toxic pest-management systems, and was more attractive to state and private funders. Additionally, many leaders reported feeling compelled to abandon their farmworker justice projects because farmers in alternative marketing systems depended on and fought to maintain the same labor relations as conventional farmers (Getz et al. 2008, Guthman 2004, Shreck et al. 2006).

At the same time that labor relations have become the elephant in the room for the sustainable agriculture movement, pesticide reform has become increasingly dislocated from questions of farmworker justice and the spaces of conventional agriculture itself. The organic food movement has brought considerable attention to the health effects of pesticides, yet it has done so by squarely defining those effects in terms of consumer health and food safety. In their discursive embrace of, and reliance on, voluntary and market-based measures, and their concomitant dismissal and abandonment of pesticide regulatory reform, sustainable agriculture advocates treat the avoidance of pesticide exposure as a personal choice, not as a right to be ensured by the state. This approach is undemocratic, as only those individuals with extra money to spend get to "vote" and secure protections from pesticide exposure. The protections secured by organics and other market-based efforts are spatially and temporally uneven, as they are tethered to isolated, individualized purchases and contingent upon ever-shifting consumer and industry whims and abilities. Claims that we can address our food system's problems through our own individual food politics dismiss the important regulatory protections that do exist and the essential role of the state in protecting environmental and social justice. Organic's gains are also geographically limited; despite rapid growth in the organic food industry, organic farming accounts for only 4 percent of California's harvested cropland.[1] Obscured in the shadow of organic's spectacular rise remain the recurring pesticide drift incidents as well as troubling data about pesticide use in the other 96 percent of California's agricultural acres.

Pesticide Drift Activism

Another group of politically active residents—pesticide drift activists—are frustrated by the state's failure to reduce the threats to human health posed by agricultural pesticides. However, they apply their anger through an approach that differs from that of the sustainable agriculture movement. Pesticide drift activists fight for regulatory restrictions on the use of the most toxic and drift-prone pesticides to reduce pesticide drift and the associated illnesses in California's agricultural communities.

Starting in the early 1990s, but gaining considerable strength after several particularly egregious pesticide drift events in 1999 and the early 2000s, pesticide drift victims and other outspoken community members (initially along the Central Coast and later in the San Joaquin Valley) began to form community-based organizations to address their shared concerns about lingering health problems and inadequate emergency and regulatory response. To confront the problem of pesticide drift, these grassroots organizations (including the Committee for the Wellbeing of Earlimart, and Save Our Shafter) soon joined forces with other non-governmental organizations (including the Association of Irritated Residents; California Rural Legal Assistance; Californians for Pesticide Reform; Center on Race, Poverty, and Environment; Fresno Metro Ministries; Pesticide Action Network [PAN]; Pesticide Watch; and the UFW). Many of these organizations are also now linked through regional coalitions such as the Central California Environmental Justice Network, California Environmental Justice Alliance, and Environmental Justice Coalition for Water.

Although active statewide, environmental justice activism around pesticide drift is most vibrant in the San Joaquin Valley, which produces half of all U.S. fruits and vegetables. To pursue their primary goal of regulatory restrictions on the most toxic and unruly pesticides, they hold press conferences and public rallies, give testimony at regulatory hearings, prepare research reports, bring lawsuits and administrative complaints against regulatory agencies, collect their own original health and pesticide exposure data, do grassroots organizing and education, and lead "toxic tours" to educate the press, regulatory staff, and elected officials about the multiple environmental hazards in contaminated communities.[2]

The UFW participates in pesticide drift activism, and campaigns to improve farmworkers' livelihoods can spur their participation in activism around pesticides and other issues (Pulido 1996; see also chapters 4, 5, and 7, this volume). That said, pesticide drift activism is more expansive in focus than the 1960s pesticide campaigns and targets the pesticide exposures exacerbated by farmworker injustice without wading into the political quagmire of the farm-labor market itself. Reaching out to *residents* engages a broader array of pesticide exposures as well as a more politically enfranchised constituency. Although pesticide drift activists staunchly criticize agencies' demonstrated proclivity to disproportionately represent industry interests and the roll-back of environmental regulations, they recognize *possibilities* for regulatory reform that were unimaginable to the UFW in the 1960s.

Drawing on their experiences living and working in agricultural communities, pesticide drift activists emphasize the everyday nature of pesticide drift. In interviews with me and in community meetings that I observed, resident-activists recounted innumerable stories of suspected pesticide exposure and described life in the San Joaquin Valley as drenched in a mist of pesticides. One activist remarked that new scientific research demonstrating high levels of certain pesticides in her neighborhood failed to shock many of her neighbors: "It's like telling people that it's windy. We are so used to it." Pesticide drift, exposure, and illness are part of normal, everyday life in agricultural communities.

These activists also emphasize the ways in which the material inequalities and social relations of oppression that characterize life in agricultural communities undermine existing regulations. Poverty exacerbates the likelihood of pesticide exposure and prevents people from reporting suspected exposures. As one farmworker with two young children explained:

> We live in a trailer park in a mobile home, surrounded by orange groves. At night during the spraying season we get sick, with symptoms that wake us up. We have asked the owner of the trailer park to do something about this problem, at least let us know when spraying is going to happen, but the owner always tells us we can leave if we don't like the situation, that we should look for another place to live. But we can't afford to rent a lot in another park.

Another explained that she could not afford to go the doctor when she was exposed to pesticides: "They said they need sufficient proof. How do you prove it with no money? No money, no doctor!" Without enough resources, her illness went unreported. Others explained that many residents' lack of legal status deters some from reporting their pesticide exposures, as does the fact that jobs are scarce and valuable. As one organizer explained, "There's incidents that are happening all of the time, they just go on not reported. Sometimes the people don't want to get involved—fear of retaliation—or they just simply don't know what it is. Especially the undocumented. You know, 'We're not saying anything. We'll get deported. We'll get fired. Our families back home depend on us working.' [So they are] afraid to speak out and have the fear that they're going to be deported or going to be fired."

Activists emphasize also that employers, medical professionals, and regulatory officials dismiss residents' concerns about possible pesticide exposures or take a long time to investigate. Pesticide drift activists explain that a slow, inadequate, or disrespectful regulatory response to residents' reports of pesticide drift creates a negative feedback of suppressing other pesticide exposures: "If people see that the officials do not do anything when other people report pesticide exposure, then they say, 'Why should I report this? Nothing will be done.'" I, too, witnessed this dismissive behavior in my interviews with regulatory representatives. They typically referred to residents' concerns about pesticide drift as "complaints" (rather than "concerns"); framed many "complaints" as unreasonable, stemming from what they see as irrational, uneducated, or uninformed anxiety; and discussed residents' concerns with a condescending and exasperated tone.

These social constraints work in concert with a range of more technical factors (e.g., many acute symptoms of pesticide exposure mimic common ailments and thus seem unremarkable to victims and their doctors, and some pesticides do not cause any acute symptoms at all), together obscuring most pesticide drift and illness from public view and from official statistics and causing pesticide regulations to be underinformed by the experiences of those who interface with pesticide drift most acutely. Pesticide drift activists thus argue for stronger regulations to account for these dynamics: more uniform enforcement of existing regulations, greater public influence over regulatory decision making to balance industry influence, standardized protections across California's counties, and new, strengthened restrictions on pesticide use to account for the widespread but unreported pesticide exposures and illnesses. In demanding these regulatory reforms, they reject the market-based approaches favored by both the state and the sustainable agriculture movement. Pesticide drift activists call on the regulatory state to ensure rights-based protections from pesticide exposure for all of California's residents—not just those able to afford organic food or work on organic farms.

Many pesticide drift activists conceptualize their work as part of the broader sustainable agriculture movement and at times work as allies with other sustainable agriculture organizations, the type of connection that Alkon (2014), Gottlieb and Joshi (2010), and others have advocated. Yet, to be clear, pesticide drift activists' efforts to help incentivize sustainable agriculture *augment*—but do not replace—their demands for regulatory restrictions on pesticide use. For example, PAN has helped develop the Equitable Food Initiative, a voluntary labeling program in which participating industry actors promise to meet certain labor, food-safety, and pest-management standards. That effort augments PAN's regulatory reform work. The continued role of both approaches is reflected, for example, in PAN's spring 2014 newsletter, which describes their Equitable Food Initiative efforts alongside an article about the organization's efforts to strengthen the Worker Protection Standard, a key set of laws providing basic health protections for farmworkers (PAN 2014, 1). Similarly, a representative of Californians for Pesticide Reform described how they are working to help incentivize sustainable agriculture but emphasized that they are not abandoning their regulatory reform work: "We are not dropping the stick just to pick up the carrot."

Some pesticide drift activists acknowledge that these different models of change are not always in harmony with each other. In an interview with me, one PAN representative reflected on the tensions that "will always be there" between fighting for the "stick" of regulatory reform and encouraging the "carrot" of alternative agriculture: "We do not historically have a good relationship with growers, because we have been all about the stick. . . . Until you get rid of the tools, there's no incentive for farmers to change. On the other hand, it is really hard for us to both be the stick, which we continue at the regulatory level, especially federal but also within California, [and the carrot]. . . . It's really hard for us to do both. But we want to do both, because we know full well and absolutely that the only real solution is sustainable agriculture. . . . So we have to play both, and it's a real challenge." Indeed, this relationship between pesticide drift activism and sustainable agriculture advocacy is an inherently uneasy one. Guthman and Brown's work (chapter 4, this volume) shows that the framing of pesticides as a threat to consumer health privileges consumers' bodies over those of farmworkers and drops pesticide drift out of the picture.

Additionally, sustainable agriculture organizations' demonstrated preference for farmer-friendly educational and marketing tactics makes many of them unwilling to also pursue restrictions on pesticides and other tactics that would alienate their farmer-organization partners. One pesticide drift activist explained to me this tension between sustainable agriculture advocates and pesticide drift activists:

> They were pretty scared of us, I would say. Because we were calling farmers bad people because they were poisoning people. And that was not their— One, they didn't want to be political. Two, they didn't want to be associated with environmental wackos who were causing problems in the grower

community. They had a different method for trying to get farmers to transition to sustainable agriculture. The organic community—or the sustainable ag activists—are trying to expand the numbers of farmers who are practicing sustainable agriculture or organic production, and certainly the pesticide drift activists want that to happen as well, but how you get there is very different. . . . You'd think they would be natural allies but they weren't just because the sustainable ag folks, well, the pesticide drift activists were so, I mean, *they were sick!* They were poisoned. And they were angry, and they were going to be confrontational. And the sustainable agriculture folks had a very different thing. They weren't *living* pesticide use like the pesticide drift activists were, so they weren't compelled in the same way to work on these issues as someone who's poisoned or whose child is poisoned. So strategies were really different, and messages were really different.

Despite the overlap between the goals of these activists, many pesticide drift activists feel that sustainable agriculture advocates' industry-friendly approach does not sufficiently confront the pesticide exposures that poison and terrify people in agricultural communities. Most pesticide drift activists thus express ambivalence about sustainable agriculture advocacy and insist on the need for pesticide regulatory reform.

Pesticide drift activists struggle with their own internal conflicts about goals and tactics, even greater budget constraints than those faced by other activists, the challenges of grassroots organizing in disadvantaged communities, and the constraints posed by an increasingly disabled regulatory apparatus. Although pesticide regulations and institutions are far from reaching their full health-protective potential, the baroque vestige of a progressive regulatory apparatus provides a preexisting framework that relieves the politically active public from having to reinvent the regulatory wheel. Pesticide drift activists have made numerous accomplishments, including securing, in 2004, the passage of the Pesticide Drift Exposure Response Act, which provides for improved response to pesticide drift incidents and processes to pay the uncompensated medical bills of pesticide drift victims; helping halt the registration of methyl iodide, a new and highly toxic soil fumigant, in 2011 (Guthman and Brown 2016b; chapter 4, this volume); and pressuring CDPR and U.S. EPA to implement significant regulatory restrictions on some of the most toxic and drift-prone pesticides, including chloropicrin and chlorpyrifos.[3] Pesticide drift activists also spearheaded the development of the Kern Environmental Enforcement Network, which includes a hotline for anonymously reporting environmental health hazards (including but not limited to pesticides) and monthly meetings in which agency representatives together work to solve problems reported through the hotline (KEEN 2014). Pesticide drift activists have also constructively influenced California EPA's new Environmental Justice Initiative, helping shape the ways in which environmental justice is conceptualized and operationalized within the California regulatory arena (Liévanos 2012, London et al. 2008).

CONCLUSION

I have argued that California's pesticide drift activism can be understood as a reaction to the deadly hazards deepened by both neoliberal regulatory roll-back and the sustainable agriculture movement's preoccupation with market-based practices. Neoliberal regulatory reforms further undermined the ability of regulatory agencies to protect public health—agencies that have always been better at getting pesticides to market than reducing their fallout. At the same time, while the sustainable agriculture movement evolved out of frustration with an inadequate regulatory apparatus and raises concerns about pesticides, its turn to market-based politics privileges the bodies of relatively wealthy and well-informed consumers, sidelines exposures near the site of production, absolves the state of its failure to protect the health of California's most marginalized residents, and structures protections from pesticide exposure as a *privilege* rather than a right.

This analysis thus problematizes not so much the door-opening "carrots" of alternative food movements but rather the lack of regulatory "sticks" so necessary for closing the door to the most toxic and drift-prone chemicals. The danger lies in the moment that alternatives become severed from the broader fights for responsible and fair government protections—protections that markets cannot provide and that are beyond the scope and scale of volunteer activities. In casting light on people and places abandoned by the state and by the sustainable agriculture movement alike, pesticide drift events demonstrate that alternative markets and technologies represent necessary but insufficient solutions, thereby highlighting the erroneous presumption of trickle-down justice embedded in neoliberal ideology. This is why pesticide drift activism is so important: it helps us see that remedying the pesticide problem for all people requires regulatory restrictions on the most toxic and drift-prone pesticides.

NOTES

1. The 405,473 acres of certified organic cropland (USDA 2011) account for 4.2 percent of all 9,591,783 acres of cropland in California (USDA 2012).

2. Many food justice organizations that fight to secure a right to food for all people employ similar practices (Alkon 2014, Alkon and Agyeman 2011, Alkon and Norgaard 2009, Gottlieb and Joshi 2010).

3. Partly as a result of pesticide drift activism, CDPR designated chloropicrin as a Toxic Air Contaminant in 2011; proposed tightened regulations for chloropicrin to protect bystanders in 2014; and proposed making chlorpyrifos a restricted-use material in 2014. In response to a 2007 lawsuit filed by Earthjustice on behalf of PAN and the Natural Resources Defense Council, U.S. EPA announced in 2015 that it would ban nearly all uses of chlorpyrifos.

REFERENCES

Alkon, Alison Hope. 2014. "Food Justice and the Challenge to Neoliberalism." *Gastronomica* 14(2): 27–40.

Alkon, Alison Hope, and Julian Agyeman, Eds. 2011. *Cultivating Food Justice: Race, Class, and Sustainability*. Cambridge, MA: MIT Press.

Alkon, Alison Hope, and Kari Marie Norgaard. 2009. "Breaking the Food Chains: An Investigation of Food Justice Activism." *Sociological Inquiry* 79: 289–305.

Allen, Patricia. 1999. "Reweaving the Food Security Safety Net: Mediating Entitlement and Entrepreneurship." *Agriculture and Human Values* 16: 117–129.

Allen, Patricia, Margaret Fitzsimmons, Michael K. Goodman, and Keith Warner. 2003. "Shifting Plates in the Agrifood Landscape: The Tectonics of Alternative Food Initiatives in California." *Journal of Rural Studies* 19: 61–75.

Allen, Patricia, and Julie Guthman. 2006. "From 'Old School' to 'Farm-to-School': Neoliberalization From the Ground Up." *Agriculture and Human Values* 23: 401–415.

Allen, Patricia, and Martin Kovach. 2000. "The Capitalist Composition of Organic: The Potential of Markets in Fulfilling the Promise of Organic Agriculture." *Agriculture and Human Values* 17: 221–232.

Andreas, Peter. 2001. "The Transformation of Migrant Smuggling across the U.S.–Mexican Border." In *Global Human Smuggling: Comparative Perspectives,* ed. D. Kyle and R. Koslowski, 107–125. Baltimore, MD: Johns Hopkins University Press.

Baker, Brian P. 1988. "Pest Control in the Public Interest: Crop Protection in California." *Journal of Environmental Law and Policy* 8: 31–77.

Barry, Tom. 1995. *Zapata's Revenge: Free Trade and the Farm Crisis in Mexico*. Boston: South End Press.

Bednarz, Colleen. 2007. "Protecting Sustainable Resources: Voting Organic with Your Dollars and Sense." *California Certified Organic Farmers Magazine,* winter.

Bittman, Mark. 2014. "(Only) Two Rules for a Good Diet." *The New York Times,* October 21.

Bobrow-Strain, Aaron. 2012. *White Bread: A Social History of the Store-Bought Loaf.* Boston: Beacon Press.

Brown, Sandy, and Christy Getz. 2008. "Privatizing Farm Worker Justice: Regulating Labor through Voluntary Certification and Labeling." *Geoforum* 39: 1184–1196.

California Department of Pesticide Regulation. 2001. "Regulating Pesticides: The California Story." Sacramento: CDPR.

———. 2003. "Funding California's Pesticide Regulatory Program: A Report to the Legislature." Sacramento: CDPR.

———. 2006a. "DPR Director: Mary-Ann Warmerdam." Sacramento: CDPR. www.cdpr.ca.gov/dprbios.htm. Accessed May 1, 2006.

———. 2006b. "Summary of Pesticide Use Report Data 2004, Indexed by Commodity." Sacramento: CDPR.

———. 2012. Pesticide Illness Surveillance Program data [online]. Sacramento: CDPR. www.cdpr.ca.gov/docs/whs/pisp.htm. Accessed January 13, 2012.

———. 2014. "Summary of Pesticide Use Report Data 2012." Sacramento: CDPR. www.cdpr.ca.gov/docs/pur/pur12rep/12sum.htm. Accessed November 24, 2014.

Center for Food Safety. 2014. "EPA Approves New 2,4-D Herbicide Blend, Paving Way for Controversial GE Crops." Press release, October 15. www.centerfor foodsafety.org/press-releases/3536/epa-approves-new-2-4-d-herbicide-blend-paving-way-for-controversial-ge-crops# Accessed 11/25/14.

Coleman, Mat. 2009. "What Counts as the Politics and Practice of Security, and Where? Devolution and Immigrant Insecurity after 9/11." *Annals of the Association of American Geographers* 99: 904–913.

Cornelius, Wayne A. 2001. "Death at the Border: Efficacy and Unintended Consequences of U.S. Immigration Control Policy." *Population and Development Review* 27: 661–685.

DuPuis, E. Melanie. 2007. "Angels and Vegetables: A Brief History of Food Advice in America." *Gastronomica* 7(2): 34–44.

DuPuis, E. Melanie, and David Goodman. 2005. "Should We Go 'Home' to Eat? Toward a Reflexive Politics of Localism." *Journal of Rural Studies* 21: 359–371.

Faber, Daniel R. 2008. *Capitalizing on Environmental Injustice: The Polluter-Industrial Complex in the Age of Globalization.* Lanham, MD: Rowman and Littlefield.

Gareau, Brian. 2013. *From Precaution to Profit: Contemporary Challenges to Environmental Protection in the Montreal Protocol.* New Haven, CT: Yale University Press.

Getz, Christy, Sandy Brown, and Aimee Shreck. 2008. "Class Politics and Agricultural Exceptionalism in California's Organic Agriculture Movement." *Politics and Society* 36: 478–507.

Golash-Boza, Tanya. 2012. *Due Process Denied: Detentions and Deportations in the United States.* New York: Routledge.

Gottlieb, Robert, and Anupama Joshi. 2010. *Food Justice.* Cambridge, MA: MIT Press.

Guthman, Julie. 2004. *Agrarian Dreams: The Paradox of Organic Farming in California.* Berkeley: University of California Press.

———. 2007. "Can't Stomach It: How Michael Pollan et al. Made Me Want to Eat Cheetos." *Gastronomica* 7(2): 75–79.

———. 2008. "Neoliberalism and the Making of Food Politics in California." *Geoforum* 39: 1171–1183.

———. 2011. *Weighing In: Obesity, Food Justice, and the Limits of Capitalism.* Berkeley: University of California Press.

Guthman, Julie, and Sandy Brown. 2016a. "I Will Never Eat Another Strawberry Again: The Biopolitics of Consumer-Citizenship in the Fight against Methyl Iodide in California." *Agriculture and Human Values* 33: 575–585.

———. 2016b. "Midas' Not-So-Golden Touch: On the Demise of Methyl Iodide as a Soil Fumigant in California." *Journal of Environmental Policy & Planning* 18: 324–341.

Harris, Gardiner, and Robert Pear. 2007. "Ex-officials Tell of Tension over Science and Politics." *The New York Times,* July 12.

Harrison, Jill Lindsey. 2006. "'Accidents' and Invisibilities: Scaled Discourse and the Naturalization of Regulatory Neglect in California's Pesticide Drift Conflict." *Political Geography* 25: 506–529.

———. 2011. *Pesticide Drift and the Pursuit of Environmental Justice.* Cambridge, MA: MIT Press.

———. 2014. "Neoliberal Environmental Justice: Mainstream Ideas of Justice in Political Conflict over Agricultural Pesticides in the United States." *Environmental Politics* 23: 650–669.

KEEN. 2014. Kern Environmental Enforcement Network website. www.kernreport.org/. Accessed November 25, 2014.

Kegley, Susan, Anne Katten, and Marion Moses. 2003. "Secondhand Pesticides: Airborne Pesticide Drift in California." San Francisco, CA: Pesticide Action Network, California Rural Legal Assistance Fund, and Californians for Pesticide Reform.

Khokha, Sasha. 2009. "Reporter's Notes: Catching the Drift." *KQED Radio,* October 16. www.kqed.org/quest/radio/catching-the-drift. Accessed October 31, 2009.

Lake, Robert, and Lisa Disch. 1992. "Structural Constraints and Pluralist Contradictions in Hazardous Waste Regulation." *Environment and Planning A* 24: 663–681.

Leitner, Helga, Jamie Peck, and Eric Sheppard, Eds. 2007. *Contesting Neoliberalism: Urban Frontiers.* New York: Guilford.

Liévanos, Raoul. 2012. "Certainty, Fairness, and Balance: State Resonance and Environmental Justice Policy Implementation." *Sociological Forum* 27: 481–503.

Locavores. 2013. "Top Twelve Reasons to Eat Locally." www.locavores.com/how /why.php. Accessed April 20, 2013.

London, Jonathan K., Julie Sze, and Raoul S. Liévanos. 2008. "Problems, Promise, Progress, and Perils: Critical Reflections on Environmental Justice Policy Implementation in California." *UCLA Journal of Environmental Law & Policy* 26: 255–289.

Majka, Linda C., and Theo J. Majka. 2000. "Organizing U.S. Farm Workers: A Continuous Struggle." In *Hungry for Profit: The Agribusiness Threat to Farmers, Food, and the Environment,* ed. Fred Magdoff, John Bellamy Foster, and Frederick H. Buttel. New York: Monthly Review Press.

McWilliams, Carey. 1999 [1935]. *Factories in the Field: The Story of Migratory Farm Labor in California.* Berkeley: University of California Press.

Nevins, Joseph. 2002. *Operation Gatekeeper: The Rise of the "Illegal Alien" and the Making of the U.S.–Mexico Boundary.* New York: Routledge.

New York Times. 2006. "Editorial: Muzzling Those Pesky Scientists." December 11.

NSAC. 2013. "Conservation, energy, and environment." National Sustainable Agriculture Coalition. http://sustainableagriculture.net/our-work/con-servation-environment/. Accessed August 26, 2013.

O'Malley, Michael. 2004. "Pesticides." In *Current Occupational and Environmental Medicine,* ed. Joseph LaDou, 554–601. New York: Lange Medical Books/ McGraw-Hill.

PAN. 2014. *Pesticide Action Network News,* spring. www.panna.org/issues/pan-mag /pan-newsletter-spring-2014. Accessed November 25, 2014.

Park, Lisa Sun-Hee, and David Naguib Pellow. 2011. *The Slums of Aspen: Immigrants vs. the Environment in America's Eden.* New York: NYU Press.

PEER. 2006. "EPA Is Hastily Disposing of Its Library Collections: Orders to Trash Library Holdings Stirs Protests." November 20. Public Employees for Environmental Responsibility. www.peer.org/news/news_id.php?row_id=786.

Pulido, Laura. 1996. *Environmentalism and Economic Justice: Two Chicano Struggles in the Southwest.* Tucson: University of Arizona.

Rosas, Gilberto. 2006. "The Managed Violences of the Borderlands: Treacherous Geographies, Policeability, and the Politics of Race." *Latino Studies* 4: 401–418.

Sass, Jennifer Beth. 2008. "USDA Cuts Budget to Its Pesticide Use Data Program." *NDRC Switchboard* (Natural Resources Defense Council staff blog), May 20. http://switch-board.nrdc.org/blogs/jsass/_a_coalition_of_public.html. Accessed May 7, 2013.

Shreck, Aimee, Christy Getz, and Gail Feenstra. 2006. "Social Sustainability, Farm Labor, and Organic Agriculture: Findings from an Exploratory Analysis." *Agriculture and Human Values* 23: 439–449.

Slesinger, Scott. 2014. "EPA Spending in the President's Budget: Where Does the 0.22% of Federal Spending Go?" Natural Resources Defense Council staff blog, March 21. www.nrdc.org/experts/scott-slesinger/epa-spending-presidents-budget-where-does-022-federal-spending-go.

U.S. Department of Agriculture. 2002. "Census of Agriculture, Volume 1, Chapter 1: California State Level Data." www.nass.usda.gov/census/census02/volume1 /ca/index1.htm. Accessed March 26, 2006.

———. 2011. "Organic Production Overview," Table 4. USDA Economic Research Service. http://ers.usda.gov/data-products/organic-production.aspx#2424. Accessed March 30, 2015.

———. 2012. "Census of Agriculture, Volume 1, Chapter 1, Table 1: Historical Highlights." www.agcensus.usda.gov/Publications/2012/Full_Report/Volume_ 1,_Chapter_1_State_Level/California/. Accessed March 30, 2015.

U.S. Department of Labor. 2005. "Findings from the National Agricultural Workers Survey (NAWS) 2001–2002: A Demographic and Employment Profile of United States Farm Workers." Research Report 9. www.doleta.gov/agworker /report9/naws_rpt9.pdf.

U.S. Environmental Protection Agency. 2004. "Pesticides Industry Sales and Usage 2000 and 2001 Market Estimates." Office of Prevention, Pesticides, and Toxic Substances. www.epa.gov/oppbead1/pestsales/01pestsales/table_of_contents2001 .html.

———. 2005. "EPA's Pesticide Program FY 2005 Annual Report." www.epa.gov /oppfead1/annual/. Accessed December 13, 2006.

———. 2014a. "EPA Launches a Voluntary Star-Rating Program to Reduce Pesticide Drift and Protect People, Wildlife and the Environment." News release, October 21. http://yosemite.epa.gov/opa/admpress.nsf/bd4379a92ceceeac852573 5900400c27/7f55633c82cd009285257d78005b932e!OpenDocument. Accessed November 25, 2014.

———. 2014b. "EPA's Budget and Spending." www2.epa.gov/planandbudget /budget. Accessed November 28, 2014.

———. 2014c. "Jim Jones, Assistant Administrator for the Office of Chemical Safety and Pollution Prevention." www2.epa.gov/aboutepa/jim-jones-assistant- administrator-office-chemical-safety-and-pollution-prevention. Accessed November 28, 2014.

Warner, Keith. 2007. *Agroecology in Action: Extending Alternative Agriculture through Social Networks.* Cambridge, MA: MIT Press.

Welch, Dwight, et al. 2006. "Letter to US EPA Administrator Stephen Johnson from Local Presidents of EPA Unions Representing Scientists, Risk Managers, and Related Staff." May 24. www.panna.org/resources/fqpa. Accessed December 20, 2009.

Wells, Miriam. 1996. *Strawberry Fields: Politics, Class, and Work in California Agriculture.* Ithaca, NY: Cornell University Press.

Wright, Angus. 2005. *The Death of Ramon Gonzalez.* Austin: University of Texas Press.

THREE

How Canadian Farmers Fought and Won the Battle against GM Wheat

Emily Eaton

INTRODUCTION

On May 10, 2004, agricultural giant Monsanto conceded defeat to a coalition of organizations opposing the introduction of transgenic Roundup Ready (RR) wheat in Canada by announcing that it would "discontinue breeding and field level research of Roundup Ready wheat" (Monsanto Company 2004). The withdrawal of RR wheat from North America marked a significant victory for the global movement against genetically modified (GM) crops. One of the world's most powerful agrochemical companies had decided to abandon commercialization of a crop that it had spent years and significant resources developing and advancing through the Canadian and American regulatory systems. Moreover, this marked the first defeat of an RR crop; Monsanto had already successfully commercialized the RR trait in other major crops such as soybeans, cotton, and canola.

Monsanto's concession to social opposition in North America, and especially to the Canadian anti-RR-wheat coalition, dominated by rural and farm groups, provides a dramatic example of the power of collective organizing. This example of a collective campaign challenges the conception of social change offered by neoliberal governmentality, wherein subjects are expected to exercise their opposition and express their values through the mechanism of individual choice by "voting with their dollars" in the market. As I will show in this chapter, the producers at the center of the anti-RR-wheat coalition eschewed the neoliberal understanding of social change that posits the market as the only appropriate site and mechanism of change. Instead, they insisted that their distinct and collective interests as producers of food should be reflected in Canadian biotech policy and argued that wheat should remain a crop that farmers could reproduce outside of markets through the practice of seed saving. Working strategically and with a specific and achievable goal, the coalition successfully dealt a blow to Monsanto's power and influence in industrial agriculture and state regulatory systems. In what follows, I tell the story of how the producer-led coalition defeated RR wheat. I begin with an introduction to the regulatory process for genetically modified organisms (GMOs) in Canada and move on to describe the nature and strengths of the coalition. The bulk of the chapter analyzes how producers successfully rejected the notion of individual consumer agency in favor of a collective campaign that asserted their common interests as producers of wheat.

REGULATING GM WHEAT IN CANADA

Unlike in many European jurisdictions, where GMOs trigger environmental, health, and safety assessments because of the novel *processes* and technologies through which they are made, in Canada only plants deemed to have novel traits trigger regulatory assessment. This *product*-based approach insists on understanding genetic engineering as the latest technology in a long trajectory of plant breeding, rather than as an inherently risky and novel process. In this view, it is not the method of production that requires regulation; rather, "plants with novel traits" (PNTs), regardless of the processes through which they are derived, are subject to safety assessment, whereas those found to be "substantially equivalent" to their nontransgenic counterparts escape regulatory assessment entirely. This product-based approach to the regulation of biotechnology has allowed the Canadian state to explicitly refrain from introducing new legislation targeting GMOs, relying instead on existing legislation and processes to regulate the introduction of plants that possess new characteristics.

When Monsanto withdrew its GM wheat from North America in 2004, the variety was already under review by the Canadian Food Inspection Agency (CFIA), the country's environmental regulator for PNTs. Having been found to possess a novel trait (herbicide resistance), Monsanto's RR wheat had triggered an environmental safety assessment and had been under review since 2002. During this time, RR wheat was being assessed according to the CFIA's criteria for PNTs, including the potential for it to become a weed of agriculture, invasive of natural habitats, or a plant pest; the potential for gene flow to wild relatives; and the potential impacts of RR wheat on nontarget species, including humans, and on biodiversity more broadly (Marcoux and Létourneau 2013). Since RR wheat was destined for human consumption, it had also triggered a novel-food assessment that would have been conducted by Health Canada; however, it had yet to begin when the company withdrew its application for unconfined release in 2004.

The Canadian state's product-based approach to the regulation of GMOs has been met with opposition by both civil-society groups and scientific-policy experts. In 2001, for example, the Expert Panel on the Future of Food Biotechnology convened by the Royal Society of Canada (Canada's senior national body of preeminent scientists and scholars) released a report titled "Elements of Precaution: Recommendations for the Regulation of Food Biotechnology in Canada" that challenged the principle of substantial equivalence whereby GM plants found to a have "familiar" traits are deemed equivalent to their non-GM counterparts and, therefore, require no new safety assessments. Importantly, the report also advocated that socioeconomic and ethical concerns be taken into account in regulatory decisions, a recommendation that ran counter to the CFIA's insistence that such concerns are outside the scope of their professed "sound science" approach. Despite such reports and civil-society pressure, Andrée and Sharratt (2004) argue that the government has not moved toward a precautionary approach to biotechnology, nor has it recognized the principle of substantial equivalence as inherently biased and inadequate. Instead, Canadian victories against GMOs have been won on a case-by-case basis through targeted social-movement campaigns. According to the Canadian Biotechnology Action Network (n.d.), which emerged from the collaborative work of twenty-three environmental, social justice, and consumer groups dating back to 1999, social-movement pressure in Canada has resulted both in the CFIA denying the approval of GMOs (e.g., bovine growth hormone) and in biotech companies voluntarily withdrawing GMOs from the regulatory approval process, as was the case with Monsanto's withdrawal of RR wheat.

CANADA'S ANTI-RR-WHEAT COALITION AND CAMPAIGN

In July 2001, a coalition of farm, consumer, environmental, health, and industry organizations announced their opposition to Monsanto's RR wheat at a press conference in Winnipeg, Manitoba (for an outline of the organizations and their positions, see table 3.1). Over the next four years, the organizations involved in the coalition launched coordinated but organizationally distinct challenges to both Monsanto and the CFIA, which ultimately resulted in Monsanto abandoning RR wheat. Unlike the urban and health-driven movements that dominate the politics of opposition to GMOs elsewhere in the Global North, this coalition was composed primarily of rural and farm groups (six of the nine coalition members). From the beginning, then, the campaign against RR wheat in Canada incorporated, but also subordinated, consumer and health discourses about the dangers of "frankenfoods" that more typically characterize the urban and consumer anti-GMO campaigns of the Global North. Instead, rural and farm groups brought agronomic and stewardship concerns to the forefront of their campaign by highlighting how RR weeds and gene flow would disrupt their cropping and land-management practices; how the proprietary nature of the technology would threaten their ability to save wheat seed from year to year; and how widespread GMO contamination of wheat crops would threaten both organic and conventional export wheat markets because of the nonacceptance of GMO contamination by major trading partners, including Japan and the European Union.

Although their coordinated work was ultimately successful, there were significant disagreements between factions within the coalition. Rural farm groups were at odds because they disagreed on their broader positions on GM crops. For example, general farm and rural organizations representing all producers and rural municipalities in Saskatchewan and all producers in Manitoba took pains to ensure that their positions of opposition to RR wheat were not understood as a broader rejection of GMOs or other RR crops. After all, a large majority of their members were, by this time, planting transgenic, herbicide-tolerant canola, including RR varieties. In fact, by 2005, herbicide-tolerant, transgenic varieties accounted for 78 percent of all canola grown nationally (Beckie et al. 2006). Other coalition members representing smaller rural constituencies took more categorical positions against all GMOs. For example, the National Farmers Union (NFU), a more left-wing farm organization with roots in the agrarian populist organizing of the early twentieth century, was demanding a moratorium on all GMOs in Canada until they could be brought under democratic, not-for-profit, collective control. Similarly, the Saskatchewan Organic Directorate (SOD) advocated for a ban on all GMOs, arguing that GMO agriculture was incompatible with organic agriculture because of the inevitability of contamination that occurs when GM crops are produced in the same ecological setting as non-GM crops. In fact, during the early 2000s, SOD was receiving significant media attention for its (ultimately unsuccessful) attempt to certify a class-action lawsuit against Monsanto and Bayer for contamination of organic canola with GM varieties.

Also strongly dividing coalition members were producer concerns about the agronomic and economic viability of RR wheat versus urban concerns related to health and environmental risks. Indeed, many farm groups did not want to be seen to be working with consumer and environmental groups like the Council of Canadians (a multi-issue NGO with a large urban base) and Greenpeace. Interviewees from many farm-based groups expressed sentiments similar to those voiced by a member of the Agricultural Producers Association of Saskatchewan: "If they [Greenpeace] would grandstand that press release that we were having down in Winnipeg we would pull out, meaning some stupid Greenpeacer was climbing a tower or something like, that you know, we were out." Another interviewee from the Council of Canadians emphasized that the coalition operated "behind closed doors" because farm-based groups understood organizations such as theirs and Greenpeace as being composed of "crop pullers" and as therefore potentially threatening to conventional agriculture. Given this tension, the coalition served less to bring together members in public displays of unity and strength; instead, it worked primarily to coordinate actions and messaging while maintaining the diversity of positions and methods of opposition advanced by the different organizations.

Despite the tenuous and fractious nature of the coalition, farm groups were reluctantly ready to set aside their differences. They recognized that they had a clear and tangible goal—to stop the introduction of RR wheat—that all member organizations agreed on, despite their differing positions on the broader question of GMOs. Producer organizations also recognized that the issue of GM wheat was not only a farm issue and, thus, they could not stop it alone. With this understanding, the coalition began mobilizing strategically and collectively in order to achieve their goal. This involved identifying appropriate targets that could concede to their demand and putting pressure on those targets through a broad and diverse base of supporters. In other words, the coalition acted as a *social movement,* defined by theorist Doug McAdam (1982, 20) as "rational attempts by excluded groups to mobilize sufficient political leverage to advance collective interests through non-institutionalized means."

The two main targets of the coalition's four-year campaign were the CFIA and Monsanto Company. Both targets had the ability to deliver on the campaign's demand—to keep RR wheat out of Canada. The CFIA had the power to deny Monsanto's application for unconfined release of RR wheat, and Monsanto could withdraw its application. While ultimately it was Monsanto that abandoned RR wheat, the CFIA also succumbed to the pressure of the anti-RR-wheat campaign by notifying Monsanto in 2003 that the agency would need additional data in order to assess possible changes in agricultural practices resulting from the adoption of RR wheat. According to Marcoux and Létourneau (2013), this request for more data, which had the effect of delaying the regulatory acceptance of RR wheat, was a direct result of the pressure being put on the state agency by members of the coalition and the public. After all, the CFIA was not authorized to consider "socioeconomic" matters, but it used the flexibility of the Canadian regulatory system to pursue the public's socioeconomic concerns as a matter of environmental safety (Marcoux and Létourneau 2013). The CFIA's request for more information also signaled to Monsanto that the agency was being influenced by public concerns and that Monsanto's seed might endure extra scrutiny and take more time to receive regulatory approval.

In choosing to mount a collective opposition to RR wheat, and in insisting that producers have collective interests, the coalition challenged neoliberal conceptions of social change. In fact, perhaps the greatest hurdle for the coalition was countering the view—held by biotech companies, trade associations and lobby groups, plant breeders, scientists, regulators, and some farm organizations—that the fate of RR wheat should be decided in the marketplace through the mechanism of individual demand. Interestingly, this logic of market demand was applied not just to consumers of food, but also to farmers as buyers of seed. Biotech companies claimed that producers could register any concerns with RR wheat by choosing not to buy and plant RR seed, while food consumers could also choose not to buy GM products in grocery stores.

In supporting their argument about farmers as consumers of farm inputs, RR-wheat proponents cited the success of RR canola and the widespread adoption of the technology among prairie farmers. They therefore insisted that the only impartial method to decide the future of GM wheat was to introduce it into the market and let individual producers and consumers choose whether to buy it, based on their own specific needs. The marketplace was here represented as the only appropriate site and mechanism for social change. According to this reasoning, the proper role of the state was to make individual choice the organizing principle of the economy.

Directly in opposition to the idea that the fate of RR wheat should be decided in the market, farmers and citizens argued for a negotiated and collective decision to ban RR wheat. In advocating against commercialization, opponents of RR wheat advanced notions and examples of collective action and common good. For example, by recalling their history of cooperative organizing, representatives of farm organizations asserted their capacity to act collectively. At the same time, citizen, environmental, and health groups reinforced the idea that the public should be able to choose to keep certain products and technologies out of the market for enough time to make definitive conclusions about their safety and environmental effects. In other words, opponents of RR wheat argued that producers and citizens should have the right to decide the fate of RR wheat through collective processes, including public-policy measures.

GOVERNING THROUGH CONSUMPTION

There is no doubt that consumers can change the world in some way; however, it is important to think carefully about the nature of change that is based on individual market action. Social theorists Nikolas Rose (1999) and Mitchell Dean (1999) have both written extensively about the way in which the concepts of individual choice and freedom underpin modern approaches to governing society. Their insights help explain what was at stake in the argument that individual eaters and farmers should decide the fate of RR wheat by voting with their dollars. Rose and Dean draw on the concept of governmentality derived from the work of Michel Foucault to emphasize how the act of governing (that is, of directing, managing, controlling, and regulating human conduct) is not only centered in the power of the state and its bureaucracy but is also pursued by a variety of nonstate actors and institutions (for example, by markets, health-care practitioners, or community organizations) and is even perpetuated by individuals themselves.

For Dean (1999, 16), governmentality "deals with how we think about governing ... [and] emphasizes the way in which the thought involved in practices of government is collective and relatively taken for granted." In this respect, current practices of governing society can be understood as involving specific ways of thinking about how to manage the conduct of people. For example, under neoliberal economic relations, the discourse of individual market choice becomes a principle or vocabulary through which individuals regulate their own behavior, hopes, and desires. Government (managing oneself in relation to market choice) is here understood as an active process that individuals will exercise in their everyday lives. The notion of consumer choice is a diffuse discourse that shapes neoliberal subjectivity writ large; it is taken for granted in how individuals and groups act in the world. As Rose (1999, 87) suggests, subjects of neoliberalism (what he calls "advanced liberalism") necessarily understand themselves and their relationships to the world around them as constituted by personal choices and the exercise of freedom.

As chapter 1 of this volume makes clear, notions of personal choice and the exercise of freedom are essential to understanding contemporary food politics. For example, Guthman (2008, 1176) writes that "probably the most central organizing theme in contemporary food politics is consumer choice. That this seems to go without saying suggests the extent to which this notion has become taken for granted." Food activists and scholars alike seem to be quite taken with the possibility that consumers might express their politics and identities by means of their consumption and, through this practice of voting with their dollars, force meaningful social and environmental change in food systems. Yet a brief history of consumer activism shows that it is only under neoliberal governmentality that the notion of voting with one's dollar has come to dominate all forms of consumer activism.

As Lang and Gabriel (2005, 39–53) show, other waves of consumer activism have challenged the very logic of the market and the individualism that characterizes current consumer activism. For example, Lang and Gabriel highlight how, in the early nineteenth century, the British co-operative movement mobilized to supply working-class families with the basic consumer necessities of life at affordable prices that excluded profit. The goal then was explicitly to organize outside of regular market imperatives like competition and profit-seeking in a collective practice of self-help (for more on food co-ops, see chapters 8 and 9, this volume). In the 1930s, when food corporations were increasing their market shares through mergers, American consumers mobilized against that growing power by forming organizations (e.g., Consumers' Research, Inc.) that would offer product safety information so that consumers could more effectively pursue the best value for their money in the market. And in another wave of activism, consumers built grassroots public pressure directed at all levels of government, demanding stronger regulations and standards of corporate conduct in order to protect the individual citizen from corporate power.

So while the idea of consumers as self-conscious actors intervening in and shaping markets is not new, a decidedly neoliberal form of consumer action abandons targets such as state regulation and corporate power, and rejects tactics such as collective organizing around notions of a common good. Instead, individual acts of market consumption have come to dominate the current wave of consumer activism that Lang and Gabriel (2005) call "alternative consumerism." Growing out of the 1970s European "green" movement, alternative consumerism also gives up on earlier environmental-movement commitments to curbing consumption, in favor of seeing consumption itself as a conscious, strategic, and ethical practice.

The argument that individuals can be persuaded to understand and act according to a common good is fundamental to notions of citizenship (including social, legal, and political conceptions). This perspective sees citizens not only as exercising civil, political, and social rights but also as responsible to carry out the ethical obligations that accompany such rights (Rose 1999, 134). What happens, then, when the ethical obligations of citizenship are reconceptualized as "voting with your dollar," as they have been under neoliberal governance? There is mounting evidence that the ethics practiced through neoliberal consumption result in less-than-favorable outcomes. In fact, many social scientists (e.g., Guthman 2004, 2003b, Johnston 2008, Roff 2007) have found that promoting ethics through shopping results in encouraging the cultural ideology of consumerism, denying the political-economic inequality between social classes, and leaving many pressing environmental issues unaddressed (see also chapter 2, this volume). There are thus good reasons to doubt whether individual market choices can result in significant social and environmental change.

For this reason, it is concerning that scholars have noted a shift in which people are no longer addressed as citizens, but rather are understood, and are being prompted to understand themselves, as consumers first and foremost (Clarke and Newman 2007, Slocum 2004). Indeed, as Rose (1999, 141–142) emphatically shows, under neoliberal governance, consumerism and the logic of choice extend themselves to *all* aspects of social behavior, such that people are expected to use calculating economic behavior, previously reserved for the marketplace, in all interactions everywhere. Rose (ibid.) and Dean (1999, 57) argue that the neoliberal subject is an entrepreneur of herself. The interests that she registers on nondiscriminating markets are now expected to change on the basis of her capacity to be influenced by her environment. She is continually engaged in acquiring new skills and making active choices that will influence all aspects of her future (psychic, material, social, etc.). Calculating actions, weighing costs and benefits, investing in the future, and accounting for external contingencies characterize the neoliberal subject active in governing herself through the mechanism of choice. This is a subjectivity that draws on the assumptions of liberal subjectivity but that intensifies expectations of flexibility and change.

ROUNDUP READY WHEAT AS A MATTER OF INDIVIDUAL MARKET CHOICE

The idea that voting with your dollar in the market is the only appropriate site and mechanism for social change was abundantly clear in my interviews with proponents of RR wheat. Such supporters argued that any collective or political decisions about RR wheat would unfairly impede individuals from making their own market decisions, whatever the shortcomings of the crop. In fact, in interviews with me, RR-wheat proponents did not even attempt to refute the widely publicized and diverse criticisms that surround the debate about genetic modification. Few felt it necessary to convince me that the health and environmental risks associated with GMOs are overblown, or that the corporate control associated with GM crops is benign. On the contrary, even the most vocal supporters of RR wheat admitted that seed companies pursue their own interests and do not produce the types of traits that farmers find most useful. Instead, they argued that it is up to individuals to weigh their concerns against any possible private benefits; the risks associated with RR wheat should not preclude private assessments of its merits, which could be registered through (non)consumption in both seed and food markets.

Many proponents of RR wheat echoed the sentiments expressed by a representative of the Grain Growers of Canada who described the voluntary non-adoption or non-purchase of RR wheat by producers as impartial and attained through the mechanism of the market, while labeling government decision-making processes as ineffective and biased. According to this interviewee,

> what we were actually hoping for was the government to be able to say we support a voluntary approach to dealing with this issue. So give a clear signal to

push it back into industry . . . because some were arguing no let's let the government take it on, that they initiate [and] coordinate all the meetings and assign people to the topic and you know consult and blah, blah, blah. . . . So we were hoping . . . for them to say our policy is to pursue a voluntary option at this time, an industry driven approach . . . just [leave] that to the market for the industry to decide as opposed to the Canadian Grain Commission getting involved, the CFIA and all of that.

Rather than a matter for public policy, the adoption of RR wheat was understood by its proponents as an individual business decision to be left to those whose families and economic well-being depended on the profitability of their farms. For a participant representing the Grain Growers of Canada, the fate of RR wheat was "just a business decision—no more, no less, and that's it." Similarly, a representative of the Western Canadian Wheat Growers underscored his organization's approach to the issue as "working with those companies and seeing it as having solutions that producers may choose to utilize or not, and that was a choice for farmers to make." For these RR-wheat proponents, the farmer is the privileged actor and is best able to make decisions at the scale of the individual family farm.

The logic that markets rather than political movements and governments should decide the fate of RR wheat was also applied to food consumers. A representative from the CFIA explained that as long as a product passes the agency's health and environmental safety risk analysis, it can be sold in Canada, and wary food consumers would have to register their concerns through the market. This same respondent elaborated that no consumer is being forced to buy GMOs and that it is always a consumer's right not to buy what she or he does not want to eat.

A member of the Canadian Biotechnology Advisory Committee (a panel of "experts" tasked with organizing consultations about the regulation of GMOs in Canada) also preferred a market-based approach. This interviewee argued that liability laws incentivize against the production of dangerous or ineffective products, because of the threat that the company could be sued if its product fails. "They're not just betting the product line, they're betting the company and so, in fact, they usually exceed the requirements of the regulatory regime, at least the big ones, because they know there's no tolerance for failure." For supporters of GM technologies, precluding the introduction of RR wheat to the market unfairly punished companies and consumers that wanted to take advantage of the possible individual rewards associated with genetic modification.

Closely related to the notion of markets as the only reasonable arbiters of individual choice was the conviction that market dynamics support progress. Citing examples of technological development, proponents of RR wheat argued against the use of market impact assessment by regulators in evaluating RR wheat. In these market enthusiasts' views, preventing the introduction of RR wheat would threaten investment and breeding progress in the crop. According to this logic, producers should simply adjust to, rather than resist, changing market conditions. A participant from the Canadian Biotechnology Advisory Committee said in an interview:

> We don't compensate people who are losing. . . . When CDs, or DVDs, became the standard, we didn't compensate the Betamax people who couldn't get videos anymore, we didn't compensate the movie theaters for the fact that they couldn't sell seats anymore. Those resources had to be reallocated. . . . It's just accelerated depreciation and then it's a wash. So you didn't get as much benefit out of it as you might have, that's just the way the world works. That's the mentality that we now have, and it has real power, *because it pushes things forward* [emphasis added].

As this brief overview shows, variously positioned proponents of RR wheat used the "let the markets decide" approach to advance the idea that neither governments nor collectivities should intervene in the approval and commercialization of RR wheat. Rather than engaging and refuting farmer and citizen concerns about the environmental, economic, and agronomic impacts of RR wheat, the neoliberal discourse of individual choice was used to advance the proponents' case. This discourse transforms farmers, who are producers of food, into consumers of farm inputs, their agency constrained to individual market decisions. In this view, farmers are encouraged to manage themselves and their operations in relation to personal market choices, in the name of maximizing freedom and avoiding constraining regulation and public policy.

CHALLENGING INDIVIDUAL MARKET CHOICE

In their campaign, the coalition against RR wheat countered this discourse of the market as a just mechanism for registering and ensuring the right of individual choice, as already encompassing the correct incentives to ensure food and environmental safety, and as motivating technological progress.

Opponents of RR wheat worked hard to convey the shortcomings of the "let the markets decide" approach to politicians, regulators, and the general public. Through a variety of avenues and tactics, opponents of RR wheat countered market choice by pointing to the limited seed options already available on the market, the potential and real harm of RR crops to already existing production systems, and the fact that GM foods are not identifiable in the marketplace because Canada has not adopted mandatory labeling.

In presentations to government and political parties and in dialogues with urban publics, producers challenged the idea that markets are just mechanisms for farmers to freely express their individual choice. For example, rural and farm groups traveled to Ottawa to testify to both the House and Senate standing committees, and they organized a speaking tour focused on the agronomic and economic arguments against RR crops in order to broaden their base of allies. While such organizing efforts necessitated much time and effort, coalition members expressed the ease with which market arguments could be challenged. In an interview, a representative from Croplife Canada (a trade association representing numerous plant biotech companies) used the market logic that opponents of RR wheat found so easy to dispel:

> Right now canola is moving . . . from open-pollinated, which is where farmers can save their seed . . . to hybrid seed because they get better yields and better return on their investment. . . . The choice is there . . . a farmer can choose to grow an open-pollinated variety, but increasingly hybrids are what the farmers are buying because they get better yields, they've got better traits, because again the research and the development is going into the hybrids where the company can capture its investment. So, just like you and I buying quality products or CDs or anything like that, if the artist doesn't get the money back from what they've produced then they can't produce anymore.

Here the interviewee uses the example of hybrid varieties, instead of GM varieties, in order to make the point that farmers, through their market actions, are determining which varieties succeed and fail. In the initial section of the quotation this participant presents the planting of hybrid versus open-pollinated seed as the individual choice of the farmer. However, in the next breath the participant goes on to explain that it is the proprietary and profit-driven nature of research and investment that determines which varieties make it to market. While farmers may have the opportunity to choose between the products on the market, their spectrum of choices is narrowly constrained by the capacity of potential varieties to earn profits for agricultural corporations. In a breeding environment where patents on genes are increasingly the norm, products of genetic modification promise opportunities for enhanced accumulation of corporate profit. Thus, opponents of RR wheat argued that GM crops are, like hybrids, overrepresented in the spectrum of market choices.

Another proponent of genetic modification, representing the Canola Council of Canada, was equally contradictory in his enthusiasm for market choice, celebrating that "in canola there are really four systems available . . . so farmers absolutely have a choice about what chemistries they want to and don't want to use on their farm." The respondent here asserts the importance of individual farmers choosing the production systems that best suit them and claims that plenty of agronomic options exist. "If they are relying very heavily on one product . . . they're probably doing that because it's the most cost-effective option for them." However, as producers made clear in their testimony to the standing committees, in the speaking tour, and in their own published materials, the choice that the interviewee celebrates involves only four options, controlled and marketed as complete management systems by four large agrochemical companies. Instead, farm organizations characterized this narrow set of GM seed varieties, revolving almost singularly around herbicide resistance and marketed by just a few large companies, as a lack of choice. In fact, in campaign literature the NFU emphasized that at the same time that yields are improving because of the hybridization of canola, the spectrum of seed choice is dwindling for that crop. After all, farmers cannot buy seeds that retailers are not offering. In an interview, a representative of the NFU suggested that the result of this narrowed choice is the deskilling of the farmer and a loss of knowledge about biodiversity and productive practices. Once farmers have lost the ability and tradition of saving seed and selecting for characteristics that suit their local environments, future options are narrowed. Rather than a multiplicity of traits for which farmers select, herbicide resistance comes to dominate the market and the professional breeding agendas.

The second argument that opponents of RR wheat used to counter the discourse of individual market choice emphasized the threats that RR crops pose to existing systems of production. The argument that RR wheat threatened current agriculture, and thus narrowed the spectrum of choice for farmers, was advanced through at least two examples. First, farmers and the Canadian Wheat Board (CWB) felt that the introduction of RR wheat jeopardized existing wheat markets, especially those in Japan and the EU that had little tolerance for GMO contamination in their imports. This argument was driven home by farm groups in all their public presentations and literature, and in resolutions adopted by member organizations. In fact, the argument was even profiled by a leading national newspaper, the *Globe and Mail,* which published an op-ed by four professors of agricultural economics, applied microbiology, and food science:

> It would seem logical to adopt a strategy of letting wheat farmers choose between growing GM and non-GM wheat, depending on market signals. For one thing, GM wheat will provide agronomic benefits to some wheat producers. As for the price of GM wheat—which we initially would expect to be lower than non-GM because of consumer resistance—the market will sort out how much of each type is produced to best satisfy its requirements. The trouble with this strategy is that it depends on farmers' ability to segregate the two types of wheat. But farmers' experience with GM canola shows how tricky that can be. And there's virtual consensus in the scientific community that it would be costly and difficult to keep GM and non-GM wheat separate for long. (Fulton et al. 2003)

Not only did RR wheat threaten existing conventional wheat markets, but it also posed a serious threat to organic production. Opponents of RR wheat, and especially those supporting and involved in organic production, pointed to the loss of canola as an organic crop, through widespread contamination of seed stocks, as evidence of the noncompatibility of RR and organic systems. In fact, during the campaign against RR wheat, SOD had applied to certify a class-action lawsuit that would seek compensation for the loss of canola as an organic crop and an injunction against the introduction of GM wheat. The lawsuit was a method of exerting pressure on Monsanto and of increasing the profile of the RR-wheat campaign and message. If the class action had succeeded, the company would have had to account for significant increases in liability associated with the contamination of non-GM crops with GM material. However, in 2005, Saskatchewan courts denied the certification of the class action.

For SOD, the capacity to produce organically was not an individual choice, but rather the product of a long-standing movement under threat. An interviewee from SOD said:

> Organic farmers . . . had the ability and the tradition of being able to supply non-GMO crops and food to the public . . . go[ing] back thousands of years to the dawn of agriculture. And when an upstart like the biotech companies

come along and destroy that ability they should be held accountable. I think the Canadian public should be outraged that their ability to choose to eat non-GMO food is being destroyed . . . we've had this tradition, this history, this ability to eat non-GMO food, and it's like saying an oil company had a spill in this river, but you know the damage has been done, and so we're just going to sit back and let a certain amount of damage happen every year because . . . it's just part of modern life, so suck it up.

Drawing on the expertise of scientists and the accumulated knowledge associated with widespread contamination of canola on the prairies, anti-RR-wheat activists argued that the introduction of RR wheat would threaten the entire wheat industry and all wheat farmers, and so the decision could not be left to individual producers and consumers.

In order to counter proponents' claims that consumers of food could choose not to buy and eat GM wheat, the coalition opted to emphasize Canada's rejection of mandatory labeling of GM products. While recognizing the neoliberal nature of labeling as a method of regulation (Guthman 2003a), coalition members engaged the discourse of consumer choice in a strategic manner in order to argue that individual market decisions were undermined by the fact that consumers did not have complete information on GM products. For example, a representative from the Council of Canadians emphasized that

if that bill came into play and they actually were to put a mandatory labeling policy then we wouldn't have a soap box anymore. Our game plan was never to regulate GE foods, we wanted a moratorium on them right? We didn't want dumb labeling, who cares about labels, that's not gonna solve the problem. But it was just an obvious thing to highlight and to educate people, because right away they were like "why don't I have the right to choose, why won't you tell me which food contains this and which food doesn't?" . . . So it was very easy for us to mobilize consumers and the average citizen on this issue. Not a problem.

While urban and citizen-based coalition members did strategically engage with the discourse of market choice, it was only one of the arguments put forward by such groups. Ultimately they argued that Canadian regulators should follow the precautionary principle and put a moratorium on GM crops. However, mandatory labeling of GM products was leveraged strategically because labeling had widespread public support. For example, in 2003 the Consumers' Association of Canada made public the results of a national poll that found that 91 percent of Canadian consumers wanted government-enforced labeling on all GM products (Wilson 2003). This result flew in the face of the voluntary labeling standards upon which the Canadian General Standards Board had finally agreed just months before. The establishment of the voluntary standard was mired in controversy and took a full four years to negotiate. Consumer advocates such as the Consumers' Association of Canada walked away from discussions because the possibility of mandatory labeling had been foreclosed from the beginning.

According to anti-RR-wheat activists, the market mechanism could not be understood as a just arbiter of consumer preferences, especially when the information that food consumers needed to register their opposition to GMOs was withheld. Two strategic moves meant to quell any possibility for citizen resistance were in plain view. First, the mechanism for citizen agency was placed in the market rather than in the realms of public policy and social movements. Second, the possibility of opposing GMOs, even through market action, was squashed through the deliberate nonidentification of GM products.

INSISTING ON COLLECTIVE ACTION AND INTERESTS

In order to counter the discourses of consumer choice advanced by proponents of RR wheat, activists highlighted their own history of collective action and insisted that the contemporary introduction of RR wheat should be a decision based on producers' collective interests. In interviews and campaign literature, participants mobilized examples of collective organizing in wheat commodity chains dating back to the twentieth century, which had established many collective institutions such as marketing boards and grain-handling cooperatives. They celebrated this oppositional positionality in which producers fought for a common interest as producers of food, and rejected RR-wheat proponents' understandings of them as consumers of farm inputs.

Central to any contribution to food justice, it should be underscored that the form of populist collective action that characterized early-twentieth-century farm organizing on the Canadian prairies was only possible because of the violent process of "clearing the plains" that forced Indigenous populations onto reserves through a policy of starvation (Daschuk 2013). Indigenous economies and bodies were eliminated in favor of wheat and settlers. Furthermore, the populist collective action that is commonly celebrated as evidence of the prairie's radical past was limited, primarily, to the realms of marketing and credit. Farmers remained vehemently protective of private property in land and the exploitation of their own (individual and familial) labor. Practices of collectivity were accepted and embraced only to the extent that they did not undermine the independent landowning farmer—the master of his own domain. Neither example of collectivity that I mobilize in this section is radical or socially just, but both do the work of denaturalizing the notion of agency as necessarily individual.

It is not a surprise that some interviewees cast back to the first half of the twentieth century, when many of the cooperative institutions associated with wheat were formed in Canada. In fact, talk of past rounds of collective action in agriculture usually surfaced during interviews with farmers when I asked questions about their involvement in farm politics. Several participants emphasized that their families had roots in the cooperative movement or with the NFU and that they brought this inherited experience and understanding to organizing against RR wheat. The following participant from the NFU thought it imperative to communicate that prairie farm history is a history of collective struggle and cooperation. Any attempt by contemporary farmers to understand themselves as individual entrepreneurial subjects is only possible by erasing the past and the institutional legacy of collective action:

> [There has been a] shift from farmers seeing themselves as having a collective interest into one where they really adopted a mythology about how they came and developed here as sort of entrepreneurs on the frontier. Rather [they really have had] a lot of institutional things in place, and a requirement for cooperatives, and a requirement for governments, and a requirement for things like the Manitoba Grains Act, and the weight of the Canadian Seeds Act, and the whole construction to allow them to prosper, and the Canadian Wheat Board being one of them.

This quotation begins with an explicit reference to farmers as having collective interests. Here it is not just that producers have the same interests; rather, their welfare is explicitly intertwined through common structures (seed acts, marketing boards, etc.) and experiences. Such common interests are not the aggregation of interests and preferences at the individual level, as is assumed in theories of consumer choice. Instead, they are the result of interconnected practices whereby the conduct of one or many farmers affects the conduct of others. For example, to the extent that a group of farmers sells their commodities below the market price, the bargaining capacity of all producers of those commodities is affected.

The above participant describes producers as being able to act collectively in order to build and secure institutional supports for their common good. Here, agency can be understood as the *product* of relationships and, thus, as intersubjective. Unlike in theories of market choice, subjects do not come to the public arena with fully formed preferences that can be sufficiently fulfilled through the market mechanism; rather, their preferences are forged in and through their social lives. Production is thus understood as fundamentally social, even if, as the participant above described, a mythology exists about farmers as individual entrepreneurs tackling the frontier in isolation. Certainly, the spatial arrangement of production in the early twentieth century (with individual family units producing on separate homesteads) imposed certain barriers to collectivity. But producers did labor together; they often shared equipment and worked each other's land in teams, and they built and relied on cooperative marketing, distribution, and credit structures.

During the campaign against RR wheat, this history of collective farm organizing was emphasized and practiced through the CWB's prominence in the mobilizing efforts. Born of producer agitation and established as a voluntary government marketing agency in 1935, the CWB gained a monopoly on the export of all western Canadian wheat for human consumption during World War II. While the CWB act was changed in 1998 to allow "shared governance" between farmers and the federal government, during the campaign against RR wheat it was still a quasi-state entity mandated first and foremost to market grain in producers' collective interests (it was dismantled by the federal Conservative government in 2012). The CWB took a leadership role in the campaign against RR wheat and, early on in the debate, it announced that over two thirds of its customers would have reservations about buying Canadian wheat if Canada were also growing RR varieties. Based on surveys it conducted with wheat farmers, the CWB was also able to communicate that the majority of farmers did not want RR wheat. It used its significant clout and connections in the wheat industry to put forward a conclusive case about collective farmer nonacceptance of the crop, and producer organizations emphasized its legitimacy as a collective voice for farmers in their campaign documents, in public presentations, and in testimony to government committees. Moreover, in 2001 the CWB convened a group of farmer, grain-industry, technology-developer, customer, and federal-government representatives to form the Canadian Grain Industry Working Group on Genetically Modified Wheat, through which the organization was able to advance producer interests and put pressure on key constituencies in the debate.

More broadly, farmers worked through their collective farm and rural organizations to pass resolutions and set policy based on the notion of a collective farming good. The Saskatchewan Association of Rural Municipalities, for example, passed a resolution in 2002 to pressure the federal government to put a moratorium on the release of all GM crops until international buyers had agreed to accept them. Farmer organizations brought the issue to national associations as well, and the Canadian Federation of Agriculture passed a resolution in 2003 that opposed the introduction of RR wheat, based on the agronomic concerns of western farmers and the nonacceptance of GM wheat in major markets. In all of this work, farm organizations emphasized their common interests as producers of food and rejected the idea that individual farmers could choose to grow RR wheat if they wished. Instead, coalition members argued that any unconfined release of RR wheat threatened wheat growers as a whole. Such was also the argument put forward by SOD in their attempt at winning an injunction against RR wheat, as discussed above.

While the coalition was dominated by producer organizations that used their democratic structures to advance their collective concerns, the three more urban and environmental organizations also eschewed the notion of individual choice and worked hard to conceptualize RR wheat as a threat not just to individual consumers, but also to broader issues of social justice. An interviewee from the Canadian Biotechnology Action Network suggested that

> initially the debate about labeling was so important because it worked in the UK, it kept GM off the shelf and consumers were really mobilized and were really concerned. And here we tried for ten years to get mandatory labeling and failed. And in the process it really kept urban people's minds focused on food safety, you know individual needs, your family, your children when really it's issues of democracy, social justice, what role does agriculture play in the policy life of our country, where and how are farmers' lives impacted by new technologies that matter.

Here, the interviewee finds the subjectivity that is associated with individual needs and individual assessments of food safety politically ineffective and proposes a common project between urban and rural constituencies around principles of democracy and social justice. Similarly, a representative from the

NFU suggested that urban and rural people should examine the issue of GMOs in a collective fashion:

> I think it's a social good to have urban and rural people thinking together about an environmental and a food issue and respecting each other's point of view and taking a collective look at it. So for me it isn't just political convenience and necessity. . . . I mean these movements are not just short-term, politically expedient fights. For me it's a change of perspective, and that's a social project, that's a social and spiritual transformation project.

The participants quoted above use the case of coordinated action to work against the logic of market choice. They advocate for a common good while recognizing that such a common good involves differently positioned and interested actors. Still, they strive to identify a coherent unity in "farmers" or "citizens" and insist that broad-based general farm organizations or citizens' groups do not represent the aggregation of individual, fully formed interests and preferences. Instead, these participants show that resolutions, policies, alliances, and campaigns are the result of contestation; they are negotiated and formed through intersubjective processes.

The practice of political subjectivity in the examples of collective action described above is social: it is oriented around the possibility of action that supports a negotiated, yet fraught, common good. This is radically different from the political subjectivity associated with consumer choice, which posits agency as an individual calculation of costs and benefits. Consumer choice supports a notion of subjectivity that is fundamentally asocial, in the sense that what is best for the sum of individuals is best for society: there is no need for a public sphere, for negotiation, or for a conception of a common good.

Importantly, when agency is exercised by voting with your dollar in the market, only consumers (either as consumers of food or consumers of farm inputs) can have their say. There exists no possibility for a politics of production, since farmers can only register their dissent as consumers of farm inputs. While farmers understand themselves first and foremost as producers, entering the market in order to buy the necessary factors of production, seed and fertilizer companies understand them chiefly as consumers. In *Grundrisse,* Karl Marx (1973, 421) outlines exactly this process with regard to the industrial laborer vis-à-vis the capitalist: "What precisely distinguishes capital from the master–servant relation is that the *worker* confronts him as consumer and possessor of exchange values, and that in the form of the *possessor of money,* in the form of money he becomes a simple centre of circulation—

one of its infinitely many centres, in which his specificity as worker is extinguished" (emphasis in original). While the relationship of input corporations to farmers is not one of capitalist to laborer, the implications in the two cases are similar. For biotech lobby groups, corporations like Monsanto, and other RR-wheat supporters, farmers are, as Marx suggested, simply "centres of circulation." They have agency only inasmuch as they make free choices in the market. Indeed, their specificity as producers/workers is extinguished.

Given Marx's insightful observations in the nineteenth century, there seems to be nothing new about the discourse of individual market choice advocated by proponents of RR wheat. However, those studying neoliberalism have shown that the imperative of market choice increasingly pervades more aspects of social life and has become central to the broader concept of freedom. That RR-wheat supporters adopted the discourse of farmers as consumers (a very specific positionality of farmers in relation to input suppliers) reflects the incursion of market choice into more and more aspects of social and political life. The capacity to choose through market action was represented as the practice of freedom itself. In this line of thinking, individuals understand themselves as entrepreneurs, obliged to navigate through, and demand, an ongoing series of choices that make them who they are. As the quotation from the NFU representative above demonstrates, even past forms of commonality get reconceptualized through this lens. The subjectivity of farmers as collective actors and producers is extinguished in both the past and the present.

CONCLUSION

The story of the successful campaign against RR wheat told in this chapter is an important example of a coalition defeating an agro-industrial giant through a concerted and collective campaign. In advocating that the appropriate mechanism for registering opposition to RR wheat was for farmers to vote with their dollars in the market, RR-wheat proponents attempted to deny the commonality of farmers as producers of food. In response, producers refused to express their agency through individual acts of consumption and insisted on their common positionality as producers of food. Countering neoliberal discourse that posits the market as the most just arbiter of individual preferences, farmers and consumers instead targeted Monsanto and

TABLE 3.1 Organizations Involved in the Coalition to Stop the Introduction of Roundup Ready (RR) Wheat

Name of Organization and Date of Founding	Type of Lobby	Main Complaint(s) about RR Wheat	Proposed Action
National Farmers Union, 1969	Left-wing farm organization formed to unite provincial Farmers Unions, which had led radical farm organizing since World War I	Loss of control of the food/seed system to multinationals; threat to profitability and autonomy of the family farm	Moratorium on all GMOs; all GMOs must be subject to democratic control, collective ownership, and not-for-profit distribution
Saskatchewan Association of Rural Municipalities, 1905	Advocate of rural municipalities to senior levels of government	Loss of markets, secrecy of field-trial locations	Ban GM wheat until segregation and detection systems, tolerance levels, markets, and changes to regulatory system are established
Saskatchewan Organic Directorate, 1998	Producer-controlled umbrella organization for producers, processors, buyers, traders, certifiers, and consumers	Liability in cases of contamination and loss of ability to farm organically	Complete ban on all GMOs because contamination is inevitable
Agricultural Producers Association of Saskatchewan, 1999	General farm organization with representatives from all rural municipalities in Saskatchewan	Market impact; agronomic issues such as effects on zero till	All GM wheats must be approved on the basis of merit (markets, agronomy)
Keystone Agricultural Producers, 1984	General farm organization in Manitoba	Market impact, agronomic issues, segregation	Prevent registration until consumer acceptance
Canadian Wheat Board, 1935	Western Canadian single-desk marketing organization jointly governed by producers and the federal government	Loss of markets (≥80% of customers are concerned about GM wheat)	Add cost-benefit analysis to regulations; do not release RR wheat at this time
Canadian Health Coalition, 1979	NGO primarily concerned with public health care	GMOs may have negative health impacts; regulatory system is antidemocratic and serves life-sciences industry	Regulatory system must be overhauled and serve the public
Greenpeace Canada, 1971	International environmental NGO founded in Canada	GMOs will harm the environment and may have negative health impacts; life should not be patented	Stop all GMOs and reform the regulatory system
Council of Canadians, 1985	Multi-issue nationalist NGO	Consumers don't want GM wheat; long-term impacts on health and the environment are unknown	Stop all GMOs until labeling, long-term studies, and regulatory reform

the CFIA through collective organizing strategies that asserted a common good, however fraught and negotiated.

The coalition against RR wheat can, however, be understood as a militant particularism (Harvey 1996), a necessarily local and particular struggle against dominant institutions (the Canadian state and Monsanto) over a single issue. Indeed, the opposition to RR wheat was rooted, to a large extent, in local rationality (Gunvald Nilsen and Cox 2013), including the agronomic particularities of viable rotations, local contamination, and access to specific wheat markets. In other words, while coalition members could unite behind opposing the introduction of RR wheat, they could not agree on or articulate a broader vision of a more just food system, or even a common position on biotechnology. Nevertheless, struggles for food justice ought to be inspired by the way in which the coalition countered neoliberal market-choice arguments by insisting on the collective positionality of farmers and by engaging in collective action.

NOTE

This chapter draws on work included in my book *Growing Resistance: Canadian Farmers and the Politics of Genetically Modified Wheat* (2013), published by the University of Manitoba Press, and on my article "Let the Market Decide: Canadian Farmers Fight the Logic of Market Choice in GM Wheat," published in *ACME: An International E-Journal for Critical Geographies*. Both are used here with permission.

REFERENCES

Andrée, Peter, and Lucy Sharratt. 2004. "Genetically Modified Organisms and Precaution: Is the Canadian Government Implementing the Royal Society of Canada's Recommendations?" Ottawa: Polaris Institute.

Beckie, H. J., K. N. Harker, L. M. Hall, S. I. Warwick, A. Légère, P. H. Sikkema, et al. 2006. "A Decade of Herbicide-Resistant Crops in Canada." *Canadian Journal of Plant Science* 86: 1243–1264.

Canadian Biotechnology Action Network. n.d. "History and Accomplishments." www.cban.ca/About/History. Accessed April 25, 2015.

Clarke, John, and Janet Newman. 2007. "What's in a Name? New Labour's Citizen-Consumers and the Remaking of Public Services." *Cultural Studies* 21: 738–757.

Daschuk, James. 2013. *Clearing the Plains: Disease, Politics of Starvation, and the Loss of Aboriginal Life.* Regina, Saskatchewan: University of Regina Press.

Dean, Mitchell. 1999. *Governmentality: Power and Rule in Modern Society.* London: Sage.

Fulton, Murray, Hartley Furtan, Richard Grey, and George Khachatourians. 2003. "Genetically Modified Wheat." *Globe and Mail,* August 11.

Gunvald Nilsen, Alf, and Laurence Cox. 2013. "What Would a Marxist Theory of Social Movements Look Like?" *In Marxism and Social Movements,* ed. Colin Barker, Laurence Cox, John Krinsky, and Alf Gunvald Nilsen, 63–82. Leiden, The Netherlands: Brill.

Guthman, Julie. 2003a. "Eating Risk." In *Engineering Trouble,* ed. Rachel Schurman, Dennis Doyle, and Takahashi Kelso, 130–151. Berkeley: University of California Press.

———. 2003b. "Fast Food/Organic Food: Reflexive Tastes and the Making of 'Yuppie Chow.'" *Social and Cultural Geography* 4: 45–58.

———. 2004. "The 'Organic Commodity' and Other Anomalies in the Politics of Consumption." In *Geographies of Commodity Chains,* ed. Alex Hughes and Suzanne Reimer, 233–249. New York: Routledge.

———. 2008. "Neoliberalism and the Making of Food Politics in California." *Geoforum* 39: 1171–1183.

Harvey, David. 1996. *Justice Nature and the Geography of Difference.* Oxford: Blackwell.

Johnston, Josée. 2008. "The Citizen-Consumer Hybrid: Ideological Tensions and the Case of Whole Foods Market." *Theory and Society* 37: 229–270.

Lang, Tim, and Yiannis Gabriel. 2005. "A Brief History of Consumer Activism." In *The Ethical Consumer,* ed. Rob Harrison, Terry Newholm, and Deirdre Shaw, 39–53. London: Sage.

Marcoux, Jean-Michel, and Lyne Létourneau. 2013. "A Distorted Regulatory Landscape: Genetically Modified Wheat and the Influence of Non-Safety Issues in Canada." *Science and Public Policy* 40: 514–528.

Marx, Karl. 1973. *Grundrisse.* Translated by Martin Nicolaus. London: Penguin.

McAdam, Doug. 1982. *Political Process and the Development of Black Insurgency, 1930–1970.* Chicago: University of Chicago Press.

Monsanto Company. 2004. "Monsanto to Realign Research Portfolio: Development of Roundup Ready Wheat Deferred." http://news.monsanto.com/press-release/monsanto-realign-research-portfolio-development-roundup-ready-wheat-deferred. Accessed April 15, 2015.

Roff, Robin Jane. 2007. "Shopping for Change? Neoliberalizing Activism and the Limits to Eating Non-GMO." *Agriculture and Human Values* 24: 511–522.

Rose, Nikolas. 1999. *Powers of Freedom: Reframing Political Thought.* Cambridge, UK: Cambridge University Press.

Slocum, Rachel. 2004. "Consumer Citizens and the Cities for Climate Protection Campaign." *Environment and Planning A* 36: 763–782.

Wilson, Barry. 2003. "Consumers Demand GM Labels." *The Western Producer,* December 11.

FOUR

How Midas Lost Its Golden Touch

NEOLIBERALISM AND ACTIVIST STRATEGY
IN THE DEMISE OF METHYL IODIDE IN CALIFORNIA

Julie Guthman and Sandy Brown

IN MARCH 2012, AFTER MORE than a decade of seeking regulatory approval for the soil fumigant Midas—registered brand name for methyl iodide—Arysta LifeScience, the largest privately held agrochemical company in the world, withdrew it from the United States and other markets. Midas was designed to replace methyl bromide, a fumigant favored by strawberry growers in California and tomato growers in Florida that was destined for phaseout in compliance with the international Montreal Protocol on Substances that Deplete the Ozone Layer. Methyl iodide was touted as a suitable alternative because it shares important qualities with methyl bromide, in terms of soil sterilization, but does not make it into the upper atmosphere. These same qualities, however, made it less desirable for those who would come in contact with the chemical, for, as many argued, it is even more acutely toxic and environmentally degrading than methyl bromide. Pesticide Action Network (PAN) North America, for example, reported it to be a known neurotoxin and carcinogen, associated with suppression of thyroid hormone synthesis, respiratory illness, and lung tumors, and a probable cause of miscarriages and birth defects (PAN 2011).

During regulatory review for use in California, Midas met considerable opposition from regulatory scientists as well as environmental and farmworker advocacy groups, which organized over fifty-three thousand public comments on proposed registration, with all but a handful opposing it. In addition, these groups organized highly visible public actions, designed to capture the attention of the media, and perhaps scare growers out of adopting it. When it was finally approved, many of these same organizations filed a lawsuit against both regulators and Arysta for failing to abide by California environmental law. Just in advance of a court ruling on the lawsuit, Arysta voluntarily withdrew its request for registration of the chemical in California and announced its plans to suspend operations in the U.S. market, publicly stating that the chemical was no longer economically viable.

This chain of events has been read by activists and scholars alike as a major achievement of the anti-pesticide movement, in which protestors successfully embarrassed the strawberry industry into nonadoption, leading to Arysta's subsequent withdrawal. Paul Towers, spokesperson for PAN, called it "a tremendous victory," in which "scientific integrity has outweighed pesticide industry pull when it comes to food and farming. This decision is born of the tireless work of farmers, farmworkers, rural high school students and mothers who are keeping strawberries safe" (Earthjustice 2012). Medical anthropologist Dvera Saxton (2015, 13) called it a "historic victory for health, environmental, and farmworker activists" owing to "massive public concern and grower hesitancy to use an unfamiliar and publicly unpopular product." In an industry in which Goliath usually wins (cf. Ganz 2009), the success of this campaign is indeed something of an anomaly. As Harrison (2011) has argued, many things have conspired to allow highly toxic agrochemicals to remain on the market, not least of which are frameworks of risk assessment that underrepresent the threats they pose, allowing industry to prevail (see also Robbins 2007, Suryanarayanan and Kleinman 2013).

The methyl iodide campaign was significant also because, at least at first glance, it appeared that the food movement pushed back against neoliberalism using contentious tactics (Alkon 2014). This is significant for a movement that has tended to embrace "neoliberal," market-oriented alternatives, such as organics, that allow those with the means to "vote with their fork" and "shop their way to safety," while giving up on regulatory battles (Guthman 2008, Harrison 2014, Szasz 2007). In keeping with that analysis, Jill Lindsey Harrison (chapter 2, this volume) pointedly shows how pesticide drift activism more generally has reacted not only to the neoliberalization of the pesticide regulatory apparatus, but also to the neoliberal subjectivity that is so prevalent in sustainable agriculture activism.

As it turns out, there are many factors that converged to cause Arysta's withdrawal, some of which were actually out of activists' hands. These included the rising costs of iodine, the continued availability of methyl bromide despite the phaseout, and Arysta's miscalculations about the time it would take to get the chemical approved and widely adopted (for a complete account, see Guthman and Brown 2016b). As it also turns out, neoliberal subjectivities and forms of action were not entirely abandoned in this campaign. To the contrary, the public-comment campaign evinced a significant degree of "fork voting" sensibility, very much associated with neoliberal governmentality, and this came to matter in the final result. In our view, what made this case different and important, then, was that the activists were strategic in their efforts: they identified a winnable fight, named their opponents, played on the weaknesses of those opponents (e.g., Arysta's miscalculations and other factors out of activists' hands), and drew on their own strengths, including a public educated in fork voting, to marshal a victory. While the outcome of the campaign was in no way determined—the activists could just as easily have lost—this case nevertheless suggests that it is not necessarily the tactics of neoliberalism that limit the politics of the possible in food movements; rather, the problem may lie with a failure to think and act strategically—to refuse, that is, to name and pursue an opponent. It is the neglect of the political, in other words, that may be the true hallmark of neoliberal governmentality as it applies to food movements.

In this chapter, we look more closely at the activist campaign against registration of methyl iodide, focusing on the primary tactics employed and the degree to which these played on industry (and regulator) weaknesses and movement strengths. Our research included review of lawsuit documents and interviews with key players for the plaintiff in the lawsuit, coding and analysis of public comments regarding methyl iodide registration, and approximately 120 interviews with growers, grower–shippers (buyers), extension agents, pest control advisors, and activists that included questions on the industry's proclivities to adopt methyl iodide. We pay particularly close attention to the lawsuit, not only for its overall significance, but also because it provided important data we could not obtain elsewhere, namely about the perspectives (and weaknesses) of the defendants.

NEOLIBERALISM, FOOD MOVEMENTS, STRATEGY

The win against methyl iodide is significant, if for no other reason than that it's been a long time since a U.S. social or environmental movement has appeared to make a visible difference in pushing back against a toxic agrochemical. In the broadest terms, it was most definitely a fight against neoliberalism, especially if we follow those who define neoliberalism not in terms of what market fundamentalists claim they are doing—minimizing state interference to let markets do their magic—but, rather, in terms of what they are actually doing: developing new regulatory mechanisms and bending the rules so as to shore up corporate profitability (Harvey 2010, Mann 2013). Insofar as the regulatory agency charged with protecting public health against toxic pesticides did its best to register Midas by skirting still-existing regulations, activists were indeed fighting another instance of "roll-back neo-liberalism" in which regulations remain in place but are not enforced (Peck and Tickell 2002)—what Harrison (2011, 2008, 2006) has documented at length in terms of California pesticide regulation.

Still, as discussed in Alkon (2014) and in this volume, food activists are not only working against neoliberal policy these days; they are ostensibly doing so in ways that are both resistant and collective, going beyond the limited set of tools that have come to be associated with contemporary food movements, such as creating nonthreatening alternatives and promoting fork voting as the primary means to effect change. These latter approaches, as many scholars have argued, indicate the pervasiveness of neoliberal govern-mentality in food movements, in which messages that encourage the exercise of ethical preferences through highly individualized purchasing decisions (i.e., fork voting) and projects that encourage entrepreneurialism and self-improvement through gardening, cooking, and selling food have become favored modes of food activism (Alkon 2014, Allen 1999, Allen and Guthman 2006, Allen et al. 2003, Guthman 2011, 2008, Johnston 2008, Lavin 2009). As they pertain to environmental and labor regulation, such approaches devolve or even privatize decisions over environmental and labor standards to voluntary, nonprofit, non-governmental organizations and even to indi-vidual consumers who use their buying power, ostensibly, to affect firm behavior (Brown and Getz 2008, Guthman 2007, 2003, Harrison 2008). A critical problem, as Guthman (2008) wrote, is that these approaches delimit the politics of the possible. At the same time, they appear to be all that remains when more collective forms of action have been made more politically difficult and even illegitimate (Guthman 2008, Jessop 2002, Larner 2003, Peck and Tickell 2002). Yet that is the point: it is this very depoliticization of social action to which neoliberalism aspires (Dean 1999, Rose 1999).

It is in this last way that we find it useful to think about movement strat-egy, especially in light of our observation that the fight against methyl iodide did not completely put aside approaches, or even tactics, associated with neo-liberal governmentality. Following those few scholars who have actually studied strategic action as it relates to food movements, we see that strategy is arguably anathema to neoliberal governmentality—and indeed to the tenor of most food activism. This is because strategy often entails naming and sizing up an opponent (as demonstrated in Ganz 2009, 2000, Schurman 2004, Schurman and Munro 2010). In that way, it is inherently political, quite contrary to the neoliberal conceit of "win-win" solutions. Writing about the 1960s movement to organize farmworkers in California, Ganz (2009, 9) emphasizes additionally that strategy requires intention, a focused choice to commit resources to specific outcomes—and a willingness to risk failure.

Scholarship on the movement to oppose agricultural biotechnology is particularly apt to understand the win against methyl iodide, not only because it has involved strategic action to contest corporate-generated technologies and the regulatory institutions and frameworks that have allowed them, but also because some of the same actors have been involved (e.g., agrochemical giants, anti-pesticide activists) (Eaton 2013, Kinchy 2012, Schurman 2004, Schurman and Munro 2010). Schurman and Munro define that movement's success by asking what the degree of commercialization would have been for genetically engineered crops without the movement. They discuss the array of tactics used by the anti-biotechnology movement, including organizing media-oriented protests, deploying dissident scientists in making the case against biotechnology, and pursuing legal action—tactics that were all used in the campaign against methyl iodide as well. Yet they particularly emphasize how these tactics played on industry weaknesses and thus were strategically informed. These weaknesses included massive up-front investment costs and hubristic expectations that their technologies would be welcomed, as well as industry characteristics vulnerable to consumer sentiment. Here they specifically note that applications that were more geared toward consumers—coincidentally a strawberry that was designed to withstand a freeze by the insertion of a flounder gene—gained much less acceptance than those that were attractive to farmers, such as herbicide-resistant commodity crop varieties. They also note that industry actors who were closer to the consumers (e.g., food manufacturers and retailers) were more vulnerable to movement action than those close to farmers (e.g., suppliers). As we shall show, the methyl iodide campaign was able to draw on similar dynamics in the strawberry industry, even though this was achieved through means that could be considered neoliberal. In addition, it successfully exploited the missteps of the key regulatory agency in its scientific evaluation of the chemical. To make this case, we first present some relevant background.

The story of methyl iodide must be understood in the context of the role of soil fumigation in making California's strawberry industry what it is today. As of 2014, strawberries were the fifth-highest-grossing crop in California, representing $2.6 billion in annual revenues to the state's economy and 88 percent of the production in the United States (California Strawberry Commission n.d.). The strawberry is also one of the highest-value crops grown in California, one in which growers expect to receive upwards of $50,000 in annual revenue per acre, revenues that also cover the high labor costs of strawberry production (Bolda et al. 2010). Since agricultural land values are directly related to crop values, strawberries are grown on some of the highest-priced agricultural land in the state, making alternatives that compromise yields or increase costs necessarily nonviable.

The industry's success owes much to the use of soil fumigants (Gianessi and Williams 2011, Wells 1996). These chemicals sterilize the soil and allow growers to plant on the same block year after year or, in regions capable of long strawberry harvests, to rotate with vegetables every other year. Fumigants became especially important for controlling a set of soil pathogens that attack the root system of strawberry plants, causing them to wilt and die. For over half a century, methyl bromide had been the preferred fumigant for strawberry growers. No other fumigants had proved as reliably effective as methyl bromide, and methyl bromide had also been widely appreciated for its ability to improve yields for reasons not well understood. However, in 1991, the Montreal Protocol, initially signed in 1987, mandated the phaseout of methyl bromide. As a signatory to the Montreal Protocol, the United States agreed to stop producing and importing methyl bromide by 2005. This deadline was extended to 2015 when the United States began requesting critical-use exemptions (CUEs) for growers who claimed that no viable alternative was available, which would thus affect future profits. For Gareau (2008), allowing the economic impact on a particular industry to trump broader health and social concerns, as the rules on CUEs did, was itself a sign of the degree to which neoliberalism has infiltrated global environmental governance. As of this writing, the U.S. Environmental Protection Agency (U.S. EPA) accepted CUE requests through 2016, although at substantially lower quantities than ever before, after which they were to end (U.S. EPA n.d.). Nevertheless, owing in part to CUEs, the industry has been slow to develop and test nonchemical alternatives, and, thus far, none have proved reliable and cost-effective on a commercial scale—or, at least, at the scale and in the style the industry is accustomed to.

In this context, the arrival of methyl iodide seemed a godsend for the industry. Methyl iodide was developed by researchers at the University of California, Riverside, and licensed by Arysta LifeScience. Beginning in 2002, Arysta moved aggressively to get methyl iodide approved for commercial use, first seeking registration with the U.S. EPA, then with the California Department of Pesticide Regulation (CDPR) in 2005. Emerging controversy, including a September 2007 letter from over fifty scientists, including several Nobel laureates in chemistry, caused the EPA to deny registration at first. However, a month later the agency reversed course, granting a one-year registration that was extended without time limitations in 2008. In 2009, the EPA even gave Arysta and the methyl iodide research team an Ozone Protection Layer Award! Things looked promising for Arysta and for an industry in need of a solution.

Things were trickier in California, though, where the vast majority of strawberries are grown, and where numerous state environmental laws go above and beyond federal standards. This includes a stronger pesticide-surveillance system that is administered by CDPR. By virtue of the California Environmental Quality Act (CEQA), all "projects," including pesticide registrations, must be subject to thorough reviews and analyses of risks, and responsible agencies must prepare a risk-characterization document. Notably, scholars have characterized California's pesticide-surveillance system, as well as scientific risk-assessment more generally, as neoliberal because (a) it depoliticizes regulatory battles by privileging scientific data as the primary bases of dispute; (b) it rejects notions of zero risk in favor of "acceptable risks" in relation to costs and benefits, and hence industry well-being; and (c) it is primarily performative rather than preventive—giving the appearance of doing something while curtailing very little (Boudia 2014, Harrison 2011, Kinchy et al. 2008). At the same time, these laws continue to exist on the books, and while there has been much talk of reforming or even repealing CEQA, thus far it has not been rolled back to the point of being meaningless.

In any case, because potentially hazardous chemicals first require federal approval, CDPR's staff did not begin the risk-analysis process for methyl iodide until early 2005. It completed an initial first draft in 2009, which was then distributed to the Office of Environmental Health Hazard Assessment and an independent, eight-person scientific review committee (SRC) convened by CDPR. These committees provided extensive comments on the draft document by the end of 2009. Both committees expressed extreme skepticism of the chemical's safety. In their report of the risk assessment they initially conducted, agency scientists concluded "that the application of MeI [methyl iodide] in field fumigation under the conditions evaluated could result in significant health risks for workers and the general population" (Lim and Nu-May 2010). As for the SRC, they wrote that "based on the available data, we know that methyl iodide is a highly toxic chemical and we expect that any anticipated scenario for the agricultural or structural fumigation use of this agent would result in exposures to a large number of the public and thus would have a significant adverse impact on the public health" (CDPR 2010c).

In April 2010, then director of CDPR Mary Ann Warmerdam announced her intent to register the chemical, neglecting the recommendations of CDPR staff and external review panels. This announcement was a necessary step to kick off a CEQA-required public-comment period. It was during this period that activist organizations, including anti-pesticide, environmental, public health, and farmworker groups, mounted a major Internet campaign to encourage members of the general public to comment on methyl iodide registration. Despite this surge of opposition, Warmerdam approved methyl iodide for use as an emergency registration in December 2010, albeit with stricter mitigation measures than the U.S. EPA label (CDPR 2010a). The approval came, notably, just before the new Democratic governor, Jerry Brown, was to take office, and it spurred a second round of movement activity that largely revolved around media events and public hearings. Meanwhile, activists had already retained attorneys, so that immediately following the registration of methyl iodide, on December 30, 2010, Earthjustice (a nonprofit law firm) and California Rural Legal Assistance filed a lawsuit against CDPR Director Warmerdam and against Arysta LifeScience as the real party in interest. Most of the counts were about the failure to register methyl iodide in accordance with California environmental laws for transparency in decision making and robust assessment of potential health and environmental effects. By failing to exercise due diligence, in short, CDPR had made itself a target of activists equal, at least, to the industry it was supposed to regulate.

As much as methyl iodide was a godsend for the industry, it was arguably also one for the anti-pesticide movement. The toxic profile of Midas was beyond the pale—after all, it was used to induce cancer in laboratory rats—which was bound to raise hackles. At the same time, industry and regulator hubris opened up additional opportunities for the movement to exploit. The campaign against methyl iodide took place in three phases, employing three primary approaches. All three incorporated some elements of neoliberal governmentality, albeit not necessarily intentionally, and yet, as we shall see, even these became strategically useful.

Massive Public Comments

Upon Warmerdam's announcement of her intent to register the chemical, multiple organizations representing labor, environmental, and public health interests, including the Sierra Club, PAN, and United Farm Workers (UFW), took up the charge of submitting comments. These highly tailored comments focused mostly on the scientific research regarding methyl iodide's adverse health and environmental effects and the insufficiency of the proposed mitigation measures to protect health. Some of these comments also raised the procedural issue that CDPR had strayed far from the recommendations of its own SRC. In addition, these organizations ran Internet campaigns to generate comments from the general public. They were joined by dedicated Internet activism organizations with very large reach, such as CREDO Action. Virtually all of these organizations provided scripts (or prompts) that commenters could use verbatim or alter slightly. In addition, many individuals wrote articles and blogs and pointed readers to those organizations' action alerts. Through this effort, CDPR received an unprecedented number of written comments (over fifty-three thousand), with all but a handful writing in opposition to the registration of Midas.

Apparently, the idea that methyl iodide would affect a food crop resonated most with the public. Using a public records request, we had the opportunity to code and analyze some thirty-five hundred comments that were submitted to CDPR, representing, according to CDPR, all of the "substantive comments" received and retained by the department that were not "generic or repetitive" (for a more extensive analysis, see Guthman and Brown 2016a). Through this exercise, we found that although many comments appealed to a policy decision and mentioned some of the key issues that had emerged in the regulatory debates, the most common concern, mentioned by over one-third of those writing, was about consumer health. This emerged, moreover, despite the fact that soil fumigants like methyl iodide dissipate long before plants produce fruit, so that consumers are at minute, if any, risk of exposure compared to farmworkers and nearby communities—and none of the leading organizations suggested otherwise. However, many of the blogs and Internet articles that circulated news of the campaign did insinuate that methyl iodide might be found in food.[1] For instance, the online magazine *Civil Eats* relayed information about the public-comment period in an article called "Strawberry Show Down: No Methyl Iodide with My Shortcake, Please" (Starkman 2010). The article went on to say that the CDPR was "accepting public comments on its proposal through June 14, so unless you'd like some more toxins with your strawberry smoothie, you might want to urge CDPR to immediately withdraw the recommendation to approve its agricultural use."

A significant number of commenters were inclined to express their concerns as future supermarket choices. An overlapping 20 percent wrote that were the state to register methyl iodide, they would no longer buy strawberries—or they would buy only organic strawberries. Again, we found no evidence that the leading organizations had provided language in their prompts suggesting that people change their individual consumption behavior. Yet the strength of these fairly typical comments speaks to the salience of ideas associated with neoliberal governmentality:

- "I will never buy strawberries treated with Methyl Iodide. Period. My family's health and wellness trump corporate profits."
- "I will not feed these toxins to my family."
- "As the parent of a very picky eater, I will tell you that I purchase fresh strawberries twice a week, dried strawberries every two weeks or so. If you move forward on this proposal, I will ensure that I either purchase berries that were not turned into cancer carriers or omit the fruit from my daughter's diet."

In other words, many of these letter writers, though nominally acting in their capacity as citizens by providing comments, substantively were acting as individual consumers and expecting that their supermarket choices were the key point of leverage for affecting industry behavior (cf. Johnston 2008).

In terms of the registration decision, apparently these comments had minimal impact. This is in large part because they were recognized as "slacktivism" (Christensen 2011), in which taking action involves little more than reading an alert and pressing a button. Indeed, following the 2010 decision to register methyl iodide, CDPR released an FAQ document that acknowledged the volume of comments received but stated that "most of the comments received were similar and generated through social media campaigns" (CDPR 2010b). They were also discounted because, as stated in this same document, "they provided no evidence that CDPR's stringent use restrictions will not keep exposures to methyl iodide within safe levels," here suggesting that nonscientific considerations are irrelevant in a case for or against a technology—a classic case of "scientization" of a regulatory controversy that we discuss further below (Kinchy et al. 2008). As such, CDPR addressed, in its detailed written evaluation and response, only those comments that raised significant environmental points, "as required by law."

CDPR's disregard of the vast majority of comments was, in many ways, the movement's gain. As we discuss in the next section, the movement made much in the media of CDPR's disdain for the regulatory process—which ultimately affected grower adoption of the chemical and, hence, Arysta's sales. In that way, the campaign was able to capitalize on the public's display of neoliberal governmentality even if unsolicited.

Public Media/Demonstrations/Protests

In writing about how the anti-biotechnology movement exploited industry weaknesses, Schurman (2004) enumerates a number of strategies that activists in Europe undertook. Although the movement had always mobilized scientific expertise that countered industry science (as has the anti-pesticide movement), at one point their tactics became more contentious, as they embraced more symbolic and direct forms of action. These attracted a great deal of media coverage and helped to eventually turn public opinion against the industry. Activists in the fight against methyl iodide were also contentious in this way, albeit not on the same scale.

One thing they did is to make much of CDPR's foibles in the public media. For instance, they trumpeted the fact that CDPR went ahead with registering the chemical despite the fifty-three thousand comments received in opposition. They also characterized the decision to make an emergency registration of methyl iodide a few days before the new Democratic governor was to take office as an eleventh-hour move. And they routinely reminded the press that Director Warmerdam had ignored her own agency's scientists. All of these facts allowed the press to cast aspersions on the process by which methyl iodide was registered.

Activists organized direct actions as well. They held mock fumigations on the steps of the state capitol and at Arysta's offices (Greenaway 2011). At the capitol, they delivered a letter to Governor Jerry Brown signed by forty-four legislators and a petition signed by thirty thousand people asking him to suspend registration. They held protests at one county's agricultural commissioner's office and picketed beside farmers' fields. They also participated in a two-hundred-mile march for fairness, organized by UFW, in which the methyl iodide fight figured large. In addition, they helped organize several hearings before legislative bodies, including the California Assembly's committees on Environmental Safety and Toxic Materials and Health and the boards of supervisors of Monterey and Santa Cruz counties.

All of this activity had a modest impact on the regulatory process post-registration. In March 2011, a week after Warmerdam's resignation to accept a position with the chemical company Clorox, Governor Brown announced that he would take a "fresh look" at methyl iodide (Herdt 2011). In response to a petition filed a year earlier by nearly a dozen advocacy organizations, a request by California Senator Diane Feinstein, and a letter signed by thirty-seven California legislators, the EPA agreed to open a two-month public-comment period in March 2011. Following those public hearings in late 2011, both the Santa Cruz and Monterey boards of supervisors passed resolutions requesting that the State of California withdraw approval of methyl iodide until additional research was completed, published, and peer reviewed. Notwithstanding these minor victories, CDPR did not reverse its position, probably to prevent a lawsuit from Arysta.

The more salient impact was thus on the strawberry industry itself. As of December 2011, a year after registration, there had been only six permits issued in California, and, aside from field trials, the chemical had been applied on less than twenty acres, for which Arysta had allegedly paid. All applications were on less than five acres, and only one was on strawberries (Wozniacka 2012). One reason there was marginal adoption is that there was a very small window of time in which growers could have used methyl iodide. Given the uncertainty surrounding the chemical's fate, many growers were just waiting it out. Nevertheless, among the growers we interviewed who knew about the chemical, a plurality expressed concern about the push-back they would face had they adopted methyl iodide. Several mentioned that they did not want to see people picketing by their fields. Several of the shippers with whom we spoke were particularly sensitive about being associated with a controversial chemical, having received word from retailers that the latter would not take their strawberries. As such, these shippers appeared to advise their growers not to use it. The California Strawberry Commission—a grower trade group—did not enthusiastically endorse its use, nor did university extension agents. Some growers concurred with activists and felt that the chemical probably was too harmful—unusual stances in an industry that has largely normalized the use of dangerous toxins. Yet some growers were disappointed by the outcome, and a few were visibly angered by the protests. Referring to media reports that methyl iodide was a carcinogen, one grower was adamant in stating that it was the intent of the activists to misinform. The one strawberry grower who had actively sought out and used a methyl iodide permit was equally frustrated by the activism. He thought the chemical had worked very well and was angered by the "harassment" he had received from Earthjustice and reporters. This grower also mentioned a meeting where all the growers in attendance voiced their need for the chemical. Still, they didn't adopt it in the brief period in which they could have.

In short, contentious politics clearly played a role in thwarting adoption of the chemical. At the same time, what concerned the industry most was not protest per se, but the potential loss of markets. Here it is important to highlight that it was also retailers and shippers that were discouraging grower adoption, responding, even if not directly, to the public commenters who threatened never to buy strawberries treated with methyl iodide. This is in keeping with Schurman and Munro's (2010) observations that industry players closer to (skeptical) consumers were more reluctant to sell products made with GMOs and thus helped subvert the spread of agricultural biotechnology into new arenas. Neoliberal fork voting there and here, in other words, was impactful in terms of a larger strategy that played on industry weakness. Since Arysta was counting on widespread and immediate adoption, especially given its investments in seeking approval for the chemical, growers' reluctance to adopt based on consumer sentiment contributed to rendering methyl iodide economically nonviable for the company. The lawsuit that ensued further darkened Midas's prospects.

The lawsuit against CDPR and Arysta, as the real party in interest, was filed on behalf of several organizations, including PAN, UFW, and Californians for Pesticide Reform, as well as two named farmworkers.[2] The plaintiffs alleged that the registration violated CEQA's requirements for a meaningful evaluation of alternatives, a cumulative risk assessment, and full public transparency in decision making for the proposed action. They also alleged that the registration violated California's Birth Defect Prevention Act, which prohibits registration of a pesticide when any of the mandatory studies of health effects is missing, incomplete, or of questionable validity. In addition, they claimed that it violated the state's Pesticide Contamination Prevention Act, which prohibits registration of a pesticide if information related to potential for groundwater contamination is missing. In short, the lawsuit largely revolved on whether sufficient evidence had been gathered and analyzed to determine if methyl iodide would be made safe enough by the mitigation measures that would be required.

As elucidated by those who study scientific controversies that involve regulatory issues, such battles are often won or lost on competing assessments of the practice of science itself: for example, the credibility of actors, the robustness and replicability of data, the adherence to formal procedures, and the standards of proof (Kinchy 2012, 2010, Sismondo 2011, Suryanarayanan and Kleinman 2013). According to Kinchy, many movement actors are loath to reduce their contentions to science-based issues because such battles tend to work in favor of industries that have the resources to cast doubt on science that shows harm. Norms of risk assessment in the United States tend to be particularly kinder to industry because different views are weighed to ascertain a preponderance of evidence, rather than using the precautionary principle, and the risks must outweigh the benefits to justify regulatory restrictions (Boudia 2014, Harrison 2011, Hoffman 2013). As such, some have suggested that the move to scientific risk assessment is itself neoliberal, especially in the case of soil fumigants (DuPuis and Gareau 2008, Harrison 2011). For Kinchy (2012), going to court is doubly a gamble for activists: not only does it necessarily narrow concerns to those that can be established factually; judges and juries are hard to predict, making it a risky strategy for activists. In this case, however, scientific risk assessment did not work in favor of the industry.

Given the nature of the claims, the merits of the case were to be based on the administrative record—which is the information that the agency obtains and reviews before it makes a decision. The case, that is, would rest on whether the agency had done due diligence in reviewing and evaluating all relevant material and whether it had made those reviews public. To establish the appropriate administrative record, the court held a set of hearings in the fall of 2011 about what documents to admit into evidence. Arysta and CDPR wanted to keep the investigation narrow; the plaintiffs wanted to include as much as possible in the record. According to Greg Loarie, lead attorney for the plaintiffs, a capacious investigation can be a bit of a fishing expedition, but "when the agency doesn't want you to see stuff you know there's something there" (personal communication, July 7, 2014). In the end, the judge agreed to accept all additional documents, including internal documents from CDPR staff that proved quite damning.

As we have already mentioned, both CDPR's own scientists and the SRC were on record as opposing registration of the chemical given the level of risk it posed. The SRC was equally concerned that the science that industry had provided was inadequate. In a letter dated February 5, 2010, transmitting its final report to CDPR, the committee noted grave concerns that the data they "would have wished to assess . . . was insufficient or non-existent altogether." Nevertheless, the two issues that received the most attention during briefing and oral proceedings were about adequate attention to the alternatives and the methodology for determining the target concentration of the chemical.

Regarding alternatives, the lawsuit had emphasized CDPR's failure to consider a range of alternatives to the registration of methyl iodide. The director of CDPR was quoted as saying that the only alternatives were either to register methyl iodide or not. In making their oral arguments, the plaintiffs emphasized the existence of additional alternatives that could have been considered, such as deferring registration until additional studies were completed or registering it for different target levels of chemical concentration. A smoking gun on this issue was an internal agency memo that showed that CDPR scientists had indeed explored numerous alternatives. This forty-four-page "pre-decisional document" of April 15, 2010, outlined a range of scenarios and mitigation measures for different target levels of exposure. According to the plaintiff's reply brief, the CDPR director had chosen to omit these in the final report.

The second major issue emerged from the revelation that the final registration decision for methyl iodide sanctioned target concentrations of the chemical that were orders of magnitude higher than CDPR staff scientists had recommended. How that change happened was revealed by another smoking gun. As narrated in oral arguments on January 12, 2012, CDPR had received a memo from Arysta on February 16, 2010, that stated:

> There is still a gap between the current [CDPR] view and the scenarios that would lead to acceptable labels. It is also clear that this gap cannot be closed by label mitigation measures. It is essential to revisit the toxicology assessments to come up with less conservative assumptions.

In other words, Arysta had recognized that the required mitigation measures (buffer zones) were too onerous given the target air-concentration levels that CDPR had recommended, and so they were asking CDPR to change the acceptable air-concentration levels to ones that would not trigger such large buffer zones.

Critical to the case is how the CDPR director arrived at those substantially revised numbers to satisfy Arysta's request. As noted by CDPR's own toxicologists, the director apparently used a "mix and match" method to come up with a desired "acceptable" level of exposure. A memo dated April 28, 2010, described in the plaintiff's opening brief, was the smoking gun for this action. Here the primary state toxicologist wrote that he was puzzled by some of the numbers in the draft regulation for inhalation exposure. "They appear to have been extracted from different MeI risk assessment methodologies that are not interchangeable." Not only did the mix of two different methods lack scientific credibility; it abandoned an additional uncertainty factor that CDPR's toxicologists and the SRC indicated was necessary because essential data were unavailable for determining methyl iodide's potential to impair neurological development. Ignoring its own scientists and review panels, CDPR had appeared, in short, to negotiate an agreement with Arysta behind closed doors and then "cook the books."

In an interesting twist on scientization, many of Arysta's defenses were political, not scientific. For instance, they said that they had already submitted to mitigation measures to have the chemical registered in the first place. They also complained that California's requirements were more protective than those of the U.S. EPA. In addition, they argued that methyl iodide was needed because of the phaseout of methyl bromide; indeed, they found it ironic that the plaintiffs made a case about not considering alternatives when methyl iodide was itself an alternative (according to Arysta's memorandum in opposition). Finally, they boasted that methyl iodide was protective of the ozone layer and prevented skin cancer. The plaintiffs claimed all of these to be irrelevant in terms of compliance with the law and stuck with the science.

The main hearing on the merits of the case, held on January 12, 2012, showed that the court clearly had grave concerns. For example, at one point an attorney for Arysta said that she rejected the petitioners' argument that CDPR had capitulated to Arysta and given the company all that it wanted to get the project registered. The judge's response was that it made no difference because "the legal issue here is whether you violated the CEQA, not whether the agency capitulated to one side or another." During the same hearing, the judge became testy about the defendant's claim that they had explored alternatives, noting that the record did not include even an environmental evaluation of the "no register alternative," required by the guidelines. If indeed methyl iodide was so necessary, the judge suggested, you would have to show what would have happened without it. When the defendant's attorneys were unable to provide an adequate response, the judge said, "I have to tell you, if you had not done that [provided the evaluation of not registering], this is a granted petition [plaintiffs win]. I just don't see how if you didn't do that, you can say that you are CEQA compliant."

It was after that statement but before the judge had ruled that Arysta made its decision to withdraw its request to register methyl iodide. Specifically, on March 20, 2012, Arysta requested that all parties appear in court the next day, based on "a late breaking fact." At the beginning of that court session, the judge stated that he did not understand how any late-breaking fact could have bearing on a case decided by an administrative record. But before giving defendants a chance to speak, the judge informed the courtroom that he was preparing to rule against them for violation of CEQA on the grounds that alternatives were not studied. In addition, he was intending to grant the petition because of lack of evidence that the actual methodology used by the CDPR director had scientific validity, noting that there was no evidence he could find that would justify cobbling together two different methodologies. He went on to say that he thought that the Birth Defect Prevention Act was also violated, but he probably would not get that far with his writing. "I will probably limit it to those two grounds. I don't know that I need to go any further." The judge then turned to Arysta's attorney to ask why they had called everyone to court. At that point the attorneys announced that Arysta was withdrawing its methyl iodide products from the U.S. market and had just voluntarily canceled its registration with CDPR that afternoon. The company had, in fact, issued a press release the previous day stating that it was withdrawing Midas, owing to its economic nonviability.

Since Arysta withdrew its request to register the chemical, the case was eventually declared moot, with the judge stating that the plaintiffs had received all the relief they could get. As such, the judge declined to issue a written statement, claiming that attorney fees would be enough of an incentive to prevent a reoccurrence. There is some question about the significance of the judge's decision not to issue a ruling. The discourse among activists is that Arysta's decision to withdraw its registration petition and make the petitioners' claims moot avoided a larger defeat, by failing to set precedent for the registration of other chemicals. Even before this final hearing, Paul Towers of PAN had postulated that "If the judge dismisses the case . . . California will have let a pesticide corporation off the hook and failed to fix our broken regulatory system" (Standen 2012). In the end, though, activists were, in the words of the plaintiff's attorney, "ecstatic" about the outcome.

The lawsuit was clearly consequential to the fate of methyl iodide, and it is unlikely that Arysta would have withdrawn its request to register methyl iodide had the lawsuit been going well for them. Nevertheless, Arysta had made many miscalculations in respect to the economic viability of methyl iodide, which also affected their decision to withdraw at that time. Many of these were outlined in the Declaration of Thomas Blaser in support of the real party in interest, a motion that was filed for the explicit purpose of not having to pay attorney fees to Earthjustice.[3] This included a registration process that was slower and more costly than expected and an expectation that methyl iodide would be broadly welcomed by both growers and the public. They also apparently did not calculate that growers needed to test the chemical before using it and went on record as expecting broad and swift adoption. Here, the lawsuit itself affected the economic viability of the chemical, since many growers were waiting it out, hoping to use methyl iodide once the lawsuit was resolved. Other factors also hurt Arysta's business plan: methyl bromide had continued to be available because of the CUE process; CDPR had imposed mitigation measures stricter than U.S. EPA requirements; and the company had seen volatility in the world market for iodine. Arysta's hubris, in other words, was a significant weakness, and the movement's legal strategy, which deepened the climate of uncertainty around the chemical, played on that weakness, even if inadvertently.

In sum, pursuing a lawsuit was effective for the activists because it cast yet more aspersions on the chemical, further delaying grower adoption, to the point that Arysta opted to bail and cut its losses in seeking approval. Yet it was successful through means generally not favorable to activists. While a lawsuit of this kind uses the court system (the state) to uphold real regulations, it does so within the framework of scientific risk assessment—a framework that scholars have argued is both neoliberal in its performativity and also in effect, since it often favors industry *tout court*. And yet the activists prevailed—and prevailed by marshaling the science in their favor, while the regulators and industry played politics in ways that undermined their case. With another judge, however, and without the evidence they were able to present, things could have gone quite differently. It was a risky strategy indeed.

CONCLUSION: HOW THE ACTIVISTS WON

The win against methyl iodide was surprising in many ways. We contend that it was successful, in part, because it took the form of a campaign—a focused campaign in which activists were willing to name and take on an opponent and risk defeat. It was also strategic in relation to industry weaknesses—most notably Arysta's need to bring methyl iodide to quick commercial fruition in order to recoup its development costs. While the fifty-three thousand comments turned out to be insignificant legally, many of the comments suggesting a future boycott surely contributed to the strawberry industry's wait-and-see stance. Moreover, the degree of public outrage expressed at public hearings and media events definitely scared some growers into nonadoption, and grower–shippers with brand names were particularly sensitive to reputational risk. Many others who would have otherwise adopted the chemical chose to wait it out given the climate of uncertainty that surrounded the lawsuit. As with the commercialization of biotechnology discussed by Schurman and Munro (2010), Arysta clearly miscalculated the degree of opposition and was working on the assumption that they were bringing the public something that it wanted by replacing a known environmentally destructive chemical.

Yet it was the lawsuit that ultimately caused Midas to lose its golden touch. While there was no final ruling, Arysta smelled its own defeat and opted to cut its losses, perhaps precluding a larger defeat (a claim that has yet to be tested). Still, as Kinchy (2012) attests, legal strategies are a gamble in scientific controversies, and the activists could easily have lost, had not Warmerdam mismanaged the case and failed to adhere to scientific norms in order to suit Arysta's ideas of acceptable buffer zones. So there was also a great deal of luck involved, including having a judge willing to bring the smoking-gun memos into evidence.

Whether this campaign veered from neoliberal forms of action is a separate question. As we have shown, activists used a combination of tactics and strategies, not all of which are easily categorized as resistant, collective, and/or nonmarket action. To the contrary, consumer "fork voting" sentiment apparently had a big impact on industry reluctance to move forward with methyl iodide. And the lawsuit ultimately revolved on activists having science on their side in the exercise of scientific risk assessment associated with neoliberal environmental governance. The key, though, is that these approaches were used strategically, in relationship to industry weakness and agency incompetence. We thus suggest that it is not necessarily the tactics of neoliberalism that limit the politics of the possible in food movements; rather, the problem may lie with a failure to think and act strategically and, hence, politically—the true hallmark of neoliberal governmentality.

All of this ought to be good news for food-movement activists who largely pursue alternatives because they have given up on the possibility of having regulatory impact. If anything, the case of Midas shows that potential outcomes are radically underdetermined, even in the difficult politics of going up against a powerful corporation and thus contesting neoliberalism as it is actually practiced. In an ironic way, we thus agree with Harris (2009), who has argued that those who critique neoliberal activism (specifically building local alternatives) read them for difference. Here we have read for difference to show the difference that both good strategy and luck made, regardless of whether it involved neoliberal means. Of course, only time will tell whether this was a one-off occurrence or if activists will build on this victory to turn the tide on the use of fumigants and other highly toxic pesticides.

NOTES

This chapter is derived in part from an article published in the *Journal of Environmental Policy & Planning* 18 (2016), copyright Taylor & Francis; the article is available online at www.tandfonline.com/10.1080/1523908X.2015.1077441. Funding for the research contained in that article and in this chapter was provided by the National Science Foundation (award no. 1228478). We are grateful for the comments of several anonymous reviewers who inspired several improvements to the manuscript.

1. Unfortunately, some of the prompts had been taken down from the Internet by the time we conducted our analysis, so we cannot say assuredly that these "personal boycotts," as some put it, were not prompted.

2. The lawsuit was filed as *Pesticide Action Network of North America v. California Department of Pesticide Regulation* in the Superior Court for the State of California, Alameda County, on December 30, 2010. Records of the lawsuit can be obtained from the court, or possibly through the plaintiff's attorneys from whom we received them.

3. As explained in the May 2, 2012, oral arguments about this motion, California law awards attorney's fees to the prevailing party in suits that protect a large class of persons, the idea being that it is in the public interest to pursue such suits. Although Earthjustice could not be the prevailing party because there was no ruling, it could still be the "catalyzing party," in which case their fees would still be recoupable.

REFERENCES

Alkon, Alison Hope. 2014. "Food Justice and the Challenge to Neoliberalism." *Gastronomica* 14(2): 27–40.

Allen, Patricia. 1999. "Reweaving the Food Security Safety Net: Mediating Entitlement and Entrepreneurship." *Agriculture and Human Values* 16: 117–129.

Allen, Patricia, Margaret Fitzsimmons, Michael K. Goodman, and Keith Warner. 2003. "Shifting Plates in the Agrifood Landscape: The Tectonics of Alternative Food Initiatives in California." *Journal of Rural Studies* 19: 61–75.

Allen, Patricia, and Julie Guthman. 2006. "From 'Old School' to 'Farm-to-School': Neoliberalization From the Ground Up." *Agriculture and Human Values* 23: 401–415.

Bolda, Marl, Laura Tourte, Karen Klonsky, and Richard De Moura. 2010. "Sample Costs to Produce Strawberries, Central Coast Region." University of California Cooperative Extension.

Boudia, Soraya. 2014. "Managing Scientific and Political Uncertainty: Environmental Risk Assessment in a Historical Perspective." In *Powerless Science? Science and Politics in a Toxic World,* ed. Soraya Boudia and Nathalie Jas, 95–112. New York: Berghahn.

Brown, Sandy, and Christy Getz. 2008. "Privatizing Farm Worker Justice: Regulating Labor through Voluntary Certification and Labeling." *Geoforum* 39: 1184–1196.

California Department of Pesticide Regulation. 2010a. "About DPR's Decision to Register Methyl Iodide." Sacramento: CDPR.

———. 2010b. "Methyl Iodide: Frequently Asked Questions." Sacramento: CDPR. www.cdpr.ca.gov/docs/registration/mei_pdfs/mei_faqs.pdf.

———. 2010c. "Report of the Scientific Review Committee on Methyl Iodide to the Department of Pesticide Regulation." Sacramento: CDPR.

California Strawberry Commission. n.d. "About Strawberries." www.californiastraw berries.com/about_strawberries. Accessed May 28, 2015.

Christensen, Henrik S. 2011. "Political Activities on the Internet: Slacktivism or Political Participation by Other Means?" *First Monday* 16(2).

Dean, Mitchell. 1999. *Governmentality: Power and Rule in Modern Society.* London: Sage.

DuPuis, E. Melanie, and Brian J. Gareau. 2008. "Neoliberal Knowledge: The Decline of Technocracy and the Weakening of the Montreal Protocol." *Social Science Quarterly* 89: 1212–1229.

Earthjustice. 2012. "Cancer-Causing Methyl Iodide Pulled." March 21. http://earthjustice.org/news/press/2012/cancer-causing-methyl-iodide-pulled. Accessed November 25, 2014.

Eaton, Emily. 2013. *Growing Resistance: Canadian Farmers and the Politics of Genetically Modified Wheat.* Winnipeg: University of Manitoba Press.

Ganz, Marshall. 2000. "Resources and Resourcefulness: Strategic Capacity in the Unionization of California Agriculture, 1959–1966." *American Journal of Sociology* 105: 1003–1062.

———. 2009. *Why David Sometimes Wins: Leadership, Organization, and Strategy in the California Farm Worker Movement.* New York: Oxford University Press.

Gareau, Brian J. 2008. "Dangerous Holes in Global Environmental Governance: The Roles of Neoliberal Discourse, Science, and California Agriculture in the Montreal Protocol." *Antipode* 40: 102–130.

Gianessi, Leonard, and Ashley Williams. 2011. "Fumigation Makes California the #1 Producer of Strawberries in the World." Washington, DC: CropLife Foundation.

Greenaway, Twilight. 2011. "Run and Hide from Methyl Iodide." *Grist,* August 30. http://grist.org/scary-food/2011-08-29-methyl-iodide-mock-fumigation/.

Guthman, Julie. 2003. "Eating Risk: The Politics of Labeling Transgenic Foods." In *Remaking the World: Genetic Engineering and Its Discontents,* ed. Rachel Schurman and Dennis Takahashi-Kelso, 130–151. Berkeley: University of California Press.

———. 2007. "The Polanyian Way? Voluntary Food Labels as Neoliberal Governance." *Antipode* 39: 456–478.

———. 2008. "Neoliberalism and the Making of Food Politics in California." *Geoforum* 39: 1171–1183.

———. 2011. *Weighing In: Obesity, Food Justice, and the Limits of Capitalism.* Berkeley: University of California Press.

Guthman, Julie, and Sandy Brown. 2016a. "I Will Never Eat Another Strawberry Again: The Biopolitics of Consumer-Citizenship in the Fight against Methyl Iodide in California." *Agriculture and Human Values* 33: 575–585.

———. 2016b. "Midas' Not-So-Golden Touch: On the Demise of Methyl Iodide as a Soil Fumigant in California." *Journal of Environmental Policy & Planning* 18: 324–341.

Harris, Edmund. 2009. "Neoliberal Subjectivities or a Politics of the Possible? Reading for Difference in Alternative Food Networks." *Area* 41: 55–63.

Harrison, Jill Lindsey. 2006. "'Accidents' and Invisibilities: Scaled Discourse and the Naturalization of Regulatory Neglect in California's Pesticide Drift Conflict." *Political Geography* 25: 506–529.

———. 2008. "Abandoned Bodies and Spaces of Sacrifice: Pesticide Drift Activism and the Contestation of Neoliberal Environmental Politics in California." *Geoforum* 30: 1197–1214.

———. 2011. *Pesticide Drift and the Pursuit of Environmental Justice.* Cambridge, MA: MIT Press.

———. 2014. "Neoliberal Environmental Justice: Mainstream Ideas of Justice in Political Conflict over Agricultural Pesticides in the United States." *Environmental Politics* 23: 650–669.

Harvey, David. 2010. *The Enigma of Capital and the Crises of Capitalism.* London: Oxford University Press.

Herdt, Timm. 2011. "Brown Will Take a 'Fresh Look' at Methyl Iodide Decision." *Ventura County Star.* www.vcstar.com/news/brown-will-take-a-145fresh-look-at-methyl-iodide.

Hoffman, Karen. 2013. "Unheeded Science: Taking Precaution out of Toxic Water Pollutants Policy." *Science, Technology & Human Values* 38: 829–850.

Jessop, Bob. 2002. "Liberalism, Neoliberalism, and Urban Governance: A State Theoretical Perspective." *Antipode* 34: 452–472.

Johnston, Josée. 2008. "The Citizen-Consumer Hybrid: Ideological Tensions and the Case of Whole Foods Market." *Theory and Society* 37: 229–270.

Kinchy, Abby J. 2010. "Anti-Genetic Engineering Activism and Scientized Politics in the Case of 'Contaminated' Mexican Maize." *Agriculture and Human Values* 27: 505–517.

———. 2012. *Seeds, Science, and Struggle: The Global Politics of Transgenic Crops.* Cambridge, MA: MIT Press.

Kinchy, Abby J., Daniel L. Kleinman, and Robyn Autry. 2008. "Against Free Markets, against Science? Regulating the Socio-Economic Effects of Biotechnology." *Rural Sociology* 73: 147–179.

Larner, W. 2003. "Neoliberalism?" *Environment and Planning D: Society and Space* 21: 509–512.

Lavin, Chad. 2009. "Pollanated Politics, or, the Neoliberal's Dilemma." *Politics and Culture* 2: 57–67.

Lim, L. O., and R. R. Nu-May. 2010. "Methyl Iodide (Iodomethane): Risk Characterization Document for Inhalation Exposure, vol. 1: Health Risk Assessment." Sacramento: California Department of Pesticide Regulation.

Mann, G. 2013. *Disassembly Required: A Field Guide to Actually Existing Capitalism.* Oakland, CA: AK Press.

PAN. 2011. "Methyl Iodide." Pesticide Action Network North America. www.panna.org/resources/methyl-iodide.

Peck, Jamie, and Adam Tickell. 2002. "Neoliberalizing Space." *Antipode* 34: 380–404.

Robbins, Paul. 2007. *Lawn People: How Grasses, Weeds, and Chemicals Make Us Who We Are*. Philadelphia: Temple University.

Rose, Nikolas. 1999. *Powers of Freedom: Reframing Political Thought*. Cambridge, UK: Cambridge University Press.

Saxton, Dvera I. 2015. "Strawberry Fields as Extreme Environments: The Ecobiopolitics of Farmworker Health." *Medical Anthropology* 34: 166–183.

Schurman, Rachel. 2004. "Fighting Frankenfoods: Industry Structures and the Efficacy of the Anti-Biotech Movement in Western Europe." *Social Problems* 51: 243–268.

Schurman, Rachel, and William A. Munro. 2010. *Fighting for the Future of Food: Activists versus Agribusiness in the Struggle over Biotechnology*. Minneapolis: University of Minnesota Press.

Sismondo, Sergio. 2011. *An Introduction to Science and Technology Studies*. Chichester, UK: Wiley.

Standen, Amy. 2012. "Fumigant Maker Pulled Disputed Product Facing Court Defeat." *California Watch,* March 23. http://californiawatch.org/dailyreport/fumigant-maker-pulled-disputed-product-facing-court-defeat-15451.

Starkman, Naomi. 2010. "Strawberry Show Down: No Methyl Iodide with My Shortcake, Please." *Civil Eats,* May 20. http://civileats.com/2010/05/20/strawberry-show-down-no-methyl-iodide-with-my-shortcake-please/.

Suryanarayanan, Sainath, and Daniel L. Kleinman. 2013. "Be(e)coming Experts: The Controversy over Insecticides in the Honey Bee Colony Collapse Disorder." *Social Studies of Science* 43: 215–240.

Szasz, Andrew. 2007. *Shopping Our Way to Safety: How We Changed from Protecting the Environment to Protecting Ourselves*. Minneapolis: University of Minnesota Press.

U.S. Environmental Protection Agency. n.d. "Critical Use Exemption Information." www.epa.gov/ozone/mbr/cueinfo.html. Accessed November 24, 2014.

Wells, Miriam. 1996. *Strawberry Fields: Politics, Class, and Work in California Agriculture*. Ithaca, NY: Cornell University Press.

Wozniacka, Gosia. 2012. "Midas, Strawberry Pesticide Methyl Iodide, Will Be Pulled from Market by Arysta Lifescience Inc." *Huffington Post,* March 21. www.huffingtonpost.com/2012/03/21/midas-strawberry-pesticide-methyl-iodide_n_1370789.html.

PART TWO

Working for Workers

FIVE

Resetting the "Good Food" Table

LABOR AND FOOD JUSTICE ALLIANCES
IN LOS ANGELES

Joshua Sbicca

INTRODUCTION

In a 2013 public service announcement (PSA) created by the Food Chain Workers Alliance, titled *Guess Who's Coming to Breakfast,* the son of an interracial couple asks where bacon comes from, to which they respond, "It came from the store." The next moment, a Black woman walks through the front door and says, "Wrong again." Those who have been following the past several decades' explosive growth of interest in food politics might expect to learn about the farm the pig was raised on, and the environmental hazards created by corporate-owned factory farms. But this PSA pushes viewers beyond typical food politics. As the scene unfolds, a racially diverse group of men and women, most of whom are actual food workers, represent the various sectors of the food supply chain. They act out their respective jobs as we learn about their poor pay and working conditions, after which the mother says, "We had no idea." The PSA centers the importance of labor by then asking, "Where does your food come from?" The answer: "It comes from twenty million people who work in the food system in the U.S."

Throughout the United States, the food movement has typically focused on organic food production, farm-to-table initiatives, educating people about the importance of healthy eating, and encouraging the growing of one's own food (Allen et al. 2003, Allen 2004). More recently, movement goals have expanded to include food security, particularly with the rise of antihunger and food justice activists challenging structural inequalities and demanding healthy and culturally appropriate food for all (Alkon 2012, Sbicca 2014). The plight of food workers on farms and in factories, warehouses, grocery stores, and restaurants, depicted in the PSA, has largely been ignored by food activists and has been the purview of the labor movement. Yet such divisions are beginning to dissolve as food justice activists increasingly highlight labor-related racial and class inequalities, and as the demands of food workers and their advocates grow louder. For example in Los Angeles (L.A.), strategic alliances have emerged between the United Food and Commercial Workers Local 770 (UFCW 770), the labor advocacy group Los Angeles Alliance for a New Economy (LAANE), and food activists over the shared concerns of poverty and food access. While new movement linkages do not eliminate old divisions, as labor-oriented activists enter the food movement they stimulate a cross-pollination of ideas and strategies that produces greater class con-sciousness[1] and a commitment to confrontational food politics. Such alli-ances also motivate an engagement with the sphere of formal politics to address the intensifying economic inequality and occupational restructuring resulting from the Great Recession.

In this chapter, I argue that the formation of labor–food justice alliances in L.A. pushes food politics beyond a focus on food access, culturally appro-priate food, and self-determination by strategically emphasizing economic inequalities and working conditions and engaging in confrontational politics.[2] This has taken place in a few key ways. First, labor campaigns have increased awareness of the economic struggles faced by service-sector and food workers. Second, many labor and food justice activists' collabora-tive food politics reflect direct knowledge or experience of food work *and* food insecurity. These activists temper the secessionist proclivity—that is, the desire to remove oneself from, rather than engage, formal politics—that tends to characterize middle- to upper-class white segments of the food movement. Instead they encourage direct confrontation with the state through marches, rallies, press conferences, lobbying, and political organizing around specific policies and elections. Third, labor advocates and unions such as UFCW 770 recognize the need to collaborate with the food movement to combat food insecurity and food deserts, which they do through the lens of poverty.[3] Because of these alliances, L.A.'s food move-ment has become noteworthy among U.S. cities for its racially diverse leader-ship, its commitment to economic justice, and its more politically opposi-tional tactics. These activists offer important lessons that are essential to the building of a movement that can fight to take care of the hands that grow, process, deliver, and sell the food meant to nourish the "good food revolution."

FOOD JUSTICE, FOOD WORKERS, AND EXPANDING
THE FOOD MOVEMENT

Although many food activists support social justice and understand, often firsthand, the economic marginalization exacerbated by the Great Recession, the food movement has historically been less concerned with class considerations, economic inequality, or food workers (Allen 2004). For example, the movement often frames its development of a network of markets for local and organic food as a method to improve environmental and human health. Yet the fact that food remains a commodity to be exchanged in a decentralized but still capitalist system can perpetuate economic marginalization and intensify class inequality (Alkon 2012, Allen and Guthman 2006, Hinrichs 2000, Hinrichs and Allen 2008, Hinrichs and Kremer 2002). Critiquing this state of affairs as it pertains to urban food and health gaps, Holt-Giménez et al. (2011, 133) contend that economic and labor problems will remain unless there are "changes in the structures of ownership . . . and a reversal of the diminished political and economic power of the poor and lower working-class."

Critical food studies attentive to this economic inequality follow a tradition of ecologically informed anarchism (Bookchin 2005, Heller 1999, Kropotkin 1990) and Marxism (Foster 2000, Harvey 1996, Smith 2008). That is, they recognize that the exploitation of labor and nature is inherent to capitalism—say, in how strawberry pickers are poorly paid and exposed to pesticides that simultaneously poison the land. Emphasis diverges, however, over how to surmount this alienation. On the one hand, food activists can create alternative food jobs or third-party governance systems like fair trade that do not require confrontation with the state. On the other hand, food activists can demand state intervention or fight against global free-trade agreements to advance or protect the livelihoods of food workers. Because food labor stands at the crux of society–environment relations, the food movement is positioned strategically to advocate for justice and sustainability for food workers (Gottlieb and Joshi 2010, Gray 2014, Harrison 2011). Nonetheless, it is difficult to bridge environmental, health, and labor concerns across entire movements (Gould et al. 1996), let alone within one place, given the particularities of local ethnic, race, class, and gender politics.

Historically, food labor struggles were part of a larger labor movement less concerned with environmental and health issues. In the United States, meatpackers made significant gains through industrial unions between World War II and the early 1980s; grocery workers fought to create the most prominent upwardly mobile food industry; and farmworkers achieved victories in California through the United Farm Workers between 1960 and the early 1980s. These campaigns, however, were largely peripheral to the food movement, which prioritized the development of organic agriculture and healthy eating (Allen 2004). Moreover, with the declining power of U.S. labor unions and an increasingly hostile social climate for immigrants, support for food workers has dwindled in favor of market-based alternatives devoid of a class analysis (Harrison 2011, Hinrichs 2000, Hinrichs and Allen 2008). It is not only that the food movement emerged from a privileged social location with a focus on environmental protection and health. Organic and small family farms have essentially failed to create cooperative ownership or fair labor standards that combat the class, racial, and gender inequalities experienced by farmworkers (Getz et al. 2008, Gray 2014, Sbicca 2015a).

That said, there are efforts to reimagine food politics as a process of class struggle that benefits eaters *and* workers. For example, some recent campaigns by food workers and their allies strive to improve labor conditions. Prominent among these are the antislavery and fair-food campaigns of the Coalition of Immokalee Workers (CIW). The antislavery campaign educates the public about the practices of modern-day slavery in agriculture, prosecutes farmworker slavery rings, and challenges major corporate buyers to pressure their supply chain to end slavery (see chapter 7, this volume). Such worker empowerment is also important to the fair-food campaign. Beginning in 2001, CIW led a boycott against Taco Bell in order to improve wages and working conditions for tomato pickers. Four years later, Taco Bell agreed to all of CIW's demands. Since then, corporations such as McDonald's, Burger King, Subway, Bon Appétit Management Company, Compass Group, Aramark, Sodexo, Trader Joe's, Whole Foods, and Walmart also signed agreements. Perhaps the most fruitful labor campaign of the past twenty years culminated in 2010 with a victory for 90 percent of Florida tomato pickers covered under a fair-food agreement signed with the Florida Tomato Growers Exchange.[4] These campaigns are important because they show how workers' idea of justice includes a "capacity to critique the conditions of production and their contexts and to visualize ways in which people might transcend those conditions" (Besky 2014, 20).

Activists are also mobilizing other segments of the supply chain through organizations such as Food Chain Workers Alliance, Restaurant Opportunities Centers United, and fair trade associations. This reflects a process of food workers fighting, as a class, for themselves through an array of strategies. This could include working on federal legislation that phases out the tipped mini-mum wage for restaurant workers and challenging corporate-friendly trade associations, while also filing lawsuits against discriminatory employers. As an alternative to the lack of labor standards in organic labeling, activists are also bridging labor to food justice through third-party arrangements. Although imperfect in its reliance on voluntary guidelines when there need to be stronger labor laws, the Agricultural Justice Project developed a certification system for farmers to label their produce "food justice certified" if they meet both ecologi-cal and strict labor standards (Brown and Getz 2008). All these examples rep-resent a blossoming commitment to food labor issues by labor and food justice activists.

In addition to these labor-led campaigns, alliances between mainstream labor unions and community-based and food justice organizations are push-ing for economic justice (Myers and Sbicca 2015, Sbicca 2015b). While not without its challenges, the cross-pollination between such differently situ-ated groups, evident in the increasingly visible perspective of food workers, inspires greater class consciousness.[5] On a panel at the first annual Food Tank Summit called "Recognizing Workers in the Food System," Jose Oliva, a codirector of the Food Chain Workers Alliance, called out food activists for overemphasizing alternatives: "We have a humongous food system that is already in place that is not going to go away by us just growing our own food. . . . There are corporations out there that are making a lot of money on the sweat and exploitation of human beings . . . [and] destroying our health . . . and environment" (Nierenberg 2015). As I argue below, this linking of worker campaigns to traditional food-movement concerns is central to alli-ance building in L.A. Moreover, after three years of strikes and protests by Walmart workers and two years of strikes by fast-food workers, food justice activists started supporting these campaigns. This required listening to work-ers convey how the Great Recession exacerbated food insecurity and eco-nomic inequality for the city's working-class communities of color.

THE GREAT RECESSION, ECONOMIC INEQUALITY, AND ALLIANCE BUILDING

The Great Recession and uneven recovery have exacerbated already rising levels of racial and economic inequality, and, as evidenced by job losses and decreased earning power among the working class, L.A. is among the U.S.

cities hardest hit (Fry and Kocchar 2014, Kocchar and Fry 2014, Owens and Sampson 2012). One of the major reasons is the historical unevenness of development in L.A. Manufacturing decline left the working class vulnerable to a low-wage service economy. At the same time, wealthy coastal and hip neighborhoods continue to overinflate property values, while public services are underfunded (Davis 2006). These increasing inequalities provide the backdrop against which L.A. labor and food justice alliances have coalesced and begun to link food justice to broader visions of economic justice.

A series of recent economic trends imbricates L.A.'s high levels of inequality. Internationally, there were greater increases in inequality in the three years after the Great Recession than in the preceding twelve (Organisation for Economic Co-operation and Development 2013). Domestically, wages stagnated or dropped over the past thirty years for a majority of Americans, while the wealthiest accumulated a greater share of the surplus, even after the "official" recovery (Saez 2016). For example, the minimum wage should be $21.72 an hour if it kept up with increases in worker productivity, or $10.52 an hour if it kept up with inflation (Schmitt 2012).[6] About one-quarter of Americans hold no wealth or are in debt (Allegretto 2011), and despite the safety net preventing millions more people from living in poverty (Fox et al. 2015), the level of poverty relief is less than in comparable countries (Jusko 2016). Meanwhile, food workers are among the lowest-paid workers (Food Chain Workers Alliance 2012). In Los Angeles County, they make up 13 percent of the overall workforce (Los Angeles Food Policy Council 2013).

The class fallout from this capitalist crisis also led to greater food insecurity nationwide (Ruel et al. 2010, von Braun 2008). In 2010, there were more food-insecure people in the United States than ever before: 7.2 million households (14.5 percent of households; Coleman-Jensen et al. 2011). California has 4.1 million food-insecure adults, with Los Angeles County accounting for 1.2 million of these people (California Food Policy Advocates 2014). Food workers disproportionately experience these realities; for example, in California, 18 percent of food workers were considered food-insecure in 2011 (Los Angeles Food Policy Council 2013). Moreover, 23 percent of food workers in California were using CalFresh food assistance, compared to 11 percent of the general population, while 54 percent of California's nonsupervisory food workers lacked health insurance (ibid.).

In California overall, and Southern California in particular, the economic outlook for many people appears bleak as both income and job-access trends remain stratified, while the middle class shrinks (Mordechay 2011). Blacks,

Latino/as, and women have higher levels of underemployment and poverty, and lower average incomes, than their white and male counterparts (Mordechay 2014, 2011). Even workers in more economically stable industries such as grocery retail have experienced a decline in wages and higher-than-average levels of food insecurity, which in California is racially stratified: Latino/as make up 40 percent of grocery workers (Jayaraman 2014).

Compared to other major cities, L.A. is struggling far more to make up for jobs lost by the Great Recession, which increased the gap between those who can afford the city's high cost of living and those who cannot (Bergman 2014). For those with jobs, the top 7 percent of households earn 31 percent of the city's income while the bottom 67 percent earn only 29 percent (Economic Roundtable 2015). There is also more poverty in L.A. than in any other metropolitan area in the country, rising 4.4 percent between 2007 and 2012 to 19.1 percent; this jumps to 28 percent if those with wages just above the poverty level are included (Los Angeles 2020 Commission 2013). Despite adding over 800,000 residents between 1980 and 2010, the city has lost 165,000 jobs (Los Angeles County Economic Development Corporation 2012). Yet the food service sector is one of only five major industries to see job growth since 1993 (Los Angeles 2020 Commission 2013). This industry is rife with low wages, few benefits, and widespread racial and gender discrimination and sexual harassment (Jayaraman 2013). For example, over the past thirty years, restaurant workers have lost a third of their buying power (Economic Roundtable 2015).

Labor and food justice activists draw on these realities to illuminate that those disproportionately working in low-wage food industries are the same people disproportionately experiencing food insecurity (Food Chain Workers Alliance 2012). Blacks, Latino/as, the poor, and women are oftentimes working part-time food jobs in order to weather economic blows suffered in the Great Recession. This crisis opened up an opportunity in L.A. to bridge interests, deepen and foster alliances that represent food workers, and increase overall labor mobilization for economic justice.

Buoying these hopeful glimmers in the midst of such dire circumstances is the revitalization of L.A.'s labor movement, and the strength of unions such as UFCW 770. As Ruth Milkman shows, L.A. became a center of labor-movement resurgence in the late twentieth century for three reasons: "the historical predominance of the AFL [American Federation of Labor], low-road employment restructuring strategies, and a massive immigrant influx" (Milkman 2006, 6). The AFL unions were built primarily around occupational culture in industries such as trucking, construction, textiles, janitorial, and grocery retail. As such, they were less threatened by deindustrialization. These unions made many gains until the 1970s, when neoliberal restructuring led to lower wages, more casualized employment, white outflight, and deunionization. After such trends were underway, immigrants began to take these jobs. In response, former AFL unions started using grassroots organizing strategies and top-down comprehensive campaigns to bring in a new generation of union members. These trends directly inform current campaigns to mobilize food workers, such as the Service Employees International Union's support of fast-food workers and UFCW's support of grocery workers.

In the following sections, I contend that there are three reasons why labor–food justice alliances emerged in the context of a post–Great Recession economy that reflect a class-conscious and confrontational food politics. These include the increased visibility of workers due to publicly prominent labor campaigns, the entrance of activists who bring an understanding of the relationship between food and economic insecurity, and the commitment by the labor movement to engage the issue of food deserts. Although presented individually, these three factors overlap in different times and places as part of a larger shift in L.A. food-movement politics. More broadly, this shift offers an example to the food movement in the United States of how to engage in a more combative food politics that does not sacrifice either food security or the concerns of workers.

Confrontational Labor Campaigns Increase the Visibility of Workers

One reason for the emergence of labor–food justice alliances is that high-profile labor campaigns have increased recognition of otherwise invisible workers and the poverty they often experience. These confrontational labor campaigns offer effective tactics and have successfully drawn support from vocal segments of the public and from politicians (Cummings and Boutcher 2009). In addition, because food workers are often food-insecure, these campaigns provide entry for food activists into broader economic justice campaigns. With victories by workers in L.A., labor groups are increasingly seen as important allies for the food movement, despite the fact that labor is historically outside the purview of the food movement.

A number of campaigns illustrate the power of workers and a well-organized L.A. labor movement. In 1997, after public pressure by LAANE and their union and community allies, the L.A. City Council passed a living-wage ordinance that covers workers hired by businesses that receive city contracts. This victory improved the lives of over ten thousand low-wage workers, including large percentages of Blacks, women, and single mothers (Fairris et al. 2005). The campaign was a watershed moment in the renewal of labor organizing and political activism, at a time when marginalized workers such as janitors and drywallers were unionizing (Dreier 2011, Milkman 2006). Continuing to build on a string of triumphs for low-wage workers in other industries, in 2014 Mayor Eric Garcetti announced a plan to raise L.A.'s minimum wage to $13.25 in 2017. Then, in 2015, labor unions and their allies pushed the City Council and mayor to pass an ordinance creating a $15 minimum wage by 2020. These labor victories cultivate an amenable context within which food labor and food justice activists mobilize for food workers.

A prime example of labor, community, and food activists fighting alongside food workers is in grocery retail—one food industry that offers some semblance of economic security, largely due to decades of successful union organizing, which is currently under threat. Many antiunion corporations, such as Walmart and even Whole Foods, are increasing the prevalence of low-wage grocery jobs. Reflecting on these conditions, Luciana, an organizer with LAANE, explains that a unionized grocery industry offers a respectable economic path to working-class people of color: "You need a high school degree to get a union grocery job. When you look at issues of access to education and resources provided to communities of color, this is just one more door that would be shut on them if this industry goes away." Although the industry is not at risk of going away absolutely, it is at risk of weakening labor standards as nonunion and low-wage grocery chains enter a growing Southern California market. Luciana's insight highlights the coupling of disadvantages experienced by working-class communities of color and therefore the importance of labor unions for resisting economic exploitation and marginalization. Jae, a political operative for UFCW 770, puts this pointedly, arguing that "Bad standards in nonunion stores become the status quo. It's a race to the bottom." Labor unions and the communities they represent see this as a front-line struggle in need of highly visible campaigns.

When the entrance of Walmart or contract negotiations have threatened unionized grocery workers, alliances have formed to protect worker gains and ensure food security (Myers and Sbicca 2015). Beginning in 2002 and culminating in 2004, LAANE and UFCW 770 successfully fought off

FIGURE 5.1. Thousands march in Chinatown, near the heart of Los Angeles, in the largest protest against Walmart in U.S. history. Photo by Neil Jacobs.

Walmart in the primarily Black community of Inglewood after the corporation attempted to circumvent impact assessments with a ballot initiative. This widely reported defeat inspired future cross-movement alliances, as it showed that Walmart's low-wage urban-growth strategy could be defeated in a pro-labor city. Resistance to Walmart manifested itself in other ways as well. In 2003, Albertsons, Kroger, and Safeway tried gutting health benefits, arguing that big-box retailers like Walmart made it hard to compete. UFCW 770 members refused to accept these cuts, which led to a disruptive, 141-day strike supported by a wide cross section of Angelenos. While ultimately accepting some cuts, UFCW 770 members worked in future contract negotiations to win back losses. It was easier to resist a race to the bottom because many allies of UFCW 770 helped push the City Council to pass a "Superstore Ordinance" in 2004 that requires economic impact assessments for stores exceeding one hundred square feet. Unionized grocery chains no longer had the convenient excuse that low-wage competition from the likes of Walmart required concessions from workers.

The high visibility of these community-supported labor campaigns facilitated the formation, in 2007, of the Alliance for Healthy and Responsible Grocery Stores (2010), which consisted of thirty organizations. The formation of this alliance was pivotal to the inclusion of food justice concerns such as access to grocery stores that provide good food. It brought together the usual labor stakeholders, such as UFCW 770 and LAANE, with groups—like Community Services Unlimited, Inc., and Hunger Action Los Angeles—that would later sit on the Los Angeles Food Policy Council. At first, the alliance produced a report linking issues of food insecurity, nutrition, and unfair labor practices. With this foundation, they fought to keep Tesco's Fresh & Easy, a nonunion and automated-checkout grocery chain, out of the city. The alliance also offered tours of food deserts for local politicians and the media in order to build support for bringing in unionized grocery chains. This is significant, given that politicians and certain grocery chains have used food deserts to ignore poor labor practices in the name of food security and support corporate urban landgrabs that harm working-class communities of color (Holt-Giménez et al. 2011).

These alliance-building efforts reflect a politics of reciprocity that continues to produce results. In 2012, for example, a number of mayoral candidates, including the eventual winner, Eric Garcetti, refused campaign contributions from Walmart. Labor groups connected issues of food security to economic justice, partially to foster support for maintaining high levels of union membership in grocery retail, while many food security advocates recognized that tying their concerns to poverty and labor made for a strong alliance (Myers and Sbicca 2015, Sbicca 2015b). To conclude, a wide range of groups that recognize the mutual benefit of working together have backed grocery workers and waged disruptive campaigns against corporations that would increase poverty and economic inequality in L.A. (Cummings 2007).

New Class-Conscious Food Politics
Reflect Interconnected Inequalities

Food workers are often food-insecure, given the economic precariousness of most jobs in the food system. Labor and food justice activists in L.A. increasingly recognize this interconnection. For example, the Los Angeles Food Policy Council (LAFPC), one of the most powerful voices for food justice in the city, describes its two most important goals as "good food economy" and "good food access" (LAFPC 2015). This is striking, given that food policy councils in other major cities are often characterized by the ecological or color-blind concerns of many middle- or upper-class white activists (Alkon 2012, Guthman 2008a, Harper et al. 2009). But in L.A., activists from communities designated food deserts and their allies are infiltrating the LAFPC, as well as the broader food movement, to rectify the lack of equitable access to healthy food, land for urban agriculture, good food jobs, and sidewalk space to sell food. This is not to suggest that conflict disappears, but rather that alliance formation is enriched through the experience of and affirmation of difference (Young 2000). Not only do labor-oriented voices and experiences inform the food movement, but also those with different privileges learn to fight alongside food workers and the food-insecure.

The LAFPC is central to nurturing greater class consciousness in the city's food movement. Although former mayor Antonio Villaraigosa's initial 2009 task force did not directly include a food-worker member, it did include key people dedicated to economic justice, such as Professor Robert Gottlieb, executive director of the Urban & Environmental Policy Institute at Occidental College.[7] Since 2010, then, the LAFPC has increasingly included members such as United Farm Workers to represent the concerns of food workers.[8] While many other members may not advocate directly for food workers, they often come from and know food-insecure communities that would benefit from good food jobs. Groups such as Community Health Councils have a commitment to social justice in working-class neighborhoods and thus see the importance of quality employment. Over a five-year period, such voices have ensured greater mobilization to ameliorate the lack of good food jobs *and* food access in working-class communities of color. Representative of such shifts was the creation of the Good Food Economy Working Group, the addition of people such as Joann Lo from the Food Chain Workers Alliance (see chapter 6, this volume), the promotion of reports on food workers, active discussion of food labor politics at networking meetings and on Facebook and Twitter, and public promotion of forty "labor and worker justice" organizations.[9]

This alliance convergence space now amplifies and echoes labor voices historically marginalized in the food movement. In 2014, the LAFPC invited John Grant, the secretary-treasurer of UFCW 770, to sit on the Leadership Board. This formal relationship furthers the perspective of food labor activists. Diego, an organizer with UFCW 770, asserts that "We are new to the conversation [i.e. the food movement]. . . . We bring a narrative that they haven't heard before." Given the centrality of this union to the overall L.A. labor movement, their voice pushes the food movement to develop a class-conscious food politics. Frank Tamborello (2011), the founder of Hunger

Action Los Angeles, a group that has supported UFCW 770[10] and LAANE, reflects on learning about the working conditions of Walmart employees:

> As someone who works on food justice and economic issues, I was already aware that wages at Walmart are so low that most employees qualify for federal benefits such as SNAP. . . . But what I found appalling was that some of the women had worked for years under the promise of wage increases which never materialized. They moved from department to department, acquiring skills, taking up the slack for other workers who had been laid off, eventually managing a wide variety of departments. And they hardly got any increase in pay over years of time for what they did.

This statement reveals the power of consciousness-raising to expand conceptions of food justice to consider not only how "economic issues" lead to food insecurity, but how economic inequality is often gendered, which requires a nuanced analysis of what constitutes a "good food job."

The infiltration of a class-conscious food politics that elevates labor also converges with the concerns of food justice activists regarding access to culturally appropriate food. Among the ten most populous U.S. cities, only L.A. prevented street vending, which disproportionately undermined many Latino/a livelihood strategies (Vallianatos 2015). Yet the city had ten thousand food vendors raking in over $100 million a year (Liu 2015). While food trucks pepper L.A. streets, immobile and resource-strapped immigrants were confined to food vending on sidewalks, where they faced criminalization and social marginalization. In response, labor and food justice activists sought to pave "a pathway to food justice" through participatory policymaking that centered the perspectives of food vendors in order to compel the City Council to legalize street vending (Fox 2015). On the one hand, activists such as Rudy Espinoza link economic justice and food access by arguing that food vendors "could be an army of entrepreneurs that could help us get affordable and healthy food into low-income neighborhoods" (KCET 2012). On the other hand, activists understand street vending as a labor issue. Clare Fox (2015), the Director of Policy and Innovation at the LAFPC, advocates that food justice "includes supporting local food economies that provide pathways out of poverty . . . supporting the self-determination of food workers and decriminalizing low-income, working people." Political organizing and protests on these fronts set in motion a process that forced politicians to take sides, and led the City Council to decriminalize sidewalk sales and draft an ordinance to legalize street vending (Alpert Reyes 2014, Mejia 2015, Martinez 2017).

The Los Angeles Street Vending Campaign—a campaign that challenged a set of intersecting inequalities that would have remained unaddressed without labor and food justice movements joining in the push for policy reform—can now claim victory (Torres 2016).

Reflecting the interconnectedness of social inequalities, there are two empowered councilmembers who have fought for other policy reforms that would increase food *and* economic security. Councilmember Curren Price Jr. (representing District 9 in historically Black South L.A.) helped lead the City Council to adopt the $15 minimum wage increase, a demand-side solution to the problem of food insecurity. In the Northeast Valley of L.A., Councilmember Felipe Fuentes (District 7) also supported the minimum-wage increase. Their support for better labor policies dovetails with a class-conscious orientation toward food security. These two councilmembers jointly introduced a motion in 2014 that would provide tax incentives to landowners to encourage urban agriculture on unused or underutilized land. In a public statement, Fuentes reasoned that "By converting empty parcels into urban farms, we can encourage local economic development, green our communities and provide produce in neighborhoods that lack access to fresh foods" (Jennings 2014).[11] In short, political support for working-class communities of color exists because activists from these communities are entering movement spaces, drawing connections between interconnected inequalities, and advocating for concrete political reforms.

Labor Adopts Food Justice Goals through the Lens of Poverty

A third reason for labor–food justice alliances is that some labor leaders recognize the need to tackle food insecurity and food deserts, and therefore participate in local food politics. This participation is a kind of political capital exchanged for the food movement's attention to concerns of the labor movement. That is, the exchange encourages a class-conscious, confrontational food politics more likely to reform local practices and institutions. Meanwhile, labor unions such as UFCW 770 are responding to the needs of their members and their members' families, many of whom live in food deserts or experience food insecurity. Below, I explain this process and the importance of movement brokers who help weave alliances around the issue of poverty.

Behind UFCW 770's commitment to food security is the hope that participation in the food movement will contribute to a stronger labor movement and greater political engagement. Diego contends that "The labor movement's future depends on its ability to think outside of the box and become part of the solution." For Mark, a longtime labor leader with UFCW 770, such solutions include combating the flight of unionized grocery stores in what he sees as "a system of food apartheid . . . where communities of color and communities of working poor are being denied access to food." He goes on to note that "besides the fact of mortality, obesity and a whole slew of other ills that constitute a food desert is that you have . . . poverty." This is a challenge, but one that union organizers such as Dave believe must be addressed. He asserts: "To the extent that we have the resources, expertise and ability to facilitate building this into a juggernaut as opposed to just a narrowly focused union . . . you know, first contracts and better contracts, into something bigger and broader on a consciousness level. . . . It's long overdue." Taken together, these positions reflect a shifting desire to participate with the food movement.[12]

Movement brokers who can translate the positions of many stakeholders and find common ground fortify union commitment to combating food deserts. In an early effort to build ties with the food movement, UFCW 770 joined the Food Chain Workers Alliance, which strengthened connections with people like Joann Lo, a current codirector and active participant in food justice networks. Emiliano, a UFCW 770 union representative, believes that these kinds of actions signify a shift to deeper community engagement, which is "one of the biggest steps we've made as a labor movement. . . . [W]e need these alliances because we need people to help us." Other community-based organizations translate the experience of poverty into concrete issues. Emiliano notes the importance of these brokers: "In South Central we have ACORN, who do housing [and] we have Community Coalition. . . . They've been helping us with the food desert situation." Given some of the historical tensions between the labor movement and other movements, new creative partnerships can support food workers within their social and economic context.

Finding common frames of reference is therefore important, because labor unions and public health activists historically approach food insecurity from different directions. One sees good jobs, and the other good food, as the solution. Attention to poverty has helped UFCW 770 work with groups such as Policy Link and Community Health Councils to address food insecurity and food deserts. Low-wage jobs perpetuate poverty, and poverty produces food insecurity. Therefore, solving poverty is of paramount importance. Making these connections is vital, given that food deserts are often in the same communities that unionized grocery stores have left, but where UFCW 770 refuses to accept low-wage corporations like Walmart, even if the latter would increase food security. Brokers such as Joann Lo help focus different stakeholders on poverty. As she told me in an interview, "ultimately everyone [in the LAFPC] is concerned about poverty; it's the root cause of various problems, whether they are bad jobs, lack of access to good food, not being able to afford good food. We have used that as a starting point for other conversations." Labor activists work with food justice activists because poverty influences dietary health, reflects the spatial organization of food access, and implicates economic exploitation in the food system (Myers and Sbicca 2015).

While the labor movement seeks to gain from supporting the food movement, community-based organizations, and its own members concerning food deserts, the process of expanding a class-conscious food politics is uneven. For example, during a widespread campaign to keep Walmart out of L.A., a report called "Food Desert to Food Oasis" was published by Community Health Councils, a member of which sits on the LAFPC.[13] The report states that

> the City should be very cautious in adopting policies that require new grocery stores to provide employees a living wage or allow for unionization. While these policies are well intentioned to ensure employees receive sufficient compensation to afford life in Los Angeles, they also pose higher labor costs that prospective new grocery retailers may not be able to afford. (Bassford et al. 2010, 24)

Labor activists had difficulty accepting such a position, given its potential to roll back victories and accelerate the influx of low-wage grocery stores. To sidestep this division, activists tackling economic and racial disparities in access to healthy food are attending more to short- and mid-term solutions. For example, a major initiative called the Healthy Neighborhood Market Network is supporting immigrant and small convenience, corner, and grocery stores to sell healthy and affordable food in neighborhoods like South L.A. Many labor activists support these initiatives because they are necessary in the short term but see them as insufficient in the long term, instead preferring full-scale grocery retailers that offer union or living-wage jobs. Adrian, an organizer with LAANE, argues that "part of being a food desert is the fact that it's a poor area. Poor areas injected with higher wages or quality jobs are going to do a lot better and will probably attract those grocers from that point ... and would not be allowed to become food deserts." Toward such ends, a long-term, public–private project came to fruition in 2014 to bring Northgate González Market to South L.A. This store is not union, but it provides more affordable and high-quality food, as well as mandated living-wage jobs, to local residents (Xu 2014). While not always successful in building bridges, a commitment to eliminating poverty militates against only addressing symptoms such as food deserts. In turn, labor leaders' engagement with a major concern for food justice activists becomes part of a range of complementary political strategies to equitably develop communities.

TOWARD A CLASS-CONSCIOUS AND CONFRONTATIONAL FOOD POLITICS

Thinking back to the discursive intervention of the PSA with which this chapter began, I want to reiterate how these tactics stoke greater class consciousness and compel other forms of political engagement across the food movement. The major lesson offered by the formation of labor–food justice alliances in L.A. is that food politics can be more than a politics of autonomy, cultural foodways, market-based alternatives, and self-provisioning. This is not to discount the value of progressive and radical efforts by working-class communities, communities of color, and their allies to prefigure the kinds of practices that stoke our imagination of, and inspire experimentation with, more socially just food systems.[14] Rather, by turning our attention to the formation of a class-conscious food politics within L.A.'s food movement, we see that one of the roads to a socially just food system is paved with confrontation.

As I have argued, given the widespread structural inequalities in L.A., intensified by the Great Recession, there is a perceived urgency on the part of labor and food justice activists to engage in contentious forms of activism. Alliances mobilized toward such ends, particularly in the case of grocery workers, emerged because of L.A.'s powerful labor movement, the strong representation in local movement networks of activists whose food politics link labor exploitation and food insecurity, and the willingness of labor unions to combat food deserts. These alliances reveal that a deeper class consciousness is an essential ingredient for challenging political and economic elites to take care of food workers. As a result, labor–food justice alliances achieved concrete reforms such as wage and benefit increases, slowed the deterioration of labor standards within grocery retail, and made the conditions of—and political support for—food workers more visible.

These alliances certainly offer an interesting case, but, contemplated in light of their implications for the food movement—and specifically for activists with a commitment to food justice—there are three broader lessons. Consider how confrontational politics exist in other movement spaces concerning access to land, biotechnology, and pesticides (e.g., as described in parts 1 and 3 of this volume). In these cases, as well as those regarding food workers, activism contests the elites and structures that drive economic and racial inequality in the food system. Building alliances, organizing rallies, and protesting can lead to concessions and reforms otherwise unattainable through prefigurative politics.

First, there is an increased chance of restructuring economic, political, and social practices and institutions for the benefit of more people. If the food movement only works in interstitial spaces or adopts market-based strategies, hoping that these actions will eventually seep into the consciousness and practices of others, there is a missed opportunity to improve more fully the lives of food workers. Institutionalized health protections from pesticide exposure gained traction because pesticide drift activists pressured regulatory agencies to ban the most toxic pesticides and to increase monitoring of exposure for farmworkers and their local communities (Harrison 2011; chapter 2, this volume). Even when other factors may compel corporations to improve labor practices, like new or upcoming minimum-wage floors, activists can claim these victories in order to increase mobilization. Labor activists and workers took credit for Walmart's pledge in 2015 to increase wages for five hundred thousand associates. TJX Companies and Target Corporation followed suit, reinforcing the narrative that taking on Walmart prevents a race to the bottom in grocery retail.[15]

Second, if the food movement does *not* engage in confrontational politics, labor exploitation and economic inequality in the food system will continue. The logic of capitalism is growth, which requires squeezing more value out of the labor required to bring food to our tables. Similarly, the logic of the state is to consolidate power and control, not only for itself, but also for capitalists, which can limit labor protections. While there are long-standing debates on whether to engage capitalists or the state in order to bring about social change (e.g., the dispute between Karl Marx and Mikhail Bakunin), the corporatization and neoliberalization of the food system necessitates direct confrontation (Alkon 2014). Under current conditions, food activists can choose to opt out and allow the food system to continue growing and consolidating power, or they can choose to intervene. Where food activists have intervened—say, in the struggle over biotechnology—they have not been able to ban, outright, all genetically modified foods, but they have altered their deployment and spread (Schurman and Munro 2010; chapter 3, this volume). By considering the counterfactual question of what would happen if activists had not taken up a particular struggle, the importance of engaging in political contests for labor rights and reforms becomes clearer.

Third, movements that engage in more disruptive forms of politics have greater visibility. Such a strategic approach is particularly important for working-class communities and communities of color that want political reform but lack the financial resources of their opponents (Piven and Cloward 1979). We see this, for instance, in L.A. with the campaign to legalize street food vending and the movement from guerilla gardening in parkways to a campaign that pushed the City Council to legalize the planting of edible plants. Moreover, protests accompanying striking fast-food and grocery workers have included more privileged allies who help illuminate exploitative food-labor conditions, especially for those workers who cannot or will not participate, for fear of retaliation by their employers. Unlike many alternative food initiatives, such as farmers' markets and school gardens, which the media usually cover as individual and consumer-driven human interest stories, contentious politics of the sort taking place in L.A. represent distinct alternatives. Although visibility through confrontation does not immediately translate into a transformed economy or state, it can reveal a deeper commitment by the food movement to ensure food justice in conventional *and* alternative food systems.

Resetting the "good food" table to include the hands that feed deepens food justice praxis and expands food politics by elevating economic justice. This strategic pivot can lead to activism that disrupts the operations of corporations and businesses intent on exploiting workers and disrupts movement circles apathetic to worker demands for fair food systems. But as this chapter shows, the formation of labor-inclusive alliances is a deliberate and ongoing process that requires flexibility in its articulation of a class-conscious and confrontational food politics.

NOTES

1. *Class consciousness* refers explicitly to the reflexive understanding of one's economic position and, in particular, to the interests and perspectives of those with few or no material resources (e.g., food, housing, car), those who have low incomes,

and/or the working poor. A class-conscious food politics, then, is one in which economic inequality between different classes is recognized as a central social struggle.

2. This chapter draws on findings that emerged through fieldwork, interviews, and archival research. In late 2012, I interned for two months with UFCW 770, during which I assisted in grocery retail campaigns and learned how the organization interfaces with the local food movement. I also made connections with other organizations working on food labor issues, namely Food Chain Workers Alliance, Warehouse Workers United, OUR Walmart, Restaurant Opportunities Center of Los Angeles, and Los Angeles Alliance for a New Economy. I conducted nineteen interviews during my fieldwork. I also analyzed over a hundred different kinds of print and digital documents such as organizational newsletters, memos, emails, newspapers, blogs, Twitter and Facebook accounts, and videos produced by news organizations and activists. Over the two years since completing fieldwork, I maintained informal ties with some activists and organizations and analyzed new print and digital documents.

3. The term *food desert* is contested, but I use it to reflect the language of those I spoke with during interviews and fieldwork, and to reflect its use by those seeking to ameliorate the limited access to healthy food.

4. This includes "a strict code of conduct, a cooperative complaint resolution system, a participatory health and safety program, and a worker-to-worker education process" (Coalition of Immokalee Workers 2010).

5. See, for instance, Bittman (2014) and the National Food Policy tweetchat held by the Union of Concerned Scientists (2014).

6. Federal minimum wage is $7.25.

7. In the first chapter of *Food Justice* (Gottlieb and Joshi 2010), the authors assert that achieving justice for food workers is central to transforming the food system.

8. United Farm Workers is no longer a member of the LAFPC but is connected with the Good Food Purchasing Policy.

9. A list of labor and worker-justice organizations supported by LAFPC is available at http://goodfoodla.org/resources/local-good-food-organizations/labor-worker-justice/.

10. The UFCW is the chief supporter of OUR Walmart. They have paid organizers who help these employees develop campaigns and worker empowerment. Such connections help bring Walmart workers out to public education events.

11. The LAFPC estimates that L.A. contains about 8,600 parcels where urban agriculture could take place.

12. Along with the California Labor Federation, UFCW 770 endorsed Proposition 37 in 2012, which would have required labeling genetically engineered foods.

13. The report relied on a workgroup that included a few other members of the LAFPC, such as PolicyLink.

14. Such efforts are reported on in "Part III: Will Work for Food Justice" in Alkon and Agyeman's (2011) edited collection *Cultivating Food Justice: Race, Class, and Sustainability.*

15. McDonald's announced in early 2015 that it would raise its pay in the roughly 1,500 stores it owns in the United States. Workers in nearly 90 percent of stores will not see a raise, because franchisees are free to set their own pay structures.

REFERENCES

Alkon, Alison Hope. 2012. *Black, White, and Green: Farmers Markets, Race, and the Green Economy.* Athens: University of Georgia Press.

———. 2014. "Food Justice and the Challenge to Neoliberalism." *Gastronomica* 14(2): 27–40.

Alkon, Alison Hope, and Julian Agyeman, Eds. 2011. *Cultivating Food Justice: Race, Class, and Sustainability.* Cambridge, MA: MIT Press.

Allegretto, Sylvia A. 2011. "The State of Working America's Wealth, 2011" (Briefing Paper 292). March 23. Washington, DC: Economic Policy Institute.

Allen, Patricia. 2004. *Together at the Table: Sustainability and Sustenance in the American Agrifood System,* new edition. University Park, PA: Penn State University Press.

Allen, Patricia, Margaret Fitzsimmons, Michael K. Goodman, and Keith Warner. 2003. "Shifting Plates in the Agrifood Landscape: The Tectonics of Alternative Food Initiatives in California." *Journal of Rural Studies* 19: 61–75.

Allen, Patricia, and Julie Guthman. 2006. "From 'Old School' to 'Farm-to-School': Neoliberalization From the Ground Up." *Agriculture and Human Values* 23: 401–415.

Alliance for Healthy and Responsible Grocery Stores. 2010. "Not Making the Grade: A Community Evaluation of Grocery Chains' Impact on Los Angeles Neighborhoods." www.laane.org/wp-content/uploads/2010/03/GroceryChain-RptCard11-30-10.pdf.

Alpert Reyes, Emily. 2014. "L.A. Officials Take a Step toward Legalizing Street Vending." *Los Angeles Times,* December 2. www.latimes.com/local/cityhall/la-me-street-vending-20141203-story.html. Accessed March 2, 2015.

Bassford, Nicky, Lark Galloway-Gilliam, Gwendolyn Flynn, and CHC Food Resource Development Workgroup. 2010. "Food Desert to Food Oasis: Promoting Grocery Store Development in South Los Angeles." Los Angeles: Community Health Councils, Inc.

Bergman, Ben. 2014. "Los Angeles Job Growth Falling Behind Other Cities, Study Says." *Southern California Public Radio,* September 11. www.scpr.org/blogs/economy/2014/09/11/17281/los-angeles-job-growth-falling-behind-other-cities/. Accessed December 3, 2014.

Besky, Sarah. 2014. *The Darjeeling Distinction: Labor and Justice on Fair-Trade Tea Plantations in India.* Berkeley: University of California Press.

Bittman, Mark. 2014. "Rethinking the Word 'Foodie.'" *The New York Times,* June 24. www.nytimes.com/2014/06/25/opinion/mark-bittman-rethinking-the-word-foodie.html.

Bookchin, Murray. 2005. *The Ecology of Freedom: The Emergence and Dissolution of Hierarchy.* Oakland, CA: AK Press.

Brown, Sandy, and Christy Getz. 2008. "Privatizing Farm Worker Justice: Regulating Labor through Voluntary Certification and Labeling." *Geoforum* 39: 1184–1196.

California Food Policy Advocates. 2014. *Nutrition & Food Insecurity Profiles,* July 30. http://cfpa.net/county-profiles. Accessed December 3, 2014.

Coalition of Immokalee Workers. 2010. "A Watershed Moment...." www.ciw-online.org/blog/2010/11/watershed_moment/. Accessed August 10, 2014.

Coleman-Jensen, Alisha, Mark Nord, Margaret Andrews, and Steven Carlson. 2011. "Household Food Security in the United States in 2010." Washington, DC: U.S. Department of Agriculture, Economic Research Service.

Cummings, Scott L. 2007. "Law in the Labor Movement's Challenge to Wal-Mart: A Case Study of the Inglewood Site Fight." *California Law Review* 95: 1927–1998.

Cummings, Scott L., and Steven A. Boutcher. 2009. "Mobilizing Local Government Law for Low-Wage Workers." *University of Chicago Legal Forum Paper* 09–23: 187–246.

Davis, Mike. 2006. *City of Quartz: Excavating the Future in Los Angeles,* second edition. London, UK: Verso.

Dreier, Peter. 2011. "Moving in the Labor LAANE." *New Labor Forum* 20: 88–92.

Economic Roundtable. 2015. "Los Angeles Rising: A City That Works for Everyone." Los Angeles: UCLA Labor Center, Institute for Research on Labor and Employment.

Fairris, David, David Runsten, Carolina Briones, and Jessica Goodheart. 2005. "Examining the Evidence: The Impact of the Los Angeles Living Wage Ordinance on Workers and Businesses." Los Angeles Alliance for a New Economy. www.irle.ucla.edu/publications/documents/LivingWage_fullreport.pdf.

Food Chain Workers Alliance. 2012. "The Hands That Feed Us: Challenges and Opportunities for Workers along the Food Chain." June 6. Los Angeles: FCWA. http://foodchainworkers.org/wp-content/uploads/2012/06/Hands-That-Feed-Us-Report.pdf.

Foster, John Bellamy. 2000. *Marx's Ecology: Materialism and Nature.* New York: Monthly Review Press.

Fox, Clare. 2015. [From the Director's Desk] "LA Street Vending Campaign as a Pathway to Food Justice." Los Angeles Food Policy Council. March 3. http://goodfoodla.org/2015/03/03/la-street-vending-campaign-as-a-pathway-to-food-justice/. Accessed March 4, 2015.

Fox, Liana, Christopher Wimer, Irwin Garfinkel, Neeraj Kaushal, and Jane Waldfogel. 2015. "Waging War on Poverty: Poverty Trends Using a Historical Supplemental Poverty Measure." *Journal of Policy Analysis and Management* 34: 567–592.

Fry, Richard, and Rakesh Kocchar. 2014. "America's Wealth Gap between Middle-Income and Upper-Income Families Is Widest on Record." Pew Research Center. December 17. www.pewresearch.org/fact-tank/2014/12/17/wealth-gap-upper-middle-income/.

Getz, Christy, Sandy Brown, and Aimee Shreck. 2008. "Class Politics and Agricultural Exceptionalism in California's Organic Agriculture Movement." *Politics and Society* 36: 478–507.

Gottlieb, Robert, and Anupama Joshi. 2010. *Food Justice.* Cambridge, MA: MIT Press.

Gould, Kenneth A., Allan Schnaiberg, and Adam S. Weinberg. 1996. *Local Environmental Struggles: Citizen Activism in the Treadmill of Production.* New York: Cambridge University Press.

Guthman, Julie. 2004. *Agrarian Dreams: The Paradox of Organic Farming in California.* Berkeley: University of California Press.

———. 2008a. "'If They Only Knew': Color Blindness and Universalism in California Alternative Food Institutions." *The Professional Geographer* 60: 387–397.

———. 2008b. "Neoliberalism and the Making of Food Politics in California." *Geoforum* 39: 1171–1183.

Gray, Margaret. 2014. *Labor and the Locavore: The Making of a Comprehensive Food Ethic.* Berkeley: University of California Press.

Harper, Alethea, Annie Shattuck, Eric Holt-Giménez, Alison Alkon, and Frances Lambrick. 2009. "Food Policy Councils: Lessons Learned." Oakland, CA: Food First.

Harrison, Jill Lindsey. 2011. *Pesticide Drift and the Pursuit of Environmental Justice.* Cambridge, MA: MIT Press.

Harvey, David. 1996. *Justice, Nature, and the Geography of Difference.* Oxford: Blackwell.

Heller, Chaia. 1999. *Ecology of Everyday Life: Rethinking the Desire for Nature.* Montreal, Quebec: Black Rose Books.

Hinrichs, C. Claire. 2000. "Embeddedness and Local Food Systems: Notes on Two Types of Direct Agricultural Market." *Journal of Rural Studies* 16: 295–303.

Hinrichs, C. Claire, and Patricia Allen. 2008. "Selective Patronage and Social Justice: Local Food Consumer Campaigns in Historical Context." *Journal of Agricultural and Environmental Ethics* 21: 329–352.

Hinrichs, C. Claire, and Kathy S. Kremer. 2002. "Social Inclusion in a Midwest Local Food System Project." *Journal of Poverty* 6: 65–90.

Holt-Giménez, Eric, Yi Wang, and Annie Shattuck. 2011. "The Urban and Northern Face of Global Land Grabs." Paper presented at the International Conference on Global Land Grabbing, University of Sussex, Brighton, UK.

Jayaraman, Saru. 2013. *Behind the Kitchen Door.* Ithaca, NY: Cornell University Press.

———. 2014. "Shelved: How Wages and Working Conditions for California's Food Retail Workers Have Declined as the Industry Has Thrived." Berkeley: Food Labor Research Center, University of California.

Jennings, Angel. 2014. "L.A. City Council Introduces Plan to Encourage Urban Farming." *Los Angeles Times,* October 8. www.latimes.com/local/lanow/la-me-ln—urban-farming-20141008-story.html. Accessed January 6, 2015.

Jusko, Karen. 2016. "Safety Net." *Pathways* (Special Issue): 25–31. http://inequality .stanford.edu/sites/default/files/Pathways-SOTU-2016.pdf.

KCET. 2012. "A Solution from the Streets." Video interview with Rudy Espinoza, May 3. www.kcet.org/socal/departures/good-food/changing-course/better-food-for-a-better-economy.html. Accessed March 3, 2015.

Kocchar, Rakesh, and Richard Fry. 2014. "Wealth Inequality Has Widened along Racial, Ethnic Lines since End of Great Recession." Pew Research Center, December 12. www.pewresearch.org/fact-tank/2014/12/12/racial-wealth-gaps-great-recession/. Accessed December 19, 2014.

Kropotkin, Peter. 1990. *The Conquest of Bread.* Montreal, Quebec: Black Rose Books.

Liu, Yvonne Y. 2015. "Impact of Street Vendors on Brick and Mortars." *Economic Roundtable,* February 19. http://economicrt.org/blog/impact-of-street-vendors-on-brick-and-mortars/#_ftnref1. Accessed March 3, 2015.

Los Angeles 2020 Commission. 2013. "A Time for Truth." City of Los Angeles.

Los Angeles County Economic Development Corporation. 2012. "LAEDC Urges the Los Angeles City Council to Phase-out Gross Receipts Business Tax." Press release, April 25.

Los Angeles Food Policy Council. 2013. "Los Angeles Food System Snapshot." http://goodfoodla.org/wp-content/uploads/2013/11/LA-Food-System-Snapshot-Oct-2013-small.pdf. Accessed November 3, 2014.

———. 2015. "LA City Council Candidate Briefing & Questionnaire." http://goodfoodla.org/wp-content/uploads/2015/02/LA_City_Council_Candidates-FoodPolicyQuestionnaire-Final.pdf. Accessed March 2, 2015.

Martinez, Arturo. 2017. "Los Angeles Street Vendors Eager to Be Legal." Voice of America, March 2. http://www.voanews.com/a/los-angeles-street-vendors-eager-to-be-legal/3741973.html. Accessed March 9, 2017.

Mejia, Brittny. 2015. "L.A. Street Vendor Protest: 'We Are Not Criminals.'" *Los Angeles Times,* March 21. www.latimes.com/local/lanow/la-me-ln-street-vendor-protest-20150331-story.html. Accessed April 27, 2015.

Milkman, Ruth. 2006. *L.A. Story: Immigrant Workers and the Future of the U.S. Labor Movement.* New York: Russell Sage Foundation.

Mordechay, Kfir. 2011. "Fragmented Economy, Stratified Society, and the Shattered Dream." Los Angeles: Civil Rights Project/Proyecto Derechos Civile.

———. 2014. "Vast Changes and an Uneasy Future: Racial and Regional Inequality in Southern California." Los Angeles: Civil Rights Project/Proyecto Derechos Civile.

Myers, Justin, and Joshua Sbicca. 2015. "Bridging Good Food and Good Jobs: From Secession to Confrontation within Alternative Food Movement Politics." *Geoforum* 61: 17–26.

Nierenberg, Danielle. 2015. "Recognizing Workers in the Food System—Jose Oliva, Food Chain Workers Alliance." *YouTube,* February 3. www.youtube.com /watch?v=Sgp1fch3sXQ#t=34. Accessed February 23, 2015.

Organisation for Economic Co-operation and Development. 2013. "Crisis Squeezes Income and Puts Pressure on Inequality and Poverty." Results from the OECD Income Distribution Database (May). www.oecd.org/els/soc/OECD2013-Inequality-and-Poverty-8p.pdf.

Owens, Ann, and Robert J. Sampson. 2012. *Community Well-Being and the Great Recession.* Stanford, CA: Stanford Center on Poverty and Inequality.

Piven, Frances F., and Richard A. Cloward. 1979. *Poor People's Movements: Why They Succeed, How They Fail.* New York: Random House.

Ruel, Marie T., James L. Garrett, Corinna Hawkes, and Marc J. Cohen. 2010. "The Food, Fuel, and Financial Crises Affect the Urban and Rural Poor Disproportionately: A Review of the Evidence." *Journal of Nutrition* 140: 170–176.

Saez, Emmanuel. 2016. "Striking It Richer: The Evolution of Top Incomes in the United States (updated with 2015 preliminary estimates)." Published by the author, University of California, Berkeley, June 30. https://eml.berkeley.edu/~saez/saez-UStopincomes-2015.pdf.

Sbicca, Joshua. 2014. "The Need to Feed: Urban Metabolic Struggles of Actually Existing Radical Projects." *Critical Sociology* 40: 817–834.

———. 2015a. "Farming While Confronting the Other: The Production and Maintenance of Boundaries in the Borderlands." *Journal of Rural Studies* 39: 1–10.

———. 2015b. "Food Labor, Economic Inequality and the Imperfect Politics of Process in the Alternative Food Movement." *Agriculture and Human Values* 32: 675–687.

Schmitt, John. 2012. "The Minimum Wage Is Too Damn Low." Washington DC: Center for Economic and Policy Research.

Schurman, Rachel, and William A. Munro. 2010. *Fighting for the Future of Food: Activists versus Agribusiness in the Struggle over Biotechnology.* Minneapolis: University of Minnesota Press.

Shaw, Lucas. 2014. "Roy Choi Wants to Reinvent Fast Food." *Bloomberg News,* November 26. www.businessweek.com/articles/2014-11-26/food-truck-pioneer-roy-choi-plans-healthy-burger-chain. Accessed December 3, 2014.

Short, Kathleen. 2015. "The Effect of the Changes to the Current Population Survey Annual Social and Economic Supplement on Estimates of the Supplemental Poverty Measure." Washington, DC: U.S. Census Bureau.

Smith, Neil. 2008. *Uneven Development: Nature, Capital, and the Production of Space,* third edition. Athens: University of Georgia Press.

Tamborello, Frank. 2011. "Learning about the Real Walmart from the Workers' View." *Capital and Main,* October 27. http://capitalandmain.com/learning-about-the-real-walmart-from-the-workers%E2%80%99-view/. Accessed December 23, 2014.

Torres, Lucia. 2016. "Is Los Angeles Finally Legalizing Street Vending?" *KCET,* December 16. www.kcet.org/shows/departures/is-los-angeles-finally-legalizing-street-vending. Accessed December 28, 2016.

Union of Concerned Scientists. 2014. "National Food Policy Tweetchat." https://storify.com/ucsusa/national-food-policy-tweetchat?utm_medium=sfy.co-twitter&utm_content=storify-pingback&utm_campaign=&awesm=sfy.co_jo3iE&utm_source=direct-sfy.co. Accessed December 9, 2014.

Vallianatos, Mark. 2015. "Compl(eat)ing the Streets: Legalizing Sidewalk Food Vending in Los Angeles." In *Incomplete Streets: Processes, Practices, and Possibilities,* ed. Stephen Zavestoski and Julian Agyeman. New York: Routledge.

von Braun, Joachim. 2008. "Food and Financial Crises: Implications for Agriculture and the Poor." Washington, DC: International Food Policy Research Institute.

Xu, Wan. 2014. "South LA Residents Shop for Employment at Juanita Tate Marketplace." *Intersections South LA,* April 23. http://intersectionssouthla.org/story /south-la-residents-shop-for-employment-at-juanita-tate-marketplace/. Accessed March 5, 2015.

Young, Iris M. 2000. *Inclusion and Democracy.* New York: Oxford University Press.

SIX

Food Workers and Consumers Organizing Together for Food Justice

Joann Lo and Biko Koenig

> To make a long subject short, it's modern-day slavery. That's how I look at it. If you look back in the day, slavery was the colors and everything. You know, they pay us with little food, little stuff here and there. It's just like now; we're getting paid just a little bit of money to do all this heavy-ass work. What are we going to get out of it? I work Monday through Friday and only get three hundred and fifty dollars out of my checks for two weeks. So, where's it going? What's happening? Like I said, it's modern-day slavery.
>
> ERIC, *a Walmart worker*
> *from San Leandro, CA*

THE POPULAR FOOD MOVEMENT HAS made serious inroads into changing the ways our nation thinks about the food we produce, purchase, and consume. However, it often finds its highest expression as a form of individualized consumer politics—voting with your fork—in which the purchasing decisions of individual consumers are lauded as the primary tool for making changes in the food system. As demonstrated in chapter 1, this politics of consumption elevates the choices of eaters while remaining blind to how front-line communities are engaged in social change processes. In particular, consumer-centric models ignore the variety of ways that workers in the food system, who are often low-wage immigrants and people of color, are struggling today to change the conditions they face. Both at their respective workplaces and across the food system, workers throughout the food chain are partnering with long-standing labor organizations, food advocacy groups, and each other to challenge a food system built on poor wages and low-quality food.[1]

As this chapter will illustrate, however, some of the most important victories for workers throughout the food chain have come through partnerships with food consumers, citizens, and activists. These partnerships work to leverage the collective power of food consumers in ways that individualistic purchasing decisions simply cannot. Building alliances with food-worker groups further helps ensure that the experiences of those in front-line communities define both the problems and solutions to workplace issues. When workers lead and consumers support, the potential is created to widen concepts like "sustainable" and "healthy" and to incorporate a variety of issues, beyond aesthetics and consumer choice, into "good food." Most workers involved in this research truly enjoy their work and love crafting healthy and delicious food. Far from wanting companies to fail, the campaigns documented in this chapter show how food workers are fighting for the long-term goal of a food system that works for everybody.

This chapter is a project of the Food Chain Workers Alliance (FCWA), a coalition of worker-based organizations whose members plant, harvest, process, pack, transport, prepare, serve, and sell food, who are organizing to improve wages and working conditions for all workers along the food chain. The FCWA's mission is to work toward a sustainable food system that respects workers' rights and is based on the principles of social, economic, and racial justice. This chapter describes and analyzes three workplace justice campaigns across food processing, distribution, and retail to illustrate how workers are challenging the modern industrial food system, and the potential for an organized consumer base to work with them. The stories span three scales and methods of consumer engagement: the local campaign of Amy's Bread in New York City, where workers and consumers are fighting side-by-side to win better working conditions at a bakery that emphasizes artisanal, handcrafted products; the regional campaign at Taylor Farms, which is turning to institutional procurement policies to amplify the power of purchasing decisions by large buyers; and the story of OUR Walmart, a national campaign whose strategy hinges on the work of a coordinated national network of allies.

WORKERS IN THE FOOD SYSTEM—
A SYSTEMIC PROBLEM

Recent changes to the U.S. economy indicate that the social contract has changed dramatically since the 1970s: stagnant wage growth for the working class and skyrocketing wealth for the rich point to a society that is more unequal now than it was forty years ago. As the nation's largest employment sector, the U.S. food system is emblematic of such a shift. It has the distinction of employing over twenty-one million workers, making up 14 percent of the nation's workforce (FCWA and Solidarity Research Cooperative 2016, 5). The food system, encompassing the farm-to-table industries of production, processing, distribution, retail, and food service, is a large and steadily growing component of our overall economy. The industries that make up the food system produce $3.5 billion in output per year, or roughly 11 percent of the nation's annual gross output (ibid., 5).

While the growth of such a large sector through the recent recession should be cause to celebrate, front-line food workers make the lowest hourly median wage in the economy, at $10 per hour compared to the $17.53 per hour median of all other industries (ibid., 5). Further, these jobs are marred by long work hours with few breaks: 40 percent of food-system employees work more than forty hours a week, and almost a third do not receive lunch breaks (FCWA 2012, 4). Perhaps surprisingly, the workers who farm, process, transport, cook, and sell the food that we eat often do not have access to health care or sick days and must report to work even when ill. Low wages and benefits create further problems for workers outside of the workplace: it is telling that food workers use food stamps at over twice the rate of the rest of the U.S. workforce (FCWA and Solidarity Research Cooperative 2016, 3).

While some might suggest that these jobs are better than no jobs at all, many food workers face workplace environments that encourage illegal and unsafe practices. Over a third of all workers experience wage theft in a given week, and over half have suffered an injury or health problem while on the job (FCWA 2012, 4). While we would like to imagine that those workers on the front lines of our food system would be encouraged to report safety and health violations, most workers have no whistle-blower protection and, in some cases, are required to hide violations from inspectors (Gersen and Sachs 2014, Pachirat 2011). In food-processing facilities across the United States, this fear of losing one's job or being deported allows wage theft, discrimination, and abuse to run rampant. It is no surprise that many advocates say that simply enforcing our current laws would go far to increase the safety and livelihood of most workers (FCWA 2012, 77; Urban Justice Center 2014, 22).

If food workers had the opportunity to advance toward living-wage jobs, these problems might not be so sharp. Indeed, for a handful of food industries—including grocery stores and meat processing—career advancement for some is possible. Unfortunately, for the sector as a whole, opportunities are usually limited to white males, who make up the majority of supervisory and managerial positions and command the highest wages (Liu and Apollon 2012, 11). For the immigrants and people of color who make up the majority of the low-wage workforce, discrimination and segregation curtail the possibility of advancement.

The problems facing workers in the food system may seem daunting, but the campaigns presented below demonstrate that they are not insurmountable. With organizing, worker leadership, and collaboration with consumers and community allies, food-system workers are winning changes in their workplaces and gaining a seat at the table.

BRANDWORKERS: WHO MAKES AMY'S BREAD?

When we think about the problems of food workers, the first thoughts are often of restaurant workers we see everyday, or perhaps farmworkers we read about in the press. Food processing, when it comes up, is usually discussed in terms of the giant meatpacking firms or chicken processing plants of the Midwest. However, in a food system that relies heavily on processed goods, the 1.8 million workers in the food processing sector make a variety of products, such as hummus, seafood, ice cream, spices, soy milk, hot sauce, candy, juices, and bread. Further, the majority of these businesses are small: about 95 percent employ one hundred or fewer workers (U.S. Census Bureau n.d.: "2009 County Business Patterns"). Unfortunately, when consumers make a decision to know where their food comes from, that knowledge is often limited to produce purchased at a farmers' market. In anonymous, windowless processing plants across the country, workers employed in "food factories" are mostly hidden from consumers.

These issues are especially salient in the New York City metro area. With about fifteen thousand processing workers and an additional twenty thousand distribution workers across roughly nine hundred firms, the industry brings in about $5 billion a year in sales and is growing steadily (U.S. Census Bureau n.d.: "2010 Annual Survey of Manufacturers"). As traditional manufacturing continues its decline in New York, food manufacturing remains a growth industry, even during the recent recession. Much of this growth is linked to the increased demand for local and artisanal food products, from handmade pickles to local breweries. This presents a major opportunity to hold companies accountable to their workers: behind the power of a consumer base that is voting with its fork for high-quality and locally made food, the promise exists for a local food system that delivers both good food and good jobs.

Kicking Off the Campaign

On the morning of November 25, 2013, artisanal bakery workers were joined by foodies, community leaders, workers' rights activists, and fellow food workers from around the city to inaugurate a workplace justice campaign at the Amy's Bread production facility in the borough of Queens. Over a hundred allies and workers marched together to the bakery, where workers delivered a petition that called on the company to provide accessible health care, better wages, and respectful treatment.

"We take pride in the bread we bake, and it's some of the best in the city," said Luis Velesaca, a seventeen-year baker at Amy's Bread, a successful NYC-based wholesaler and retailer of handmade bread. "The image of Amy's Bread as a community-oriented company fueled its growth to the large facility where we now work. But those of us who make the bread don't have the financial security our families need or the treatment we deserve. We're asking the company to come to the table and join in a dialogue around livable wages, affordable health care, and a respectful work environment for everyone" (Brandworkers 2013). The workers at Amy's Bread had come together with the help of Brandworkers, a nonprofit organization founded in 2007 that trains workers in food processing and distribution how to plan, organize, and lead their own workplace justice campaigns. With further support from the Industrial Workers of the World (IWW),[2] Brandworkers members at Amy's Bread called on the company to live up to its image of a local and sustainable company by providing fair wages and a dignified work environment.

Amy's Bread—The Power of Worker–Consumer Dialogue

Amy's Bread had its start as a small retail bakery in the Hell's Kitchen neighborhood of Manhattan in 1992. The founder, Amy Scherber, was an early adopter of the tenets of the local food movement and sought to reintroduce handmade bread to local consumers. The strategy paid off: today, Amy's Bread boasts three Manhattan retail locations; numerous wholesale accounts with retailers such as Whole Foods and Zabar's; a new, 33,000-square-foot facility in Queens, and a reputation as one of the best bakeries in the country.

The marketing and production of Amy's Bread should be familiar to most foodie consumers: "carefully handcrafted foods" that "respect the craft of traditional baking," are local and freshly baked, and use only "ingredients and procedures that sustain the health of the planet" (Amy's Bread n.d.). Employees, for their part, are "skilled members of the baking family" who have a "professional and congenial workplace" (ibid.).

For the Amy's Bread employees who joined with Brandworkers, these promises remain unfulfilled. Many longtime workers struggle to afford basic expenses like rent, utilities, and food for their families. While the company does offer a health-care plan to its employees, many report that they cannot afford the premiums and are forced to go uninsured or rely on public assistance. As is typical for most workers in their sector, petitions and requests by the workers were met with stiff resistance. In the lead-up to the November march, workers were informed that any labor organizing could force the company to close shop and all the employees to be fired. Further, after the workers presented their petition, management initially refused to discuss the concerns of the workers. Instead, they required all workers to attend mandatory, closed meetings, a long-standing antilabor strategy whereby workers are intimidated against organizing, under the guise of "rights trainings."

Nonetheless, Brandworkers persevered through these challenges, utilizing a unique workplace-justice model, one that does not rely on the collective bargaining agreements that typify traditional unions in the United States. Brandworkers, a grassroots workers center, embraces the syndicalist model of its ally, the IWW. This approach emphasizes the importance of a committed activist workforce rather than a top-down approach to organizing. In the Brandworkers model, rank-and-file workers both design and lead the campaigns from start to finish.

While this approach has historical roots in the successes of the IWW in the early 1900s, the innovation of Brandworkers centers on the importance of good, local food to the burgeoning food movement. This is the potential of campaigns such as Amy's Bread: so long as demand for local food exists, the opportunity to connect processing workers to informed consumers on the local scale is high. Through a strategy that reaches out to customers, Brandworkers can help make the sturdy walls of these food factories transparent and give consumers the opportunity to stand alongside workers for a truly just food system. The upshot is that consumers themselves must be willing to make such a stand in order to realize this potential.

Consumer Involvement—Turning the Corner

When the initial petition was met with forced meetings and retaliation, Brandworkers reached out to allies and consumers to help raise the visibility of the campaign. Given that companies like Amy's Bread need a strong brand to stand out in a competitive market, the workers took to the Internet to bring their concerns into the conversation. Over the course of two weeks in December, workers, allies, and consumers participated in a social media "Holiday Blizzard." Through Twitter, Facebook, Instagram, and Vine, allies submitted multiple posts, videos, and memes in support of the campaign and called on Amy's Bread to respond to the petition and meet with its workers.

When the company still refused to meet with workers, consumers and allies again stepped up to support the campaign. During the spring, they joined with Brandworkers to hand out leaflets to customers at the retail stores in Manhattan. Workers challenged these consumers to think about living-wage jobs as a crucial part of a sustainable food system, asking "How can you help make Amy's Bread sustainable?" The leafleting actions asked customers to support the workers who make Amy's Bread by speaking with management, signing petitions, and volunteering with the campaign. Most importantly, the workers did not ask customers to boycott Amy's Bread. Rather than opting out of their consumer relationship with the company, the campaign asked them to opt into a just food system by actively leverage their purchasing power by combining it with vocal activism.

Nonetheless, the company remained intransigent, and the workers were forced to look for new ways to pressure the company to the table. Luckily, they were able to find a partner willing to think through new strategies to support the campaign. The main innovation was found through conversations with a grassroots organization called the Brooklyn Food Coalition (BFC). Begun as an activist committee of the sixteen-thousand-member Park Slope Food Co-op, the BFC had grown into a nonprofit focused on sustainable agriculture, healthy school food, and justice for food workers. Primarily composed of consumer activists, the Labor Committee of the BFC had been an ally of the campaign since its inception.

During the early summer of 2014, the Labor Committee took a more active role in the campaign. With the backing of the workers, the Labor Committee reached out directly to the company. Through a series of conversations, BFC members discussed their concerns with management and were able to help encourage the company to finally meet with its workers in

September 2014. As of the writing of this chapter, workers and Amy's Bread management have been involved in a series of meetings to help the company grow in sustainable ways.

Through the courage of the workers and the dedication of their BFC allies, Amy's Bread may be on a path that recognizes that good, local food must include living wages, affordable health care, and respectful treatment of workers who want to organize for a better life. This case shows both the peril and the promise of the food movement. A good marketing firm can deliver products that ostensibly meet the desires of consumers who want local, organic, or artisanal foods and who are willing to vote with their fork—and likely pay higher prices—in the process. The risk is that many companies can too easily hide the true cost of these products: an underpaid, intimidated workforce that sees little of the higher profits that come with organic and local labels.

Yet with local production comes the potential of worker–consumer alliances. If consumers want to have locally produced organic hummus and fresh-baked bread, they also have the latent power to hold these companies accountable to those workers who blend the chickpeas and knead the dough. Doing so requires following in the footsteps of those who support the Amy's Bread workers. From tweeting their support to forming groups like the BFC Labor Committee, consumers have immense power beyond their wallets and checkbooks.

TAYLOR FARMS: THE POTENTIAL OF INSTITUTIONAL STRATEGIES

Your average consumer has never heard of Taylor Farms, but they have nonetheless likely eaten their products. Based in California's Central Valley, Taylor Farms makes products for a variety of well-known customers. From organic spinach salad for Trader Joe's to private-label packaged salads for Walmart, Safeway, and Kroger, Taylor Farms is the world's largest processor of salads and fresh-cut produce and a sizable processor of organic vegetables in the United States (Sherry 2009). To put this in perspective, it sells as much salad as its next three competitors, is the largest fresh salad processor in the world, and employs ten thousand workers across its ten plants in the United States and one in Mexico (Berkeley Haas 2012, Murfreesboro Post 2013, Strom 2013, Taylor Farms n.d.).

As a multibillion-dollar corporation, Taylor Farms can set standards in its industry and in the economy—standards around the kind of food it produces, how the food is grown and processed, and how the workers are treated. Combined with the anonymity provided by private labels and institutional buyers, Taylor Farms is a company that exists beyond the influence and knowledge of most individual customers.

A Dr. Jekyll and Mr. Hyde Company

About an hour and a half south of San Francisco, near the California coastline, sits a Taylor Farms facility—modern, shiny, and clean. The 2,500 workers at the Salinas plant have been represented for twenty years by the Teamsters Local 890. With a union contract comes a situation at odds with that of most other workers in the food system: these workers receive regular raises, affordable health insurance, and paid sick days. When workplace issues arise at the plant, there is a fair grievance process in place to help resolve them. And when the company brings in temporary workers, they become permanent employees after they have worked more than thirty days.

In the Central Valley town of Tracy, conditions are much different. There, two Taylor Farms plants on Valpico and MacArthur boulevards exist in a different world than the Salinas plant. About nine hundred workers, mostly Latino, toil at these two Tracy plants, where two-thirds of the workers are employed through two temporary staffing agencies: Slingshot and Abel Mendoza. The use of temporary workers is a growing trend in the food system, from farms and warehouses to food processing plants and distribution companies and even fast-food restaurants, and these plants exemplify the problems of a disposable workforce (McCluskey et al. 2013, Mertl 2014). According to Doug Bloch, political director of the Teamsters Joint Council 7, some of these "temporary" employees have been working at Taylor Farms for up to fourteen years; most are paid the minimum wage; and, on average, the workers in Tracy earn $3 an hour less than workers in the same job classifications in Salinas.

Jose Gonzalez, who has worked for Taylor Farms for over a year through the Slingshot agency, reports of those hired through the agencies: "We work directly next to direct Taylor Farms workers and are fully intermingled in every way with those workers. We do the same work, have the same hours, and have the same supervisors as the Taylor Farms workers." Workers hired directly by the company receive slightly higher pay but still don't earn anything close to the region's living wage of $20.06 per hour for an adult with one child (Glasmeier 2015).

As in many parts of the food system, the problems at Taylor Farms go beyond poor wages to include a troubling record of labor violations. The company has accrued $80,000 in OSHA (Occupational Health and Safety Administration) penalties from 2008 to 2013 and is currently the defendant in a class-action lawsuit for wage theft that was filed in 2011 (Tierney 2014). Multiple workers have suffered injuries that make it difficult for them to work in their regular jobs or to work at all. One of these workers is Victor Borja, who slipped from a machine in 2012. His foot was crushed and he can no longer work. Victor says his first thought after his fall was that he was going to be fired, as he had seen coworkers suffer a full range of injuries, "and one thing always happened if they reported it: they would get fired." He describes a workplace where fear of termination has created an environment where instead of reporting injuries, many workers simply try to fix the problem (Teamsters 2014).

The Union Organizing Campaign

In August 2013, after months of behind-the-scenes organizing, workers at the Taylor Farms plants in Tracy came out publicly that they were organizing to join the Teamsters Local 601. A few workers had approached the union because they were concerned about how the temporary workers were being mistreated. "Workers are segregated in three different categories—the workers hired by two different staffing agencies and the different hires . . . a lot of conditions that we kept hearing about was around how the different classes were being treated," explains Veronica Diaz, former political coordinator with the Teamsters Joint Council 7, which is supporting the workers' campaign.

Once the worker leaders came out publicly that they were organizing to join the Teamsters, Taylor Farms responded with both carrots and sticks. On the stick side, the company management hired antiunion consultants, also called union-busters. The Teamsters estimate that Taylor Farms spent $500,000 on these consultants, who held meetings with the workers to scare them from supporting the union, part of a strategy that embraced intimidation, harassment, and mistreatment to break the campaign (Teamsters 2014). Marta Barrajas recalls, "They intimidated us that we couldn't vote because immigration was going to come . . . to take us away." Armida Galeana vividly

FIGURE 6.1. Protest by Taylor Farms workers. Photo by Brian Tierney, Teamsters.

remembers the humiliating feeling when one of the antiunion consultants referred to the workers as "Latinos de mierda," or "piece-of-shit Latinos." In case anyone missed the point, a warehouse manager posted images of a donkey wearing a sombrero with the caption "This is what the union means" (ibid.).

The company also fired worker leaders in the organizing campaign, sometimes creating excuses to do so and sometimes not. Victor Borja, whose foot was crushed, is one such fired leader. Another is Edibray Rodriguez. Edibray was receiving thirty cents less per hour than he had been promised when he was hired. In the break room and after work, he began discussing the possibility of organizing into a union with his coworkers. On October 29, 2013, he joined Teamster organizers in handing out fliers outside of his facility. Edibray was then questioned by two supervisors about his conversations with the Teamsters, and he described his desire to correct his pay for the last month and a half. The next day, a director at Abel Mendoza, the agency that hired Edibray for Taylor Farms, came to his house with a check, saying, as Edibray described it, "Here is the check for the thirty cents we owe you for every hour you have worked, but here is also your last paycheck . . . today was your last day" (ibid.).

On the "carrot" side, Taylor Farms began making some improvements to working conditions in what appeared to be efforts to try to convince workers they would not need the union. In January 2014, the company started providing direct-hire workers with paid sick days. On Mother's Day, the company gave roses to the women, and on Father's Day, they gave backpacks, jackets, and scarves to the men. The company also now provides transportation between the employee parking lot and the facility, which they had not done before. Taylor Farms also gave out free shirts and hats that said not to vote for the union.

Despite the company's antiunion tactics, the worker leaders and the Teamsters organizers were able to collect enough signatures on union authorization cards to file for an election through the National Labor Relations Board (NLRB). The vote on whether the workers wanted the Teamsters to be their union representative was held on March 27 and 28, 2014. Right after the vote, in an unprecedented move, the NLRB impounded the ballots because the Teamsters had filed hundreds of complaints of unfair labor practices before the vote. However, the long process at the NLRB allowed the company to fire more union supporters since the vote. In December 2015, the NLRB determined that Taylor Farms had committed so many unfair labor practices that a new election could not be conducted fairly. The NLRB issued a bargaining order to Taylor Farms, but talks have not led to a union contract (Teamsters Joint Council 7 2016). "Our campaign has demonstrated almost the complete failure of federal labor law to protect workers to organize and collectively bargain," says Doug.

Building Support from Consumers to Institutions

Since the workers and the union cannot depend on fast action by the federal labor agency and Taylor Farms continues to fight against the workers' organizing efforts, the campaign has turned toward alliances with consumers. In the words of Veronica Diaz,

> We're in a period where people are increasingly conscious of where they get their food. It's very trendy to ask if your lettuce is organic and to be concerned with whether your beef or chicken is free-range and killed humanely. But that movement, so far, I haven't really seen it to be encompassing of also asking whether the people who slaughtered the cow or picked the lettuce in the field were also treated humanely or given a fair salary. I think some of these consumer campaigns, especially with items like organic lettuce that Taylor Farms supplies . . . it's an opportune time to make that connection to consumers as well.

When facing companies that have the size, spread, and distribution of Taylor Farms, it can be a challenge to envision clear strategies for consumers to leverage their power on behalf of workers. With anonymous private-label products and large-scale food service customers, individual activist purchasing decisions are easily drowned out amid larger purchasers like schools and grocery stores. Also, it's hard to know where food comes from because of private labels like Trader Joe's. One solution involves flipping the problem on its head: by organizing around institutional buyers, citizens can amplify their individual purchasing power through collective procurement policies on the regional scale.

Advocates of the Taylor Farms campaign are embracing this strategy, utilizing a model embodied by the Good Food Purchasing Policy (GFPP). Adopted in October 2012 by the City of Los Angeles and then by the Los Angeles Unified School District (LAUSD) in November 2012, the GFPP sets purchasing guidelines across five key values: local food economies, environmental sustainability, humane animal treatment, healthy nutrition standards, and fair treatment and compensation of food-chain workers. By leveraging the purchasing power of institutional buyers—including the LAUSD, which serves over 650,000 meals a day—citizens can make major impacts on companies too large to feel the pressure of smaller-scale purchasing decisions (Lo and Delwiche 2016).

A clear example of this power can be seen in the Teamsters' strategy regarding school food. On May 1, 2014, the Teamsters organized an emergency town meeting in Oakland for Taylor Farms workers to talk about what was happening at the Tracy plant. Attendees included California Assemblymember Rob Bonta, members of the Oakland Unified School Board, and representatives of the school district's employee unions and the Oakland Food Policy Council. Without any request from the FCWA or the Teamsters, members of the Oakland Unified School Board announced at this meeting that the school district was no longer buying from Taylor Farms. In short order, a small group of committed activists were able to leverage the institutional power of a school system that serves over thirty thousand meals a day—a substantial pressure point on a company that needs these contracts to remain profitable (Oakland Unified School District n.d.).

With support from the FCWA and the new Center for Good Food Purchasing, the Teamsters are now organizing to ask school districts across California to adopt a comprehensive food-procurement policy that includes labor standards in order to hold companies like Taylor Farms accountable to provide good and safe working conditions. "We ended up looking at the Good Food Purchasing Policy in Los Angeles, which is the best model to support the food chain that we believe—where workers' rights are being respected, where the environment is being respected, local businesses are being supported, and where school districts are being smart about using the resources that they have to support an equitable, just food chain," says Bloch. "Taylor Farms is the perfect example of why school districts need a policy like this." Due to the Teamsters' leadership, both the San Francisco Unified School District (on May 24, 2016) and the Oakland Unified School District (on November 30, 2016) unanimously adopted the GFPP.

In campaigns like Taylor Farms, consumers can punch above their weight through institutional purchasers like school districts, municipalities, corporate cafeterias, and grocery co-ops. Such an approach takes the "voting with your fork" analogy to a much higher level by dramatically multiplying the number of forks in play while requiring political action in city councils and school districts.

OUR WALMART: THE POWER OF A NATIONAL CAMPAIGN

Grocery stores and supermarkets make up one of the segments of the food chain that consumers interact with directly, and they have become an integral part of our daily lives. But as with other sectors of the food chain, the wages and working conditions of grocery workers are usually unknown by the millions of shoppers who go into these stores every day. Over three million people work in food and beverage stores in the United States, and the typical grocery worker is only earning $18,800 per year, with cashiers earning less than $14,000; further, the average work-week in May 2014 was just 29.1 hours, reflecting the fact that the majority of workers in this industry are only allowed part-time work (U.S. Bureau of Labor Statistics 2014). To make matters worse, a recent report based on worker surveys in New York City, Chicago, and Los Angeles found that 23.5 percent of grocery workers were paid less than the minimum wage, and 65 percent were not paid overtime (Bernhardt et al. 2009).

This is partially due to the decline of union power in this sector. About 17 percent of grocery workers are covered by a union contract, down from 26.1 percent in 1990 (Hirsch and Macpherson n.d.). First, many food retail companies—including ones with significant union density—have opted to spend surpluses on dividend payouts, share repurchases, and capital investments while allowing wages to decline (Jayaraman 2014). Second, much of this has to do with the increased corporate consolidation in this sector and the growth of nonunion general-merchandise companies like Walmart and Target. The four largest food retailers in the United States—Walmart, Kroger, Target, and Costco—control 50 percent of all grocery sales in the country (Hauter 2012). With such a concentration of ownership, these corporations have tremendous power over the grocery industry and down the food supply chain. With only Kroger and Costco having unionized workforces (only part of Costco's labor force is unionized), nonunion Walmart and Target now dominate the grocery industry. Their low wages create a downward pressure on wages across the sector. Despite this, Walmart workers across the country are winning victories through their own courage and with the help and staunch support of their communities.

Organizing the World's Largest Company

The annual Walmart Shareholders Meeting is a huge event for which the company flies in twenty thousand employees, called "associates" in the company lingo, for a multiday celebration of everything Walmart, including visits to the Walmart Museum (at the site of the original Walton's five-and-dime store) and attendance at a pop-star-studded concert-cum-shareholder meeting held in Bud Walton Arena. Associates from around the world flood into Bentonville and Fayetteville, Arkansas, to eat, breathe, and dream the promises of the Walmart corporation, which include company founder Sam Walton's vision of how to treat his workers, captured in his oft-repeated maxim: *Share your profits with all your associates, and treat them as partners.*

June 2014 saw a long line of Walmart associates from around the country forming a picket line at the company headquarters in Bentonville. For the past five years, there had been a new component to the yearly meeting: striking workers. Members of the Organization United for Respect at Walmart (OUR Walmart), these workers did not come to town to take pictures with the bronze bust of Sam Walton or to hear Pharrell sing his latest hit at the shareholder concert. Instead, OUR Walmart members had come to call attention to how Walton's slogan had become an empty promise built on low wages, bad working conditions, and a troubling streak of disrespect by management for everyday associates.

For OUR Walmart members, the campaign boils down to three key items: better wages, an end to retaliation, and respect on the job. With an average company wage of about $15,000 per year—below the federal poverty line for working families—OUR Walmart members are asking for $25,000 a year, or $15 an hour, for full-time workers (Bradford 2012). While many might argue that low-wage jobs at places like Walmart are simply stepping-stones for young people, Walmart itself touts these jobs as part of a well-paid career path. Nonetheless, such jobs are quickly becoming the typical type of employment in the United States. National figures back this up, showing that the median age of an employee at a big-box retailer is over thirty, and that seven out of ten growth occupations are low-wage service jobs, most in food-related sectors such as service and retail (Reich 2012). Further, those workers who choose to speak to management on behalf of their stores, customers, or fellow workers often face intimidation, harassment, and termination—forms of retaliation that are usually illegal and always immoral. With this in mind, Walmart is not so much an employer of part-time teenagers looking to make some extra money, but as the country's largest private employer, it is *the* pacesetter for the careers of an increasingly larger share of working Americans. And the pace in question has a set of clear guidelines: very low wages and small, infrequent raises. Richard, a worker who staffs the overnight stocking shift in a store in Duarte, California, spoke directly to this point when thinking about what a wage increase could mean for him:

> Well, for one, it would get me out of having to go to food banks for food. It would get me off of Medi-Cal. It would probably give me some type of money, even if it's just change, to be able to save, and accumulate. To be able to buy something for myself that could be useful as far as clothes, or, say, a present for my little sister on her birthday, or a present for Mother's Day. Having money to buy soap and shampoo. Not having to water down my soap and shampoo just to take a shower, to go to work clean, and clean-cut and everything, because that's the way they want me to be.

On the picket line outside the Bentonville company headquarters, workers discussed why they were standing up to Walmart. Allison, holding a sign that called on the company to end the practice of firing associates who complained about working conditions, spoke about how Walmart thinks about its employees: "They probably still think we're just, you know, numbers on a paper," said Allison, a jewelry department worker from Oshkosh, Wisconsin.

"But hopefully we'll be showing them that … we're actual human beings that make them their money and that make them their profit."

Mark, a night-shift baker from the Yreka, California, store, agreed with her: "Yes, this isn't just for the workers. This is for all the people that work at levels of Walmart, showing them that their respect is going to be restored." He looked down the picket line, where the Day-Glo green shirts of OUR Walmart members and colorful signs demanding that the company respect pregnant workers stood in sharp contrast to the gray suits of executives walking to work and the rain-filled clouds of an impending thunderstorm. The strikers sang in unison, "I'll be buried in my grave, before I'll ever be a Walmart slave, keepin' our eyes on the prize, and holding on. . . ." Mark looked at the crowd of executives who had gathered outside the doors to gawk and point at the associates and said, "This time of tyranny is over."

Standing in Solidarity

The main challenge that is commonly voiced when consumers are asked to get involved with the OUR Walmart campaign revolves around the sheer size of the largest grocery-store chain in the world. As Silvia Fabela, a communications director with Making Change at Walmart, a national coalition of workers and community members, explains: "I think for many people, they think this is such a large company and they feel like, perhaps … the company is not changeable, that it's not a winnable campaign." While the circumstances do not always allow for the face-to-face solutions described in the Amy's Bread campaign or the regional procurement strategy at Taylor Farms, consumers are far from powerless in this situation. In fact, the very nature of Walmart's multinational corporate structure provides inroads for food activists to make their voices heard, and OUR Walmart capitalizes on this.

Silvia explains how this works in practice:

> What we find are the most impactful actions are when people deliver a letter to a store manager, highlighting any issues that are happening in an area, where perhaps a worker has illegally been fired or disciplined. The reason that going directly to those stores is important is because Walmart is so centralized that they have to report everything into the headquarters. It demonstrates to the company that there is a growing number of activists, individuals, consumers, et cetera, that care about these issues and that are taking action wherever they are. And so our theory on this has been that breadth is very, very important.

Thus, due to the hierarchical nature of the company, any solidarity action that occurs at a local Walmart will be heard throughout the chain of command. The campaign capitalizes on this system by coordinating national days of action during which workers and allies across the country protest both national company policy and problems at local stores.

The best example of how these actions can be coordinated nationally for optimal impact can be seen in the national Black Friday protests. Begun in 2012, these protests combine worker strikes and actions with letter deliveries and rallies by supporters at stores around the country. In 2014, more than 1,600 stores in forty-nine states saw protests on the busiest retail day of the year. The pressure seems to be working, as the company revised its pregnancy policy in response to these actions and OUR Walmart's popular "Respect the Bump" campaign, and also raised the lowest wage in some of its stores to $9 an hour in April 2015. As OUR Walmart members are quick to point out, these would not have been possible without ally support in communities across the country, and they show that the company can be moved by worker and consumer action.

However, these victories still fall short of the core demands of the campaign. The wage increase signals, in Paul Krugman's words, that "low wages are a political choice," and the extra dollar or two makes little difference for workers who are stuck with part-time hours as a result of company policy (Krugman 2015). OUR Walmart members are still fighting for "$15 and full time" and still calling on allies to help them win. The first step is to sign up on the Making Change at Walmart website (http://makingchangeat walmart.org/). With 90 percent of Americans living within fifteen minutes of a Walmart store, it is more than likely that interested consumers can find like-minded people to organize with locally (Forbes 2013). However, the national spread and coordination of the campaign means that even small groups can leverage power to push Walmart to change. As Silvia states, "In terms of impact, I always remind people that being out with a handful of people is going to be equally impactful as a large rally because it still sends the same message to the company: everyone's participation is really heard in a very significant way."

Beyond pressuring the company as a consumer, standing in solidarity with OUR Walmart at Black Friday protests and other events also supports and encourages workers directly. For Barbara, a long-time associate from Aurora, Colorado, knowing that she has a support network of community allies gives her the courage to overcome the fear of organizing:

I wish that every Walmart employee could go to an ally meeting. . . . Because they could see that their communities support them. Really and truly, the people that they live next door to really do support them and are willing to stand behind them, want to stand behind them, and that it's just not all in their head. Every time I leave a meeting, I'm always like, "God, I wish I could just bring my store here." Once that happens, man, Walmart's in trouble. As soon as workers find out that they really have the power, Walmart's in trouble.

FOOD WORKERS UNITE!

Solidarity between workers from different industries is not new, but the increasing solidarity and coordination between workers from different industries, particularly within the food system, is a recent innovation. In fact, the FCWA was founded in 2009 mainly to bring workers from throughout the food system together, not only in solidarity, but also to coordinate efforts and strategy. All the workers in these three case studies have taken action in support of other workers in the food system.

Perhaps most importantly, the FCWA annual retreat gives food workers from around the country the chance to meet, share their stories, and learn about each other's challenges. Workers who attend say that these conversations are the highlight of the retreat, and these talks transform into large, joint actions that call on a company to respect the rights of food workers. In April 2015, workers from across the food chain formed a picket line at a Walmart store in Washington, D.C. Cooks, bakers, farmworkers, poultry-plant workers, waiters, grocery-store clerks, warehouse workers, and street vendors called on the company to respect its own employees, as well as workers down its food supply chain. When a handful of workers tried to go into the store to deliver their letter to the manager, they represented the potential of a sustainable food system that puts the status of the worker on par with the quality of our food.

As this chapter has shown, consumers, citizens, students, and activists are crucial for the formation of a just food system, and many supporters have formed their own organization to do so. As such, the FCWA also includes consumer and ally organizations that have made food workers a priority. One such member organization is the Fair World Project (FWP), an independent campaign of the Organic Consumers Association. The FWP has been active in educating its supporters about food workers' organizing campaigns and fair trade certification programs that have high labor standards for workers. The FWP also started a pledge for consumers to sign in support of the OUR Walmart workers (Lo 2014).

PUT DOWN YOUR FORKS!

The cases above illustrate how consumers can support and stand in solidarity with workers who are organizing against exploitation and oppression every day. While front-line workers must take the lead in these campaigns, significant change calls for consumers, activists, students, and citizens to rise to the challenge. The Amy's Bread campaign exemplifies the dilemma of consumer politics—workers want their company to grow and thrive, but they desperately need living wages and affordable health care to support their families. In this instance, the decision to buy their bread (or not) simply fails to engage the problem at hand, and a "vote" cast in this way has little impact on the campaign. If anything, it can exacerbate the problems in our food system by reinforcing the importance of the consumer over that of anyone else (Barnett et al. 2005, Schudson 2007).

Luckily, other options abound. Some are as simple as signing petitions or joining social media campaigns through Twitter, Instagram, and Facebook. As with many political issues, higher-impact actions require more commitment and work on the part of consumers. OUR Walmart workers are always looking for new allies for their Black Friday strikes. The Brooklyn Food Coalition is a working model of food-worker solidarity that can be adapted and implemented in other cities to support food workers through an organized consumer base. Citizens and voters can organize and agitate for comprehensive procurement legislation, akin to the Good Food Purchasing Policy, that is pro-worker *and* supports other values key to a just and sustainable food system.

Being human, one cannot entirely opt out of food. Like it or not, we must eat every day for the entirety of our lives. As an accumulated set of purchasing decisions, it is important to have agency over where our money goes, and to own the satisfaction that can come with eating food that is both valued and appreciated. However, the aesthetic and nutritional qualities of good food cannot overshadow the fact that workers need—and are asking for— more overt, active, and direct forms of support. If our goal is to reshape the food system into something equitable, sustainable, and just, we must get out of the farmers' market and into the streets.

NOTES

1. This chapter utilizes interviews and fieldwork conducted from June 2014 through May 2015. Unless otherwise attributed, quotes are from interviews conducted by the authors during that fieldwork.

2. The IWW, a union that saw its membership peak in the early twentieth century, utilizes a syndicalist model of labor organizing, which emphasizes solidarity and direct action over collective bargaining agreements and formal union certification.

REFERENCES

Amy's Bread. n.d. "Amy's Bread: Our Story." www.amysbread.com/our_story.

Barnett, Clive, Paul Cloke, Nick Clarke, and Alice Malpass. 2005. "Consuming Ethics: Articulating the Subjects and Spaces of Ethical Consumption." *Antipode* 37: 23–45.

Berkeley Haas. Spring 2012. "Lettuce Now Praise Farming Men." http://haas .berkeley.edu/groups/pubs/berkeleyhaas/spring2012/yhn04.html.

Bernhardt, Annette, Ruth Milkman, Nik Theodore, Douglas Heckathorn, Mirabai Auer, James DeFilippis, et al. 2009. "Broken Laws, Unprotected Workers: Violations of Employment and Labor Laws in America's Cities." New York: National Employment Law Project.

Bradford, Harry. 2012. "Walmart CEO Mike Duke: We Do Pay Competitive Wages." *Huffington Post,* December 12. www.huffingtonpost.com/2012/12/12 /walmart-ceo-mike-duke_n_2286440.html.

Brandworkers. 2013. "Workers Launch Campaign Challenging Image of High-End Baking Company." Press release, November 11. www.brandworkers.org /workers-launch-o.

DuPuis, E. Melanie, and David Goodman. 2005. "Should We Go 'Home' to Eat? Toward a Reflexive Politics of Localism." *Journal of Rural Studies* 21: 359–371.

Food Chain Workers Alliance. 2012. "The Hands That Feed Us: Challenges and Opportunities for Workers along the Food Chain." June 6. Los Angeles: FCWA. http://foodchainworkers.org/wp-content/uploads/2012/06/Hands-That-Feed-Us-Report.pdf.

Food Chain Workers Alliance and Solidarity Research Cooperative. 2016. "No Piece of the Pie." November 14. Los Angeles: FCWA. http://foodchainworkers .org/wp-content/uploads/2011/05/FCWA_NoPieceOfThePie_P.pdf.

Forbes Profile. n.d. "Bruce Taylor." *Forbes Online.* www.forbes.com/profile/bruce-taylor/.

Gersen, Jacob E., and Benjamin I. Sachs. 2014. "Protect Those Who Protect Our Food." *The New York Times,* November 12. www.nytimes.com/2014/11/13/opinion /protect-those-who-protect-our-food.html.

Glasmeier, Amy. 2015. "Living Wage Calculation for San Joaquin County, California." MIT Living Wage Calculator. http://livingwage.mit.edu/counties/06077.

Guthman, Julie. 2008. "Neoliberalism and the Making of Food Politics in California." *Geoforum* 39: 1171–1183.

Hallman, Cory, Tom Temprano, and Laura Thomasby. 2014. "Op-Ed: Bad Work Conditions Hurt LGBT Employees Too." *The Advocate,* December 24. www.advocate.com/commentary/2014/12/24/op-ed-bad-work-conditions-hurt-lgbt-employees-too.

Hauter, Wenoah. 2012. *Foodopoly: The Battle over the Future of Food and Farming in America.* New York: New Press.

Hirsch, Barry, and David Macpherson. n.d. "U.S. Historical Tables: Union Membership, Coverage, Density and Employment, 1973–2012." http://unionstats.com/.

Holt-Giménez, Eric, and Yi Wang. 2011. "Reform or Transformation? The Pivotal Role of Food Justice in the U.S. Food Movement." *Race/Ethnicity: Multidisciplinary Global Contexts* 5: 83–102.

Jaffe, JoAnn, and M. Gertler. 2006. "Victual Vicissitudes: Consumer Deskilling and the (Gendered) Transformations of Food Systems." *Agricultural and Human Values* 23: 143–162.

Jayaraman, Saru. 2014. "Shelved: How Wages and Working Conditions for California's Food Retail Workers Have Declined as the Industry Has Thrived." Berkeley: University of California, Food Labor Research Center.

Krugman, Paul. 2015. "Walmart's Visible Hand." *The New York Times,* March 2. www.nytimes.com/2015/03/02/opinion/paul-krugman-walmarts-visible-hand.html.

Lang, Timothy, and Yiannis Gabriel. 1995. "The Consumer as Citizen." *Consumer Policy Review* 5: 96–102.

Liu, Yvonne Y., and Dominique Apollon. 2012. "The Color of Food." New York: Applied Research Center.

Lo, Joann. 2014. "Social Justice for Food Workers in a Foodie World." *Journal of Critical Thought and Praxis* 3: 10–11.

Lo, Joann, and Alexa Delwiche. 2016. "The Good Food Purchasing Policy: A Tool to Intertwine Worker Justice with a Sustainable Food System." *Journal of Agriculture, Food Systems, and Community Development* 6: 185–194.

Lo, Joann, and Ariel Jacobson. 2011. "Human Rights from Field to Fork: Improving Labor Conditions for Food-Sector Workers by Organizing across Boundaries." *Race/Ethnicity: Multidisciplinary Global Contexts* 5: 61–82.

McCluskey, Martha, Thomas McGarity, Sidney Shapiro, and Matthew Shudtz. 2013. "At the Company's Mercy: Protecting Contingent Workers from Unsafe Working Conditions." Washington, DC: Center for Progressive Reform.

Mertl, Steve. 2014. "Fast-food Industry's Use of Temporary Foreign Worker Program Suspended Following Damning Report." *The Daily Brew, Yahoo News Canada,* April 24. https://ca.news.yahoo.com/blogs/dailybrew/fast-food-industry-temporary-foreign-worker-program-suspended-014305363.html.

Murfreesboro Post. 2013. "Taylor Farms to Expand Smyrna Operations." *The Murfreesboro Post,* July 7. www.murfreesboropost.com/taylor-farms-to-expand-smyrna-operations-cms-36132.

Oakland Unified School District. n.d. "Nutrition Services: Overview." www.ousd.k12.ca.us/nutritionservices.

Pachirat, Timothy. 2011. *Every Twelve Seconds: Industrialized Slaughter and the Politics of Sight.* New Haven, CT: Yale University Press.

Pollan, Michael. 2006. "Voting with Your Fork." *The New York Times,* May 7. http://pollan.blogs.nytimes.com/2006/05/07/voting-with-your-fork/.

Raden, Bill, and Gary Cohen. 2014. "The Dirty Truth behind Fast Food Lettuce." *Huffington Post,* May 29. www.huffingtonpost.com/2014/05/28/taylor-farms-exploited-labor_n_5406238.html.

Reich, Robert. 2012. "Walmart & McDonald's: What's Wrong with U.S. Employment." *Salon,* November 30. www.salon.com/2012/11/30/wal_mart_and_mcdonalds_whats_wrong_with_u_s_employment/.

Schudson, Michael. 2007. "Citizen Consumers, and the Good Society." *ANNALS of the American Academy of Political and Social Science* 611: 236–249.

Sherry, Kristina. 2009. "Farmers Critical of Food Safety Bill." *Los Angeles Times,* July 17. http://articles.latimes.com/2009/jul/17/nation/na-food-safety17.

Siders, David. 2014. "Jerry Brown Signs Subcontractor Bill." *The Sacramento Bee,* October 8. www.sacbee.com/news/politics-government/capitol-alert/article2614696.html.

Smith, Rebecca, and Claire McKenna. 2014. "Temped Out: How the Domestic Outsourcing of Blue Collar Jobs Harms America's Workforce." New York: National Employment Law Project.

Strom, Stephanie. 2013. "Taylor Farms, Big Food Supplier, Grapples with Frequent Recalls." *The New York Times,* August 29. www.nytimes.com/2013/08/30/business/taylor-farms-big-food-supplier-grapples-with-frequent-recalls.html.

Taylor Farms. n.d. "Our Story." www.taylorfarms.com/our-story/.

Teamsters. 2014. "NLRB Impounds Ballots In Taylor Farms Teamster Election." April 1. International Brotherhood of Teamsters Food Processing Division. http://teamster.org/news/2014/04/nlrb-impounds-ballots-taylor-farms-teamster-election.

———. n.d. "Crimes against Workers at Taylor Farms." https://teamster.org/justice-taylor-farms/crimes-against-workers-taylor-farms.

Teamsters Joint Council 7. 2016. "Supporting the Workers at Taylor Farms." *Joint Council 7 Teamster* 61 (1): 2. http://teamstersjc7.org/newsletter/PDFs/JC7News_16-FMA.pdf.

Tierney, Brian. 2014. "Low-Wage Movement Strikes Fast Food Processing at Taylor Farms." *CounterPunch,* January 2. www.counterpunch.org/2014/01/02/low-wage-movement-strikes-fast-food-processing-at-taylor-farms.

Urban Justice Center. 2014. "Feeding New York: Challenges and Opportunities for Workers in New York City's Food Manufacturing Industry." New York: Community Development Project at the Urban Justice Center and Brandworkers.

U.S. Bureau of Labor Statistics. 2009. "Occupational Injuries and Illnesses Annual News Release 2008." October 29. Washington, DC: U.S. Census Bureau.

―――. 2014. "Industries at a Glance: Food and Beverage Stores." *NAICS 445,* June 2014 data. www.bls.gov/iag/tgs/iag445.htm.

U.S. Census Bureau. 2011. "American Community Survey 2011, 1-Year Estimates." Washington, DC: U.S. Census Bureau. http://factfinder2.census.gov/faces/nav/jsf/pages/index.xhtml.

―――. n.d. "2009 County Business Patterns." Washington, DC: U.S. Census Bureau. http://factfinder2.census.gov/faces/nav/jsf/pages/index.xhtml.

―――. n.d. "2010 Annual Survey of Manufacturers." Washington, U.S. Census Bureau. http://factfinder2.census.gov/faces/nav/jsf/pages/index.xhtml.

―――. n.d. "QWI Online." http://lehd.ces.census.gov/applications/qwi_online/.

SEVEN

Farmworker-Led Food Movements Then and Now

UNITED FARM WORKERS, THE COALITION OF IMMOKALEE WORKERS, AND THE POTENTIAL FOR FARM LABOR JUSTICE

Laura-Anne Minkoff-Zern

IN CRITICAL DISCUSSIONS CONCERNING food-movement activism, the overwhelming emphasis on consumer engagement is often scorned for drawing energy away from the growth of a more politically motivated food movement—one that, ideally, would better highlight worker rights, food access, and food justice more broadly. Although much food activism is indeed aimed at addressing the needs of relatively wealthy consumers (as suggested in chapter 1), this narrative overlooks the historical and present-day instances of consumer-based initiatives aimed at improving working conditions in the fields. In this chapter, I will outline the history of these initiatives and discuss what the recent success of consumer-based initiatives focused on workers' rights means for broader food-movement change.

Most consumer-based food initiatives utilize an approach whereby consumers (rather than boycotters, workers, or citizen-activists) are the primary organizers (Allen and Hinrichs 2007, Goodman et al. 2009, and many others). Contemporary consumer-based initiatives that address fair labor standards in the United States include domestic labor certification schemes such as the Agricultural Justice Project and the Domestic Fair Trade Working Group. They allow consumers to purchase their way into a supposedly more ethical food system. But as Brown and Getz argue (2008), in these initiatives laborers become yet another standard to be consumed, rather than being regarded as participants in the process of achieving justice. Broader farmworker movements and unionization efforts are not incorporated into these schemes, and therefore labor certification, no matter how well-meaning, can thwart efforts to create structural changes to the social relations of production (ibid.).

In contrast to consumer actions that end at the cash register, this chapter highlights campaigns that are part of a broader movement for consumer–farmworker solidarity, in which consumers are not only utilizing their purchasing power directly, but also applying their influence in boycotts, protests, and media campaigns. By refusing to purchase certain products and taking part in protests and actions, consumer–farmworker collaborations have successfully pressured producers and large-scale purchasers to improve labor conditions. These campaigns include both the United Farm Workers (UFW) boycotts of the 1960s and the contemporary Coalition of Immokalee Workers (CIW) Campaign for Fair Food (based in Immokalee, Florida). The CIW campaign employs consumer pressure to encourage restaurants, wholesalers, grocery stores, and other large buyers of produce to pay higher prices for agricultural products. These actions go beyond consumers purchasing "better" goods to make environmental or social change, and instead push consumers to see farmworkers as part of the agrarian landscape and to advocate for improving conditions.

In this chapter, I explore the progress made by these farmworker-led, consumer-supported movements for farmworker justice. After providing historical background on farmworker movements, I highlight the potential of what could be called the most active and successful farmworker-rights campaign today, the CIW's Fair Food Campaign. The campaign is a farmworker-led initiative to address labor practices on large-scale Florida tomato farms by targeting national food purchasers, such as grocers and fast-food restaurant chains. The CIW's immigrant organizers often draw on political experience from their home countries. I do not claim that a campaign like this can overturn a structurally unjust food system. Rather, I look at the ways in which the CIW's initiatives contrast with consumer-based food initiatives as they attempt to redirect the emphasis from individual consumers to large-scale food buyers. I argue that this shift in food activism toward a more worker-centered food movement creates an opening for consumers and workers alike to break down the divides between consumer and producer, urban and rural, and individual and community-based approaches to changing the food system.

Furthermore, this chapter argues for a shift in food studies research from work that highlights individual consumers (see Hassanein 2003, Kloppenburg et al. 1996, Lyson 2004) to studies that emphasize farm and food-system workers as key actors in changing the industrial food system. Much of the food systems literature does not question who has the privilege to access alternative food and, therefore, who has the implied power to change the way food is produced (Alkon and Agyeman 2011, Guthman 2008a, 2008b). Although the past several years have seen several farmworker-focused additions to the food studies literature (e.g., Gray 2014, Holmes 2013), these studies focus on the exploitation of workers rather than their potential as movement leaders. I contend that shifting the focus on agency from food consumers to food laborers and labor-solidarity activists is integral to moving the conversation in a direction that challenges the unjust class structures our food system relies on.

GETTING TO KNOW YOUR FARMER . . . AND FARMWORKER

Since the first African slaves were brought to North America in the seventeenth century, farmers have utilized vulnerable and impoverished groups as agricultural labor. Such exploitation continues today, as an estimated one-half to three-quarters of the national farmworker population are undocumented immigrants, mostly from Mexico and Central America.[1] Due to their fear of deportation, they are often afraid to speak out about their wages and working conditions.[2]

Among the farmworkers recorded in the National Agricultural Workers Survey in 2009, about one-third earned less than $7.25 an hour and only a quarter reported working more than nine months per calendar year (U.S. Department of Labor 2010). It is estimated that one-fourth live below the federal poverty line and, on average, 55 percent of farmworkers are food-insecure (Kresge and Eastman 2010, Wirth et al. 2007). In reality, farmworker conditions are often worse than is stated in surveys, as undocumented workers are less willing to fill out forms and respond to interviews because they fear attracting attention from the federal government.

Farm labor is one of few occupations exempt from the federal Fair Labor Standards Act of 1938, which established a minimum wage, a forty-hour work week, and overtime pay and prohibited child labor. Farmworkers continue to be left out of most state minimum-wage and work-hour limitations, with the exceptions of California, Oregon, and Washington. Farmworkers were also excluded from the National Labor Relations Act of 1935, which guarantees the rights of private-sector employees to join a union and engage in collective bargaining. In California, farmworkers fought for and won that right in 1975 after a prolonged effort by the UFW. They are now covered under the California Agricultural Labor Relations Act (CALRA). When laws do exist to protect workers, they are routinely ignored by employers and not enforced by relevant authorities (Gray 2014).

Despite decades of farmworker union organizing and consumer solidarity efforts, many of today's foodies are woefully unaware of farmworker struggles. Places where alternative food is sold and promoted, such as natural food stores and food-purchasing cooperatives, commonly post large, glossy photographs of local growers, encouraging consumers to familiarize themselves with farm owners. These images of "local" farmers mask historical and current-day inequalities related to labor, land, and consumer–producer relations (Allen 2008, 2004, 1993, Allen et al. 1991, Dupuis and Goodman 2005, Gray 2014, Guthman 2008a, 2008b). Bucolic depictions of farmer livelihoods draw on an "agrarian imaginary," an idealized image of the small-scale farmer (Getz et al. 2008, Gray 2014, Guthman 2004). Such portrayals appeal to the historical notion of the Jeffersonian yeoman farmer who developed the U.S. agricultural economy and landscape by working the land with his own hands. This farmer is usually rendered as white and male, and as an individual who labors alone to produce wholesome food for the nation's population. This agrarian imaginary continues to disguise the messiness of real agriculture practice and its inherent injustices (Allen 2008, 1993, Brown and Getz 2008, Getz 2011, Gray 2014, Guthman 2004, Walker 2004). Often a farmer's small-scale and local-market focus works to mask the most particularly egregious labor practices (Gray 2014).

Critics of food movements dependent on consumer-based approaches conclude that they remain limited to middle- and upper-class, mostly white, consumers, excluding those who don't have the ability to pay more for "good" food or who don't feel included by the culture of alternative food spaces (Alkon 2008, Alkon and Agyeman 2011, Guthman 2008a, 2008b, 2008c). Consumer-based politics and campaigns are often critiqued for prioritizing the economic success of farm owners over social and environmental standards (Allen 2004), reinforcing the limited accessibility of such foods, and the privilege inherent in making "conscious" food decisions. Additionally, they follow a neoliberal model, dependent on the market and non-governmental actors for creating environmental and social change, rather than applying pressure on the state to address structural inequities (Alkon 2012, Allen

2008, 2004, Guthman 2011, 2008b, Holt-Giménez and Wang 2011, Lo and Jacobson 2011). Although consumer initiatives have resulted in increased organic production, they have failed to cope with the most toxic use of pesticides, privileging the bodies of organic consumers while abandoning those of agricultural communities (Harrison 2011, 2008; chapter 2, this volume). Yet, some scholars argue, when we make linkages between production and consumption, there is more possibility for making political inroads with regard to labor. Although it has yet to be seen in practice, Hartwick (2000, 1998) proposes that when the material realities of commodity chains are taken seriously, and consumers are more directly connected with producers, they will be more likely to take action to improve the conditions of production.

The food justice movement is a direct response to the elitism and classism inherent in consumer-based food movements. Born from many of the ideals and actions of the environmental justice movement, food justice actors work with the goal of directly addressing food access and structural racism and classism, focusing on human rights in the food system (Alkon and Agyeman 2011, Gottlieb and Joshi 2010, Holt-Giménez and Wang 2011). Yet, as Allen (2008) argues, there is often a "gap between intent and outcome in food justice." Although the idea of creating a more just food system is a valiant one, many food justice organizations lack attention to workers' rights, continuing to focus on farm owners, rather than farmworkers, as the primary producers of food. The emphasis, though, often shifts to supporting farmers of color, rather than only white ones.

Though actors in the food justice movement often critique the structural inequality inherent in our domestic food system, they tend to have an urban bias, challenging inequality in urban spaces of food consumption while still fetishizing the production of food and the rural farmer. For example, at a food-themed academic conference, I was asked to moderate a farm-labor panel. At the same time that our panel was scheduled, another panel, focused on "food justice," was occurring as a completely separate discussion. While our panel focused on rural issues, the other panel discussed strictly urban ones. This experience illustrates the way that conversations about food justice and farm labor are often happening in isolation, yet in very close proximity to one another. Solutions for a more just food system often revolve around equitable access regarding consumption, not equitable production practices, therefore reinforcing the notion of a rural–urban divide in our food system (Guthman 2011, Harrison 2008). Many food justice organizations work on initiatives to enable and popularize urban gardening and to increase farmers' markets and the availability of fresh food in poor urban neighborhoods. Although these are important efforts to increase the quality of health and the well-being of often underserved urban residents, they tend to limit the conversation concerning food injustice to the urban core.

Yet this is not always the case. During the UFW's 1969 Safeway boycott, the Black Panther Party supported the campaign, as they saw a connection between their own actions to increase access to healthy food for inner-city youth and the farmworkers' movement for justice in the fields (Henderson 2011). This example could act as a model for other organizations starting to do solidarity work on food justice issues by bringing urban and rural economic injustices into closer conversation. The CIW's campaign is unique in that many actions take place in urban spaces, yet the leaders and beneficiaries of the organizing work live in rural areas. Their campaign bridges the urban–rural divide in food-related activism and consumerism, making rural injustice a reality to urban-based food consumers, while maintaining rural leadership.

HISTORY OF FARMWORKER ORGANIZING AND SOLIDARITY ACTIVISM

The CIW is not the first farmworker-based organization that has appealed to consumer engagement in order to improve domestic agricultural labor conditions. Farmworker unions such as the UFW in California, Pineros y Campesinos Unidos del Noroeste ("Northwest Treeplanters and Farmworkers United") in the Pacific Northwest, and the Farm Labor Organizing Committee in the Midwest, have been working for decades, utilizing a mix of tactics including consumer boycotts, worker strikes, and legislative pressure to improve farmworker conditions in the United States. All these groups have successfully pressured large purchasers of agricultural products to change their buying practices on the basis of farmworker treatment, ultimately resulting in worker contracts and better working conditions. They have done so by activating consumers to boycott products and engage with worker politics. Although long-term success has varied, their accomplishments prove the potential of like organizations to utilize the power of the consumer beyond individual purchasing.

The most iconic food-consumer actions in the name of labor are the grape boycotts of the late 1960s, which many food activists and workers still reminisce about today. In 1965, Filipino grape workers and members of the AFL-CIO–affiliated Agricultural Workers Organizing Committee in Delano, California, started striking against low wages and dreadful working and living conditions. They soon asked a newly formed, predominantly Latino/a union, the National Farm Workers Association (NFWA), to join them, and together they became the United Farm Workers. To gain national attention and support the strike, Cesar Chavez and other organizers orchestrated a march on Sacramento, California's capital. Over the following four years, the UFW and its collaborators organized the largest food boycott in U.S. history. By 1970, all table grape workers were under union contract, and by 1977 the UFW had secured over a hundred union contracts. These contracts guaranteed higher wages, benefits, and working conditions for farm labor (Ganz 2009). Although the worker strikes and marches were important tactics in creating worker solidarity, ultimately the boycott was the action that pushed the growers over the edge (Bardacke 2012, Ganz 2009, Garcia 2012). By affecting their public image and therefore their bottom line, the boycott not only succeeded as a tactic in inspiring consumer support of farmworker struggles, but ultimately also forced the growers to agree to worker demands (Bardacke 2012, Garcia 2012, Pulido 1996).

Solidarity work was key in creating the widespread boycott. From the beginning, civil rights and antiwar groups, such as the Student Nonviolent Coordinating Committee and Students for a Democratic Society, threw support behind the efforts, helping the NFWA establish the boycott nationwide (Bardacke 2012). Campaign materials explicitly connected consumer health and worker health by emphasizing shared exposure to pesticides. Further, their organizing and boycotts led to a court ruling stating that pesticide reports are public documents, helping to foster a national ban on the toxic pesticide DDT (Harrison 2011).

The UFW has been crucial to getting specific legislation passed to protect farmworker rights. In California, the UFW played a large role in helping pass the Agricultural Labor Relations Act and in establishing California's Agricultural Relations Board in 1975 (Martin 2003). More contemporary successes include signing labor contracts with cattle feeders in Oregon and Washington and with Dole strawberry growers in California (United Farm Workers 2012).

Unfortunately, the UFW's influence in improving agricultural workers' rights has waned in recent years. Violent antiunion tactics, as well as the entry of new immigrant labor groups throughout U.S. history, have systematically undermined farmworker organizing since the 1970s. Farm labor is currently one of the least unionized industries in the United States, with less than 2 percent of farmworkers organized (Mayer 2004). As various immigrant groups have organized and demanded better wages and working conditions, employers have replaced them with newer, differently racialized immigrant groups, effectively avoiding collective mobilization for better wages and conditions (Almaguer 1994, Ganz 2009, Henderson 1998, Mitchell 1996, Walker 2004, Wells 1996). Over the past few decades, there has been a shift from mostly mestizo workers from northern Mexico to an influx of indigenous immigrants from more southern Mexican states. These workers often speak primarily pre-Colombian languages (instead of Spanish) and are discriminated against by mestizos as well as by whites (Holmes 2013, Minkoff-Zern 2012a, Stephen 2007). This recent demographic shift has been identified as one of the many reasons that the UFW's organizing strength has diminished over the years.

There are many related explanations for why farmworker unions failed to grow in power and popularity after the 1970s. Some believe that although Cesar Chavez was a charismatic leader, the UFW lacked the practical organizing tactics to respond to the demands of union members, leading to decreasing support from the membership. Others point to the growing numbers of documented and undocumented immigrants and demands on the agricultural labor market (Wells 1996), as well as Chavez's lack of interest in incorporating indigenous and undocumented workers into the UFW's organizing strategy (Bardacke 2012, Garcia 2012). In terms of internal organization, labor historian Frank Bardacke (2012) argues that when the UFW began to devote time and attention to boycotts, it led to the ultimate demise of the grassroots organizing arm of the UFW, and the heart of the struggles. Still others argue that the downfall was directly correlated with Chavez's thirst for power, and his unwillingness to manage the union in a democratic manner (Garcia 2012). Additionally, the changing economic organization of agriculture over the past few decades includes a shift from direct hiring to contractors as middlemen (Martin 2003), as well as a broader reorganization of the produce industry, as grower–shippers were replaced by shipper–retailers, responding to the consolidation of grocery-store chains (Bardacke 2012). Both of these shifts affected hiring practices and took power away from the workers. In California specifically, the Republican attack on the California Agricultural Labor Relations Board was representative of a political shift away from farmworker support (ibid.). The ultimate effect of these combined factors has been less collective power for workers to bargain for improved wages, benefits, and working conditions.

Despite the fact that many labor supporters and activists see unions as the most direct way to improve working conditions and harness a movement around labor, it is important to note geographic differences in terms of union success. Most success in farmworker organizing in the United States has occurred in California, and, as discussed above, even there it has still been limited. Many, although not all, agricultural workers in California are hired by the season, rather than by the day. Although they are hired at will, and have no job security from season to season, this is relatively more stable than the hiring system in Florida, where there are more day laborers and fewer seasonal jobs. In the CIW's case, organizers do not see a traditional union approach as the most viable strategy. Lucas Benitez of the CIW explains: "In Immokalee we needed to look for an alternative to a union system. . . . Unions don't work there because people go farm to farm, there are no worker contracts" (Benitez 2012). This difference in hiring practices has created a situation in which, in some parts of the country, workers pursue appeals to food purchasers, rather than to growers directly. Furthermore, since they are organizing in Florida, workers are not legally protected to join a union or engage in collective bargaining, as workers are in California under the CALRA. Benitez adds: "We don't have the opportunity [to go directly to employers], because we don't have the right to a union" (ibid.). It is for these reasons that workers in the CIW's Fair Food Campaign have focused on aligning with consumers in lobbying large-scale purchasers in order to create downward pressure on the growers to change wages and working conditions.

THE CIW: FARMWORKER LED, CONSUMER SUPPORTED

The CIW campaign is unique in the broader context of present-day consumer food activism in that it is motivated and organized by farmworkers themselves. In contrast to fair trade labels and certification schemes, the CIW's campaigns do not merely encourage consumers to make better choices through their buying practices or create pressure for social change through the market. Rather, they ask consumers to use their political power as citizens to write letters and get involved with farmworker-led movements and, most importantly, to boycott products and retailers that do not adhere to the CIW's standards.

The Fair Food Campaign builds on the organizing experience that many farmworkers bring to the United States after decades of political work in their home countries. In the case presented here, farmworkers are utilizing consumers' political sway with purchasers to achieve their strategic goals, rather than the other way around. In this way, the CIW campaign, as compared to other consumer-based initiatives, shifts the agency in food movements from those who eat to those who work.

Although not all immigrants come to the United States from traditions of agrarian struggle, often those who work in agriculture, especially from Mexico, Guatemala, El Salvador, and Haiti, have been dispossessed from their own land and experienced conflict around land and labor prior to immigrating. Similarly to indigenous Oaxacan immigrants in California, who bring their experience with collective action in Mexico to their organizing of community-based groups in the United States (Fox and Rivera-Salgado 2004, Minkoff-Zern 2012b), CIW organizers have built on knowledge from peasant struggles in their home countries. Some of the CIW's original organizers were trained in the Mouvman Peyizan Papay ("Peasant Movement of Papay"), Haiti's largest peasant organization and part of the popular movement that ended Jean-Claude Duvalier's dictatorial regime. When the CIW incorporated as a nonprofit organization in 1996, it drew on members' experience with cooperatives in rural parts of Latin America in the 1970s and '80s. Inspired by liberation theology and previous social-movement activism, tactics that utilize immigrant experience include popular education, leadership development, and protest actions. CIW organizers have continuously drawn on these strategies in identifying and addressing the roots of farmworker oppression (Giagnoni 2011, Sellers 2009).

Although many doubt the ability of immigrants, particularly undocumented immigrants, to organize for better working standards and wages, union-organizing successes in Los Angeles in the 1980s and '90s show otherwise. Latino immigrants from Mexico and Central America working as janitors, garment manufacturers, and construction workers tended to be more responsive to organizing into labor unions than their native-born counterparts (Milkman 2006). Ruth Milkman (ibid.) attributes some of the organizing success to these workers being veterans of intense political struggle in their home countries and, relatedly, being less individualistic than many U.S.-born workers.

The CIW's Campaign for Fair Food has focused on corporate buyers of produce and has succeeded in gaining contracts with the nation's four largest fast-food companies (McDonald's, Yum Brands, Burger King, and Subway) and the three largest food-service providers (Compass Group, Aramark, and Sodexo), as well as grocery stores like Walmart, Trader Joe's, and others. Companies that sign on to the campaign have agreed to use their market power to force producers to increase farmworker wages (a penny more per pound of tomatoes bought goes directly to workers' paychecks), enforce a human-rights-based code of conduct for agricultural suppliers (in which ethics standards are regulated by worker groups, including zero tolerance for sexual harassment and forced labor), ongoing third-party farm audits to ensure that growers are complying with standards, and providing transparency for tomato purchases in Florida.

Although reversing the exploitation of workers inherent to the capitalist mode of production will require radical transformation, farmworker-led, consumer-oriented campaigns have the potential to directly and immediately improve agricultural workers' conditions and wages within the current system. According to labor economist Philip Martin, if farm wages increased 40 percent, individual households in the United States would spend only about $15 more a year on food, while farmworkers would be lifted above the federal poverty line (Martin 2011). The Fair Food Campaign asks corporate food purchasers to spend a penny more per pound of tomatoes, and to sign an agreement that holds growers accountable to pass on the extra profit to their workers as well as to provide humane conditions in the fields. Such improvements to wages may sound like insignificant progress to those calling for structural changes to national inequality. Nonetheless, small wage increases can mean enormous changes for farmworkers' livelihoods. Since the advent of the campaign in 2011, over $18 million has been paid in premiums directly to workers. Additionally, close to one hundred fifty thousand workers have been educated on their workplace rights and six hundred workers have filed complaints of employer abuse, holding owners accountable for abuses such as sexual harassment, sexual assault, and systematic wage theft (CIW 2015).

The campaign, now in its sixth year, has had immediate effects in the lives of workers, from making sure that workers receive the wages for hours they labored to getting their basic human needs met in the fields. In an interview with the author, Lupe Gonzalo, a tomato picker and organizer with the CIW, described these changes:

This program has made a huge impact on the life of the workers because, for example, we can now drink clean water, take breaks in places where there is shade (when it gets too hot outside), and we can talk to our bosses.... For the women, to be able to work with dignity and respect is something huge because before the program, the women would be sexually harassed. But now that the program exists there is zero tolerance for sexual harassment and women can report sexual harassment anonymously, because that did not happen before. Therefore, now women are working and our human rights are being respected.

Moreover, the campaign utilizes the political power of a "boycott," in which consumers are discouraged from purchasing a product, versus that of a "buycott," in which consumers are encouraged to purchase a product in order to redirect market power from another item (Freidman 1996). Gonzalo explains their focus on consumers:

The consumers have one of the most powerful roles in getting corporations to come on board to sign an agreement with the workers. Many corporations like to paint a pretty picture for the consumers and what we want consumers to know is that corporations do not always say the truth or show the reality.... For this reason we begin the campaign with the consumers, students or people of faith. So that they see what us workers are doing, and that is how we are able to form a union.

In addition to consumer boycotts, the CIW has enacted letter-writing campaigns, petitions, protests, and days of action at various national agrifood companies' corporate headquarters. The Fair Food Campaign identifies points of power in the food chain and applies pressure, demanding improved labor standards and practices. Large-scale buyers of produce are able to apply downward pressure on growers to produce food cheaply. The campaign is working to harness this power and reverse this trend. Despite threats from the Florida Tomato Growers Exchange after their first successful agreements with Taco Bell and McDonald's, the campaign has continued to grow, including more restaurants and grocers on a national scale.

All CIW campaign missions are decided on by farmworkers themselves. As the primary leaders of the CIW, farmworkers ensure that consumer and activist energies are utilized to directly support their daily struggles. Gerardo Reyes, an organizer with the CIW, clarifies their organizational structure:

Basically the coalition is an organization without a hierarchy—we don't have a president or vice president who decides what's best for everyone else. We function as a group collectively. We gather to talk about the work and divide the work based on the skills that people in the room have.

Most of us, who make up the organization, including myself, are farmworkers. We run the day-to-day operational structure and coordinate with the community to develop strategy and explore ideas to advance the Campaign for Fair Food. The community, through weekly community meetings, monthly retreats, and cultural activities like marimba playing, popular theater and education, develops the direction of the national campaign. These various activities are all opportunities for workers to become core members and leaders of the organization.

Further, contrary to most consumer-based food initiatives, CIW's actions do not focus solely on privileged consumers. The campaign's first target was Taco Bell, a fast-food chain that targets low-income consumers with their low-price menu items. By not limiting their base of consumer "activists" to the white middle and upper classes, there is more potential for the CIW's movement to grow in size and power. Through appealing to the large mass of consumers and producers involved in purchasing industrial agriculture, rather than the relatively small number of those involved in the small-scale specialty food industry, they are aiming at a larger target of producers—those that employ more workers and those whose workers often labor under the worst conditions.

The potential power of these actions is that they encourage consumers to recognize that their influence is not only in their conscious consumption, or voting with their dollar or fork, but in identifying ways to partner with, support, and advocate for farmworker groups. Although CIW's contracts with retailers target tomato growers specifically, their influence is more broad-based. In one example, the U.S. Senate Health, Education, Labor, and Pension Committee held a hearing on the CIW's campaign in 2008, where several senators stated they were compelled to introduce legislation to improve labor standards for farmworkers (Harrison 2011).

Through these campaigns, farmworkers collectively foster and galvanize consumer support. They are successfully forcing large buyers of produce to agree to labor contracts, which, in turn, forces suppliers to pay workers more and provide better work conditions. The farm owners are beholden to the buyers who have a contract with the farmworkers. Contrary to most consumer-based food activism, in which consumers use their privilege to make choices based on their own health and desires, Reyes highlights the ways that farmworkers are utilizing consumer–citizen power for worker needs, confronting structural inequities:

They [the contracts] are strong because the public campaign is strong. It is also strong because these are legal agreements that have been taken to court. And this is going to make it very difficult for any corporation who is currently doing the right thing to say, "You know what, we no longer want to participate in your program," because that will generate a lot of consumer energy against them.

Reyes also notes the ways that the CIW's campaign depends on consumer power, yet is still very consciously a worker-led movement:

The Campaign for Fair Food is not a movement to *help* the poor workers; it is a worker-led movement that belongs to everyone who gets involved in it. Yes, consumers have a role in shaping how corporations behave in the supply chain. Consumers have made possible the campaign victories we have had with Taco Bell, McDonald's, and the nine other major corporations who have signed onto the Fair Food Program. Public pressure brought fourteen corporations to sign Fair Food Agreements with the Coalition of Immokalee Workers. . . .[3]

None of this would have been possible if it were just workers from Immokalee asking the tomato buyers on our own. These advances have happened because we were able to connect the dots with the consumers and allow for our analysis of the supply chain to be shared with communities across the country.

The Campaign for Fair Food does not simply empower consumers as individuals by means of their purchases. Rather, it emphasizes the ways in which consumers can be part of a movement in solidarity with workers. Reyes and others at the coalition encourage and support consumers to "Protest in the streets next to us and create public pressure [to sign the agreements]." These actions not only affect wages directly, but also raise awareness among those physically detached from rural areas and struggles in the field, providing potential support for future policy changes and more stringent labor regulations. The power of farmworker grassroots organizing, combined with consumer power, has exhibited new ways that food injustice can be challenged by bridging physical and social geographical divisions. Recognizing workers as key actors in achieving social change opens new avenues for addressing inequalities in the food system.

The coalition has plans to expand the campaign beyond Florida and tomatoes. They see these contracts with growers as one step in making larger transformations in the food industry. Max Perez, a former farmworker born in Immokalee, highlights the way the CIW is making structural social change:

The coalition to me is more than just an organization working towards farmworker rights and higher wages, things like that. It's an organization that is trying to fundamentally change things. Little towns like Immokalee that are totally controlled by the environment and agricultural industry and everything else. We are changing things ourselves, showing that there's a different way. And it's working.

According to organizers and activists like Perez, this work is making day-to-day changes in the lives of farmworkers and is the beginning of substantial changes to the food system as a whole.

THE POWER OF COALITIONS

Although many consumer food activists avoid labor as an issue, there is a growing interest in labor rights among some food enthusiasts, and a developing awareness among university students in particular. Social justice is now being mentioned in the titles and mission statements of alternative agrifood organizations, a great improvement since the beginning of the movement just a few decades ago (Allen 2008). Yet justice often equates to more rights for small-scale farmers, not workers (Alkon and Agyeman 2011, Allen 2008, Brown and Getz 2008, Guthman 2008b, 2008c, 2004). Only recently have such groups started mentioning labor as a central issue.

Some consumer activists are starting to utilize consumer support for food-labor organizing and action. Former Slow Food USA president Josh Viertel spoke at a 2011 march organized by the CIW and the Student Farmworker Alliance in Boston.[4] Viertel told the audience, "I am here today because the food movement cannot be separate from the farmworkers movement" (Viertel 2011). His impassioned speech and follow-up publication in the *Atlantic Monthly* resonates with many who identify as part of the Slow Food or foodie movements and are starting to see more just farm labor as part of the movement for "good" food.[5]

Food justice activists are also starting to work more broadly on issues of farm and food-system labor, coordinating with farm, food-processing, and restaurant-worker unions, and building new coalitions, such as the Food Chain Workers Alliance, the U.S. Food Sovereignty Alliance, the Restaurant Opportunities Center United, and the Student Farmworker Alliance. Working in coalition, many groups are galvanizing more influence in motivating policy change and raising working standards, bringing worker struggles closer to the center of the food movement (Lo 2014, Lo and Jacobson 2011; chapters 6 and 8, this volume). The Student Farmworker Alliance has played a major role in the CIW protests and boycotts, fostering discussions about farmworker injustice on college campuses. Gerardo Reyes explains:

> The relationship with the organizations based here in Immokalee is very close. Together we develop plans we are considering implementing at a local and national level. For example, if we are planning a march, we ask ourselves, what does that mean for our network of allies? How can students and communities of different faiths engage? When is the most strategic time to hold an action to maximize its impact and ally participation? Which type of actions will have the strongest impact on corporate targets? These are examples of some of the questions we explore with our ally organizations. . . .
>
> We work together with different organizations all over the country that support our campaign. Our intention is not just to harness support for our campaign, but to find ways to support the struggles and work of other communities.

The Food Chain Workers Alliance is working directly with urban as well as rural food justice groups, bridging this geographic gap in the food movement. Founded by regionally diverse groups, such as the Restaurant Opportunities Center United in New York City and the Northwest Arkansas Workers' Justice Center, the Alliance organizes to improve wages and working conditions for all workers along the food chain (Food Chain Workers Alliance 2012). Coalition building is an important step for bringing together the growing food justice movement to rally political pressure around farm labor. By working in coalition, food justice activists and organizers with an urban focus are beginning to learn from rural activists, as well as the reverse. As Reyes notes, working in coalition not only helps advance the CIW's goals in the fields but also helps develop a broader movement for food justice.

CONCLUSION

In order to create a just food system, agrarian narratives and imagery that promote small, family-owned, and local farms must be pushed further: people need to ask not only "Where does my food come from?" but also "Who performs the labor to grow this food?" In order to make farmworker rights a central part of this movement, eaters must start to engage with a broader critique of our agricultural system, an agrarian structure based in exploitation, and hold small-scale farmers as well as large-scale ones accountable.

To make lasting changes to the food system, there must be more cooperation among food and labor movements, workers' rights must become central to food-movement discourses, and divisions between the rural and urban must be dissolved. Farmworker-led food movements, with deep analyses of agrarian power, class relations, and the struggle over controlling food, are primed to take this step. They are primed to do so by working in coalition with movements for food justice.

Achieving farmworker justice cannot be based on one strategy. Labor laws and hiring practices differ regionally, and what works in one part of the country may not work in another. Consumer solidarity campaigns such as the CIW's must be used to raise awareness by emboldening consumer activism beyond voting with one's fork. If just labor practices are to be included as part of sustainable food ideals, solidarity activists must demand that farm employers, large-scale food purchasers, politicians, and regulators improve field labor conditions and wages by encouraging state and national policies that support unionizing, strengthen existing labor laws, and amend laws that reinforce structural injustice. In this study of the CIW and the UFW, farmworkers collaborate with consumers and organizers to raise awareness and take action against labor injustices. Many farmworkers come to their jobs with personal histories as organizers and activists. They know the most pressing issues in the fields, and only by listening to their voices as a guide for solidarity work will such inequalities begin to be rectified.

Farmworkers aligning with the food movement will not, of course, simply undo the political power of agribusiness and other growers, who oppose unionization and other forms of labor organization. Nonetheless, stronger alliances can increase awareness of food labor abuses, creating more popular support for organizing tactics such as unionization, strikes, and boycotts. Alliances to address farm labor are growing with increased awareness of labor conditions in the food system. More alliances must form across the food chain to include not only farmworkers, but those in distribution and service as well. The knowledge and skills that exist in farmworker communities are a starting place for making structural changes. They must be included as part of these movements, not only as subjects of discussion, but as participants in creating change and a force to be respected and reckoned with.

NOTES

A version of this chapter was first published in the journal *Human Geography* 7 (2014); it is reprinted with permission from the journal. Many thanks to the staff and organizers at the Coalition of Immokalee Workers who took the time to update their interviews, and to Sara Quinteros-Fernandez for her assistance with revising the manuscript.

1. The total number is hard to determine. The National Agricultural Workers Survey conducted by the U.S. Department of Labor (2010) reports that 53 percent are unauthorized, whereas a report by Bon Appétit and United Farm Workers (2011) asserts that the number is most likely higher.

2. This is not always the case. Milkman (2006) documents the successes of Latino immigrants involved in organized labor in Los Angeles in the 1980s and '90s (discussed further below).

3. There are now twelve corporations that have signed the Fair Food Agreements.

4. Slow Food USA is a popular anchor for food consumer movements in the United States, followed by other national and regional organizations and campaigns such as Buy Fresh, Buy Local; the Food Alliance; and Local Harvest. This movement, which was founded to "counter the rise of fast food and fast life, the disappearance of local food traditions and people's dwindling interest in the food they eat," has gained speed in the United States in the past decade, promoted as a way for consumers to improve their own health and that of the environment (Slow Food 2012).

5. This progress is debated by others in the foodie movement, who argue that organizations such as Slow Food should be focused on preserving traditional food-ways, rather than getting involved in "political" debates or policy-based initiatives (Greenaway 2012). In June 2012, Viertel stepped down as president of Slow Food, presumably due to these conflicting goals within the movement.

REFERENCES

Alkon, Alison Hope. 2008. "From Value to Values: Sustainable Consumption at Farmers Markets." *Agriculture and Human Values* 25: 487–498.

———. 2012. *Black, White, and Green: Farmers Markets, Race, and the Green Economy.* Athens: University of Georgia Press.

Alkon, Alison Hope, and Julian Agyeman, Eds. 2011. *Cultivating Food Justice: Race, Class, and Sustainability.* Cambridge, MA: MIT Press.

Allen, Patricia. 1993. *Food for the Future: Conditions and Contradictions of Sustainability.* New York: Wiley.

———. 2004. *Together at the Table: Sustainability and Sustenance in the American Agrifood System,* new edition. University Park, PA: Penn State University Press.

———. 2008. "Mining for Justice in the Food System: Perceptions, Practices, and Possibilities." *Agriculture and Human Values* 25: 157–161.

Allen, Patricia, and C. Claire Hinrichs. 2007. "Buying into 'Buy Local': Engagements of United States Local Food Initiatives." In *Constructing Alternative Food Geographies: Representation and Practice,* ed. D. Maye, L. Holloway, and M. Kneafsey, 255–272. Oxford: Elsevier.

Allen, Patricia, Debra Van Dusen, Jackelyn Lundy, and Stephen Gliessman. 1991. "Integrating Social, Environmental, and Economic Issues in Sustainable Agriculture." *American Journal of Alternative Agriculture* 6: 34–39.

Almaguer, Tomás. 1994. *Racial Fault Lines: The Historical Origins of White Supremacy in California.* Berkeley: University of California Press.

Bardacke, Frank. 2012. *Trampling Out the Vintage: Cesar Chavez and the Two Souls of the United Farm Workers.* London: Verso.

Benitez, Lucas. 2012. Conference presentation. Labor Across the Food System Conference, Santa Cruz, California.

Bon Appétit and United Farm Workers. 2011. "Inventory of Farmworker Issues and Protections in the United States." www.ufw.org/pdf/farmworkerinventory_0401_2011.pdf.

Brown, Sandy, and Christy Getz. 2008. "Privatizing Farm Worker Justice: Regulating Labor through Voluntary Certification and Labeling." *Geoforum* 39: 1184–1196.

———. 2011. "Farmworker Food Insecurity and the Production of Hunger in California." In *Cultivating Food Justice: Race, Class, and Sustainability,* ed. Alison Hope Alkon and Julian Agyeman, 121–146. Cambridge, MA: MIT Press.

Coalition of Immokalee Workers. 2015. "Fair Food Program 2015 Annual Report." www.fairfoodprogram.org. Accessed March 8, 2017.

DuPuis, E. Melanie, and David Goodman. 2005. "Should We Go 'Home' to Eat? Toward a Reflexive Politics of Localism." *Journal of Rural Studies* 21: 359–371.

Food Chain Workers Alliance. "Mission." http://foodchainworkers.org/?page_id=38. Accessed March 2, 2012.

Fox, Jonathan, and Gaspar Rivera-Salgado, Eds. 2004. "Indigenous Mexican Migrants in the United States." San Diego, CA: Center for U.S.–Mexican Studies, UCSD/Center for Comparative Immigration Studies.

Friedman, Monroe. 1996. "A Positive Approach to Organized Consumer Action: The 'Buycott' as an Alternative to the Boycott." *Journal of Consumer Policy* 19: 439–451.

Ganz, Marshall. 2009. *Why David Sometimes Wins: Leadership, Organization, and Strategy in the California Farm Worker Movement.* New York: Oxford University Press.

Garcia, M. 2012. *From the Jaws of Victory: The Triumph and Tragedy of the Farm Worker Movement.* Berkeley: University of California Press.

Getz, Christy. 2011. "Social Justice in Agriculture: Exploring Contradictions." Paper presented at the UC Berkeley Law School Environmental Justice Symposium.

Getz, Christy, Sandy Brown, and Aimee Shreck. 2008. "Class Politics and Agricultural Exceptionalism in California's Organic Agriculture Movement." *Politics and Society* 36: 478–507.

Giagnoni, Silvia. 2011. *Fields of Resistance: The Struggle of Florida's Farmworkers for Justice.* Chicago: Haymarket Books.

Goodman, Mike K., David Goodman, and Michael Redclift. 2009. "Situating Consumption, Space and Place." *Environment, Politics and Development Working Paper Series.* London: Department of Geography, King's College London.

Gottlieb, Robert, and Anupama Joshi. 2010. *Food Justice.* Cambridge, MA: MIT Press.

Gray, Margaret. 2014. *Labor and the Locavore: The Making of a Comprehensive Food Ethic.* Berkeley: University of California Press.

Greenaway, Twilight. 2012. "A Fork in the Road for Slow Food." *Grist,* January 11. www.grist.org/sustainable-food/2012–01–10-fork-in-the-road-for-slow-food. Accessed February 3, 2012.

Guthman, Julie. 2004. *Agrarian Dreams: The Paradox of Organic Farming in California.* Berkeley: University of California Press.

———. 2008a. "'If They Only Knew': Color Blindness and Universalism in California Alternative Food Institutions." *The Professional Geographer* 60: 387–397.

———. 2008b. "Neoliberalism and the Making of Food Politics in California." *Geoforum* 39: 1171–1183.

———. 2008c. "Thinking inside the Neoliberal Box: The Micro-politics of Agrofood Philanthropy." *Geoforum* 39: 1241–1253.

———. 2011. *Weighing In: Obesity, Food Justice, and the Limits of Capitalism.* Berkeley: University of California Press.

Harrison, Jill Lindsey. 2008. "Lessons Learned from Pesticide Drift: A Call to Bring Production Agriculture, Farm Labor, and Social Justice Back into Agrifood Research and Activism." *Agriculture and Human Values* 25: 163–167.

———. 2011. *Pesticide Drift and the Pursuit of Environmental Justice.* Cambridge, MA: MIT Press.

Hartwick, Elaine R. 1998. "Geographies of Consumption: A Commodity-Chain Approach." *Environment and Planning D* 16: 423–438.

———. 2000. "Towards a Geographical Politics of Consumption." *Environment and Planning A* 32: 1177–1192.

Hassanein, Neva. 2003. "Practicing Food Democracy: A Pragmatic Politics of Transformation." *Journal of Rural Studies* 19: 77–86.

Henderson, George. 1998. "Nature and Fictitious Capital: The Historical Geography of an Agrarian Question." *Antipode* 30: 73–118.

Henderson, Nikki. 2011. "TEDxFruitvale—The Black Power and Farmworker Movements." *YouTube.* http://youtube.com/watch?v=qUcwytnlDsM. Accessed June 20, 2012.

Holmes, Seth. 2013. *Fresh Fruit, Broken Bodies: Migrant Farmworkers in the United States.* Berkeley: University of California Press.

Holt-Giménez, Eric, and Raj Patel. 2009. *Food Rebellions! Forging Food Sovereignty to Solve the Global Food Crisis.* Cape Town: Pambazuka Press.

Holt-Giménez, Eric, and Yi Wang. 2011. "Reform or Transformation? The Pivotal Role of Food Justice in the U.S. Food Movement." *Race/Ethnicity: Multidisciplinary Global Contexts* 5: 83–102.

Kloppenburg, Jack, Jr., John Hendrickson, and G. W. Stevenson. 1996. "Coming in to the Foodshed." *Agriculture and Human Values* 13: 33–42.

Kresge, Lisa, and Chelsea Eastman. 2010. "Increasing Food Security among Agricultural Workers in California's Salinas Valley." Davis: California Institute for Rural Studies.

Lo, Joann. 2014. "Social Justice for Food Workers in a Foodie World." *Journal of Critical Thought and Praxis* 3: 10–11.

Lo, Joann, and Ariel Jacobson. 2011. "Human Rights from Field to Fork: Improving Labor Conditions for Food-Sector Workers by Organizing across Boundaries." *Race/Ethnicity: Multidisciplinary Global Contexts* 5: 61–82.

Lyson, Thomas. 2004. *Civic Agriculture: Reconnecting Farm, Food, and Community.* Boston: Tufts University Press.

Martin, Philip. 2003. *Promise Unfulfilled: Unions, Immigration and the Farm Workers.* Ithaca, NY: Cornell University Press.

———. 2011. "The Costs and Benefits of a Raise for Field Workers." *The New York Times,* September 30. http://nytimes.com/roomfordebate/2011/08/17/could-farms-survive-without-illegal-labor/the-costs-and-benefits-of-a-raise-for-field-workers. Accessed June 5, 2012.

Mayer, Gerald. 2004. "Union Membership Trends in the United States." Federal Publications, Paper 174. http://digitalcommons.ilr.cornell.edu/key_workplace/174. Accessed June 10, 2012.

Milkman, Ruth. 2006. *L.A. Story: Immigrant Workers and the Future of the U.S. Labor Movement.* New York: Russell Sage Foundation.

Minkoff-Zern, Laura-Anne. 2012a. "Migrations of Hunger and Knowledge: Food Insecurity and California's Indigenous Farmworkers." PhD dissertation, University of California, Berkeley.

———. 2012b. "Pushing the Boundaries of Indigeneity and Agricultural Knowledge: Oaxacan Immigrant Community Gardening in California." *Agriculture and Human Values* 29: 381–392.

Mitchell, Don. 1996. *Lie of the Land: Migrant Workers and the California Landscape.* Minneapolis: University Of Minnesota Press.

Patel, Raj. 2009. "Food Sovereignty." *Journal of Peasant Studies* 36: 663–706.

Pulido, Laura. 1996. *Environmentalism and Economic Justice: Two Chicano Struggles in the Southwest.* Tucson: University of Arizona.

Sellers, Randall. 2009. "'Del Pueblo, Para El Pueblo': The Coalition of Immokalee Workers and the Fight for Fair Food." Master's thesis, University of Texas, Austin.

Slow Food. 2012. "About Us: Slow Food USA." http://slowfoodusa.org/index.php/about_us/. Accessed March 3, 2012.

Stephen, Lynn. 2007. *Transborder Lives: Indigenous Oaxacans in Mexico, California, and Oregon.* Durham, NC: Duke University Press.

United Farm Workers. 2012. "Recent Successes." http://ufw.org/_board.php?b_code=about_suc#5756. Accessed March 3, 2012.

U.S. Department of Labor. 2010. "The National Agricultural Workers Survey." www.doleta.gov/agworker/naws.cfm. Accessed March 3, 2012.

Viertel, Josh. 2011. "We Are All Farmworkers." *The Atlantic,* March 2. www
.theatlantic.com/health/archive/2011/03/we-are-all-farmworkers/71951/.
Accessed March 2, 2012.

Walker, Richard A. 2004. *The Conquest of Bread: 150 Years of Agribusiness in California.* New York: The New Press.

Wells, Miriam. 1996. *Strawberry Fields: Politics, Class, and Work in California Agriculture.* Ithaca, NY: Cornell University Press.

Wirth, Cathy, Ron Strochlic, and Christy Getz. 2007. "Hunger in the Fields: Food
Insecurity among Farmworkers in Fresno County." Davis: California Institute
for Rural Studies.

PART THREE

Collective Practices

EIGHT

Collective Purchase

FOOD COOPERATIVES AND THEIR PURSUIT OF JUSTICE

Andrew Zitcer

SHOPPING FOR FOOD IS AN everyday spatial practice. People animate city streets and suburban shopping centers by performing habitual acts of consumption, loading carts and cars with the things that nourish them and the people they love. Though these activities may be routine, even banal, the scale of consumer power they invoke is vast: personal consumption in the United States totaled more than $12 trillion in 2014 (Bureau of Economic Analysis 2014). Depending on how consumers manage their resources, these banal acts have the potential to either reproduce or transform existing social and economic relations (Hilton 2008).

Researchers have leveled appropriate critiques of the reliance on market-based strategies to foster meaningful change (Busa and Garder 2014; also see chapter 1, this volume). But shifting consumer habits can still be an effective constituent part—necessary, if not sufficient—in transforming the economy and society. While the purchase of certain goods supports large-scale factory farming and overfishing, other choices bolster the livelihoods of family farms, employee-owned businesses, and sustainable fisheries. Purchasing from retailers that exploit their workers—or price gouge their customers—is substantially different from supporting those that otherwise enrich their surroundings. Yet consumers may have a hard time discriminating among the variety of options in the marketplace. They must decide for themselves what it means to be an ethical consumer (Barnett et al. 2005, J. Clarke et al. 2007, N. Clarke 2008). But by banding together, they can pool resources and knowledge, using the power of collective action to exert greater influence. Consumers, working together, affect what appears on the shelves, how workers are treated, and even how goods are produced and brought to market. In order for consumer movements to maximize their reach, they need to be directed toward broader social, economic, and cultural transformation. But how can such goals be accomplished?

Consumer food cooperatives are one way to achieve these ends. They have been a part of the struggle for justice since the middle of the nineteenth century. Beginning as a response to the exploitation and excesses of the Industrial Revolution, co-ops seek to shift power back toward local ownership and consumer control. Co-ops are businesses owned and controlled by their members that distribute benefits based on use (Deller et al. 2009). They are different from stock corporations, as the shareholding owners are also the users of the firm's goods and services. They are different from nonprofits in that they seek to be financially self-sustaining without outside fundraising. The internationally recognized cooperative principles emphasize democratic member control, education, and concern for the broader community (International Cooperative Alliance 2013). At their best, co-ops are alternative economic spaces that complicate dominant narratives about capitalist economy and an emphasis on individual effort and achievement (Lee et al. 2008). Such narratives depict a society in which capitalism is the only available economic option—every person is compelled to maximize her income as a demonstration of personal worth. By contrast, co-ops show that other economic practices exist, and even thrive, in a capitalist framework (Gibson-Graham 2008, 1996). Co-ops can foster collective action, democratic practice, and community control of capital. However, living up to cooperative ideals is difficult in practice; the exigencies of running a thriving business can make pursuing other aims a challenge. And, in the food sector, many contemporary U.S. cooperatives are marked by their exclusivity and inaccessibility in terms of price, selection, and cultural relevance (Yee 2014, Zitcer 2014). In this chapter, I explore the efforts of cooperatives in Philadelphia to pursue their visions of social and economic justice through cooperative ideals. I assert that co-ops need to be explicitly aware of their ideological orientation, and make careful choices about how they approach their role in the economy, food system, and cultural life of their communities.

To lend credence to this assertion, I explore two co-ops in Philadelphia, Weavers Way Co-op and Mariposa Food Co-op, which have different visions of how to achieve such goals. Weavers Way is a powerful force in the retail and political landscape of Northwest Philadelphia, operating two stores that together generate $20 million in gross annual sales and employ 150 people. Weavers Way has helped seed the development of new co-ops throughout the region and has a subsidiary nonprofit organization that works on farm education. In this study, I characterize Weavers Way Co-op as a "liberal" co-op, representing the mainstream among contemporary U.S. food co-ops. It views cooperation as beneficial, perhaps preferable to capitalism, but nonetheless supports the political economic status quo through hierarchical management, sale of premium products, and cultivation of affluent customers.

I contrast Weavers Way with Mariposa Food Co-op in West Philadelphia. Mariposa has transformed from a tiny buying club in the 1970s to a significant economic force in its neighborhood over the past several years. It generates $5 million in gross sales and employs about fifty people. Unlike Weavers Way, Mariposa does not have a separate nonprofit; rather, it seeks to use the store itself as a site of activism, through educational programming and by building awareness of justice issues. I consider Mariposa a "radical" co-op, because it has committed itself to an anticapitalist agenda, workplace democracy, and grassroots local economic development. As progressive as this agenda sounds, Mariposa may not be as effective as Weavers Way in its pursuit of a cooperatively owned, just economy. At the time of this writing, Mariposa faces some management challenges; and it has a much smaller economic footprint than Weavers Way, along with significantly less in the way of programming and regional visibility.

In using the term *liberal,* I invoke doctrines skeptical of the overreliance on markets, emphasizing reciprocity and the reduction of inequality (Gaus et al. 2014). I also rely on the contemporary connotation among political progressives that *liberal* refers to those content with mere modifications to the political–economic status quo. By *radical,* I refer to those committed to uncovering systematic social, political, racial, and other forms of inequality and vowing to eradicate them through the replacement of status quo arrangements (Boggs 1989, 48–49).

In this chapter, I compare Weavers Way and Mariposa, asking whether a liberal or radical approach befits a co-op seeking to pursue justice through democratic governance, collective ownership, and community wealth building. There are a number of ways in which co-ops serve as spaces of hope (Harvey 2000) and other ways in which they fall short. I begin by profiling each of the co-ops. Then I present the perspectives of co-op stakeholders, who detail the areas of the co-ops' transformative potential and most effective strategies, which include offering quality employment and more fair distribution of economic resources. Finally, given the exclusivity of the co-ops, I discuss the limitations they face in achieving their social and economic goals. Throughout, I ask whether food cooperatives are adequately fitted to the project of justice. And if they are so fitted, should they pursue a liberal or radical path, or some combination of the two? In other words, if cooperatives represent spaces of hope, how expansive should our hope be?

THE COOPERATIVES IN PRACTICE

Philadelphia plays host to a number of cooperative enterprises, including those in housing, child care, arts, and credit unions. There are three long-standing food co-ops, and half a dozen start-ups in either the fund-raising stage or with recently opened stores. All the food co-ops in Philadelphia are consumer co-ops, which means they are owned by their members, mirroring the national trend. Worker-owned cooperatives exist in the food sector as well, but virtually all are bakeries or cafes, not grocery stores (Democracy at Work Institutes 2015). From 2009 to 2012, I undertook an ethnographic study focusing on two of the established consumer food co-ops, Weavers Way and Mariposa, and I conducted fifty-nine interviews and numerous site visits at seven other cooperatives. I also became a member of both Weavers Way and Mariposa. My research consisted of in-depth interviews, participant observation, and document review. I transcribed the interviews and coded them using qualitative-data-analysis software. All names of research participants have been changed to pseudonyms.

Co-ops have been part of the American food landscape since the mid-nineteenth century. During the 1840s, Philadelphia itself was host to the first of these stores, the Union Cooperative Association, which succeeded, in part, because it served as a community center and library as well as a store (Curl 2009). Cooperatives spread throughout the United States in the decades that followed, sometimes connected to broader movements like trade unionism, socialism, and communism (Knupfer 2013). By the 1940s, a template for mainstream food co-ops was set: stores without broader political affiliation that looked a lot like traditional supermarkets, but that were especially concerned with food labeling and fair prices, often featuring in-house dieticians or educators. Some co-ops rode the wave of suburbanization and automobile dominance, relocating to shopping centers and opening a multitude of larger-format stores.

In the 1960s and '70s, the broader transformation of society affected food co-ops as well. Frustrated by the stodginess and lack of political ambition of these "old wave" food co-ops, young people formed "new wave" co-ops that reflected their commitment to building countercultural institutions (Cox 1994, Knupfer 2013). Rather than a consistent practical program for building a new cooperative economy, many of these small co-ops prioritized organizational democracy and oppositional politics; they were explicitly utopian about both food and business (Rothschild and Whitt 1986, Zwerdling 1979). Many of these co-ops had a short shelf life—internal organizational dysfunction and broader trends in the food retail climate led to a decline of food co-ops in the 1980s. Not all disappeared, however: both Weavers Way and Mariposa have been in continuous operation since the early 1970s. In the past decade, there has been a renewed interest in food co-ops, especially in urban areas. These co-ops are working to preserve the political ambition of the 1970s co-ops while applying a lot more business acumen, but without aping capitalist arrangements.

One challenge shared by most contemporary cooperatives is the homogeneity of their membership. Many co-ops, including the ones in this chapter, are owned by white and relatively affluent members, reflecting trends in the broader alternative food movement (Guthman 2011, Slocum 2007). However, the cooperative business model and its complex history do not compel whiteness or affluence from its practitioners. When co-ops began, they were a working-class response to the oppression of industrial capitalism. In the early part of the twentieth century, various immigrant groups in America, including Finns, Italians, and Jews, relied on co-ops for food access (Knupfer 2013, 24). There is a distinguished lineage of African American food co-ops as well, in both southern and northern states (Gordon Nembhard 2014). It is only in the past few decades that some co-ops have drifted away from the mission of serving lower-income and marginalized groups—serving affluent foodies instead (for a powerful counterexample of contemporary cooperation in low-income communities, see chapter 9, this volume). This chapter will demonstrate the efforts of both co-ops to become more broadly inclusive, and offer recommendations for going further.

Weavers Way Co-op was founded in 1973 in Mount Airy, a middle-class Northwest Philadelphia neighborhood known for its pursuit of Black–white racial integration in the 1950s and beyond (Ferman and Kaylor 2000, Perkiss 2014). Weavers Way was one of a number of institutions that emerged during this period, including progressive schools, churches, and synagogues, which catered to the politically liberal, middle-class population of this section of Philadelphia. Though the co-op drew both Black and white patrons early in its history, white people tended to dominate then and still do today. A membership survey from 2013 (not a complete reflection of all shoppers, but useful nonetheless) showed 87 percent of respondents to be white, older (nearly two-thirds of respondents were more than fifty years old), longtime patrons (a quarter had been members for more than twenty years), and extraordinarily well educated (virtually all respondents had completed college, and nearly 70 percent had graduate degrees). Nearly 70 percent of respondents had a household income of more than $75,000, double Philadelphia's median household income.

For most of its history, Weavers Way required patrons to be members in order to shop, and all members had to work. In addition to functioning as a successful grocer and community gathering place, Weavers Way helped start a credit union, a health insurance co-op, and a home-heating-oil co-op. Weavers Way expanded steadily, beginning to outgrow its space by the late 1990s. But when it was ready to expand in 2002, the co-op discovered that an employee had mismanaged hundreds of thousands of dollars, halting the expansion and throwing Weavers Way into crisis. The board responded by tightening controls, asking members to make loans to the co-op, and streamlining management. The co-op rebounded and continued to grow. After a failed attempt to operate a co-op in a predominantly working-class, African American neighborhood near Mount Airy (as discussed below), the co-op successfully expanded in 2010 to Chestnut Hill, one of the most affluent areas of the city. Today, Weavers Way operates two branches and is in the process of looking for a third location. Though it still has a working member program, Weavers Way no longer requires membership or member labor. The co-op has a robust outreach and education program, operates farms and gardens, supports the development of new co-ops in the region, and chartered a subsidiary nonprofit organization to expand the scope of its impact.

Weavers Way is managed hierarchically by a strong general manager, assisted by department managers, as well as an administrative staff that includes personnel working in human resources, marketing and outreach, membership, and purchasing. There is a ten-member board of directors that represents the membership, and there are annual board elections and semiannual membership meetings, where members give voice to any concerns. Weavers Way is owned by approximately five thousand member households. Most contemporary food co-ops in the United States work this way, managed hierarchically like any other natural food store or small business. The board of Weavers Way employs policy governance, a system popular among food co-ops, which gives considerable latitude to the general manager (Carver

1997). Policy governance requires only that the general manager meet certain predetermined goals in terms of sales, product philosophy, and management. These goals are called "ends," and the means of getting there are at the general manager's discretion.

The co-op employs a fairly weak system of representative democracy, and recently a longtime member complained in the Weavers Way newsletter, the *Shuttle,* that the board is not interested in member input and leaves it up to the general manager to run the co-op. The article was provocatively titled "Long-Time Member Asks: Are We Still a Co-op?" (Bonn 2015). The governance model used by Weavers Way (and common to many food co-ops) places a firewall between the staff and the board. All staff matters are to be addressed by the general manager and his or her deputies. In one board meeting I attended, a staff member who was on the board openly confronted the general manager about operational practices, leading to an uncomfortable conflict. The board sided with the general manager. The staff member left the board soon after, and there is no staff member on the board today.

Weavers Way is liberal in character. The co-op takes left-leaning positions on issues like genetically modified food and support for local farmers. But Weavers Way is hardly agitating for wholesale societal change, and it does not model progressive politics in the way the organization is run. In contrast to Weavers Way, Mariposa Food Co-op staff and members participate in more progressive activism around issues of food justice, advancing queer issues, and other left political goals. Though the co-ops sell many of the same products, behind the scenes there are differences.

Mariposa Food Co-op, founded in 1971, is located in the mixed-income, mixed-race West Philadelphia neighborhood of Cedar Park. Despite the diversity of the neighborhood, Mariposa members are overwhelmingly white (80 percent of respondents to a 2015 member survey), young (80 percent fifty or under), extremely well educated (82 percent holding a four-year-college or advanced degree), but not wealthy (77 percent making less than $80,000 per year, the inverse of Weavers Way). Also notable is the presence of a relatively large number of respondents (3 percent) identifying as transgender (in contrast to 1 percent at Weavers Way).

The co-op grew out of the Movement for a New Society, an anarchist organization that split from the American Friends Service Committee and operated feminist radical-pacifist collectives in the 1970s and '80s (Cornell 2009). Based in Philadelphia, the organization helped launch the food co-op as well as a community land trust and a worker-owned print shop. For the first few decades, Mariposa operated as a small buyer's club where people ordered produce and other goods in advance and picked them up at a tiny West Philadelphia storefront. Eventually the pickup location became more of a grocer, with staple items (usually) in stock. There were, however, a number of practices that differentiated Mariposa from a typical grocer. Shopping in the store required membership, which entailed both an equity (ownership) investment and annual dues. Members also had to work a few hours per month in the store, usually stocking shelves or serving as cashier. The hours the co-op was open were limited, but members could let themselves in with a key and shop after hours, recording their purchases in a ledger, on the honor system. Within a few years of opening, the store began to have a few part-time employees to support member labor. The co-op grew slowly until the late 1990s, when gentrification began to take hold in the neighborhood (Etienne 2013) just as interest in local and organic food began to rise. Mariposa began to plan an expansion, which occurred in 2012. The co-op moved to a former bank building and lifted the restrictions on membership and mandatory labor. Since then, it has expanded its offerings, its staff, and its hours; Mariposa's sales have grown apace.

Today, Mariposa has over 1,500 member households. The co-op employs about fifty people and generates over $5 million in annual sales. The administrative staff, though smaller than that of Weavers Way, supports positions in purchasing, membership, marketing, and outreach. Unlike Weavers Way, Mariposa operates as a collective consisting of all staff. An operations committee made up of department managers supports the staff collective. There is a board, instituted only five years before this study, and it sets some policy for co-op activities, in areas like human resources. At all levels, from membership meetings to the board to the staff, decisions are made using consensus. This democratic arrangement means that all staff members, including entry-level cashiers, have a voice in the way the co-op is run.

There are considerable challenges to Mariposa's model. The first is that Mariposa has a relatively weak board, leaving both operational and strategic decisions mostly in the hands of the staff (which can be problematic when there is staff turnover). The second is that democratic self-management is hard to practice and sustain. There have been conflicts among staff members, and there is an implied hierarchy between the "upstairs" staff, who manage departments like finance, information technology, and education, and the floor staff, who stock shelves and assist customers. Despite the implied hierarchy, there is no difference in compensation between the more experienced managers and new entrants to the staff—a factor that drives turnover and burnout. In late 2014, Mariposa staff and membership agreed to ask two staff members to oversee the staff in lieu of running by consensus. One of the staff members is responsible for store operations; the other manages organizational development, education, and so forth. Mariposa's goal is to return to completely collective management after a year of planning and inquiry, but it is unclear whether, once a co-op embraces some level of hierarchical management, it can ever go back.

Neither co-op has completely solved the challenge of running a member-owned cooperative business. Weavers Way, in its use of managers to run the business, is efficient but encourages less member engagement. Mariposa, a radical proponent of direct democracy, encourages—requires, even—a higher level of participation. But this newly expanded co-op is still struggling with growing pains and the challenge of consensus-based management. Both are in flux: Weavers Way is working to be accountable to members on the issues of price and transparency, and Mariposa is experimenting with a bit of hierarchy in pursuit of a more sustainable organization.

MORE THAN JUST GROCERIES

Mariposa and Weavers Way differ in the activities they prioritize beyond their grocery operations. Overall, Weavers Way is able to generate broader awareness of relevant social and environmental issues through its programming and outreach, though its message is rather mainstream, focused on incremental change to existing systems. Mariposa, while promoting an agenda that calls for greater transformation, is limited by its organizational capacity, making its current reach somewhat questionable.

Weavers Way fulfills its vision through a related nonprofit organization, Weavers Way Community Programs (WWCP). Founded in 2007, WWCP supports the education programs that occur at Weavers Way's farm and gardens, as well as supporting school-based, student-run co-ops in several Philadelphia schools. Each year, thousands of school-age children benefit from WWCP's farm education programs. One of the gardens is located at a family homeless shelter, where residents learn to grow, harvest, and prepare their own fresh food. The school-based co-op marketplace program teaches young people about cooperative economics and basic business skills, as well as promoting healthy eating in the school. Being a nonprofit allows WWCP to raise money to support programs, so the co-op does not have to subsidize them. Co-op members are able to donate at the cash register to the nonprofit, and there are periodic drives within the co-op to get members to contribute to the nonprofit. The lack of direct funding from the co-op cuts both ways: it demonstrates sound financial stewardship of financial resources, but it limits the scope of what can be accomplished by WWCP. (The same is true of Weavers Way's farm operations: the co-op requires that the farms break even, pushing the farmers to sell produce at farmers markets' in higher-income neighborhoods, rather than selling the produce for less at the co-op itself.)

The staff and board of Weavers Way itself are also quite active in programming and outreach. Most of these efforts involve food and/or environmental causes, such as on-site beekeeping, electronics recycling, a farmers' market, and more. Most notable is the *Shuttle,* a full-color, twenty-four-page, monthly newsletter featuring original articles contributed by members as well as community and co-op events. The *Shuttle* is distributed around the neighborhood, not just to co-op member households. It serves for many as their local paper. Mariposa has no equivalent; it relies on periodic emails to update its members and has no paper version for non-member shoppers to peruse at the store.

Mariposa works at a much smaller scale, attempting to integrate its activism into the store itself. Through member education efforts and a Food Justice and Anti-Racism Committee, Mariposa works to educate members and people from the neighborhood about cooperation, racism and other forms of oppression, and food justice, mostly through evening meetings at the store. These efforts are not well publicized and are probably less visible to shoppers than Weavers Way's programs. However, the co-op has an extensive lending library and hosts events, such as a workshop in February 2014 that explored racism in the co-op. That event drew a capacity crowd, diverse in age, gender expression, and racial composition, to the co-op's small meeting space. There are study circles composed of members who read on food justice and other topics, though their reports to the broader co-op have been inconsistent. In its communications and outreach, Mariposa positions itself as more radical than Weavers Way, with the store (as opposed to a separate nonprofit) more central to its pursuit of social and economic transformation. Though it partners with a local farm and a couple of school-based programs, Mariposa does not have the level of dedicated staff or oversight that WWCP provides. This reflects the oppositional origins of Mariposa as a low-to-the-ground, activist buying club, not initially concerned with building an institution (Rothschild and Whitt 1986). The offerings of Weavers Way, though they are focused on less confrontational topics surrounding food, are more robust and comprehensive. But perhaps, given Mariposa's recent rapid expansion, it will grow an organizational capacity to rival that of Weavers Way.

SPACES OF HOPE

Now that I have drawn a picture of the two co-ops and their differences, I will outline the ways in which both co-ops inspire hope, even when that hope is not yet fulfilled. I will focus on the benefits of co-ops to local ownership, and their ability to serve as good employers and to expand food access. Afterward, I will detail ways in which the co-ops serve as spaces of exclusion, largely around dimensions of race, ethnicity, and age. Throughout the following sections, I will foreground the perspectives of a variety of co-op stakeholders, all speaking from their specific experience in the cooperative movement.

Democratic and Local Ownership of Cooperatives

One of the defining features of both Mariposa and Weavers Way is democratic, local ownership. Even though Weavers Way operates more than one branch, it is owned by members who hail from the store's home neighborhoods. James, the communications director of Weavers Way, concludes that the remote ownership of big-box stores is detrimental to local communities. Co-ops, in contrast, keep the money and the decision making local. He sees a positive trend in people's awareness of the benefits of cooperatives versus the Walmarts of the world:

> People have seen the negative impact that big-box stores can have on communities and this whole backlash against Walmart and those types of stores where basically you spend your money at a store and it leaves the community immediately, whereas with the co-op, it's owned by the members and the members live in the community. . . . The money's not going anywhere. It's not perfect but it's much better.

Walmart stores are a feature of many communities, but the ownership is neither local nor collectively owned. This presents two challenges to community empowerment. The first is related to democratic control: multinational corporations have tremendous difficulty being democratically managed in a way that empowers local workers and consumers in the decision-making process. This can result in policies that are good for owners and bad for workers—or good for consumers but bad for the planet. The second challenge, which affects economic justice, is that the money these corporations generate does not stay local. This is not to argue that the world only has room for small, local businesses. However, if community empowerment is the goal, locally owned and democratically managed businesses are an important tool.

In contrast to the local Philadelphia food co-ops, the wealth that Walmart generates leaves the communities where the workers reside and fills the coffers of the Walton family, based in Arkansas. In 2013, the Waltons had a fortune that equaled the wealth of the bottom 42 percent of Americans (Kertscher 2013). The wages at Walmart are so low that employees rely on government assistance to the tune of billions of dollars (O'Connor 2014). A co-op, by contrast, is both local and community controlled: it is accountable to a group of citizens, ensuring that the co-op lives up to its principles and distributes any proceeds to the people who work and shop there.

Owning the grocer means that members can get the things that they want, regardless of whether a capitalist firm sees a worthwhile market opportunity in them. That can mean the types of products on the shelves, the training and compensation of the employees in the aisles, the co-op's hours, and more. Both Weavers Way and Mariposa support small and local artisanal producers who do not achieve the scale necessary to be noticed by a chain grocer, as well as cooperative and fair trade agricultural products that may carry an "ethical premium" in their pricing (Soper 2007). Both co-ops also encourage members to buy in bulk and to special-order products they don't find on the shelves, which consumes staff resources that larger stores might not wish to provide. And members (at Mariposa especially) have begun to advocate for the board of directors to improve the overall compensation and training for workers, in solidarity with worker demands.

Local ownership also means local governance and all of the challenges and opportunities contained therein. The difference in relationship to cooperatives versus corporations is inscribed even in the language. Mariposa member Miriam explains the different feeling that comes over her as she shops at her local food co-op:

> When you walk in, you are like, "I own this place!" There is something to be said for "What do we have?" Not "What do you have?" Just difference in language, but it's significant. And it's indicative of people feeling an ownership stake in the co-op.

Participating in a community-owned co-op means that serious decisions are up to the membership. Co-ops, often small, still have the potential to meet the needs of their members and their communities. Mariposa employee Siobhan explains:

> I think that it's really important to retain that sense of democratic ownership of something. Otherwise, it's like, "I'm a little voice, nobody can hear me!" But together we have a loud shout.

This "loud shout" speaks to the sense of empowerment that co-op members feel regarding the food they buy and sell. The "loud shout" is audible only when there is someone there to hear it, which necessitates that the people in charge hold themselves accountable to local needs. In a marketplace that can be characterized by a race to the bottom in terms of wages, prices, and quality, co-ops are a hopeful bulwark. Yet there are limitations here as well. The first is the assumption that anything local is inherently just, when local businesses (including local food producers and retailers) can be just as exploitative as their corporate counterparts (Born and Purcell 2006). Another way co-ops can fall short is that the small group of people who constitute their membership can often be quite homogeneous and therefore exclusive. This is true of the co-ops in question, though Mariposa especially is making efforts to change its internal composition. But there is a danger here—a co-op existing in a mixed-income and mixed-race area that does not share those characteristics may meet its "collective needs" without meeting the needs of its neighbors.

Co-op as Employer

Cooperatives have the potential to be better workplaces than traditional, for-profit grocers. The co-op movement overall pays better than the supermarket industry, with many more employers offering fringe benefits (National Cooperative Grocers Association 2012). Co-ops often have a smaller gap between the highest- and lowest-paid employees (Jaffe 2015). Weavers Way, in particular, prides itself on paying its workers above market rate and offering comprehensive benefits, including health insurance. Weavers Way employee Gerald recognizes the advantage of working for a co-op, contrasting his co-op employer with conventional grocers:

> [We] have that mentality that we are not doing this to line somebody's pocket. We want to pay people living wages; we want to respect the people who are

here, who are [also] owners, and I think that also is a motivating factor, that we have an invested stake in the future of the co-op. That you wouldn't get if you were just working for "the man" at some grocery store.

Gerald recognizes that staff members are also owners of the co-op and have a financial stake in the success of the co-op, as a business and as a community project. This relationship is more complicated than a strict employer–employee relationship. By contrast, some employees have had similar experiences working at other health food stores that were not co-ops. One employee compares working in a for-profit health food store in Philadelphia to working at Mariposa:

> [Mentions name of local health food store] I am really ready to trash them. I worked there for a little over a year, which is an extremely long time. Probably twenty employees came and went in the time I was there. Their turnover rate is extremely high and the reason it's extremely high is because they pay a little over minimum wage, their pay rates are super low. You're probably better off working at a chain grocery store.
>
> The bullshit just became really clear after a while: "Oh, we're this macrobiotic place and here's this whole philosophy and we do everything here around this philosophy." And then they were lying and misrepresenting about the food they were making and how they were making it.

This person goes on to explain the incident that finally made it time to leave:

> And this was a minor thing but it was a sign of what was frustrating me all along. They would ask us—they had bulk goods in containers or baked goods in containers that had a date printed on them, and they would just ask you to re-date them when they were coming up to expiration—just put a new sticker on it. I was just, "I'm not doing this."

The image of employees putting new dates on expired food recalls the sort of behavior that the earliest cooperators protested in the nineteenth century (Birchall 1994). Whether it is the adulteration of ingredients, the thumb on the scale, or the food being sold past its sell-by date, mistreatment of employees and customers has occurred since the earliest days of the grocery business.

It is clear why employment relationships at the co-op are different than in other places the staff person had worked: the co-op itself is structured differently than a traditional grocer. When staff members are also part owner of the enterprise, the relationship is much more complex. This dual affiliation can lead to greater feelings of attachment to the business and lower turnover.

It can also lead to disgruntlement when things are not going well. This tension arose at Mariposa around the issue of wages and overall job satisfaction among the new, larger staff. Operating margins in grocers are notoriously thin, and Mariposa has struggled to retain highly trained managers, since hourly wages are roughly the same at Mariposa regardless of responsibilities or prior training. The collective management structure has also been seen as cumbersome and not well implemented, leading floor staff to feel unheard, which is especially problematic in an organization that considers organizational democracy a cardinal value.

Fresh-Food Availability

In addition to creating jobs, co-ops can also establish new stores in places that did not have grocers before, or where grocers have departed. Urban co-ops particularly have worked to alleviate the lack of fresh food available, including recent efforts in Greensboro, North Carolina, and Minneapolis, Minnesota. The early, smaller version of the Mariposa Co-op was located in a designated "food desert" until Mariposa's own expansion and increased sales helped the neighborhood lose that designation. Funders have been attracted to Mariposa's and Weavers Way's mission of providing access to healthy food. I asked Sarah, who ran Mariposa's capital campaign during its expansion, why a major funder gave money to a then marginal co-op. Food access was her answer: "You can argue [that] this is an incredibly mixed-wealth community, but it is technically a food desert." There are a variety of definitions for the term *food desert* (Raja et al. 2008, Walker et al. 2010), but the core of the idea revolves around inadequate access to food, based on either the quantity of nearby retailers or the quality of the products available.

The idea of a "food desert" has been criticized by scholars for stigmatizing certain bodies and neighborhoods as morally deficient (Shannon 2014; chapter 1, this volume). The fit, white body is the standard against which all people are judged, and food access is generally adequate for those people. Certainly, many of today's co-op shoppers conform to that image. In the case of Weavers Way, the co-op received low-cost loans and grants to expand to Chestnut Hill, one of the wealthiest neighborhoods in Philadelphia. The rationale used by the co-op's funders is that the urban retail market is not sufficiently served (even in some wealthy neighborhoods), and that Weavers Way can help fill that gap. But this expansion to a wealthy neighborhood does little to assuage the problems of food access experienced disproportionately by low-income communities and communities of color. And Weavers Way's biggest effort to serve these communities (a branch in the West Oak Lane neighborhood of Philadelphia) ended with the co-op pulling out after only three years.

Nevertheless, some co-ops strive to embrace the food-access mission in their communities. For example, a branch of discount grocer Bottom Dollar was welcomed into Ambler, Pennsylvania, in 2013, raising hopes for new jobs and food availability. Just a year later, Bottom Dollar announced the immediate shuttering of all thirty-two of its stores. The nascent Ambler Food Co-op intends to pick up the slack (Quigley 2014). When fresh food is made newly available under community control, the options for residents can diversify and expand. Residents can tailor and scale the operation to suit their needs, and not the needs of remote or disinterested shareholders.

SPACES OF EXCLUSION

Despite the hopeful prospects of co-ops as conveners of community, local owners of capital, creators of good jobs, and providers of quality food, there are still shortcomings in the way cooperation is often enacted. Co-ops like Weavers Way and Mariposa are often sites of exclusion around class, race, and other factors. Food co-ops face an overall paradox of exclusivity, in which co-ops need to maintain a coherent sense of group affiliation yet not discriminate against outsiders (Zitcer 2014). If the co-op's identity is too open and undefined, it is just another grocery store; there is no incentive to become a member and commit to the project. There needs to be a sense of group affiliation to keep people interested. But if too many of the same kind of people come together to support a co-op, it can lead to feelings of exclusion for anyone who is different. When co-ops are meant to support a certain group, like the immigrant-run stores of the 1920s, this may not be a problem. But in today's multicultural urban landscape, co-ops usually strive to represent the diversity they see around them, and they do not always succeed.

Achieving diversity of ages, races, classes, and incomes is a purported goal of both Weavers Way and Mariposa, but each tackles these issues a bit differently. In 2008, Weavers Way made a notable step to move beyond its demographic boundaries by opening a store in West Oak Lane, a working-class, African American neighborhood. That co-op lasted only three years, suffering from low sales and an apparent lack of connection to the neighbors. But interviewees at Weavers Way did not seem to understand that what went wrong might implicate the co-op as well as the neighborhood—that perhaps the co-op had not developed the proper relationships or thought about how it might be perceived as exclusive or out of reach. Instead, they evinced an "if they only knew what was good for them" mentality toward the neighbors (Guthman 2011). More than one person I interviewed believed that if the co-op had sold junk food and cigarettes, it would have stayed in business— that such commodities are the only things people in that neighborhood purchase. By contrast, Mariposa speaks much more openly about wanting to represent the diversity of West Philadelphia. And it has made strides to do so, such as surveying neighbors to determine the food it should sell, and running membership drives with incentives for low-income families and youth. But memories in the neighborhood are long, and as recently as a few years ago (in the old, smaller store), it alienated members of the community by not accepting cash (only credit or checks) and having a sign on the door that said "Don't let random people into the co-op." In retrospect, those actions seem clearly exclusionary, but at the time the co-op let them persist.

Another way to relate (or fail to relate) to the broader community is through young people. The two co-ops also differ here. Mariposa's staff and board are very excited about getting young people involved in co-ops, to create the next generation of co-op members and leaders. Mariposa recently instituted a youth membership policy that allows people aged fourteen to seventeen to join the co-op, receive discounts, and serve on committees. Weavers Way has school programs, but it is not necessarily as comfortable with young people shopping in the store, especially during after-school hours. One of Weavers Way's branches is across the street from an elementary school, and it has sporadically had problems with students. One Weavers Way board member, Cynthia, relates a story about young people coming into the co-op:

> When Henry School let out [for the day] and a child came to the doors of Weavers Way, managers were closing up the door to say, "Are you a member?" And if you said your parents were a member, you could come in. Well, the African American kids' parents were not members, so they were not allowed in. Well, one of my nephew's children, young son, came home and told his father—this is a mixed child, his father is African American, his mother is white—came home and said "Daddy, they won't let us in the co-op. They don't let the Black kids come in." ... We were busy ... selling the lettuce and the bread, the bottom line, were busy taking care of the needs of the co-op, and the immediate community, we forgot that Henry School also was a neighbor.

This exclusion led to the creation of WWCP and the school marketplace programs. Other stakeholders spoke with pride about the steps the co-op has taken to engage young people—yet not as fully empowered members of the co-op.

Also related to building an inclusive co-op is the hiring of staff. Recently, Mariposa explored the tension between its radicalism and its business objectives during a staff hiring process. The two finalists for the position were a seasoned natural foods worker who was white and a young community organizer of color. The personnel committee found the decision difficult and had trouble agreeing. Should they hire for experience in selling food, or should they hire someone who had intercultural experience dealing with class analysis and organizing? Mariposa employee Tom thought that the path forward was clear regarding the more conventional natural foods applicant:

> She had this incredible experience but . . . she was probably mid-thirties and a white woman and she seemed very typical in that way. Very white culture, very natural foods industry, which is something I think we are trying to not be totally consumed by.

The co-op decided to hire the young woman of color, whom they felt subsequently made a substantial contribution to the co-op's strategic direction. However, she left the co-op after a short stint, feeling that, despite its radical rhetoric, Mariposa was insufficiently progressive when it came to race. Would the other applicant have stayed longer and grown into her position at Mariposa?

Weavers Way also struggles with diversity and inclusion in hiring. The co-op's human resources manager, Jack, reinforces the impression that co-ops are a pretty white world. He describes a human resources conference for food cooperatives that he attended, where there was not one person of color in the room. He asserts that the gathering was less diverse than any such meeting he has been to in other sectors. The lack of diversity in the food co-op world is reflected by the staff at many co-ops, not just the hiring managers. Jack works hard to diversify the co-op, but it is not as simple as it seems:

> It is one thing to create a diverse applicant pool; it is another thing to create a diverse workplace. There are people that are naturally inclined and really want to work at the co-op. I could show you my inbox. They are smart, they are often college educated; they often come with great experience. Maybe they worked at Whole Foods or they worked at another co-op, or a farmers' market or whatever. And they really, really want to work at the co-op and

they will represent us extremely well. They will be passionate about the apples that we sell or the different kinds of meats that we have in our meat department. . . . And that group is overwhelmingly white.

And it is hard when you are talking about presenting candidates to department managers to present: "On the one hand is this really, really great person who is really into the co-op, who will do just about anything to work here. And then the other person, who comes from the neighborhood, who also has some decent experience, worked at Acme for a couple of years, or wherever." How do you sort of tap into the labor force that isn't naturally inclined to seek out our kind of organization as an employer, do you know what I am saying?

Jack's dilemma is getting the hiring department to step out of their comfort zone and hire people who do not have as much natural foods experience. He stated that opening another co-op in Chestnut Hill gave Weavers Way an opportunity to bring in many more people of color to the new positions. And Mariposa has worked quite consciously to hire people from the neighborhood and people who represent all manner of diversity, from age to race to gender. But as with Mariposa's previous example, putting together a staff that will last and contribute to the co-op in the long term is a nontrivial challenge.

Mariposa and Weavers Way work hard to support their members, and each creates a meaningful cooperative contrast to the extremes of capitalism. But there are many roadblocks, particularly when it comes to exclusivity. Whether liberal or radical, co-ops like these may desire members and staff from across the economic, racial, and cultural spectrum but have trouble attracting and retaining them. In the next section, I summarize and contrast the two co-ops' approaches.

LIBERAL AND RADICAL APPROACHES TO COOPERATION

Both Weavers Way and Mariposa have recently made encouraging strides toward inclusion. Weavers Way recently announced a program to offer storewide discounts to people who demonstrate financial hardship. Mariposa has a member equity fund that subsidizes member ownership for people with low incomes. Both co-ops, along with many of their peers, have begun to use the markup on higher-profit-margin items, like health and beauty products, to subsidize the prices on staple goods. And as these co-ops grow, their purchasing power increases and prices can fall. In 2014, both co-ops cut prices on a slew of items. Along with other co-ops in the region, they have chartered the member organization Philadelphia Area Cooperative Alliance (PACA), designed to foster the growth of the local cooperative economy. It is their hope that PACA can do the cooperative education, organizing, and development that busy grocers do not have the time or capacity to do.

Yet distinct differences between the two co-ops remain, and it is worth examining which philosophy (or what combination) most suits the pursuit of justice more broadly. Weavers Way is like a lot of co-ops in America, with relatively affluent shoppers, premium goods, and hierarchical management. Member participation in governance is limited and the board yields considerable power to the general manager. Their approach has paid off: the co-op is retiring debt from its expansion early, and it is seeking to open a third, much larger branch in the next few years. Weavers Way Community Program struggles like many nonprofit organizations but continues to obtain recognition for its outreach and education activities. The co-op now employs 150 people and contributes to the local economy. Because of its stability, Weavers Way can support other co-ops as they emerge or try to expand (including some very timely help offered to Mariposa to open its expanded store). Through it all, Weavers Way is a thoroughly liberal organization; it is content to serve as an example at the margins of capitalism, hopefully disciplining the market with its good behavior and clean conscience. It is really good at what it does and is, without a doubt, the strongest grocery co-op in the region.

But not everyone is satisfied with how Weavers Way has evolved in recent years. In 2011 the co-op stopped operating its branch in West Oak Lane after several years of financial losses, as discussed above. This move left some people frustrated that the co-op had not commited sufficiently to community outreach and organizing in West Oak Lane; it had failed to engage in even a modicum of democratic inclusion with the neighbors. It also didn't help that Weavers Way was simultaneously expanding to the wealthiest neighborhood in the city (that branch has succeeded financially beyond all expectations). In addition, the co-op's fiscal conservatism, even in a time of record-breaking sales, has led to tension about the status of the co-op's farms and its nonprofit, which do important work but don't get to take advantage of the co-op's stronger financial position. Finally, there has been a vigorous debate in the pages of the *Shuttle* recently about Weavers Way's commitment to affordability, democratic process, and broad inclusion. Recently, members have taken the rare step of calling for meetings to discuss prices at the co-op, as well as the prudence of expansion. They are working to hold the management and board accountable for what they see as a distortion of the co-op's historical commitments.

Mariposa is substantially different, both from Weavers Way and from most established co-ops in the United States. It is staunchly radical in its rhetoric about race, gender, age, and economics. As former employee Sam related, "[Some staff] took the position that, yeah, we might sell groceries—but we are a political organization—*that's* what we do, but we happen to do it by selling groceries." The co-op is committed to democratic worker self-management (taking into account the recent adjustments to the management structure). Since its expansion from a tiny storefront three years ago, it strives for economic and social inclusion, though sometimes it falls short of achieving this. Members and staff have braved the exhausting process of consensus in order to craft policies for youth and low-income membership. Yet the co-op is far from perfect. Recent membership meetings have uncovered significant burnout and dissatisfaction within the staff. There is a brewing schism between highly educated and trained staff and managers and those who are coming in with entry-level skills. In addition, the co-op's expansive goals for societal transformation are not matched by a concomitant roster of workshops, events, and programming. Only those members most closely involved with Mariposa's inner workings are likely to know about the co-op's long-standing and deeply held political convictions. Indeed, without an organ like the *Shuttle* in place, it is possible that the only reason I know so much about the co-op's political commitments is through attending membership meetings and interviewing stakeholders.

So what is the best way for a co-op to organize if a just society is its aim? Can a co-op like Mariposa successfully agitate against systems of oppression if its democratic management structure undermines employee morale? Can Weavers Way produce meaningful social change if its efforts stop short of calling for wholesale transformation? Advocates can learn something from both of these successful organizations and perhaps produce some hybrid of the two approaches. From Mariposa, it seems worthwhile to retain a critical analysis of race, class, and gender. That upending of convention must influence the way business is conducted at the co-op. Again, a co-op, when successful, can serve as a precursor to a more just set of institutional arrangements. But democracy at work does not have to mean total reliance on consensus and complete lack of hierarchy. It may mean that the co-op installs qualified management, with ongoing and substantive input from staff and accountability for managers. Growing the rest of what it means to be a co-op is a critical pursuit, and that should grow as the co-op does. There is an opportunity for a co-op of Weavers Way's size to do more provocative programming and outreach than it does (and maybe that will evolve with the recent creation of a Food Justice Committee by the board).

Finally, justice does not only need to emanate from the co-op's walls. The work that Weavers Way and Mariposa have done to build the regional group PACA may yield successes that neither co-op could produce on its own. Co-ops in federation are much stronger than any one individual organization. Already, PACA is exploring a cooperative leadership institute, as well as supporting new co-ops in development throughout the region. Strong co-ops have the ability to nourish individual members, literally and figuratively. One interviewee emphasized that co-ops can serve as nodes for the gathering of people who engage in meaningful advocacy and activism in the rest of their lives. The co-op is something that unites them and helps them take care of banal, quotidian needs. But shopping at the co-op should nevertheless provide them food for thought as well as food for the body.

In conclusion, the importance of co-ops lies first in their ability to transform governance and ownership in the food system. As much as advocates for transforming work or land tenure into cooperatives believe in this worthwhile goal, transforming the sites of consumption to be more accountable and democratic should be thought of as a logical next step. The dollars we use to shop are at our discretion and can be redeployed without remaking our lives completely. Successfully changing consumption in turn affects production and distribution of goods. But consumption without critical awareness of injustice is an incomplete recipe for economic and social amelioration. A vital, collectively controlled piece of the economy that manages to be broadly inclusive and politically vocal provides good purchase for communities seeking to transform themselves for the better.

REFERENCES

Barnett, Clive, Paul Cloke, Nick Clarke, and Alice Malpass. 2005. "Consuming Ethics: Articulating the Subjects and Spaces of Ethical Consumption." *Antipode* 37: 23–45.

Birchall, Johnston. 1994. *Co-Op, the People's Business.* Manchester, UK: Manchester University Press.

Boggs, Carl. 1989. *Social Movements and Political Power: Emerging Forms of Radicalism in the West.* Philadelphia: Temple University Press.

Bonn, Anne. 2015. "Long-Time Member Asks: Are We Still a Co-Op?" *Weavers Way Shuttle,* January.

Born, Branden, and Mark Purcell. 2006. "Avoiding the Local Trap Scale and Food Systems in Planning Research." *Journal of Planning Education and Research* 26: 195–207.

Bureau of Economic Analysis. 2014. "Gross Domestic Product: Third Quarter 2014 (Third Estimate)." Washington, DC: U.S. Department of Commerce. www.bea .gov/newsreleases/national/gdp/2014/pdf/gdp3q14_3rd.pdf.

Busa, Julianne H., and Rebekah Garder. 2014. "Champions of the Movement or Fair-Weather Heroes? Individualization and the (A)politics of Local Food." *Antipode* 47: 323–341.

Carver, John. 1997. *Boards That Make a Difference : A New Design for Leadership in Nonprofit and Public Organizations.* San Francisco, Ca: Jossey-Bass.

Clarke, John, Janet Newman, Nick Smith, Elizabeth Vidler, and Louise Westmarland, Eds. 2007. *Creating Citizen–Consumers: Changing Publics & Changing Public Services.* London: Thousand SAGE.

Clarke, Nick. 2008. "From Ethical Consumerism to Political Consumption." *Geography Compass* 2: 1870–1884.

Cornell, Andrew. 2009. "Anarchism and the Movement for a New Society: Direct Action and Prefigurative Community in the 1970s and 80s." *Perspectives on Anarchist Theory.* www.anarchiststudies.org/node/292.

Cox, Craig. 1994. *Storefront Revolution: Food Co-Ops and the Counterculture.* New Brunswick, NJ: Rutgers University Press.

Curl, John. 2009. *For All the People: Uncovering the Hidden History of Cooperation, Cooperative Movements, and Communalism in America.* Oakland, CA: PM Press.

Deller, Steven, Ann Hoyt, Brent Hueth, and Reka Sundaram-Stukel. 2009. "Research on the Economic Impact of Cooperatives." University of Wisconsin Center for Cooperatives. http://sowtheseedsfund.com/iatp/files/258_2_105752 .pdf.

Democracy at Work Institutes. 2015. "US Worker Cooperatives: A State of the Sector." Oakland, CA: U.S. Federation of Worker Cooperatives. http://institute .usworker.coop/sites/default/files/State_of_the_sector.pdf.

Etienne, Harley F. 2013. *Pushing Back the Gates: Neighborhood Perspectives on University-Driven Revitalization in West Philadelphia,* reprint edition. Philadelphia: Temple University Press.

Ferman, Barbara, and Patrick Kaylor. 2000. "The Role of Institutions in Community Building: The Case of West Mt. Airy, Philadelphia." In *Nonprofits in Urban America,* ed. Richard C. Hula and Cynthia Jackson-Elmoore, 93–120. Westport, CT: Quorum Books.

Gaus, Gerald, Shane D. Courtland, and David Schmidtz. 2014. "Liberalism." In *The Stanford Encyclopedia of Philosophy Archive,* ed. Edward N. Zalta. http://plato .stanford.edu/archives/spr2015/entries/liberalism/.

Gibson-Graham, J. K. 1996. *The End of Capitalism (As We Knew It): A Feminist Critique of Political Economy.* Minneapolis: University of Minnesota Press.

———. 2008. "Diverse Economies: Performative Practices for 'Other Worlds.'" *Progress in Human Geography* 32: 613–632.

Gordon Nembhard, Jessica. 2014. *Collective Courage: A History of African American Cooperative Economic Thought and Practice.* University Park, PA: Penn State University Press.

Guthman, Julie. 2011. "'If They Only Knew': The Unbearable Whiteness of Alternative Food." In *Cultivating Food Justice: Race, Class, and Sustainability,* ed. Alison Hope Alkon and Julian Agyeman, 278–296. Cambridge, MA: MIT Press.

Harvey, David. 2000. *Spaces of Hope.* Berkeley: University of California Press.

Hilton, Matthew. 2008. "The Banality of Consumption." In *Citizenship and Consumption,* ed. Kate Soper and Frank Trentmann, 87–103. New York: Palgrave Macmillan.

International Cooperative Alliance. 2013. "Co-Operative Identity, Values & Principles." http://ica.coop/en/what-co-op/co-operative-identity-values-principles. Accessed January 28, 2013.

Jaffe, Sarah. 2015. "Can Worker Cooperatives Alleviate Income Inequality?" *Al Jazeera America,* January 13. http://america.aljazeera.com/articles/2015/1/13/worker-run-cooperatives.html.

Kertscher, Tom. 2013. "Just How Wealthy Is the Wal-Mart Walton Family?" *Politifact,* December 8. www.politifact.com/wisconsin/statements/2013/dec/08/one-wisconsin-now/just-how-wealthy-wal-mart-walton-family/.

Knupfer, Anne Meis. 2013. *Food Co-Ops in America: Communities, Consumption, and Economic Democracy.* Ithaca, NY: Cornell University Press.

Lee, Roger, Andrew Leyshon, and Adrian Smith. 2008. "Rethinking Economies/Economic Geographies." *Geoforum* 39: 1111–1115.

National Cooperative Grocers Association. 2012. "Healthy Foods, Healthy Communities." http://strongertogether.coop/food-coops/food-co-op-impact-study/.

O'Connor, Claire. 2014. "Report: Walmart Workers Cost Taxpayers $6.2 Billion in Public Assistance." *Forbes,* April 15. www.forbes.com/sites/clareoconnor/2014/04/15/report-walmart-workers-cost-taxpayers-6-2-billion-in-public-assistance/.

Perkiss, Abigail. 2014. *Making Good Neighbors: Civil Rights, Liberalism, and Integration in Postwar Philadelphia.* Ithaca, NY: Cornell University Press.

Quigley, Caitlin. 2014. "Co-Op Currents: How Co-Ops Are Committed to Meeting Community Needs." *Generocity,* December 18. www.generocity.org/co-op-currents-co-ops-committed-meeting-community-needs/.

Raja, Samina, Changxing Ma, and Pavan Yadav. 2008. "Beyond Food Deserts: Measuring and Mapping Racial Disparities in Neighborhood Food Environments." *Journal of Planning Education and Research* 27: 469–482.

Rothschild, Joyce, and J. A. Whitt. 1986. *The Cooperative Workplace: Potentials and Dilemmas of Organisational Democracy and Participation.* Cambridge, UK: Cambridge University Press.

Shannon, Jerry. 2014. "Food Deserts: Governing Obesity in the Neoliberal City." *Progress in Human Geography* 38: 248–266.

Slocum, Rachel. 2007. "Whiteness, Space, and Alternative Food Practice." *Geoforum* 38: 520–533.

Soper, K. 2007. "Re-Thinking the 'Good Life': The Citizenship Dimension of Consumer Disaffection with Consumerism." *Journal of Consumer Culture* 7: 205–229.

Walker, Renee E., Christopher R. Keane, and Jessica G. Burke. 2010. "Disparities and Access to Healthy Food in the United States: A Review of Food Deserts Literature." *Health & Place* 16: 876–884.

Yee, Vivian. 2014. "Food Co-Ops in Gentrifying Areas Find They Aren't to Every Taste." *The New York Times,* February 11. www.nytimes.com/2014/02/12/nyregion/as-neighborhoods-gentrify-co-ops-find-they-are-not-to-everyones-taste.html.

Zitcer, Andrew. 2014. "Food Co-Ops and the Paradox of Exclusivity." *Antipode* 47: 812–828.

Zwerdling, Daniel. 1979. "The Uncertain Revival of Food Cooperatives." In *Co-Ops, Communes and Collectives : Experiments in Social Change in the 1960s and 1970s,* ed. John Case and Rosemary C. R. Taylor, 89–111. New York: Pantheon.

NINE

Cooperative Social Practices, Self-Determination, and the Struggle for Food Justice in Oakland and Chicago

Meleiza Figueroa and Alison Hope Alkon

FOR MORE THAN TWO DECADES NOW, academics and activists have engaged in debates about how food movements and alternative food systems should best respond to the challenges of a corporate food regime that is environmentally, socially, and, for all but the most elite actors, economically destructive (Altieri 2009, Bell 2010, McMichael 2009, Perfecto et al. 2009, Shiva 1991). Farmers and entrepreneurs have developed alternative food systems that emphasize the ethics and quality of their local, organic, artisanal, and fair trade goods, while activists have worked to create support for these products and their distribution networks (Goodman et al. 2012, Hinrichs 2003, Jarosz 2008, Watts et al. 2005). As outlined in chapter 1, these solutions have spurned a growing foodie culture but have largely failed to speak to the lived experiences of those most marginalized by the industrial food system, and have reinforced imaginaries of self-interested consumers as the primary agents of social change. We wholeheartedly agree with this volume's desire to highlight more collective approaches such as the regulation of toxic practices and worker organizing. However, we also believe that alternative food systems have important roles to play in the fight for food justice.

This chapter highlights the work of two food hubs in low-income, predominantly African American neighborhoods in Chicago, Illinois, and Oakland, California. Food hubs are organizations that provide the infrastructure to manage aggregation, distribution, and/or marketing of locally and regionally produced food. We examine food hubs in light of the food justice and neoliberalism critiques outlined in chapter 1. We argue that although alternative foods are broadly culturally coded as affluent and white, these organizations are simultaneously embedded in and draw from the cultural specificities and racialized lived experiences of their neighborhoods. We also argue that although these are markets—places to buy and sell food—the individualistic logic of consumer choice promoted by neoliberalism is tempered by an emphasis on collective practices and community benefits. Indeed, the collective nature of food provisioning in these hubs is not just an added benefit, but an essential component of their material functioning. Therefore, we believe that although they build alternative food systems rather than work to constrain the corporate food regime, their collective practices produce subjectivities that resist neoliberalism and contribute to the broader fight for food justice. Thus, in contrast to the assertion of J. K. Gibson-Graham that focusing on neoliberalism eclipses our appetites for progressive action, we highlight the ways that neoliberalism is simultaneously reproduced and contested in order to point toward progressive possibilities rooted in marginalized communities.

ELITISM AND NEOLIBERALISM IN ALTERNATIVE FOOD SYSTEMS

Broadly, the critique of alternative food systems as elitist focuses on the ways that organizations tend to hail affluent, predominantly white subjects while ignoring the collective histories, identities, and material needs of low-income communities and communities of color with regard to food and agriculture (Alkon and Agyeman 2011, Slocum 2007). The lack of a structural critique of race and class, however, does not mean that alternative food movements have not set their sights on urban communities of color, particularly in attempts to "bring good food to others" (Guthman 2008a). These well-meaning efforts often carry with them an already established notion of what "good food" is, representing a kind of utopian, perfectionist politics focused on food quality (Goodman et al. 2012).

In their missionary impulse, these projects often position urban communities of color through a "deficit" lens, requiring top-down educational, technocratic, aid-based solutions that rely on a high level of intervention on the part of outside actors. This "deficit thinking" (Valencia 1997) often doesn't recognize potentially useful forms of knowledge, talent, and social practice that already exist within those communities, leading to a reliance on outside retailers and nonprofit professionals. Moreover, this approach largely fails to engage the very communities that supporters of alternative food systems are trying to reach (Alkon 2012). While many food activists and city planners tend to explain their lack of resonance with communities of color as an issue of inadequate education and/or market failure (Cohen et al. 2011, Guthman 2008b), others point to a gap in "agendas and discourse" (Gottlieb and Fisher 1996, 28) between alternative food activism and other community-based social movements. The food hubs highlighted in this chapter maintain agendas and discourses rooted in the needs and talents of the communities that nurture them.

These are, of course, not the only two alternative food projects to have grown from marginalized communities, and we argue that this rootedness is a necessary but not sufficient component of their potential to contribute to the fight for food justice. We also believe that these projects are exemplary because their collective structures allow them to contest aspects of neoliberalism commonly embodied by many alternative food organizations even as they simultaneously reproduce others.

Neoliberalism "originated as a way of describing the resurgence of free-market economic theory, and has been extended to describe the way in which a discourse of market, quasi-market or consumer-based relationships has colonized numerous arenas of economic, social, cultural and political life" (Laurie and Bondi 2005, 8). For example, neoliberal approaches to pressing issues of food and public health in poor communities are framed within a "corporate-driven food enterprise discourse" rooted in the "belief that methods drawn from business can solve social problems and are superior to other methods in use in the public sector and civil society" (Holt-Giménez and Shattuck 2011, 119).

A telling example of this is the discourse on "food deserts" (Gallagher 2006), and the ways in which problems of access to healthy food in poor communities of color are both defined and addressed institutionally. Food deserts are primarily defined by metrics of distance between places of residence and grocery stores (ibid.). As a result, solutions sought by state officials, such as Chicago's mayor, Rahm Emanuel, have consisted of "courting [corporate] chains like Aldi, Family Dollar and even Wal-Mart to fill the void created by food deserts" (Gray 2009). While these moves are highly touted as a way to bring both food access and jobs to poor communities, they serve to elide and reproduce the deeper structural problems that contribute to the conditions experienced by people living in food deserts, and position corporate commerce as a solution to a social problem.

While many in the broader food movement are critical of the increasing corporate control of food systems, they often ignore the ways in which this enterprise discourse also colors their alternatives (Guthman 2008c). Food justice organizations have largely fallen in line with this privileging of market-based strategies for social change, such as the buying and selling of local and organic produce, to the point that they eclipse the possibility of regulatory reforms (such as those described in parts 1 and 2 of this volume). Activists in the food hubs depicted in this chapter, and in alternative food systems more generally, participate primarily as buyers and sellers of local and organic food, and seek to create social change through shifting market demand. This implicitly lends support to the notion that social change can best be pursued through market exchange relations, relieving the state of its regulatory role.

However, the food hubs we studied in Oakland and Chicago cultivate notions of community and collectivity that resist both the individualizing focus of neoliberalism and a continued dependence on the corporate food regime. These notions of collectivity are neither add-ons nor aggregates of individual choices and actions, but are materially essential to each food hub's functioning. Even as they self-identify as forms of "social enterprise," the production, procurement, and distribution of food, work, knowledge, and profit within these food hubs are fundamentally driven by collective action and a commitment to empowering their own communities. In the words of Dana Harvey, executive director of Mandela Marketplace in Oakland, "It's not about plopping a grocery store down in a community. It's about engaging and resourcing a community to solve their problems, and own those solutions."

In the search for effective and transformative alternatives to neoliberal capitalism, a common impulse is to create, or look for, utopian solutions wholly autonomous from the system—in the words of Gibson-Graham (2006, 21), to "starve capitalism's bloated body and invigorate its 'constitutive outside' . . . constituting a positive space of noncapitalist economic difference." The food hubs described in this chapter could easily be read as examples of the kinds of "emergent institutions and practices" (ibid., 56) that characterize the authors' imaginings of diverse economies and noncapitalist initiatives. And our analysis does follow their directive to "read for difference rather than dominance" (ibid., xxii) by demonstrating the ways that these organizations interpolate subjectivities—not of consumers creating social change through individual choice, but of community members engaged in collective practices (see also Harris 2009).

However, and in line with the larger aims of this volume, we strongly disagree with the notion that analyses that highlight the reproduction of neoliberal subjectivities and strategies serve to eclipse the politics of the possible. Neither of these cases exists in a space in which neoliberalism is not a defining factor of political and economic life. In fact, where performative, utopian models of alternative food systems are created, they tend to gain little traction, especially in communities of color. Rather, we believe that only by understanding the ways that neoliberalism continues to constrain alternative food systems can activists develop effective practices of resistance. We therefore orient our analysis toward the question of how alternative food projects in marginalized communities are affected by the broader context of neoliberalism, and thus simultaneously reproduce and resist its logic.

In doing so, we follow Figueroa's earlier work on the need to shift our examination of alternative food projects in marginalized communities from an approach focused on food to one that highlights everyday social practices (Figueroa 2015). She argues that critical food scholarship and discourses within food movements have mostly concentrated on the "food" in food systems—the technical, political, economic, and social developments that surround commodity chains, as the saying goes, from the field to the dining table. Instead, we offer a historically and culturally grounded approach focused on social practice and rooted in everyday life (Lefebvre 2002). We believe this can highlight the social elements that create and/or strengthen resonant, locally inflected political strategies for food provisioning in urban communities. This approach helps make explicit the connections between food and other social phenomena, such as class exploitation and racism, that shape particular experiences and struggles, making it particularly appropriate when seeking to understand alternative food projects in marginalized Black communities such as West Oakland and the South Side of Chicago.

Moreover, this more nuanced perspective moves beyond debates over whether alternative food projects are or are not neoliberal, and allows researchers to understand the ways that neoliberal logics can be simultaneously reproduced and resisted. Scholars of social movements have long considered the construction of alternative institutions as an essential part of movement building (Hess 2005, Johnston and Klandermans 1995, Tarrow 1994, Taylor et al. 1998), and we argue that projects like these, which both require collective practices and are steeped in the everyday lived experiences of marginalized communities, have the greatest potential to contribute to the broader fight for food justice.

THE HEALTHY FOOD HUB AND MANDELA
MARKETPLACE

Chicago's Healthy Food Hub and Oakland's Mandela Marketplace both work to create alternative food systems in neighborhoods historically left out of the alternative food movement, and left out of capital investment and economic development more generally. Well-documented processes of racial inequalities in urban economic development, including redlining, differential policing, and systemic underinvestment (Massey and Denton 1993, Squires and Kubrin 2006) heavily influenced these communities' trajectories. The deindustrialization of the United States since the late 1970s (Wilson 2011), a result of the spatial reconfigurations of capital due to neoliberal globalization (Harvey 2005), exacerbated existing racial inequalities by way of massive capital flight, job loss, and economic devastation in the largely Black working-class areas of major cities, including Oakland and Chicago (McClintock 2008, Wacquant 1995). Further, the most recent economic crisis, which started in 2007, has driven Black unemployment in these communities to nearly 50 percent, levels last seen during the Great Depression (Walker 2010).

We believe that these historical and structural conditions, rather than a simple lack of corporate investment, provide a more comprehensive explanation for the existence of "food deserts" in South Chicago and West Oakland. These communities, like many other poor Black communities, not only lack the presence of traditional grocery stores, but are replete with corner liquor stores and fast-food establishments that provide cheap and unhealthy food, the consumption of which can be correlated with poor health outcomes (Babey et al. 2008, Gallagher 2006, McClintock 2011). It is unclear whether these relationships are causal, or if both are effects of the racism, poverty, and unemployment described above. Nonetheless, it was the lack of available healthy food that inspired the creation of both food hubs.

Chicago's Healthy Food Hub was established in 2009 with the aim of pooling the resources of its members and surrounding communities to "bring home healthier, tastier, fresher food for less" (Healthy Food Hub n.d.). This is mainly achieved through collective purchasing of wholesale organic produce, as well as food production on rural farms in the historic Black farming community of Pembroke Township, Illinois, about sixty miles south of the city. It is a membership-based organization; one pays an annual fee of $25 to become a member and receive discounts on food products, as well as access to the Hub's main preordering mechanism on its website or over the phone. The Hub holds a Market Day every Saturday when members can pick up their preordered purchases, shop for additional food items, buy other sundries and gift items from vendors, and attend talks, workshops, and organizational meetings. Members also commit to "seek and find" ways to improve the Hub's operations and expand its membership, by engaging in five major "tasks": comparing prices, recruiting new members, bulk purchasing for friends and family, sharing knowledge and research on healthy living, and forging connections with local producers (ibid.). Decisions regarding the Hub are discussed and made collectively via a monthly "stakeholders" conference call, in which all members are invited and encouraged to participate.

Preorders are the main mechanism by which the Hub obtains its food products. There are two "rounds" to the preorder process. Members submit the first round of orders on the Monday before Market Day, over the website or over the phone. An email is then sent to members a couple of days later with details on what has been ordered, and how much more of each item must be acquired to receive the greatest bulk discount. Members can then choose to buy more, or recruit family and friends to their original order, so that everyone can receive the lowest possible price for their food.

Presentations and workshops are integral parts of the weekly Market Days and involve a range of topics, such as healthy cooking, herbal medicine (from diverse traditions), aquaponics (integrated fish and crop systems), fair trade coffee and chocolate (including presentations by African farmers), disaster preparedness, and cultivation systems that stem from old farming traditions as well as newer forms of permaculture. These not only expose members to new knowledge and ideas, they also enhance the scope of goods and services the Hub is able to provide, and present potential economic opportunities for members and presenters. While Market Days and work days on Pembroke farms are mainly run by volunteers, as well as by local youth through partnerships with local school programs, the Hub aspires to eventually be able to provide paid jobs for its members and the community at large. They have also recently begun to pursue crowd-funding measures to build infrastructure for year-round food production and training programs on their forty-acre "eco-campus" at the Black Oaks Center for Renewable Sustainable Living in Pembroke Township.

It is important to note that the Healthy Food Hub was not initially conceived as a food justice initiative; it began rather spontaneously among a group of patients in the care of Hub founder Dr. Jifunza Wright, an African American holistic practitioner based in South Chicago. Having noted that many patients' conditions stemmed from a lack of access to fresh, healthy food, Wright and her husband, Fred Carter, expanded what had been a household practice of buying food in bulk to include her patients and their families, in order to secure the best-quality food for the best available prices. As Dr. Wright states in the Healthy Food Hub's mission statement:

> To do what is best for our bodies, we must eat as close to 100% organic to rid ourselves of mounting environmental toxins, take in the highest nutrients, and prevent disease. Most of us cannot financially afford to do this going to local retail centers where prices are prohibitive. Buying wholesale, in volume allows us all to stay within our budget while getting only the best whole, natural foods. (Wright n.d.)

The success and sensibility of collective food purchasing as a means of addressing both the health and food-access issues faced by residents on the South Side attracted more participants from the community as well as partners from nearby Black churches and schools, who contributed time, space, and volunteers to the creation of the Hub. After five years of operation, the Healthy Food Hub now serves hundreds of families each week with an expanding inventory of locally and regionally sourced fresh vegetables, fruits, dry goods, pastured meats, and more.

Oakland's Mandela Marketplace is a nonprofit organization that "works in partnership with local residents, family farmers, and community-based businesses to improve health, create wealth, and build assets through cooperative food enterprises in low income communities" (Mandela Marketplace n.d.). Its centerpiece is Mandela Foods Cooperative, a worker-owned grocery store and nutrition education center that opened in 2008. Other hub programs include Earth's Produce distribution, which provides outlets for the sales of food from local, under-resourced, farmers, who are primarily farmers of color. The Healthy Neighborhood Store Alliance and community produce stands provide additional distribution points beyond the co-op, a ladder-up financing initiative that marshals Kiva microfinance loans[1] to West Oakland–based food entrepreneurs.

Mandela Marketplace grew out of the West Oakland Food Collaborative (WOFC), a collective of neighborhood residents and nonprofit organizations founded in 2001, which worked to improve access to high-quality, affordable food in the neighborhood. One of WOFC's early initiatives was a community foods assessment, a now common tool through which local residents and other interested groups can assess community food needs and resources.

FIGURE 9.1. The worker–owners of Mandela Foods Cooperative. Photo courtesy of Mandela Marketplace.

According to Dana Harvey, a long-term environmental justice activist and founding member of the WOFC who is now the executive director of Mandela Marketplace, "We did an assessment to determine what foods were and weren't available locally, and went through a community facilitation process to come up with solutions. One of the strategies that we identified to fix the food security problem was to have a grocery store, and [we felt] that it should be owned by people in the neighborhood." Notably, all the worker–owners of Mandela Foods Cooperative are African American, while the nonprofit staff and staff of other programs are multiracial.

Mandela Foods Cooperative functions as a for-profit, cooperatively owned store, while also receiving support from the nonprofit Mandela Marketplace. Mandela Marketplace's director of social entrepreneurship, Mariela Cedeño, describes this relationship:

> The reason we established ourselves as a nonprofit to support and incubate Mandela Foods was because four worker–owners from West Oakland didn't have the credit or the networks or the access to the kind of financing they would need to build out something that was going to cost $750,000, whereas, a nonprofit has the kind of the skills necessary to network through grants or to provide guarantees to help them get that financing.

Our relationship with the co-op has also changed over time. When we first established ourselves, we were trying to find them resources to launch and technical assistance to train them to be grocery operators. We've evolved as they've taken more autonomy over their business into being more ad hoc, more technical assistance, [such as] providing them their accountant or hiring business consultants to advise on various decisions.

Decision-making power is exercised primarily by the four worker–owners, each of whom has a vote on workplace policies. The nonprofit collectively has one vote as well, which allows them input but not control. In addition, it is the worker–owners who share the organization's profits, while the nonprofit can fundraise to cover any losses. Thus, the nonprofit serves as a kind of angel investor in the co-op, allowing it to operate in the red for several years. The co-op broke even for the first time in 2012, one year ahead of their business plan, and earned profits for the first time in 2014. According to their bylaws, when Mandela Marketplace begins generating larger profits, a portion will also be shared with the larger community through matched savings accounts at the West Oakland Credit Union (Tucker 2015).

The remainder of this chapter lays out the ways in which these organizations embody and resist the critiques of alternative food movements as elitist and reproducing neoliberal logics. We argue that both organizations work toward and from a deeply embedded, specifically African American cultural framework that foregrounds issues of race, health, and community development rather than the environmental concerns that dominate many alternative food projects. In Chicago, this successfully mitigates associations of organic and local foods with affluent whites; while in West Oakland, which is rapidly gentrifying, the results are more mixed. Secondly, we argue that while these food hubs are essentially markets, and offer participation mainly through consumption, their operations require collective practices and a focus on the local community in a way that pushes back against the individualizing force of neoliberal subjectivities. As we will show, each organization creates an alternative food system rooted in and committed to low-income communities of color, broadening and deepening the fight for food justice.

RACIALIZED REALITIES

In contrast to many predominantly white alternative food projects, the organizers, employees, and customers at the Healthy Food Hub and Mandela

Marketplace do not shy away from discussions of race. Indeed, understanding the effects of institutionalized racism on food systems is as essential to their goals as the promotion of healthy food. First, both projects work to combat the above-described racialized underdevelopment of the communities in which they exist, and serve to make this process visible to community members. In addition, the Healthy Food Hub creates discursive and material connections between its members and Black farmers, as well as pan-African sociocultural institutions and networks that grew out of Black Power and decolonial movements; while at Mandela Marketplace, the co-op's worker–owners feel that their presence as African Americans involved in food provisioning is inviting to long-term residents of their gentrifying neighborhood. In placing race at the center of their work, these food justice projects disrupt the association between eliteness and alternative food movements, grounding them in the everyday lived experiences of their marginalized communities.

In Chicago, the Healthy Food Hub sources much of its food from the historic Black farming community of Pembroke Township, located approximately sixty miles south of the city and home to the largest concentration of Black farmers north of the Mason-Dixon line. During the Great Depression, Pembroke Township's location along the Grand Central railroad attracted Black farmers fleeing the social ills of the rural South (Houde and Klasey 1968). In later decades, the area also received Black settlers who had initially moved up to Chicago, but who sought to escape the racism and urban blight they had found in the city (Myers 1999). Pembroke farmers benefit from their linkages with the Healthy Food Hub and other South Side organizations by producing and selling crops and livestock using organic and ecological farming techniques (Gray 2010). This is particularly noteworthy given the challenges that have plagued Black farmers throughout the twentieth century, including lack of support from the U.S. Department of Agriculture, which forced many African Americans out of farming (Gilbert et al. 2002). At the Black Oaks Center's "eco-campus" in Pembroke, organizers hold weekend seminars for urban residents, mostly youth, in ecology and permaculture. In these seminars, African American youth participate in and learn from Black agricultural traditions while providing food for their communities, linking their sustenance to racial identity.

Unlike other social groups for whom "connections with the land" have powerful, positive cultural resonances, forging these discursive and ideological links between race, food, and land has proved to be very difficult for urban youth in South Chicago. The founders of the Healthy Food Hub believe that the legacy of slavery and sharecropping has disrupted many of their community members' interest in farming, as described by cofounder Dr. Jifunza Wright:

> The sons and daughters of what used to be here in Pembroke—the largest Black farming community north of the Mason-Dixon line—came here and did not want to know how to farm. They did not want to know anything to do with dealing with the land. . . . We kept meeting this experience of people being in a lot of pain with the earth. And so we literally buried the pain here. . . . Not only did we put the pain back into the earth, we also picked up our power, of our relationship with the earth. We have strawberries for love and forgiveness, and calendula for wound healing. . . . Fellows came from Uganda and Kenya, and they shared in it. . . . Maybe we can begin to do a global process where we'll release our colonization and our suffering and regain our power again.

In this view, farming is not only a way to connect to the earth, as it often is for alternative food movements, but also a way to heal the trauma associated with forced agricultural labor and to empower a community through reimagined and reclaimed foodways.

Additionally, the strategy of a buying club has deep historical roots in longstanding African American practices of collective survival and resistance. The founders of the Healthy Food Hub, as well as many of its older members, came to Chicago with their respective families from Mississippi during the 1950s and '60s; many remember collective food purchasing as a routine family practice and a vital strategy in the process of rural–urban chain migration. In the words of Healthy Food Hub cofounder Fred Carter: "When we got to Chicago, our whole extended family, or people from our hometown, would all live together on a block. And we would all put our money together to buy a cow, and divide it up amongst ourselves. It was just cheaper that way. . . . I guess that is where the Healthy Food Hub came out of."

Collective buying also carries a specific political history for Chicago's Black migrants, including many who migrated from the Mississippi Valley, where the populist Colored Farmers' Alliance organized purchasing cooperatives to resist the power of white creditors during Reconstruction (Willis 2000). Thus, while buying clubs are not particular to African Americans, they had a strong history in the Black farming communities of the Mississippi Valley, and were already a familiar part of the cultural and social practice of many Healthy Food Hub members. This may be one reason why the Hub has been so successful at enrolling and engaging its members, while other alternative food organizations working in similar communities of color have struggled.

At Mandela, the fact that the co-op is owned and run by African Americans sends a clear message that healthy food is not just for elites. Worker–owner Adrionna Fike says that over the three years she's been at the co-op, she's seen increasing numbers of Black shoppers. "People are just starting to ask more questions and coming in, and not just being like, 'This is not for me,' and walking past. They see other Black people walking in so they'll just come in as well." Initially curious because of the presence of Black bodies in the store, what impresses these new customers the most is the way the co-op's product mix speaks to their everyday food needs. As Adrionna continues,

> Someone will come in and go to the bathroom and they'll just start walking around, [saying] "Oh y'all have greens? Oh, okay. Y'all have meat? Oh, okay." When people come in, they realize that we are in a way their typical grocery store as far as having familiar products alongside products that folks have never seen, alongside healthy products that people have seen but never really engaged with.

Adrionna adds that her customers are often pleased to learn that the co-op accepts food stamps.

Long accustomed to seeing businesses in their area owned by non-Blacks, these neighbors are particularly excited to learn that those working at the store also own it. Worker–owner James Burke, who grew up in West Oakland, describes how impressed long-term residents are when they realize this. "They say, 'Oh yeah, you all own this store?' And they'll tell their kids, 'Oh they own this store.' I always hear people telling their kids, 'You know they own this store, right?'" Adrionna expands on the reasons that Black ownership matters:

> It matters for reasons of representation, it matters for reasons of community development that the developers look like us. That we are developing our own. It matters in terms of self-determination; expressing it, demonstrating it, teaching it. It matters for the legacy of all the grocers, Black grocers that have come before in Black communities. It matters for legacies going forward, it matters for just communities of color around the world, for people trying to transform food systems or participating in their own sovereignty, in owning themselves. It matters when the Black people are trying to do that and they have examples of Black people who are doing it already. Because you can't just tell me that it's a white thing because we're here!

Clearly, Mandela Marketplace disrupts the association between healthy food and affluent whiteness by demonstrating a successful project owned and run by working-class African Americans. According to the worker–owners, this gives them a sense of connection to long-term, predominantly Black neighborhood residents who are used to seeing alternative food systems managed by people they would consider outsiders.

In sum, both the Healthy Food Hub and Mandela Marketplace are commonly home to the kinds of discussions of race and racism that are often lacking from predominantly white alternative food projects. They are grounded in the place-specific lived realities of the communities they serve, whose geographies are shaped by race in ways ranging from migration patterns to neighborhood development. Such culturally and socially grounded food systems, especially in these sites of profoundly racialized economic precarity, emerge not as utopian ideals but as concrete survival strategies built from a long and continuous history of Black struggle. Thus, access to producing and consuming healthy food becomes an issue of self-determination; a mechanism for economic survival that facilitates neighborhood residents' abilities to connect their everyday eating practices to larger political realities.

AFFORDABILITY

The logic of neoliberalism directs individuals who wish to resist the above-described racial and economic inequalities to pursue change through individual consumer choice: "voting with dollars and forks" by patronizing alternative markets such as Mandela Marketplace and the Healthy Food Hub. Here, the economic success of these food hubs—their ability to maximize profits and minimize costs—would become the key to broader socio-environmental changes. Instead, however, the Hub and Mandela are markets created primarily to prioritize community needs. Perhaps the most telling indicator of this is their prices, which are lower than for comparable goods that generally extract a price premium for being organic and locally sourced.

In Chicago, the issue of price is one of the strongest draws for members of the Hub; as one member remarked, "It's so much cheaper and less off-putting than Whole Foods." Perhaps because of this, pragmatic concerns over price can, at times, trump the organic-ness and/or local-ness of some products. Hub volunteers admit that especially in the winter, products that members need are sometimes procured from nonlocal or even international sources.

This is important to note because it is an indicator of the Hub's priorities. While the Hub seeks to source its produce from local and organic sources whenever possible, the economic concerns of the community necessitate prioritizing the immediate needs of its members, and so they must ensure that certain items are both available and affordable.

In Oakland, worker–owners at Mandela Foods Cooperative often feel torn between their own need to cover costs and keeping prices affordable. One way that the worker–owners attempt to mitigate this tension is by carrying a variety of products to appeal to people at all income levels. While West Oakland has long been a low-income, predominantly African American community, gentrification has begun to bring in white, more affluent residents as well, many of whom are already steeped in the Bay Area's strong foodie culture. According to worker–owner James Burke, who is African American and West Oakland raised, "Caucasian people help keep the blood of the business flowing. . . . These customers that we have know what we're selling. They know what organic is and why they want that."

Mariela Cedeño, the director of social enterprise for Mandela Marketplace, explains how the co-op uses these customers to keep prices affordable:

> [The worker–owners'] end goal is to make healthy food accessible to community residents and to by that, change the health indicators and dynamics of this community. And so, making sure that the healthy produce and the bulk goods like beans and grains are affordable is important to them, but they're also going to want to cater to the people who can make it profitable. So they're also going sell a fancy cheese or free-range chicken or a ten-dollar bottle of honey.

Executive Director Dana Harvey offers an example. "I think the only negative Yelp review we've ever had is that our Nutella is too expensive," she said. "And we wrote back and said 'Yes, our Nutella is expensive and this is why. It's so we can keep our apples affordable.'" Worker–owners use high-profit items to keep the produce and staple foods affordable, keeping at least some of the store's products accessible to the community.

COMMUNITY BUILDING

The reason that affordability is so important to these food hubs is that their goal is to improve their communities through healthy food. Indeed, while these are places where food is bought and sold, these sales are often inextricable from the community building that takes place in and through their distinctive social spaces.

In Chicago, some of the most celebrated aspects of the Healthy Food Hub are the face-to-face interactions between members on Market Day. At the market, people tend to know each other well, and often greet each other with a warm hug. Asking after each other's families is also a commonly heard conversation, as are exchanges of gossip and ranting about one's day or week. Unlike a typical supermarket, or even a farmers' market, where anonymity and a businesslike comportment geared toward efficiency (a desire to just buy things and leave) sets the predominant tone of the market space, people here at the Hub have a more luxurious sense of time. Relative inefficiencies in the processing of purchases—especially at busy times when the volunteer staff can be overwhelmed by the volume of people, computer problems, or confusion in the fulfillment of preorders—are generally much more tolerated by customers; even though the line can be very slow sometimes, there are never expressions of exasperation or arguments over staff inefficiency. Children often play freely within the market space and interact at will with vendors and volunteers, even though an adjoining room is designated for child care. Indeed, several people expressed a preference for taking their families to the Hub's Market Day because it "provided a safe space for children" (especially important at a time when these particular neighborhoods in South Chicago were enduring a period of extreme violence). As one of the Hub's members noted:

> Every time that I'm talking about membership and its benefits, beyond things like food discounts, I'm always saying: when you come into that Hub, there are conversations that are happening in the Hub that you're not going to get anywhere else. There's always going to be someone there that's going to be talking about something that you know you may want to connect with, whether it's ... talking about how to get children into healthy eating and cooking healthy for themselves, whether it's Divine chocolate, that fair trade chocolate, Brother T__ and fair trade coffee.... These are all interactions that bring the community closer together. Community is something that connects and holds these different people together from different arenas.

Although the Healthy Food Hub, in its original incarnation as a collective buying cooperative, was conceived as simply a means of obtaining fresh fruits, vegetables, and herbs at affordable prices, it has grown beyond food in many ways. The interactions, knowledge, and sense of community brought to the Hub by its members has helped push the concept of a "hub" beyond a strategy for food production and consumption, and recast it as a vehicle for social cohesion and community empowerment—in its own words, "using social capital to build community wealth." This overarching narrative of "building community wealth" has, to a significant extent, been developed in opposition to corporate "food desert" initiatives that have targeted the same areas in South Chicago. Healthy Food Hub members explicitly seek to "transform the food deserts from within themselves, not from . . . people who don't live in their communities and carry the majority of the wealth out of their communities."

In Oakland, a similar sense of community-based social change pervades Mandela Marketplace's larger mission and a similar sense of warmth characterizes the store. Worker–owner James Burke explains that "There is a camaraderie, and a relationship that exists between us that's friendlier than just doing business for the customers and for the people that work there." Adrionna, another worker–owner, continues: "One of our customers that lives upstairs says, 'This is like a community center, I come in here, I see people I know, I meet people, I make connections, I buy meat, I buy my food, I come in here for the air conditioner, recreation.'"

"I hope that when we get more seating," says James, "that we'll see more of that kind of communal environment. When you're in a line and you have to just pay and leave, there's not as much time to really relate with other people." The co-op has recently created a prepared-foods counter and is, at the time of this writing, applying for the necessary permits to add seating.

In addition, Mandela Marketplace strongly emphasizes community ownership. According to Director of Social Entrepreneurship Mariela Cedeño, this was the reason a cooperative structure was chosen for the grocery store:

> The worker co-op model is a strategy that we felt could bring people from the community together as owners and have a support network for owning the business. . . . The ideology [of cooperative ownership] is important, but [we were thinking about] how can we have a business that is owned by the community, that people have equal power in how it's run, and have equal profits from how it's run and have equal say in how it's run. And so, that, by definition, is a cooperative. It's really what makes the most sense so there is both a distribution of profits but also a distribution of responsibility and shared knowledge across worker–owners.

Community ownership becomes especially important as the neighborhood gentrifies. In the past decade, increasing numbers of young, white residents have been moving to West Oakland, and artists and punks renting warehouses have been joined by professionals buying recently built condominiums.

In some ways, the co-op's dependence on new customers makes its status as a business owned by Black, long-term residents all the more important. Mariela explains:

> We're a cooperative, but we're working in a capitalist system. [Mandela's programs] can make sure that community residents who have been part of the history of West Oakland can own the economy so that they can stay in [the neighborhood] and profit from the people who are coming in who have higher levels of income. You know, [James] Burke grew up here, and Mandela Marketplace is going to become profitable and he's going to get a share of those profits and be able to afford to stay in West Oakland. That's part of making a national model about how to fight these dynamics and work within the system even if it's flawed.

This model of community building through the buying and selling of food has the potential, like other alternative food initiatives, to reproduce neoliberal logics and subjectivities by designating the individual consumer as the locus of social change. Indeed, given the erosion of the welfare state and the public sector in general, and the inability of neoliberalized state institutions to recognize, much less support, the needs and capacities of these communities, forms of "social enterprise" are perhaps the only avenues left through which community-level structures for needs such as healthy food can be realized.

At the same time, however, these projects have other priorities besides their economic bottom lines, including promoting health, resisting racism, and serving their communities; and it does not appear that these priorities have been subsumed by neoliberal logics of individualism and the profit motive. In both cases, a primary emphasis on accruing and keeping both the benefits and the profits of their operations within their communities allows these food hubs to simultaneously articulate with and subvert the hegemonic market-based paradigms that shape the circumstances of their operation. For this reason, we argue that these cases complicate scholarly interpretations of the role neoliberalism plays in alternative food projects, particularly in communities that have long been marginalized by capitalist development.

COOPERATIVE PRACTICES

Neoliberalism interpolates the subject of the self-maximizing individual expressing himself through the free market while delegitimizing all forms of action other than entrepreneurial ones (Lavin 2009). By keeping community at the forefront, these organizations resist this logic, asserting that individuals need one another in order to better themselves. This is clearly demonstrated through the cooperative practices of each food hub. Cooperative practices are neither merely add-ons to their capitalist practices nor an aggregation of individual purchasing decisions, but are functionally and materially essential to their continued existence.

In Chicago, the Healthy Food Hub's procurement model requires that individuals work together to purchase their food, reinforcing the participatory and cooperative culture that supports its aims for community building. The two "rounds" of preorders, in which members are informed of the status of items and potential needs in the bulk procurement process, involves a significant amount of communication and cooperation among members to get what they need. One of the Hub's volunteers described the collective buying process as the "reverse" of community-supported agriculture: "In other words, it's not the farmer selling memberships. It's the eaters determining what they want to eat. And they're creating a system to support that. So, it's not like a farmers' market, securing the farmer, and people have no say in it. We eat. So we should determine what we want to eat. And create a system around that." The Hub is thus participatory by nature; preorders are an important part of how the Hub is able to procure affordable food for its members, and preordering is one of the principal ways that members demonstrate their commitment to the project. As a Hub volunteer noted, "It's part of the old general store model. I know what you need, that way I only have to get what it is that my community recognizes they need."

While coordinating the growing bank of people and resources that are incorporated into the Hub is the responsibility of a core group of organizers, the open-ended structure of the "hub" allows for a particular openness to the diverse kinds of knowledge and experience that those at the Hub encounter. The Hub's core model is based on African American practices, as well as concepts of cooperative economics derived from the African socialist tradition of *ujamaa,* but other influences, such as permaculture and peak-oil transition movements, have also formed parts of their knowledge and resource base. In a model reminiscent of the "rhizomic" structure described by Deleuze and Guattari (2004), organizers use "mycelium" as an ecological metaphor for demonstrating how the Hub gains its power through building relationships, and how the structure of the Hub emerges from the initiative of its members:

It's the power of relationships. That's what I got. You know, in permaculture, this is what I learned, it so transformed me. So [starts drawing] you have trees over there, and you have trees over here. Above the ground, everything looks different. But below the surface, they're all connected. And so, when this tree here is having problems, the whole community knows, and helps, through the mycelia. It just blew me away—I thought, wow! That's intelligence! Now, on the surface of the earth, we all look separate. But beneath, we're intricately tied to the same energy system, the same life system. We're not separate. It's been proven. And the violation of the trees here impact the whole community. . . . They will send electromagnetic, chemicals, and all that, to support that tree when it's stressed. It just knocked me out. . . . On the surface we look separate, but underneath we're tied to the same system. So we need to act like that.

Here, the material and social ecology of permaculture and the "rhizome" serves as a powerful heuristic illustrating the Healthy Food Hub's support for and reliance on cooperative, community-based practices.

At Mandela Marketplace, consumption remains conceptualized as an individual activity, but the organization of work is collectivized. This is most clearly seen at Mandela Foods Cooperative. The co-op currently has four worker–owners, though it hopes to add more as profits grow. As in many co-ops, there is an initial review period in which a potential worker–owner begins as an employee and is entitled to apply for membership after working a thousand hours. A $2,000 buy-in (relatively minimal compared to other Bay Area cooperative businesses) can be paid through a combination of cash and sweat equity, either up front or over a number of years, making ownership relatively accessible to low-income people. Each worker–owner supervises a particular area of the store such as produce or bulk goods. Pay is flat among the worker–owners and employees, and tied only to hours worked. Decisions are made by vote: each worker–owner has one vote, and a representative from the nonprofit also has a vote.

In many ways, Mandela Foods Cooperative does work similar to that of many other food justice organizations, focusing on bringing healthy food into neighborhoods with few other options. But as a worker-owned business, the co-op does more than provide a place to shop. Worker–owner James Burke explains:

I think a lot of people in the community are happy just to have another place to shop that offers a different kind of variety than what you see in the other locations here, but for those that understand more about who we are and what we're trying to do and who we are because you're seeing people from the community, people you might even see on a regular basis and now they're part of something. They're not just employees, but this is their business and they're opening in their community trying to support their neighbors.

While the emphasis on business ownership is very much a part of the entrepreneurial focus common to neoliberal subjectivities, Mandela's cooperative structure makes this association much less straightforward.

Indeed, worker-owned businesses are not straightforward capitalist enterprises. According to Marx, they are not capitalist enterprises at all, as no one sells their labor in exchange for a wage. In his Inaugural Address to the Working Men's International Association in London in 1864, Marx said: "The value of these great social experiments cannot be overrated. By deed, instead of by argument, they have shown that production . . . may be carried on without the existence of a class of masters employing a class of hands." In a contemporary sense, cooperatives are one way to resist the reproduction of proletarianization, as worker–owners avoid the alienation from the means of production necessary under capital.

CONCLUSIONS

This chapter has examined the Healthy Food Hub and Mandela Marketplace through the lens of everyday social practices. Rather than a focus on the authenticity of the food itself, this lens emphasizes the lived experiences of those working to create local food systems. In marginalized communities, the creation of alternative foodways can be intimately linked to institutional racism, underdevelopment, and desires for community uplift. These local-food-system initiatives not only emphasize these linkages, but are formed out of the particular combination of challenges, resources, and aspirations that exist in their communities, and thus are able to connect to their respective constituencies in intimate and exciting ways.

With regard to neoliberalism, these cases embody the complex question of how food systems can push back against the subsumption of social life to the logic of free-market fundamentalism and the atomized consumer subject, while operating within essentially entrepreneurial forms of production, exchange, and consumption. We argue that although these food hubs have prioritized their social goals of racial empowerment and community development, they do so as "markets" that buy and sell goods, and depend on non-market inputs, such as foundation funding or volunteer labor, to supplement their ability to succeed in a capitalist context. Perhaps most importantly, we believe these organizations are particularly noteworthy for their emphasis on collectivism over individualism, which challenges the individualizing nature of neoliberal subjectivities in a way that goes beyond many food justice projects.

Many, if not most, consumer-driven social justice projects emphasize "collective" values by applying a kind of moral discourse that benefits the individual consumer. By purchasing fair trade coffee or locally sourced organic food at a Whole Foods, for example, a consumer expresses support for small farmers and assumes a performative role as a "conscious consumer," while leaving intact the basic and unequal economic structure in which their "conscious" market transactions take place. The crucial difference between such food practices, centered on the ethics and aesthetics of consumption, and those observed in the cases of Mandela Marketplace and the Healthy Food Hub, is that practices of collectivity are embedded in the material functions and requirements of the organizations themselves. Instead of encouraging change through an aggregation of individual market practices and behaviors, cooperative practices are not simply performative, but are fundamental to how the organizations examined in this chapter work. The Healthy Food Hub's dependence on bulk discounts requires the collective effort of its members to secure the lowest possible price for healthy food; individual benefit is inextricably tied to the benefit of the whole. For Mandela Marketplace, which operates on a more conventional grocery-store model, its worker–owner structure collectivizes profits and decision making; and operational decisions, such as its pricing rules, are consciously oriented toward providing access and opportunity for those who need it most.

The differences between these cases also illuminate the importance of local specificity in how food justice initiatives navigate between their ideological or aspirational values and the concrete realities and challenges encountered in serving their communities. These cases are significant in that they are markets that compete within a neoliberal market economy, yet they undeniably prioritize the distribution of material and social benefits to their respective communities, above and beyond the commodities they provide, in ways that resonate powerfully with the people they serve. We have argued that specific factors contribute crucially to their successes—for the Healthy Food Hub, family histories and practices carried over from rural Mississippi became constitutive organizational features of its operations in South Chicago, while in Oakland, Mandela Marketplace's unique structure and mission gains crucial support from the Bay Area's strong food culture as well as a well-developed network of social justice activists and organizations.

According to Gibson-Graham, analyses highlighting the constraining forces of neoliberalism on the development of alternative economic forms, such as the food hubs described in this chapter, contribute "to an affect and attitude of entrenched opposition ... a habit of thinking and feeling that [leaves] little emotional space for alternatives" (Gibson-Graham 2006, xxii). In contrast, our analysis highlights, rather than minimizes, the ways in which the food hubs we studied can reproduce neoliberal strategies and structures, but also remains optimistic in terms of their abilities to simultaneously resist neoliberalism in other ways.

Organizations rooted in low-income communities of color such as West Oakland and the South Side of Chicago do not have the luxury of creating utopian forms of resistance out of thin air, nor do the utopian visions of many alternative food projects appeal to these communities. What seems to work is an approach grounded in everyday material practices, acknowledging the neighborhoods' racialized histories and present-day realities in which appeals to state institutions and policies are no longer viable options. In these sacrifice zones, where capital has largely left the people who inhabit them behind, organizations are necessarily privatized and market based. These cases work explicitly to push back against the perceived eliteness of many alternative food projects by directly addressing the specific needs of their communities, sharing resources and knowledge, and empowering members of marginalized groups to create collective solutions to the challenges they face, in ways that *work for them*.

Worker–owners at Mandela Marketplace and Healthy Food Hub members embody the belief that one's business does not succeed or fail on its economic merits alone, and recognize that community improvement is a collective endeavor. While they remain enterprises within capitalism, and food remains a commodity to be bought and sold, their cultures of collectivity can be read as implicit challenges to the status quo. In creating these subjectivities, these food hubs are finding cracks in the concrete of neoliberal capitalism in which they can sow seeds of collective resistance.

NOTE

1. Kiva is a nonprofit organization that allows individual donors to make small-scale loans to entrepreneurs across the globe. Donors can select recipients on the

basis of profiles listed on the organization's website, and Kiva maintains a worldwide network of field partners to administer the donations. Mandela Marketplace is one such field partner, focused on loans to those looking to develop food-based businesses in West Oakland.

REFERENCES

Alkon, Alison Hope. 2012. *Black, White, and Green: Farmers Markets, Race, and the Green Economy.* Athens: University of Georgia Press.

Alkon, Alison Hope, and Julian Agyeman, Eds. 2011. *Cultivating Food Justice: Race, Class, and Sustainability.* Cambridge, MA: MIT Press.

Altieri, Miguel A. 2009. "Agroecology, Small Farms, and Food Sovereignty." *Monthly Review* 61: 102–113.

Babey, Susan H., Allison L. Diamant, Theresa A. Hastert, and Stefan Harvey. 2008. "Designed for Disease: The Link between Local Food Environments and Obesity and Diabetes." Los Angeles: California Center for Public Health Advocacy, Policy Link, and UCLA Center for Health Policy Research.

Barnett, Clive. 2005. "The Consolations of 'Neoliberalism.'" *Geoforum* 36: 7–12.

Bell, Michael M. 2010. *Farming for Us All: Practical Agriculture and the Cultivation of Sustainability.* State College, PA: Penn State University Press.

Cohen, Pam, Mari Gallagher, and Pamela Martin. 2011. "The Urban Food Model: Perspectives on Economics, Science and Policy." Chicago: Franke Institute for the Humanities, University of Chicago.

Deleuze, Gilles, and Félix Guattari. 2004. *A Thousand Plateaus: Capitalism and Schizophrenia,* trans. Brian Massumi. London: Continuum International.

Figueroa, Meleiza. 2015. "Food Sovereignty in Everyday Life: Toward a People-Centered Approach to Food Systems." *Globalizations* 15(4): 1–15.

Gallagher, M. 2006. "Examining the Impact of Food Deserts on Public Health in Chicago." Chicago: Mari Gallagher Research and Consulting Group.

Gibson-Graham, J.K. 2006. *The End of Capitalism (As We Knew It): A Feminist Critique of Political Economy,* new edition. Minneapolis: University of Minnesota Press.

Gilbert, Jess, Gwen Sharp, and M. Sindy Felin. 2002. "The Loss and Persistence of Black-Owned Farms and Farmland: A Review of the Research Literature and Its Implications." *Southern Rural Sociology* 18(2): 1–30.

Goodman, David, E. Melanie DuPuis, and Michael K. Goodman. 2012. *Alternative Food Networks: Knowledge, Practice, and Politics.* London: Routledge.

Gottlieb, Robert, and Andrew Fisher. 1996. "Community Food Security and Environmental Justice: Searching for a Common Discourse." *Agriculture and Human Values* 13: 23–32.

Gray, Steven. 2009. "Can America's Urban Food Deserts Bloom?" *Time,* May 26.

Gray, Topher. 2010. "From Farm to Food Desert." *Chicago Reader.*

Guthman, Julie. 2008a. "Bringing Good Food to Others: Investigating the Subjects of Alternative Food Practice." *Cultural Geographies* 15: 431–447. www.chicagoreader .com/chicago/chicago-food-deserts-hopkins-park-black-farmers/Content?oid= 2272825.

———. 2008b. "'If They Only Knew': Color Blindness and Universalism in California Alternative Food Institutions." *The Professional Geographer* 60: 387–397.

———. 2008c. "Neoliberalism and the Making of Food Politics in California." *Geoforum* 39: 1171–1183.

———. 2011. *Weighing In: Obesity, Food Justice, and the Limits of Capitalism.* Berkeley: University of California Press.

Harris, Edmund. 2009. "Neoliberal Subjectivities or a Politics of the Possible? Reading for Difference in Alternative Food Networks." *Area* 41: 55–63.

Harvey, David. 2005. *A Brief History of Neoliberalism.* New York: Oxford University Press.

Healthy Food Hub. n.d. "Become a Member." *Healthy Food Hub.* www.healthy foodhub.org/become_member.

———. n.d. "Welcome." www.healthyfoodhub.org.

Hess, David J. 2005. "Technology-and Product-Oriented Movements: Approximating Social Movement Studies and Science and Technology Studies." *Science, Technology & Human Values* 30: 515–535.

Hinrichs, C. Claire. 2003. "The Practice and Politics of Food System Localization." *Journal of Rural Studies* 19: 33–45.

Holt-Giménez, Eric, and Annie Shattuck. 2011. "Food Crises, Food Regimes and Food Movements: Rumblings of Reform or Tides of Transformation?" *Journal of Peasant Studies* 38: 109–144.

Houde, Mary Jane, and John Klasey. 1968. *Of the People: A Popular History of Kankakee County.* Chicago: General Printing.

Jarosz, Lucy. 2008. "The City in the Country: Growing Alternative Food Networks in Metropolitan Areas." *Journal of Rural Studies* 24: 231–244.

Johnston, Hank, and Bert Klandermans. 1995. "The Cultural Analysis of Social Movements." *Social Movements and Culture* 4: 3–24.

Laurie, Nina, and Liz Bondi, Eds. 2005. *Working the Spaces of Neoliberalism.* Malden, MA: Blackwell.

Lavin, Chad. 2009. "Pollanated Politics, or, the Neoliberal's Dilemma." *Politics and Culture* 2: 57–67.

Lefebvre, Henri. 2002. *Critique of Everyday Life: Foundations for a Sociology of the Everyday.* London: Verso Books.

Mandela Marketplace. n.d. "About Us." www.mandelamarketplace.org/#!about_ us/csgz.

Massey, Douglas S., and Nancy A. Denton. 1993. *American Apartheid : Segregation and the Making of the Underclass.* Cambridge, MA: Harvard University Press.

McClintock, Nathan. 2008. "From Industrial Garden to Food Desert: Unearthing the Root Structure of Urban Agriculture in Oakland, California." ISSI Fellows Working Papers Series, Institute for the Study of Social Claims.

———. 2011. "From Industrial Garden to Food Desert: Demarcated Devaluation in the Flatlands of Oakland, California." In *Cultivating Food Justice: Race, Class, and Sustainability,* ed. Alison Hope Alkon and Julian Agyeman. Cambridge, MA: MIT Press.

McMichael, Philip. 2009. "A Food Regime Analysis of the 'World Food Crisis.'" *Agriculture and Human Values* 26: 281–295.

Myers, Linnet. 1999. "Dirt Poor." *Chicago Tribune,* February 28.

Perfecto, Ivette, John H. Vandermeer, and Angus Lindsay Wright. 2009. *Nature's Matrix : Linking Agriculture, Conservation and Food Sovereignty.* Sterling, VA: Earthscan. http://lib.myilibrary.com/detail.asp?ID=240231.

Shiva, Vandana. 1991. *Biodiversity: Social & Ecological Perspectives.* London: Zed Books.

Slocum, Rachel. 2007. "Whiteness, Space, and Alternative Food Practice." *Geoforum* 38: 520–533.

Squires, Gregory D., and Charis E. Kubrin. 2006. *Privileged Places: Race, Residence, and the Structure of Opportunity.* Boulder, CO: Lynne Rienner.

Tarrow, Sidney. 1994. *Power in Movement: Social Movements, Collective Action and Politics.* Cambridge, UK: Cambridge University Press.

Taylor, Verta, Nancy Whittier, A. D. Morris, and C. M. Mueller. 1998. "Collective Identity in Social Movement Communities: Lesbian Feminist Mobilization." In *Social Perspectives in Lesbian and Gay Studies,* ed. Peter M. Nardi and Beth E. Schneider, 349–365. New York: Routledge.

Tucker, Zoe O. 2015. "The Expanders: Groceries and Greywater." Grassroots Economic Organizing. www.geo.coop/story/expanders-groceries-and-greywater. Accessed June 8, 2015.

Valencia, Richard R. 1997. *The Evolution of Deficit Thinking: Educational Thought and Practice.* New York: Routledge.

Wacquant, Loïc J. D. 1995. "The Ghetto, the State, and the New Capitalist Economy." In *Metropolis: Center and Symbol of Our Times,* ed. Philip Kasinitz, 418–449. New York: New York University Press.

Walker, Devona. 2010. "The Unreported Economic Depression in Black America." *Alternet,* November 29. www.alternet.org/speakeasy/2010/11/29/the-unreported-economic-depression-in-black-america.

Watts, David C. H., Brian Ilbery, and Damian Maye. 2005. "Making Reconnections in Agro-Food Geography: Alternative Systems of Food Provision." *Progress in Human Geography* 29: 22–40.

Willis, John C. 2000. *Forgotten Time: The Yazoo-Mississippi Delta after the Civil War.* Charlottesville: University Press of Virginia.

Wilson, William Julius. 2011. *When Work Disappears: The World of the New Urban Poor.* New York: Vintage Books.

Wright, Jifunza. n.d. "Healthy Food Hub—Welcome." www.healthyfoodhub.org.

TEN

Urban Agriculture, Food Justice, and Neoliberal Urbanization

REBUILDING THE INSTITUTION OF PROPERTY

Michelle Glowa

URBAN AGRICULTURE HAS ARISEN AS a popular strategy in food movements to build alternatives to industrial food systems. Food justice advocates embrace gardening as one strategy in larger battles to address affordability and access to healthy food, community self-determination, and racial and economic inequality. And in the San Francisco Bay Area, the geographic focus of this chapter, urban agriculture has gained tremendous popularity, with hundreds of gardens dotting the landscape. Today's urban agriculture is situated within a national history in which gardening has been popularized at moments of crisis or social need but only as a form of temporary and interim land use. Gardening has generally been allowed or encouraged for short periods on vacant urban land, with the expectation that gardens would be removed when landlords chose to develop the land, typically once the crisis passed (Drake and Lawson 2014). In the Bay Area, contemporary garden projects follow a similar trend. While urban agriculture has been immensely popular in the region, highly competitive land markets increasingly compel landowners, both public and private, to put their properties to uses other than gardening. This poses a problem for food justice advocates trying to carve out spaces for gardening in their communities in the long term or aiming to create immediate benefits in the short term.

Gardening has thus become an entry to a land politics that asks who should have access to, and decision-making power over, particular properties. Contemporary property relations limit the ambitions of gardeners who have faced evictions by private landlords and government agencies, who have been impacted by over a century of racial exclusion in land ownership, and who hold limited financial resources to purchase desirable land. Private property is a social institution with enormous power and a central place in neoliberal urban governance dominated by growth logics. But far from settled or cemented, I argue that property relations are continually in the process of being remade. Gardeners thus enact land politics that can either reimagine or reinforce contemporary property relations, by both drawing on threads of neoliberal privatization and development and resisting those threads.

In order to understand how gardeners may be changing the socio-spatial landscapes of cities, this chapter explores the strategies that activists use to enact, and thus build anew, the institution of property. I tell the stories of multiple organized garden projects that, over the past five years, have enacted property relations that favor the success of their projects through protest, negotiation, collaboration, and legislative change. I examine three land-access strategies that gardeners have employed: backyard-garden activism, reclaiming public land, and developing flexible, short-term relationships to particular pieces of land. These land-access strategies are shared across many projects; in fact, many of the organizations described use more than one of these strategies. While this chapter does not attempt to survey all forms of land-access arrangements or property enactments utilized by gardeners, it does outline dominant themes and debates over strategy in urban agricultural communities. By reimagining property in service of social justice and community control, urban gardeners build opportunities for connection with broader movements such as food sovereignty and right to the city.

GARDENS SHAPING CITIES

Gardening is a socio-ecological process that can create urban space through struggles for the transformation of landscapes. Space is socially produced through a history of practices, representations, and experiences (Heynen et al. 2006). Gardeners change the production of urban spaces by advocating the use of public land, changing investor decisions about buying particular parcels, and working with policymakers to create legislation to increase space for gardens. Through gardening, the subjects analyzed in this chapter work not only to change the physical, everyday urban spaces of today, but also are changing the trajectories and orientations of relationships between municipal governments, developers, and urban agriculturalists, thus changing the processes of the production of space. In this study, *gardeners* refers to a broad set of roles played by people engaged in organized garden projects, including the producers with their hands in the dirt doing the everyday work of reproducing vegetative life, project leaders managing relationships with landowners, and garden advocates working with broader political organizations to create social movement and political change. I use this one term because during my ethnographic research I frequently, though not universally, saw participants wearing these different hats throughout the course of their work, shifting between roles and engaging in multiple projects: these are individuals committed to urban gardening as a significant part of their lives. The gardeners depicted in this chapter consciously seek to address a number of political and philosophical questions: What kind of city do we want to live in? How do we want to eat and work, interact with nature, and engage with our neighbors and governmental agencies within that city? How can gardens help us transform cities today and prefigure new cities of our futures? Can we change the economic, political, social, and ecological landscapes of cities through garden projects?

Since the 1970s, urban spaces in industrial nations have undergone radical transformation through processes of neoliberalization. In the United States, the phase of "roll-back neoliberalism" that began in the 1970s saw a loose coalition of actors dismantling social programs and defunding the welfare state (Peck and Tickell 2002). For example, several traditional municipal community-garden programs in the Bay Area were defunded starting in the late 1970s. More recently, the processes of "roll-out neoliberalization" created new modes of governance that both empower the market as authority and assert the power of the state in differing ways. States increasingly are charged with the responsibility of creating a policy and social environment for secure investment and market exchange. In this vein, market-oriented food justice projects have been critiqued as engaging neoliberal logics that emphasize social change through consumption (Allen 2004, Guthman 2008, Pudup 2008). This chapter looks to gardeners' orientation toward consumption of land and property as a commodity exchanged in land markets, the role of municipalities in facilitating and promoting this exchange, and potential alternatives to this perspective on land relations.

While neoliberalization processes have been heterogeneous and uneven in their development, critical scholars have noted the strategic role that cities have played in neoliberalization (Brenner and Theodore 2002, Smith 2002). In what those authors termed "the urbanization of neoliberalism," cities have become both the targets and the experimental terrains of neoliberal policies such as place-marketing, enterprise zones, urban development corporations, market-oriented restructuring projects, public–private partnerships, entrepreneurial project promotion, and new strategies for social control (Smith 2002, 21). Creative destruction and the urban built environment are key components of neoliberal processes. Surplus value is no longer primarily generated through industrial production as described by Marx in *Capital,* but by spatial production instead (Lefebvre 1974).

In the Bay Area region, the growth of the tech industry, among other factors, has led to a real estate boom and highly competitive land markets. In the 1970s and '80s, Silicon Valley was rich with venture capital and tech innovation; by 2013, scholars asked "Is San Francisco the new Silicon Valley?" (Florida 2013, Florida and Kenney 1988). The region continues to attract venture-capital-backed high-tech industry at a higher rate than any other location in the world, with more than $13.5 billion invested in 2011 alone (Florida 2013). Bridging technology and real estate development, commercial-real-estate tech start-ups based in the region brought in $74 million of capital investment between 2012 and 2014 (Samtani 2014). Silicon Valley is the national leader in these investments and, with New York, represents 36 percent of real estate tech start-ups worldwide (ibid.). Today San Francisco boasts the highest and fastest-growing property values in the nation, with regional property values rising quickly as well (Sankin 2012).

Gardening is one response from communities facing food injustices within neoliberal urban regimes. But in the Bay Area, gardening over the past ten years has been thriving in both devalorized landscapes, such as the flatland of West Oakland, and the competitive land markets of places like downtown San Francisco (McClintock 2011). Now, as property values rise across the region and a regional housing crisis unfolds, food justice projects engaged in urban gardening are faced with greater tenure insecurity as new development pushes gardeners off vacant land. Drawing inspiration from over five decades of rich social-movement activism using food production projects in the region, gardeners are resisting eviction and tenure insecurity. In fact, gardening in the Bay Area has been a key tactic in collective-living, urban ecological, and student social movements as well as in Black and Chicano liberation work. Those histories are alive and well in today's food justice work in Oakland, San Francisco, and San Jose.

Yet gardening has also become a key tool in entrepreneurial and cost-saving policies that encourage urban development throughout the uneven economic geographies of the region. Regardless of the intention of gardeners, the presence of urban agriculture tends to increase property values (Voicu and Been 2008). And, as they are in other locales, real estate companies and developers are aware of this opportunity (Quastel 2009). Some gardeners have actively developed relationships with municipal governments and developers in order to gain access to parcels of land for short-term leases until such time as the owner is able to sell or build on the land. And gardeners have worked with local politicians to pass legislation and incentives for temporary land use, helping create a culture of comfort and security for landowners.

Thus, how gardeners position themselves in relation to urban development and the rights and priorities of landowners matters. When gardeners assert they can change the economic, political, social, and ecological landscapes of cities, it is essential to interrogate the land politics they enact and are entangled within. Gardeners particularly impact the continuous development of property as a social institution that assigns rights, authority, and resources to individuals and groups in contemporary society. Urban agriculture cultivates property regimes as much as local and sustainable foods.

Gardeners recognize that their strategies are shaped by contemporary property relations. Many gardeners also contend that they are active participants in shaping the property relations that may determine the fates of their projects. Gardeners stress that their projects are making an impact on how local municipalities are embracing urban gardening as land use, how residents view the use of land for food production, and how gardening can challenge the priority of land value for development. As such, some gardeners wish to and do contribute to versions of property that challenge neoliberal, land-ownership-based relations of land use that many see as a barrier to better urban forms. By analyzing these property practices, we can see property enacted more as a continual and somewhat open process of "doing" than as a closed collection of laws (Blomley 2003).

ENACTING PROPERTY

To understand gardeners' land claims, we must first understand something about private property as it is institutionalized and practiced in the United States. Emphasis on private property within contemporary economic policy revives liberal and utilitarian arguments that assert property as a stabilizing and productive social force (Rose 1994). Neo-utilitarians draw from Jeremy Bentham's thesis that when individuals have clear and secure ownership they feel free to participate in economic activity (i.e., trade). Bentham's assertion is part of what Joseph Singer (2000) terms the "ownership model," which makes clear and distinct categories of public and private property. Singer argues that this model of property has become the dominant and guiding view of property in social and political life.

The ownership model identifies property as a set of rights over particular things, and the holder of those rights as the property owner (Singer 2000). The set of rights implies that owners have the freedom to use the property, sell it, or otherwise transfer title, exclude others from its use, and experience security that others will not attempt to take their property without the owner's consent. As such, the freedom to property is conceived as a negative freedom, a freedom from intrusion (ibid.). Clear and discrete boundaries between private and state property become a means of securing owner rights. The state is responsible for creating stable frameworks of enforcement and protection of an owner's right to property. Blomley (2003) cites Laclau and Mouffe as arguing that rights offer a means of acknowledging and measuring power relations in their political and conditional contexts. As we will see in this chapter, when particular communities assert rights to property, either as discursive tools or as legal claims, we can observe their struggles for legitimization.

Yet within the ownership model, both space and property are represented as "fixed, natural, and objective" (ibid.). Objective representations of property, space, and law make current property relations "appear pre-political, obvious, and unproblematic" (ibid.). But property can take on complex meanings: alternative property dynamics may exist within our current society that are not completely outside the capitalist ownership model nor completely capitalist (Gibson-Graham 1996, Mansfield 2007). Rose considers property relations as plural, interrelated, and unfixed, describing "unreal estate" as when people make property claims or recognize others' claims despite their knowledge that the claims are legally illegitimate (Rose 1994). The ownership model thus sits side-by-side with these resistant practices. As such, gardeners can contribute to what Blomley (2003, 14) argues is the need to "depict property 'at its loose ends,'" thus destabilizing the ownership model, which occupies a hegemonic place in today's society. Blomley (2005) offers this example: in Vancouver, private gardeners are planting beyond their yards by taking over the soil in the space between the sidewalk and street. An artist collective used this space to place an old bathtub and other creative planters as a way to disrupt ideas of normal use of the space. The legal categories of private and public space had little relevance to these gardeners who used land in their daily practices, practices that through their doing make relationships to property.

The land-access strategies that gardeners engage are their processes of enacting property. As an object of social and political ambiguity and contest, property can become a site of resistance, a tool of resistance, and also that which must be resisted (Blomley 2003). For the gardeners in this chapter, property is all three. In the rest of this chapter, I depict stories of gardener entanglements with spatial production and the enactment of property through their use of three strategies of land access: backyard gardening, reclaiming public land for community management, and embracing interim use. These provide an initial, though incomplete, view into the land politics that urban agriculturalists are developing in the Bay Area.

BACKYARD GARDENING: ASSERTING NEW RELATIONSHIPS TO PRIVATE LANDOWNERS

Several organizations have embraced backyard gardens to achieve a variety of social goals, including cultural empowerment, food security, and transformation of urban ecology. The scale of these projects is significant. The combined efforts of La Mesa Verde, Valley Verde, and Planting Justice have resulted in the development of over a thousand home gardens in San Jose and Oakland since 2008.

La Mesa Verde (LMV) is an example of one gardening project that has developed a complicated relationship to the way land access is conceived and practiced. The organization works with low-income San Jose residents to build gardens in their backyards, whether they own or rent the land. In its ambitious beginnings, former executive director Raul Lozano used LMV to advocate within city government. His version imagined placing urban gardening prominently in the city plans by encouraging the development of twenty thousand home gardens by 2020. At least half of the gardens would be in homes of lower-income residents. He has since formed another project, "Valley Verde," with this aim. Planning documents that would mandate or support the use of backyards for gardening in rental property could challenge the autonomy of property owners. As such, this type of political engagement complicates a simplified understanding of backyard food production on rented land and challenges the ownership model.

Lozano viewed LMV as distinct from community gardening organizations: "We are going to the families" by placing the gardens in participants' yards. For Lozano, this was an explicit food justice commitment to the

Latino community, whereby he hoped to support gardeners in continuing agroecological and culinary traditions as well as increasing food security. A current LMV staff member, Patty Guzman, believes that while many program participants might want to participate in community gardens, backyard gardens are more realistic, given other commitments and time constraints like work and family schedules or limited access to transportation. Additionally, in Guzman's words, community gardens "may not be culturally relevant to some." However, Guzman acknowledges that the strategy of using backyards limits who can engage in the program: "It's a double-edged sword. Backyard gardens aren't accessible to some, many people who live in apartments or projects and just don't have the space. By the same token, a lot of people who do have the space and have their own homes don't have the luxury of time or the ability to pay the fee to go to a community garden" (all quotations not followed by a citation are from interviews conducted by the author during 2013–14).

In theory, the LMV effort to change the control parameters for backyards might upend the ownership model of property; however, logistical and training challenges make this difficult. For instance, for LMV's program participants to have yard space with sufficient sunlight where the raised beds can be built, they need permission to use the property. Of the more than 350 families that have participated in LMV, the vast majority have been renters. Participants are expected to have the discussions or negotiations necessary with their landlord to gain permission. However, program staff lament that they currently do not have the capacity to offer assistance to participants when they are seeking permission from their landlords. Interested families have been turned away because they were unable to get permission or find an adequate space in their yard. Program staff see this as an unfortunate parameter that they must work within. Guzman explains: "We just haven't approached the beast of land-ownership and rights around land access. We're trying to get the gardens up and running and get everyone the materials. We just can't address the issue of land rights. Ultimately, it's their responsibility to deal with the land question." She goes on to explain that several families, including one of the primary leaders in the program who had previously hosted a demonstration garden, have lost their gardens as a result of eviction or having to move. In 2013, LMV worked with student researchers to develop a set of tools to assist interested families in approaching their landlords.

In spite of these challenges, the gardening of LMV has resulted in some resistant property narratives. For instance, several gardeners expressed a lack of concern about normative property boundaries. They explicitly rejected the need to ask permission to access space in the houses they cultivated. Many gardeners described planting outside of the agreed-upon planting areas and using the yard space for other gardening-related projects that were not preapproved by the landlord. In a few interviews, Mexican-American gardeners cited long-held beliefs that they deserved access to the land because, after all, they were the ones who worked it in order to produce food for survival. One gardener cited Mexican revolutionary Emiliano Zapata: "La tierra es de quien la trabaja con sus manos—The land belongs to those that work it with their own hands." This was echoed by vacant-lot gardeners of Mexican descent in Oakland as well. In other words, the gardens became sites for nurturing alternative expressions of property relations.

Concerns and complaints from organizations like LMV that use backyard-gardening strategies, regarding the ability of landlords to limit their work, inspired the Sustainable Economies Law Center (SELC) to pursue legislative change, resulting in a measured victory in 2014. The SELC worked with lawmakers to introduce California bill AB 2561, the California Neighborhood Food Act, to ensure that renters have access to their yard space for home food production. Initially, the bill aimed toward significant gains for tenants' rights to grow produce on rental-property land, including making it illegal for individual landlords and homeowners' associations to prohibit home food gardens. Through the legislative committee process and as a result of resistance from the homeowners' lobby, the bill was amended to restrict rights to backyard gardens to backyards of single-family and duplex homes, requiring tenant gardens to be in movable containers that the landlord approves, and allowing the landlord to restrict the number and location of containers. Even so, SELC organizers believe this is an important first step in shifting the landscape of rights for non-property-owners to grow food on rented land. Neil Thapar, SELC lead campaign staffer, was encouraged that many legislators were surprised that there would be resistance to allowing tenants and homeowners' association members to grow food to feed themselves. While some assume that the work of promoting sustainable home food production is universally supported, SELC made visible the tension of landlord concerns about liability and decreasing property value in contrast with the long-held ideal of a backyard garden providing supplemental food resources and a space for family betterment.

Thus, while LMV and the California Neighborhood Food Act have had a limited impact on shifting actual access to land for renters, their work contributes to the cultivation of property subjectivities that decenter the landlord. Their efforts spotlight the question of "who has access to land in order to produce their own food." Backyard gardening was popularized as a national hobby in the post–World War II era, at the same time that racially discriminatory selling and lending practices excluded many non-white families from becoming homeowners. The consequence of decades of racism in housing markets and in access to educational and economic opportunities is a landscape where home ownership is still an opportunity available to many more white and economically advantaged families. At the same time, home food production in the United States has a long and rich history in many communities that were denied land access. Food justice movements, which work to confront racial and economic inequality, are problematizing the popular food movement's assumption that everyone has legal access to land on which they can "grow it yourself." And in the case of LMV and SELC, organizers and gardeners are working to ensure that the landlord does not have the final word on the construction of the limits of property. Gardeners are promoting an engagement with space that prioritizes land for food production, similar to the stories of gardeners taking back public land in the next section.

PRIORITIZING USE OF PUBLIC LANDS

Gardeners use various land-access strategies that emphasize the need to use public or state-owned land. Some have focused on the responsibility of municipalities or other governmental agencies to provide access to, manage, or actively cultivate space for the purposes of food justice. For example, two of the more prominent urban-agriculture land-inventory projects conducted in the region in the past five years were designed to advocate for increased access to public space by local residents (McClintock and Cooper 2010, Zigas 2012). While some efforts emphasize the need for state responsibility, many gardeners approach the question of public land as an opportunity to increase community management of local resources. This is especially pertinent to gardeners who have seen urban agriculture pushed aside by municipal governments seeking financial benefits, as in the case of the more than $5 million public sale and eviction of gardeners at the South Central Farm of East Los Angeles or the evictions of hundreds of gardeners in the sale of public gardens in the New York City development boom of the 1990s. Two contemporary examples of projects using public land to promote community land management are the Edible Parks Taskforce in Oakland and the alliance of actors trying to take back the Gill Tract Farm, including Occupy the Farm.

The Edible Parks Taskforce arose in an environment where collective gardening and education projects are finding success working with the City of Oakland through public–private partnerships. Various nonprofits are partnering with the City of Oakland Office of Parks and Recreation to use and manage currently existing park space (see City of Oakland 2014, fig. 4.5). For these projects, which currently hold temporary use agreements, access to space on public land is meaningful. Max Cadji describes the once weedy, underutilized land located in a city park now used by Phat Beets: "It was not a lawn; it didn't have a *use.*" Gardeners, neighbors, and organizers planted a large area with vegetable beds and fruit trees, and made art in the public space. For Cadji, gardening thus is a means to revitalize underfunded and undermanaged public areas. When two neighbors complained to the city that the project was "Peoples' Park-ifying the park," allowing younger, politically oriented residents to take over public space, more than two hundred neighbors responded by supporting the project.

In 2011, seeing the success of gardens on park land, community members began organizing the Edible Parks Taskforce, a coalition of individuals and organizations including Phat Beets, PUEBLO, City Slicker Farms, Acta Non Verba, the Victory Gardens Foundation, Planting Justice, Oakland Food Policy Council, and many others. They joined together to propose an Edible Parks Community Stewardship Program, which would promote the use of public space for edible landscaping for community self-determination. The program is inspired by Oakland's Adopt-a-Spot program, in which individuals, groups, and businesses can volunteer to manage pieces of public land and help reduce city costs. Yet for activists the program is an opportunity to engage people in managing public land. As Cadji describes,

> We're trying to come up with a way that we can make the park more interactive and meet these huge concerns of literally food apartheid in some communities. A public park is for everyone so we want everyone to access it.

For gardeners in the Taskforce, bringing neighbors into urban agriculture in parks begins a process of reinspiring these neighbors to embrace the public management of space, taking back local land resources to address community needs.

TABLE 10.1 Oakland Office of Parks and Recreation Garden Partnerships

Organization	Location
Acta Non Verba	Tassafaronga Park Urban Farm
City Slicker Farms	Fitzgerald Park Urban Farm
Oakland Based Urban Gardens	Marston Campbell Park Youth Gardens
People United for a Better Life in Oakland	Kings Estates Community Gardens
Phat Beets Produce	Dover Street Park Community Garden
Stonehurst Edible Schoolyard	Esperanza Elementary School and Korematsu Discovery Academy

At the center of their work is community self-determination, built through legacies of struggles for Black and Latino liberation. Histories of environmental justice and antihunger organizing that built toward garden activism today are founded in radical Black power, student, and environmental movements of the 1960s. While local-food-production projects have been critiqued as isolationist, individualistic, conservative, and in tension with social justice desires, for many in the food justice movement, localist politics do not manifest as an unexamined commitment to communalistic ideals. Instead, in marginalized communities, mistrust of dominant power structures and understanding of historical, systemic, and currently institutionalized racism have influenced some organizers to emphasize strategies that promote the self-reliance and self-determination of local communities (Alkon and Norgaard 2009, Bradley and Galt 2014).

The Taskforce wants the city to standardize and clarify the process for use of public land. Some feel that the process for accessing parkland for gardening has varied depending on the political support of different organizations. Despite conversations for over a year and the presentation of a concrete proposal with support from three City Council members, gardeners claim the city has been slow to engage with the Taskforce and has yet to offer support. Stephanie Benavidez of the Office of Parks and Recreation argued, "We have different goals and objectives. It's about finding common ground" (Key 2014). Both city officials and some neighbors worry that this interest in urban gardening is held by only a small subsector of the population. City planner Heather Klein, for instance, asks: "Who's the community and how is the community defined? Some people see that, those groups as just sort of taking over those resources." There is concern that gardeners may intentionally or unintentionally exclude certain people or practices from the area they garden or that the projects may be adopted and then discarded, creating more work for city employees. Changing park priorities and their physical landscapes has long-term consequences and impacts for the broader community, not just for advocates of urban agriculture. But overall, Klein has been impressed by the remarkable energy and ability of gardening projects to spring up without relying on city infrastructure: "They seem to be able to move these things forward on their own. I think with the city's limited resources, it's just difficult for us to be able to commit to providing some of the things that they want to have us provide. It's a whole level of review that we just don't have staff for or the capacity to do."

In a city with limited resources and staffing, gardeners are demanding access to underutilized public land. But activists and nonprofits are not just participating in roll-out neoliberalism by taking over governmental duties as the state withdraws community support; instead, they are putting pressure on municipal departments to develop and administer fair processes that empower residents to take greater responsibility in the care and decision making for public land. Organizers are insisting that public voices guide the use of public property, arguing that city officials and technocrats are out of touch with the desires of many community members who would manage community land resources if given the chance. Similarly, just a few miles to the north, Gill Tract Farm activists envision public land in control of student and community members.

In Albany, just north of Berkeley, urban-agriculture advocates struggled from 1997 to 2013 to gain a ten-year agreement for a garden on University of California (UC) property, with the intention of promoting community land management. Hoping to attract commercial development funds, UC Berkeley had decided to sell the development rights to the south side of Gill Tract Farm, which was adjacent to UC Berkeley family student housing. In 1997, after learning of UC's plans, a coalition of over thirty groups began resisting the development and proposed instead an urban-agriculture research and education center. UC students, neighbors, and urban-garden advocates led by Peter Rosset and others at Food First organized to resist the development and advocated for the creation of a sustainable urban-agriculture training center (Bay Area Coalition for Urban Agriculture 1997).

For over seven decades, the farm had been used by the Division of Biological Control for research on integrated pest management, but in 1998, just a year after the decision to sell the development rights to the south side of Gill Tract Farm, a research agreement was made between the UC Department of Plant and Molecular Biology and Novartis, a biotechnology corporation, which granted Novartis the right to license discoveries in exchange for a $25 million donation to the department (Press and Washburn 2000). As a result, by 2001 the Division of Biological Control was no longer allowed to use the land and was defunded by the university, opening more land to potential development. In 2004 the UC regents released a Master Plan for Developing the University Village that included the entire tract. In spite of community and student objections, between 2004 and the early 2010s the UC moved ahead with planning the development. At the same time, neoliberal privatization of the university unfurled in other ways: unprecedented tuition hikes, recruitment of out-of-state students to augment tuition profits, and increased investment in real estate and development on UC campuses (Roman-Alcalá 2013, Watson 2012).

In April 2012, a group of students and activists occupied the south part of the Gill Tract, naming the action Occupy the Farm (OTF). They were outraged that public land owned by UC would be used to generate revenue instead of promoting the public education mission of the institution. As one OTF activist explained:

> This is a land grant university . . . the privileges and benefits that they enjoy now are because they were created as a public institution. And so [it's] best to hold them to that through this project. [It] feels like really engaged civic duty or action.

The occupation initially lasted three weeks during April 2012, until UC police stepped in to end the occupation. Subsequent reoccupations and other actions have continued on the tract.

At the same time, students and garden advocates from the newly forming Students for Engaged and Active Learning were working with faculty such as Miguel Altieri, an internationally renowned agroecologist, to develop a community–university partnership for use of the land. Today that partnership project manages a collectively run garden called the Gill Tract Community Farm, located on part of the northern portion of the land. The garden is embraced as a territory in which to relearn more collective decision making and share governing power. Murray (2014) argued that OTF activists develop counterinstitutions of commons management—a space for community land management that engages local residents, students, and researchers in a project that redefines how public university space should be prioritized. Gardeners would like to see more of the land re-devoted to agroecology research and practice. In making a claim to UC property, OTF highlights UC's shift toward increasing privatization while little support is given to projects for agroecology, food security, or purposes that otherwise serve the local ecological and human communities. OTF activists protested the hiring of the first "vice chancellor for real estate," articulating that UC land is for community benefit, not development. OTF activists have also developed a connection with the MST (Movimento dos Trabalhadores Rurais Sem Terra, or Landless Workers Movement),[1] organizing events that connect food and land sovereignty work in the Global South to the struggle for the Gill Tract Farm.

Both the Edible Parks Taskforce and the campaign for the Gill Tract Farm are examples of people prioritizing and redefining the use of public land, in their terms "reclaiming" public space. They emphasize the need for greater community management of land resources for self-determination, education, and livelihoods. When gardeners organize to demand parcels of public space and make community land management a priority, they open opportunities to connect their work to other justice-oriented urban social movements, including housing justice, transportation justice, and the like. Recently in the United States, some of the urban movements have united under the banner of the "right to the city," creating demands for an end of displacement and for rights to govern the city. Local organizations like Movement Generation, which participated in the Right to the City Alliance, stress that gardening has its place in these urban social movements. For Esperanza Pallana of the Oakland Food Policy Council, gardeners contribute to food movements that ask:

> Who gets to say how the land is used? Why is it way above our heads? Why are we not involved in saying what our city looks like? The built environment is directly impacting our ability to feed ourselves, our ability to get around, move around within the city without a car, our ability to access school education.

Gardener and food justice advocates that work to increase community power through land management and access are building bridges between urban movements confronting the dominance of private property and neoliberal governance in Bay Area cities. Yet not all projects are advocating this orientation.

Many urban-agriculture projects in the region have embraced projects with limited access to particular tracts of land. Thus, some develop technology to be able to move gardens easily when their lease or use agreement is up; others accept that any given garden will be temporary but hope that each temporary space can be the seed to inspire many other gardeners to grow. What connects these gardeners is a lack of permanence on any given piece of land.

For instance, AB 551, the Urban Agriculture Incentive Zones legislation, incentivizes the use of urban land for agriculture by allowing a property to be assessed at a lower tax rate (i.e., based on the agricultural value rather than the market value), in exchange for a five-year commitment to using the land for farming or gardening. SPUR and Little City Gardens, both significant supporters of AB 551, were inspired by the state's 1965 Williamson Act, which allowed local governments to assess rural land at lower rates in exchange for ten-year agreements to keep land in open space or agricultural land use (Mazurek 2013). Thus, AB 551 was based on the recognition that property tax rates are one of many barriers to landowners engaged in imagining urban farms on their land. Although AB 551 passed, it still requires counties to choose to opt in and to create local policies that will facilitate private landowners' participation. On August 7, 2014, San Francisco became the first county and city to implement AB 551 (Zigas 2014).

Eli Zigas, manager of SPUR's Food Systems and Urban Agriculture program, acknowledges that this legislation will not create a sufficient financial advantage to outweigh other options but argues that it will reduce the costs to landowners, which may soften their hesitation to form a partnership with gardeners: "It's a carrot to bring someone [landowner] to the table, but only in a few situations will it be enough to bring them to the table." One such project to benefit from the new legislation is the Urban Permaculture Institute, which is located on private property owned by a San Francisco doctor, Aaron Roland, who is currently committed to allowing the garden to continue on his land in order to improve food security and healthy food consumption within the city. Roland was quoted as saying, "There's a huge opportunity cost in letting your property be used for a garden. I'm delighted that the property has some use, but I'm paying over $6,000 year for the privilege of saying no to high offers to sell it" (Mazurek 2013). Garden projects across the Bay Area have been inspired by the legislation and are working with local officials toward implementation, while others are innovating new approaches to temporary access.

For San Francisco–based NOMADgardens, the use of portable metal garden containers is designed to aid the nonprofit in "roam(ing) seamlessly from vacant lot to vacant lot" (NOMADgardens 2012). They aim to "activate vacant lots in developing neighborhoods" and build community through workshops, movie screenings, art events, picnics, and gardening. NOMAD founder Stephanie Goodson was motivated to create spaces where neighbors can connect outside of home and work. After difficulties in reaching out to a local developer to use a piece of vacant land, she decided a new approach to land use was needed. Goodson argues that gardeners grow attached to their garden on a particular piece of land and that this makes it dangerous for developers who intend to eventually construct projects on the property to allow gardening as a temporary use. Instead, "By creating a 'roaming community garden' developers would be able to reclaim the land easily" (ibid.). Similarly, before buying the land for their current farm, Berkeley-based Urban Adamah had a two-year lease on private land owned by the founder of Wareham Development. The farm developed its infrastructure to be portable and has since trained others in portable-bed construction (Adam Berman, personal communication, 2014). One San Jose project leader states that "People need to be clever—we build mobile beds so you can move—we build it into the concept. We're lucky to have this—we need to make owners/developers feel comfortable." Portability facilitates temporary land use and beneficial relationships with owners who are concerned that gardeners may resist.

Another approach advocated by some gardeners is to work with city offices to develop interim-use projects. In 2009 the mayor of San Francisco, Gavin Newsom, issued the Executive Directive on Healthy and Sustainable Food, which outlined the city's support of urban agriculture and the sustainable food movement. Through the directive, two lots in downtown were allocated for temporary garden development, which became the Hayes Valley Farm and the Growing Home Garden. Both projects ended when the city sold the properties for housing development. From project organizers of these particular projects to gardeners across the region, the value and role of interim use in the future of urban gardening is hotly debated.

The Hayes Valley Farm (HVF) was a high-profile urban garden located in downtown San Francisco. After the 1989 Loma Prieta earthquake, the Central Freeway was damaged and torn down on the 2.2-acre site that later became the farm. In January 2010, after two decades of slow cleanup with the land lying vacant, HVF opened. Leading up to the opening of the farm, the ownership of the land had changed hands from Cal Trans to the former Redevelopment Agency, and then to the City of San Francisco's Office of Housing, and the two parcels had been slotted for future development. In 2010, with a $52,950 grant from San Francisco's Office of Economic and Workforce Development, HVF was started as an interim-use project to last between three and eighteen years (City of San Francisco 2014). In June 2013 the farm closed its doors, and two real estate developers—Avalon Bay Communities, a national company, and Build Inc., a small San Francisco–based company—bought one of the parcels (half of the 2.2 acres) for $9 million and made plans to start construction on a housing project (Roth 2013).

For the original organizers of HVF and many others, interim use offers an innovative approach to creating temporary yet vibrant projects in the context of a highly competitive land market.

> Hayes Valley Farm is a champion of interim-use farming. Not only does interim-use provide an opportunity to rethink how we use the land and demonstrate how much food can be grown in a given area, it also allows us to engage in education, outreach, community building, and to develop broader, transportable, resiliency models that we feel are essential in this era of transition and transformation. (HVF 2013)

The knowledge that the project was temporary motivated volunteers and organizers to use the momentum from the HVF to start various other projects in the city. Jay Rosenberg of the leadership team stated: "I'd love to see it explode into fireworks so that little farm projects start popping up all over, as a space to grow food, recycle, create compost, take classes and share tools." For organizers, the proliferation of projects resulted from a process of inspiration predicated on impending closure. For one organizer who self-identified as an anarchist, it was inspired by a conception of resiliency that embraced this form of inspiration: "We are interested in creating a resiliency model where you don't have to be permanent—you can respond to changes—respond to emergencies and otherwise—tactical permaculture. Also to show that we can work outside ownership models."

While these organizers embraced interim use, others had concerns about the impacts short-term projects could have. These gardeners advocated for "developing roots" in particular communities, with particular pieces of land. Markos Major, organizer with Growing Home, the other interim-use project, asked how the homeless community served by their garden could interpret the information that their garden would be temporary, other than concluding they are not a priority to the city. When discussing the desire of other gardeners that Growing Home leave their project quietly when the city ended their arrangement, Major stated: "Frankly, I'm not interested in interim use. I mean it's not useless of course, but it's not really extremely beneficial in the long run by any means, except for developers who really do have a lot to gain from it."

Gardeners also cite the ecology of the garden as a reason for long-term tenure. Evan Krokowski, of the Farm2Market Farm, describes the necessity of long-term access for their project:

> I think also going back to the agroecology, the reality is it takes a long time to eliminate weed seed banks and build up soil fertility and get the till and the layout of the space that you want. For us, it's happened over six years and I finally feel like we're getting to this point where things are the way that I would like them to be, but we're still refining things all the time. You really have to think about a long-term sustainability and building your own soil and creating systems that will support life on the site.

This conception of an agroecological, resilient site differed from interim-use promoters' visions of projects generously creating environmental benefits in the now, with flexible communities of gardeners able to inspire the creation of new projects when old ones come to an end.

While the leadership team of HVF embraced the interim-use quality of the project as an opportunity, some garden volunteers and other Bay Area activists did not, and questioned why the lot should be sold. A protest was organized, "Liberate the Land," with the claim that "We are being called to defend the land we grow on. While 36,000 housing units are left empty in San Francisco, property owners and developers plan to build condominiums and high-end housing structures at the cost of displacing *urban farms and gardens*." This occurred shortly after the Taksim Gezi Park mass protests in Turkey, which opposed the development of one of the few green spaces left and open to the public in Istanbul's Beyoglu district. Inspired by Istanbul, protesters occupied HVF and renamed the farm Gezi Garden in solidarity with the Turkish activist efforts. Protesters spoke to the necessity of defending urban green space as open space for people to connect with the soil, and of valuing the land for its ecological importance and not its development potential. The occupation lasted two weeks, when the gardeners and three tree sitters were forcibly removed from the site.

The occupation sparked a powerful and sometimes quite contentious debate within urban agricultural communities across the Bay Area. Erin

Dage, in the *San Francisco Bay Guardian* blog, frames the debate: "might it [the Gezi Garden occupation] actually make property owners less likely to allow community-based temporary uses on land awaiting development?" (Dage 2013). For those opposed, the occupation represented a naive and shortsighted action aimed at agitating instead of growing food. One garden advocate argued: "I don't think the people who squatted Hayes Valley after the actual organizers left had a sense of how we were going to get from where they were and where we are as a society to where they wanted us to be which is a society without private property—their feeling was the land is for the people but that's not how we've set up society—I don't think it's happening anytime soon." For another, the opposition to private property and the idea that urban residents should reclaim control of urban green space were even more problematic: "They took it for granted—felt like it was their right to be there. That can't happen. It's a privilege to be able to garden. The time that it's there is a gift. That's the classic example of why landowners don't want to do this." As this interviewee's argument indicates, a major anxiety for many gardeners after the occupation was whether this action, or similar ones like OTF outside of Berkeley, would scare landlords or municipal agencies out of wanting to work with gardeners.

Other gardeners appreciated the work of the occupiers, claiming that the conversations about development and the evictions of gardens is something the urban-agriculture community needs to face directly. Interim use demands an accommodating approach from gardeners that can be seen mirrored in neoliberal discourse of "flexibility." Scholars over the past several decades have studied neoliberalism as social processes elevating the flexibility of real estate markets and municipal decision making around land use, labor, and production systems (Harvey 1978, Vives Miró 2011). As one self-identified anarchist gardener, critical of flexibility and interim projects, argued:

> It's definitely not a long-term solution to the need for places to grow food, places to connect with the earth, places to live in balance with one's environment because every single interim-use project is pretty much almost immediately slated to be removed and turned into something that's the antithesis of what they're doing now, which is more concrete, more asphalt, more development. So yeah, I think it's a great thing to do if we want to temporarily model these systems but it's not in any way a solution to what's a big problem, which is that people are talking a lot these days about needing to grow food locally and sustainably and organically, close to home, and the biggest thing getting in the way of that is people's access to land.

In the highly competitive land markets in the region, some gardeners advocate short-term land-access agreements as a means of practicality and are attempting to cultivate a new relationship to land, one built not on long-term access but on a form of generosity that encourages practitioners to both benefit from the garden and give to the place and community, even for a short period. In so doing, these activists have described interim use as a model that can challenge private property, taking the wind out of the sails of a system that derives power from exclusive rights to land. Yet interim use clearly delineates a strategy oriented toward short-term projects with immediate gains and amicable relationships for landowners who want flexible options for future land uses. While gardeners are able to demonstrate innovative ecological and community projects, this model relies on politics that bolster the authority of public and private landlords as the ultimate decision-makers for land management and access. It places gardening in the position of supporting development policies and practices that value land as an economic commodity.

CONCLUSION

In each of these strategies—backyard-garden activism, reclaiming public land, and developing flexible, short-term relationships to particular pieces of land—gardeners and garden advocates are creating relations to property as a living and changing social institution. In all of these strategies, activists are engaging, or meeting head-on, state agencies or actors. For some, their demands challenge urban regimes determined by growth politics. For others, collaborations or attempts at legislative reform trust in a process of citizen input. But on the question of property, activists invariably must face the state as the rule-maker and enforcer of property laws and norms. Thus, through their politics of land, garden projects do not remain on the margins of neoliberal urban political economy, but play important roles in creating or reinforcing private and state property as social institutions.

Backyard-gardening advocates and the public land projects described in the first two strategies are examples of food justice projects that are working to recreate property as a more just set of relations. In the case of backyard-garden advocacy, gardeners at times ignore the authority of the landlord and propose to base land access on use values. Recent legislation ties tenants' rights with the right to food access, especially for communities that have limited access to home ownership. The two projects documented in the East

Bay in this chapter are working to confront state agencies and demand access to public land for community management and benefit. While limited by the land politics of the region, neither of these strategies takes property, as it is currently enacted, as something that must just be worked around. Instead, they are reworking property, both public and private.

And in the case of activists developing flexible, short-term relationships to particular pieces of land, some believe that this can undermine the emphasis put on ownership, acting as a form of resistance to neoliberalization of the city. Yet this model does not challenge the power landowners have in making land-use decisions, or take as problematic the driving force of development in urban politics. It is a model that has been less associated with food justice communities, and more with garden advocates able to mobilize cooperative relationships with developers. In order to not exist at the margins of neoliberal political economy, these projects are positioned in a supportive role, allowing landlords to benefit until such time as they choose to sell or develop the land.

This chapter contributes to understanding the work of food-justice and urban-agriculture activists as social-movement actors engaged in institution building. The praxis enacted through the land politics of gardening is important for understanding how these actors are entangled within, and also influence, shifts in the socio-spatial terrain of U.S. cities in economies increasingly steered, and communities increasingly galvanized, by financial and real estate investment. In the Bay Area, this praxis develops through tensions, debate, and critique of how to approach the institution of property as an essential base from which the possibilities of more just urban ecologies will be built.

NOTE

1. The MST, one of the largest contemporary social movements in Latin America, fights for land access for poor workers (see Robles 2001).

REFERENCES

Alkon, Alison Hope, and Kari Marie Norgaard. 2009. "Breaking the Food Chains: An Investigation of Food Justice Activism." *Sociological Inquiry* 79: 289–305.
Allen, Patricia. 2004. *Together at the Table: Sustainability and Sustenance in the American Agrifood System,* new edition. University Park, PA: Penn State University Press.

Bay Area Coalition for Urban Agriculture. 1997. "Creating a Center for Sustainable Urban Agriculture and Food Systems at the University of California Gill Tract in Albany." Berkeley, CA: BACUA. http://nature.berkeley.edu/srr/BACUA /bacua_proposal.htm.

Blomley, Nicholas. 2003. *Unsettling the City: Urban Land and the Politics of Property.* New York: Routledge.

———. 2005. "Flowers in the Bathtub: Boundary Crossings at the Public–Private Divide." *Geoforum* 36: 281–296.

Bradley, Katharine, and Ryan E. Galt. 2013. "Practicing Food Justice at Dig Deep Farms & Produce, East Bay Area, California: Self-Determination as a Guiding Value and Intersections with Foodie Logics." *Local Environment: The International Journal of Justice and Sustainability* 19: 172–186.

Brenner, Neil, and Nik Theodore. 2002. "Cities and the Geographies of 'Actually Existing Neoliberalism.'" *Antipode* 34: 349–379.

Cadji, Josh, and Alison Hope Alkon. 2015. "'One Day, the White People Are Going to Want These Houses Again': Understanding Gentrification through the North Oakland Farmers Market." In *Incomplete Streets: Processes, Practices, and Possibilities,* ed. Stephen Zavestoski and Julian Agyeman. New York: Routledge.

City of Oakland. 2014. "Community Gardening Program." www2.oaklandnet .com/government/o/opr/s/cgardening/index.htm.

City of San Francisco. 2014. "Community Challenge Grants." https://data.sfgov. org/api/views/nddu-z4m8/rows.pdf?app_token=U29jcmFoYSotd2VraWNrY XNzo.

Dage, Erin. 2013. "Did the Hayes Valley Farm Occupation Help or Hurt the Cause of Liberating Urban Space?" Blog post. *San Francisco Bay Guardian,* June 24. www.sfbg.com/politics/2013/06/24/did-hayes-valley-farm-occupation-help-or-hurt-cause-liberating-urban-space.

Drake, Luke, and Laura J. Lawson. 2014. "Validating Verdancy or Vacancy? The Relationship of Community Gardens and Vacant Lands in the U.S." *Cities* 40 (Part B): 133–142.

Florida, Richard. 2013. "Why San Francisco May Be the New Silicon Valley." *CityLab,* August 5. www.theatlanticcities.com/jobs-and-economy/2013/08/why-san-francisco-may-be-new-silicon-valley/6295/.

Florida, Richard, and Martin Kenney. 1988. "Venture Capital-Financed Innovation and Technological Change in the USA." *Research Policy* 17: 119–137.

Gibson-Graham, J. K. 1996. *The End of Capitalism (As We Knew It): A Feminist Critique of Political Economy.* Minneapolis: University of Minnesota Press.

Guthman, Julie. 2008. "Neoliberalism and the Making of Food Politics in California." *Geoforum* 39: 1171–1183.

Harvey, David. 1978. "The Urban Process under Capitalism: A Framework for Analysis." *International Journal of Urban and Regional Research* 2: 101–131.

Hayes Valley Farm. 2013. "Hayes Valley Farm Seeds Urban Agriculture, Biodiversity, and Youth Education Projects across San Francisco as It Bids Farewell." June 3. http://hayesvalleyfarm.tumblr.com/?og=1.

Heynen, Nik, Maria Kaika, and Erik Swyngedouw, Eds. 2006. *In the Nature of Cities: Urban Political Ecology and the Politics of Urban Metabolism.* New York: Routledge.

Key, Madeleine. 2014. "Oakland Slow to Okay More Public Urban Gardens." *East Bay Express,* June 3. www.eastbayexpress.com/oakland/oakland-slow-to-okay-more-public-urban-gardens/Content?oid=3939495.

Lefebvre, Henri. 1974. *The Production of Space.* Oxford: Wiley-Blackwell.

Mansfield, Becky. 2007. "Privatization: Property and the Remaking of Nature–Society Relations Introduction to the Special Issue." *Antipode* 39: 393–405.

Mazurek, Brie. 2013. "New Law Breaks Ground for Urban Ag." October 4. San Francisco: CUESA. www.cuesa.org/article/new-law-breaks-ground-urban-ag.

McClintock, Nathan C. 2011. "Cultivation, Capital, and Contamination: Urban Agriculture in Oakland, California." PhD dissertation, University of California, Berkeley. http://search.proquest.com.oca.ucsc.edu/docview/929198964/abstract/ABEB10C04F744DC6PQ/4?accountid=14523.

McClintock, Nathan, and Jenny Cooper. 2010. "Cultivating the Commons: An Assessment of the Potential for Urban Agriculture on Oakland's Public Land." Department of Geography, University of California, Berkeley.

Murray, Daniel. 2014. "Prefiguration or Actualization? Radical Democracy and Counter-Institution in the Occupy Movement." *Berkeley Journal of Sociology,* November. http://berkeleyjournal.org/2014/11/prefiguration-or-actualization-radical-democracy-and-counter-institution-in-the-occupy-movement/.

NOMADgardens. 2012. "Our Story." www.nomadgardens.org/about/.

Peck, Jamie, and Adam Tickell. 2002. "Neoliberalizing Space." *Antipode* 34: 380–404.

Press, Eyal, and Jennifer Washburn. 2000. "The Kept University." *The Atlantic,* March. www.theatlantic.com/magazine/archive/2000/03/the-kept-university/306629/.

Pudup, Mary B. 2008. "It Takes a Garden: Cultivating Citizen-Subjects in Organized Garden Projects." *Geoforum* 39: 1228–1240.

Quastel, Noah. 2009. "Political Ecologies of Gentrification." *Urban Geography* 30: 694–725.

Robles, Wilder. 2001. "The Landless Rural Workers Movement (MST) in Brazil." *Journal of Peasant Studies* 28: 146–161.

Roman-Alcalá, Antonio. 2013. "Occupy the Farm: A Study of Civil Society Tactics to Cultivate Commons and Construct Food Sovereignty in the United States." Paper presented at the conference "Food Sovereignty: A Critical Dialogue," Yale University, New Haven, CT.

Rose, Carol M. 1994. *Property and Persuasion: Essays on the History, Theory, and Rhetoric of Ownership.* Boulder, CO: Westview Press.

Roth, Anna. 2013. "Down and Dirty: Activists Occupy Hayes Valley Farm to Keep Developers Out." *SF Weekly,* June 13. www.sfweekly.com/sanfrancisco/down-and-dirty-activists-occupy-hayes-valley-farm-to-keep-developers-out/Content?oid=2826342.

Samtani, Hiten. 2014. "Real Estate Tech Startups Raised over $700M since 2012: Report." July 17. http://therealdeal.com/blog/2014/07/17/real-estate-tech-startups-raised-over-700m-since-2012-report/.

Sankin, Aaron. 2012. "San Francisco Rents the Highest of Any City in Country." *Huffington Post,* March 14. www.huffingtonpost.com/2012/03/14/san-francisco-rents-the-highest-in-nation_n_1345275.html.

Singer, Joseph W. 2000. *Entitlement: The Paradoxes of Property.* New Haven, CT: Yale University Press.

Smith, Neil. 2002. "New Globalism, New Urbanism: Gentrification as Global Urban Strategy." *Antipode* 34: 427–450.

Vives Miró, Sònia. 2011. "Producing a 'Successful City': Neoliberal Urbanism and Gentrification in the Tourist City—The Case of Palma (Majorca)." *Urban Studies Research* (September): e989676.

Voicu, Ioan, and Vicki Been. 2008. "The Effect of Community Gardens on Neighboring Property Values." *Real Estate Economics* 36: 241–283.

Watson, Mary V. 2012. "Teach the Budget." UC Santa Cruz. http://teachthe budgetdotcom.files.wordpress.com/2012/11/ttb-fall-2012-public.pdf.

Zigas, Eli. 2012. "Public Harvest: Expanding the Use of Public Land for Urban Agriculture in San Francisco." *SPUR Report,* April. SPUR, San Francisco.

———. 2014. "San Francisco Establishes California's First Urban Agriculture Incentive Zone." *Urban Agriculture—ANR Blogs,* August 18. http://ucanr.edu /blogs/blogcore/postdetail.cfm?postnum=15017.

ELEVEN

Boston's Emerging Food Solidarity Economy

Penn Loh and Julian Agyeman

INTRODUCTION

A FOOD JUSTICE MOVEMENT with a difference has been quietly blossoming in Boston. It is springing forth from Roxbury and Dorchester, two adjoining lower-income neighborhoods of color, where for decades residents have been organizing and struggling for community control over development. This movement encompasses a variety of initiatives to take back land; to grow, process, distribute, and sell food; and to repurpose organic wastes. It is driven by desires for a more just, sustainable, and democratic local food economy.

One poignant example is the Garrison-Trotter Farm in Roxbury, which broke ground in July 2014. This farm was the first to be permitted under Boston's 2013 "Right-to-Farm" zoning ordinance (Article 89) and was named after abolitionist William Lloyd Garrison and civil rights activist William Monroe Trotter. For decades, neighbors had been stewarding the land, which had lain vacant as a result of urban disinvestment and had fallen into city ownership. When a local commercial farming venture, City Growers, approached the neighbors about converting the land into a for-profit farm, they eagerly embraced the idea. But first City Growers and the neighbors had to get commercial farming in the city legalized, working with—and sometimes struggling against—city agencies that were used to pursuing the "highest and best use" for city-owned land. Along the way, they won support from political leaders, including former mayor Tom Menino, who started Boston's Urban Agriculture Initiative to increase access to fresh, healthy food, create economic opportunities, and decrease the environmental impacts of food transport.

To launch the Garrison-Trotter Farm, an innovative model had to be developed, wherein city-owned vacant land is first converted into a farmable condition and conveyed to a community land trust, which then provides long-term leases to urban farmers. This form of ownership insulates the land from the pressures of Boston's ferocious real estate market and ensures democratic governance and long-term access for urban growing. In this case, a national nonprofit, the Trust for Public Land, will convert the lot into farmable condition, which involves the costly step of importing clean soil. Then the Dudley Street Neighborhood Initiative's (DSNI) land trust, founded in 1988, will take ownership of the land. In turn, DSNI will provide a ninety-nine-year ground lease to the nonprofit training affiliate of City Growers, the Urban Farming Institute of Boston. Finally, the institute will rent the land affordably to its trained farmers, most of whom hail from the local community and are people of color.

As remarkable as this model is in overcoming barriers to land access, it also reveals a fundamental contradiction between for-profit farming and affordable access to local fresh food. In order to earn a decent living, urban farmers must sell their product for the highest price possible. Under City Growers' model, that means selling greens to Boston's flourishing high-end restaurants and groceries, most of which lower-income residents can rarely afford. Thus, while the City of Boston touts the Garrison-Trotter Farm as a way to both "bring healthy foods back to the communities to make it more accessible, and to also create jobs and give opportunities to folks who would like to get into farming" (Boston Neighborhood Network News 2014), the latter goal trumps the former.

In this chapter, we offer a critical but hopeful examination of the successes and challenges of the increasingly influential food justice movement in Boston. In particular, we explore the tensions inherent in challenging and transforming the neoliberal landscape within which food injustice and other inequalities are produced and reproduced. The Garrison-Trotter Farm represents just one strand in an emerging web of local initiatives that we call a "food solidarity economy." Other elements include nonprofit farms, guerilla gardens, a catering company, a food business incubator, a cooperative grocery, a bakery-café, and a recycling cooperative, all derived from diverse social-enterprise, nonprofit, and cooperative sectors.

We draw on the theory and practice of solidarity economics and diverse community economies (Gibson-Graham 2006, 1996) to show the possibilities for these food justice projects to enact and grow an economy that goes beyond the constraints of capitalism. But we also use an urban political ecology lens to foreground the challenges of neoliberalism to a food solidarity economy. For example, the Garrison-Trotter Farm model advances noncapitalist practices by de-commoditizing land via a land trust, but at the same time remains constrained by a commercial farming model premised on the commoditization of food. By examining both the possibilities and the constraints, we hope to support activists, practitioners, policymakers, and researchers in Boston and beyond in developing strategies to help solidarity economies proliferate. We conclude that moving toward this economy will require the creation of new alternatives, building on existing practices while challenging and transforming current institutions.

We begin with a more detailed articulation of our approach to food justice and neoliberalism. We then lay out our framework for understanding solidarity economies, followed by an overview of the various elements of the emerging Boston Food Solidarity Economy. The second half of the chapter unpacks and analyzes the tensions of growing this economy within the current neoliberal landscape. We look at how these challenges play out through the case of the legalization of commercial farming in Boston. Finally, we discuss how some of these constraints might be overcome and possibilities realized, with an emphasis on organizing and shifting power relations.

FOOD JUSTICE AND NEOLIBERALISM

We view food justice broadly as a movement that extends beyond the politics of consumption. Not only does it include the fight for low-wage workers within the current food economy, but food justice is about the right to control the food system itself—also referred to as food sovereignty (Holt-Giménez 2011). This approach to food justice sees race and class as central to the causes of inequality in the food system (Alkon and Agyeman 2011, Gottlieb and Joshi 2010, Morales 2011, White 2010). In particular, race is not reducible to or apart from economic structures, but "in actuality, structural and institutional racisms are embedded in the market itself" (Agyeman and McEntee 2014, 216).

We use an urban political ecology lens to understand and analyze the ideological, political, and economic processes that produce and reproduce injustice over time and across space (Agyeman and McEntee 2014, Heynen et al. 2012). These processes "together go to form highly uneven and deeply unjust urban landscapes" (Swyngedouw and Heynen 2003, 898). This lens allows us to analyze food justice movements and their transformative potential in relation to neoliberal ideology and its incomplete manifestations in political and economic institutions.

Not only are food justice projects struggling against neoliberalization and its effects, but as was explained in chapter 1, neoliberalism has also shaped the politics of food. Agyeman and McEntee (2014, 211) point to how the food justice movement can be coopted by being "folded into neoliberalization processes through state involvement and an underlying assumption that food injustice can be solved by private market forces, namely the presence of transnational food companies with increasingly dominant retail arms as well as new types of food provisioning at the geographically localized scale."

Similarly, many community development initiatives, including ones focused on food, have been "solidly in the grips of the idea that we simply need to figure out how to make the capitalist market work for the benefit of communities" (Loh and Shear 2015, 4). Neoliberalization, then, constrains possibilities by narrowing the focus to local solutions while eliding the global and regional forces that shape the local. It also prioritizes market exchange-value over community use-value in an effort to attract private investment (Kirkpatrick 2007, Stoecker 1997). Privatization has resulted in more services being contracted out to nonprofits, which has increased expectations that nonprofits operate with more business-like efficiency and subjected them to more competition for funding (Holland et al. 2007). These dynamics have led to professionalization of nonprofit community-development organizations, leading to a decrease in democratic control and a shift to less confrontational approaches that reduce the focus on power relations (DeFilippis et al. 2010, Stoecker 1997). From this view, many of the efforts to localize the food system, support food entrepreneurs, and shift food aid to nonprofits can be seen as part of neoliberalization processes.

McClintock (2014) sees urban agriculture as necessarily *both* neoliberal and radical and encourages the rejection of this dualism. While urban agriculture is "filling the void left by the 'rolling back' of the social safety net" (ibid., 147), it also represents a countermovement to re-embed the food system within social relations that have been obliterated or taken over by the capitalist market economy. We agree with McClintock on the need to examine these internal contradictions as part of a dialectical process and to understand them across multiple scales and over time. Any potentially transformative project necessarily begins within a neoliberal landscape. Guthman

(2008, 1181) emphasizes that "the politics of the possible lies in the indeterminacy of neoliberalism, the dialectical relationship between activist projects and their objects, and the always possible unintended consequences." It is this space of possibility to which we now turn with the concept of a solidarity economy.

WHAT IS A SOLIDARITY ECONOMY?

The solidarity economy (SE) concept provides a framework for understanding the possibilities and challenges of the emerging food economy in Boston. A set of theories and practices that aspire toward democratic, just, and sustainable development, SE has been defined as creating "a socio-economic order and new way of life that deliberately chooses serving the needs of people and ecological sustainability as the goal of economic activity rather than maximization of profits under the unfettered rule of the market" (Quiñones 2008, 13). While SE movements exist throughout the world, they are most well established in Latin America, Canada, and Europe. In Latin America, SE has emerged from social movements struggling explicitly against neoliberalism (Allard and Matthaei 2008, Miller 2006). Under leftist progressive regimes, SE has become incorporated into government policy, for instance with the establishment in Brazil of the National Secretariat of Solidarity Economy in 2003, and the recognition of SE in Ecuador's 2008 constitution.[1]

In Europe, SE is often described as the "third sector" of the economy, or the *social economy*[2] (Laville 2010), a term whose origins are often associated with utopian socialists such as Owen, Fourier, Saint-Simon, and Proudhon. Well-known SE practices can be found in cooperative economies in the Basque region of Spain (Mondragon) and the Emilia-Romagna region of Italy (Hancock 2008, Restakis 2010). In Canada, SE has been particularly visible in Quebec, where labor unions, nonprofits, and social movements established the Social Economy Task Force. Since 1996, this network has financed and organized around the creation of jobs in new sectors, such as the home care industry, which employs more than six thousand in over a hundred cooperatives and nonprofits (Mendell 2009). In the United States, SE movements are still in a nascent phase (though SE practices have long existed), but SE ideas can be seen in efforts labeled *new economy, local living economy, generative economy,* and *sharing economy.*

Currently, SE practices span all three sectors of the economy: the private sector (market driven, profit oriented), public sector (planned), and third sector (social economy) (Lewis and Conaty 2012). These practices include cooperatives of all kinds, participatory budgeting, fair trade, community land trusts, mutual associations, community banks, alternative currencies, time banks, and more.

There are many definitions of SE, arising from diverse intellectual and social-movement roots (Kawano 2013, Miller 2010).[3] Though SE is not a singular theory or framework, we see four cornerstone ideas that underlie the concept. First is a view of humans as *interdependent, social beings.* Individuals are more than self-interested utility-maximizers, the *Homo economicus* of neoclassical economic theory (Graeber 2010, Mauss 1990, Polanyi 2001); economic motivations also include collective well-being, ethical concerns, and moral values.

Second, *solidarity* is the core value basis for social relations. Solidarity is about "broadening the sense of us" to balance collective and individual interests (Altuna-Gabilondo 2013). Race, class, gender, and other differences must always be negotiated in enacting solidarity. Solidarity also encompasses our relations with nonhuman entities, thus incorporating notions of environmental sustainability.

Third is *democratic practice.* Collective ownership and cooperative management are central to SE institutions like cooperatives, community land trusts, and credit unions. But beyond these enterprises, SE also favors more participatory and deliberative forms of democracy in state governance, such as participatory budgeting. Thus, democratic practice infuses both the economic and political spheres and is about the empowerment and agency of people to change the conditions affecting their lives.

Fourth is seeing a *diverse and plural economy,* beyond simply the market. There are many existing forms of exchange, production, and ownership that function within different value frames than those of the capitalist market. Simply acknowledging their existence can cut through the ideological constraints of capitalism, opening up new ways for people to understand and act in the world (Gibson-Graham et al. 2013, Miller 2010). At the same time, this "pluralist approach, eschew[s] rigid blueprints and the belief in a single, correct path ... [and] builds on concrete practices, many of which are quite old, rather than seeking to create utopia out of theory and thin air" (Kawano 2013).

The SE concept has been particularly influential in food movements. Food justice and sovereignty movements have been at the forefront of challenging the dominant food economy, which is based on corporate control of global industrialized production and informed by "free market" ideology (Agyeman and McEntee 2014, Holt-Giménez 2011, McClintock 2014). These movements have pioneered solidarity-based approaches to taking back land, creating cooperative institutions, and forging fair and direct trade networks. Anderson et al. (2014, 4) see the development of cooperative alternative food networks that go beyond the "more individualistic and inward focused 'first generation' localization efforts in the food movement." We see the emerging Boston Food Solidarity Economy as one example of a cooperative alternative food network.

As our case study illustrates, the development of a solidarity economy entails sustaining and creating solidarity practices and institutions *and* reforming and transforming current neoliberal capitalist logics. Solidarity economy is often conceived of as sprouting from the margins or cracks of capitalism, where it poses little threat to elite power. But these SE practices show that "another world is possible" that can gain strength and may eventually degrade capitalist logics, though not without other strategies to transform and challenge capitalism (Wright 2010).

THE BOSTON FOOD SOLIDARITY ECONOMY

Neoliberal landscapes of inequality and injustice are drivers of food injustice in Massachusetts. Though they live in one of the wealthiest states in the nation, 11.9 percent of Massachusetts residents are food-insecure; this rises to 16.6 percent in children (Gunderson et al. 2014). Allegretto et al. (2013) found that 46 percent of fast-food workers in Massachusetts had to rely on public programs—the Supplemental Nutrition Assistance Program (SNAP, formerly called Food Stamps), Medicaid, and the Earned Income Tax Credit—to meet their basic expenses in 2011.

Yet, in the neighborhoods most affected in Boston, the state's biggest city, an array of food justice initiatives has emerged from the nonprofit, social-enterprise, and cooperative sectors to form what we are calling the Boston Food Solidarity Economy (figure 11.1). This network encompasses all phases of the food system, including a community land trust, for-profit and nonprofit farming and community gardening, processing by a kitchen

FIGURE 11.1. The emerging Boston Food Solidarity Economy.

incubator and catering firm, retail through a social-enterprise café and a newly forming food cooperative, and finally waste processing by a worker-owned cooperative that processes organic waste back into compost. These are all initiated and led by local residents, mostly people of color, but also in partnership with other resources.

This chapter is focused on the initiatives that are sprouting in Roxbury and Dorchester, two adjoining neighborhoods that are home to about a quarter of Boston residents. More than 75 percent of those who live in these two neighborhoods are people of color, mostly African American and Latino. These are among the city's lowest-income communities. In 2011 Roxbury's per capita income was just over half of Boston's, and more than 35 percent of households received SNAP benefits.[4]

We describe this emerging food solidarity economy from the perspective of possibility and a pluralist view of diverse economies. We first root this economy in the history of community struggles over land in these neighborhoods. Then we show how this diverse network of initiatives, some decades old and others still forming, is an example of how a solidarity economy can grow from the merger of existing and new institutions and practices.

Community Control of Land

Crucially, the emerging Boston Food Solidarity Economy starts with collective ownership of land in the Dudley neighborhood through a community land trust. The roots of this land trust trace back to decades of neighborhood struggles over land and development. Following World War II, Roxbury and Dorchester, like many other inner-city areas, suffered from disinvestment and neglect. Racist banking and housing policies ("redlining") and practices such as "block busting" further segregated people of color from opportunity. "Urban renewal" programs and highway building dealt a further blow to these neighborhoods by taking land and, in some cases, removing residents (Agyeman and Alkon 2014).

By the 1980s, Roxbury and North Dorchester had been devastated by the disinvestment and white flight of the 1960s and '70s. More than a third of the land lay vacant—1,300 parcels covering 1.5 square miles. In 1984, residents and community organizations came together as DSNI to revitalize the Dudley neighborhood and resist city redevelopment plans that would have gentrified and transformed the area into hotels and offices serving downtown Boston. They successfully pushed the City of Boston to adopt their own plan for the neighborhood and give DSNI the power of eminent domain[5] over a sixty-acre parcel in the core of the Dudley neighborhood. In 1988 they established their own community land trust to take ownership and develop the vacant land (Medoff and Sklar 1994).

A community land trust is a nonprofit organization governed by community members[6] that owns and stewards land for long-term public benefit. It protects land from the pressures of the real estate market, as the land is never resold. By separating ownership of land from human improvements to the land (such as housing), a land trust allows the community to retain the value of land appreciation. Land trusts then rent land to leaseholders, often for long terms (typically ninety-nine years), to build housing, operate farms or other businesses, and develop other community-benefiting uses. The terms of the lease can include limits on resale in order to preserve affordability. The first community land trust in the United States, New Communities, Inc., was started in 1969 in rural Georgia, born of the civil rights movement. Established to secure land for Black farmers, the trust owned more than 5,600 acres of farmland that was farmed cooperatively for fifteen years (Rosenberg and Yuen 2012). There are now almost 250 community land trusts across forty-six states and Washington, D.C. (Thaden 2012).

In the more than twenty-five years since establishing their own land trust, DSNI has built 225 permanently affordable homes, as well as parks, a town common, a community center, and a charter school. The land trust also hosts a variety of urban agricultural activities. These include a 10,000-square-foot community greenhouse and two farm sites operated by the nonprofit The Food Project, as well as dozens of home and community gardens. These developments are remarkable, given that the land in this neighborhood is no longer inexpensive, because real estate prices (and property taxes) have sky-rocketed across Boston. But as it does for housing, the land trust keeps land affordable for community uses, such as food production, that would otherwise be priced out of the real estate market. Because the land trust is a non-profit, the land it owns is not taxed, thus keeping property taxes affordable. And farmers can gain long-term access, such as through the ninety-nine-year lease that DSNI recently granted to one of the Food Project farms. This control of land has enabled DSNI and its community partners to guide development that goes beyond the constraints of the private real estate market.

Bringing Together the New and the Existing in the Boston Food Solidarity Economy

Control of land is just the beginning of a food solidarity economy. In addition to the nonprofit greenhouse[7] and farms, the land also supports resident gardens and for-profit farming. A 2013 survey found more than sixty-five resident gardens, some more than forty years old, in DSNI's core area, growing more than fifty types of vegetables and fruits and yielding an estimated 4,400 pounds of produce (Loh et al. 2013). A guerilla gardening campaign launched in 2011 by youth organizers of the environmental justice group Alternatives for Community and Environment (ACE) has reclaimed nine vacant lots and built raised-bed gardens now tended by more than a hundred families in Roxbury and Dorchester. Some of these lots had been vacant for more than forty years. "We've grown up next to all these vacant lots that were just collecting trash. We can take back the land and provide for ourselves," said Hakim Sutherland, a youth organizer with ACE (Loh 2014). This initiative is an example of self-provisioning (without market exchange) as part of a solidarity economy.

Founded in 2009, City Growers is a for-profit farming business that operates four sites in Roxbury and Dorchester. As detailed above, it is a partner in developing the Garrison-Trotter Farm, which will be owned by the Dudley land trust. It is proving a commercial model for growing on plots as small as a quarter acre. City Growers is also exploring the development of a producer cooperative among the farmers they train, to pool resources and market under one brand (Loh and Lloyd 2013).

This emerging food solidarity economy also has food-processing initiatives. City Fresh Foods is a for-profit catering company cofounded in 1994 by Glynn Lloyd, who wanted to create jobs for young people in the neighborhood. Lloyd also cofounded City Growers out of the desire to source locally grown produce for City Fresh, which delivers fresh, healthy, and culturally appropriate meals to nursing homes, schools, and other institutions. They employ about a hundred, have a profit-sharing program for employees, and are looking toward worker ownership in the long term. In spring 2014, CommonWealth Kitchen opened a kitchen incubator facility in Dorchester at the site of the former Bornstein and Pearl Meat factory. This $14 million redevelopment project was guided by Dorchester Bay Economic Development Corporation. The center provides shared and private kitchen space, business development support, and a commissary kitchen serving the food-preparation needs of institutions, restaurants, and the food truck industry. It hopes to produce 150 jobs within five years.

On the retail end of the economy, the Dorchester Community Food Co-op has been organizing since 2011 to launch a member- and worker-owned store providing affordable, fresh, and healthy foods and green products, as well as space for community education and cultural activities. Unlike many food cooperatives that cater to more white and middle- to upper-class populations, this effort is dedicated to serving a culturally and economically diverse community.[8] So far, they have over four hundred member–owners, run a winter farmers' market, and hold weekly "Fresh Fridays" festivals in the summer. They are now developing the physical site for their store, set to open in 2017. The Haley House Bakery Café, a social enterprise opened in 2005 by a nonprofit serving the homeless, has become a vibrant community space, provides dining and catering services, and also runs a bakery training program for ex-prisoners and education programs for youth.

At the waste-processing end of the food system is a worker cooperative, CERO (Cooperative Energy, Recycling, and Organics), which was formed in 2013 to help local businesses separate their wastes, increase recycling, and reprocess their food scraps. CERO was started by African American and Latino/a workers who wanted to create their own green jobs. The founders were members of economic justice programs at two community nonprofits,[9] which raised the funds for business development. CERO raised more than $370,000 from over eighty investors through a direct public offering in 2014.

While these initiatives are not all fully functioning or collaborating explicitly within an SE framework, the political and business ties between them are growing. The community land trust and cooperatives are most explicit about their connection to solidarity values and have more directly democratic forms. As cooperatives, the Dorchester Food Co-op and CERO are governed by their members, who make decisions about how to operate the business, invest surplus (or address deficits), and care for the community. While DSNI and its land trust are nonprofits, they have a robust process whereby several thousand members elect a board of directors into seats representing the various racial/ethnic groups and other stakeholders in the neighborhood.

The other enterprises in the emerging Boston Food Solidarity Economy arise out of the nonprofit and social-enterprise sectors. While these sectors may be more challenged under neoliberalism than the cooperatives, they nonetheless represent desires and actual practices of solidarity. They are creating space and access for more community control over the food system, from growing to selling to eating. They have access to more mainstream sources of foundation, government, and private-capital funding, which was crucial for CommonWealth Kitchen and for growing enterprises to larger scales. Collectively, these initiatives have built growing political power to influence policies and garner public resources, such as legalizing commercial farming in Boston.

An SE framework helps illuminate the desires to go beyond neoliberal capitalism and show how solidarity practices already exist. It also helps in envisioning the potential collective impact of these initiatives. Each, alone, may seem small and fragile, but as a network they are building political power and embedding their own supply chains. Perhaps most importantly, they are a breeding ground for cutting through the ideological constraints of neoliberalism. They show that another world is not only possible, but already here in some ways. The pluralist view provided by SE encourages us to see how initiatives coming out of more neoliberalized sectors, such as nonprofits and social enterprise, enact and strive toward transformative practices. For example, City Fresh and City Growers, both for-profit small businesses, are attempting to evolve toward employee control and ownership.

As important as it is to see the potential, it is also crucial to analyze the constraints and contradictions in birthing a solidarity economy. The central challenge is sustaining the existing and creating the new while resisting and transforming neoliberalization processes. The emerging food solidarity economy must navigate across ideological, political, and economic dimensions, each of which is influenced by neoliberalism. In the ideological (or discursive) dimension, the mere existence of solidarity initiatives counters the idea that "there is no alternative" (a phrase often used by British Prime Minister Margaret Thatcher). But simply embodying values of democracy, justice, and sustainability is not enough because neoliberalism has so deeply and comprehensively infused the social-enterprise and nonprofit sectors (as well as the public sector), thereby reinforcing ideas around individualism, market efficiency, privatization, and small government.

In the political realm, solidarity initiatives can gain supportive policy and other resources from the state. But they must also build power among various stakeholders to counter "corporate welfare" and transform neoliberalized government policies. Thus, organizing and movement building are essential to the further growth of SE. And with a wide diversity of actors involved in these efforts (which is a strength), attention must be paid to differences in socioeconomic and racial privilege within the movement.

Economically (or materially), there arise questions of financing, resources, business models, and competition. All the entities described above, while building on local assets, rely to some degree on outside resources, whether from philanthropy, private capital, or public funding. This reliance can lead to a taming of resistance and to less confrontational forms of organizing. The initiatives that fit better within neoliberal discourse on entrepreneurship and job training—for instance, City Fresh and CommonWealth Kitchen—may have easier access to public and private capital. Each of these entities faces some level of market competition and must balance its goals of sustaining the enterprise, supporting good jobs, and operating in an environmental manner.

Constraints in any of these dimensions can stymie or undermine the growth of a solidarity economy. Oftentimes, food justice efforts are strong in advancing along one or two of these dimensions but are hampered by a third. For instance, the Garrison-Trotter Farm has built strong political support and is changing ideas about property and ownership, but it remains embedded within an economy that drives it to sell produce to the highest bidder. ACE's guerilla gardens produce modest food returns and, more importantly, are helping shift ideas about who land should benefit. However, without ownership, the land remains at risk of being taken for other purposes.

Legalizing Urban Farming

In the remainder of this section, we explore these contradictions and challenges through the case of the city's process to legalize commercial farming in Boston. Legalization was a crucial step toward enabling the Garrison-Trotter Farm and similar efforts. But the victory was only partial, in that the new zoning code supports only commercial farming, thereby staying within the constraints of a neoliberal for-profit logic and managing land for its "highest and best" use. The city's approach shows the importance of community political struggles and power relations in the battle to shift public policy and planning, which have been neoliberalized to a great extent. These legal and planning structures have historically upheld private property rights and maximized real estate market values, further enhancing and embedding racial hierarchies at the expense of low-income communities of color. Yet legalization eventually helped build more political power in the community to acquire land at less-than-market value for farming. This is, in fact, the process that led to the Garrison-Trotter Farm model, in which one city agency is giving vacant parcels to a community land trust.

Prior to Article 89, for-profit urban agriculture was forbidden by the Boston Zoning Code, though the city's community gardens were covered under its Open Space Zoning District. In November 2010 the city, at the behest of Mayor Menino, initiated a process to establish an Urban Agriculture Overlay District to allow the cultivation of fruits and vegetables. Phase 1 included a pilot project to attract for-profit farms to four city-owned lots in the Codman Square area of Dorchester. The program was administered by the Boston Redevelopment Authority (BRA), the city's planning agency.

There is an assumption among those in racially and economically privileged groups that urban agriculture is "good for you," and "if *they* only knew" (Guthman 2011, 263), *they* would be healthier. This thinking has become something of a universal given; it is simply accepted, which means that urban agriculture, as a universal good, can bypass planning and public-participation processes. But this assumption was not held by all community residents and leaders. During the city's planning process—which was initially on an aggressive timetable—concerns emerged around neighborhood impacts, particularly regarding farm animals, rodents, and soil contamination. In addressing the zoning commission, City Councilman Charles Yancey, whose district included the Dorchester area, argued that one of the sites was home to a former oil company and that the soil could "poison people down the line" (Gaffin 2011).

Conflict also flared over the lack of process and community input. This initial lack of participation continued a history of antagonism between the city and the community. The city, and particularly the BRA, were remembered by long-time residents as contributing to the disinvestment and white flight that occurred in the decades following World War II. Neighborhoods had to wage intense struggles over the BRA's urban renewal plans and projects that either displaced or could have displaced many residents in the name of revitalization and economic development. As Agyeman and Alkon (2014) report:

> Perhaps the strongest words on this topic were spoken by Councillor Yancey, who, when addressing the members of the BRA, specifically referenced racial inequalities—*"I think there was a level of arrogance displayed in this process . . . The BRA totally ignored the community concerns when they voted to approve this project, which in reality had been already approved by assigning their staff to do it. But that's not a legitimate process . . . This is not a colonial regime! This is not a plantation! These are residents who deserve respect."*

In invoking the plantation, and thereby slavery, Yancey reveals what Ramírez (2014, 19) describes as "the complex relationship between African Americans and farming, and how the plantation bears the roots of the global racial capitalist system."

While most Dorchester residents were generally supportive of urban agriculture, they did not believe that they would benefit directly from the new farms. Agyeman and Alkon (2014) found that residents spoke favorably about school and community gardens and expressed hope that urban farms could lead to economic development. But some Dorchester residents objected to the new farms because they did not believe this project would increase their access to either the potential jobs or the produce from the farms. When Glynn Lloyd of City Growers came to a meeting and shared that estimated start-up costs would be between $5,000 and $10,000, one resident described his reaction: "Nobody in this community that I know of can afford to do the

kind of farming that was talked about for this community" (ibid.). The pro-
hibitive costs of commercial farming furthered the impression that this
project was, in the words of one resident, "about maybe rich white people
coming into our neighborhood, taking over the community and making
money off of our people" (ibid.).

Community residents also began to realize that the vegetables grown on
the farm would have to be sold at high prices, given the high start-up costs of
farming. Thus, they might not even be able to access the produce grown on
the farms. As Agyeman and Alkon (ibid.) document:

> As one resident put it, "We couldn't afford it at the prices they'll have to
> charge." "So who are you building it for?" chimed in another. "For poor folks?
> Or the types of people who can buy that?"

To the city's credit, however, once it was obvious that the "process," such as it
was, was going nowhere, the whole process was slowed down to allow for
more genuine participation and collaboration. Key players in this volte-face
included community organizers, city officials, and the community-rooted
organizations that eventually won the leases to the pilot sites (including City
Growers and the nonprofit Victory Programs). Tangible community gains
under the new process included the BRA permitting plant cultivation only
and eliminating one original site where residents wanted to create a play-
ground. Crucially, the request for proposals (RFP) by which City Growers
and Victory Programs got their lots, was written to require ongoing community participation and engagement in any farm's operations. Addressing
"poison" concerns, the RFP specified that farmers will be required to follow
"established practices of the Boston gardening community" for separating
the existing soil from contact with people and produce.

Ultimately, the struggle over the pilot siting process yielded a stronger collaboration among stakeholders in shaping the second phase of the process—
drafting the urban-farming zoning ordinance. A working group of twenty-
two people, including community representatives, was convened and met
eighteen times. In addition, the city held eleven neighborhood meetings in the
summer of 2013. Article 89 was finally adopted by the city in December 2013.
The ordinance sets out rules for where and what kinds of commercial farming
are allowed, rules and design standards for farm structures, soil safety regulations, rules for farm markets and stands, and permitting processes.

Immediately after adoption of Article 89, the city's Department of
Neighborhood Development (DND) started the process to develop several

urban farms on city-owned land in Roxbury and Dorchester. Three RFPs were released, including for the Garrison-Trotter site and another location known as Tommy's Rock. These two sites were ones that had active neighborhood support, where neighborhood groups were already working with City Growers to establish urban farms. In fact, the neighborhood association in Tommy's Rock and City Growers met with the mayor in 2010 about trying to establish an urban farm on an urban renewal site controlled by the BRA (Hachmyer 2013). While this first meeting did not yield immediate results for the neighborhood, it may have influenced Mayor Menino, who launched the Urban Agriculture Initiative later that same year.

It is important to note that these first urban farming sites are being administered through the DND, not the BRA. The DND is the city's affordable-housing agency and was originally established in 1966 as the Public Facilities Department. Thus, its mission and role contrast sharply with those of the BRA, which was established in 1957, during the era of urban renewal. Whereas the BRA's role is seen as facilitating economic development (measured in more conventional neoliberal terms), the DND can sell off surplus public land under its Community Facilities Assistance Program at $100 a parcel for purposes of public benefit. That public benefit must be retained for at least fifty years under a deed restriction, and ownership reverts to the DND if the public benefit is not sustained.

Thus, with Article 89 in place and under the guidance of the DND, innovative partnerships like the one for Garrison-Trotter Farm are now possible. Transfer of public property to a land trust helps comply with the DND's fifty-year use restriction. The Urban Farming Institute (UFI) and City Growers are able to engage community residents and organizations beforehand to ensure that neighborhood support for an urban farm is already secured before the city's development process begins.

But this story of the legalization of urban farming in Boston also points to the bias that cities have toward maximizing real estate value. Cities like Boston depend on property taxes for a majority of their operating revenues, and the appreciation of property values leads directly to increased property-tax revenues. This dependence by cities on property taxes is further heightened by neoliberal roll-backs, and specifically cutbacks in federal aid and programs for cities. Yet this increase in land values (and property taxes) drove out urban agriculture in the first place. Farmers did not make enough money to stay on the land; under private property ownership, the land eventually ended up in the hands of the highest bidders seeking to convert it to its "highest and best" use.

Discussion of Tensions

As the Boston Food Solidarity Economy struggles to emerge, it contends with the challenges of neoliberalism as an ideology, as well as with Boston's political and economic institutions that are shaped by it. Neoliberal ideas about free markets and privatization of resources hold a privileged position, which in turn shapes policy and investment. For example, Article 89 was premised on a for-profit farming model, which fits well with Boston's neoliberal discourse around entrepreneurship and jobs in both the Menino and the current Walsh administrations. It is also consistent with the BRA's economic development approach, which relies on Boston's prowess in attracting capital investment. This commercial agricultural approach then reinforces the commoditization of food and its sale for highest return. And it bolsters a food system in which "voting with your fork" also means being wealthy enough to buy more local and organic produce. So, while growing local for the market can contribute to food justice through decent wages for farmers, it does little to increase affordability and access.

To be fair, City Growers and UFI are not claiming to solve the food access problem. According to one member of UFI, "In order for us to make money, we have to sell to market. . . . Your local bodega cannot pay 8 to 13, 16 dollars per pound for mesclun mix. So when you talk about food access, you have to be honest and truthful about what that really, really means. We're not solving food access" (Oorthuys 2015). Yet efforts like Garrison-Trotter Farm are touted publicly by the city as helping to provide more access.

On one hand, City Growers and UFI can tap into political and economic support for entrepreneurship and job creation, but on the other, they argue for de-commoditization of land and the privileging of labor over capital. To create decent wages for farmers, they need access to land at very low cost, which is why they have partnered with DSNI's land trust. They also rely on UFI's nonprofit farmer-training program for apprentices and skilled workers. The land and labor aspects of this urban-farming model challenge the neoliberal tenets around private property and profit logic. While the land-ownership model may be more transformative, the idea of public support for generating good-paying jobs is a critical reform and push-back against deregulation.

Political support for this model appears to be growing in Boston, with the election of Mayor Marty Walsh and his appointment of John Barros, former executive director of DSNI, as chief of economic development. The mayor's housing plan includes community land trusts as a strategy for mitigating gentrification (Walsh 2014). Thus, there are opportunities emerging to challenge the neoliberalization of city governance and the idea of maximizing the exchange value of land.

The role of nonprofits in this emerging Boston Food Solidarity Economy needs parsing out. They are central players in the Garrison-Trotter Farm, and their roles raise questions about local autonomy and democratic control. For example, the Trust for Public Land (TPL) was brought into the partnership because of its ability to raise the capital necessary to rehabilitate the land for farming. Does this reliance on funding from a largely white, national nonprofit lead to more or to less autonomy for the local partners? So far, it appears that the TPL has been playing a critical role in raising the funds from sources that the local groups would otherwise not be able to access and then transferring permanent ownership to the locally controlled DSNI land trust. Even among local nonprofits, there is a diversity of intent and practice of democratic and solidarity values. The Food Project, for instance, operates in the neighborhood but is not democratically controlled by residents, in contrast to DSNI, which is democratically governed by members. But as DSNI's land trust starts to acquire land outside of its area, as in the case of the Garrison-Trotter Farm, there are questions around how the interests of those neighborhoods can be adequately represented in DSNI's governance structure.

Finally, we will discuss the race and class dynamics that play out in these cases. In popular discourse, lower-income people of color are seen as the recipients of the benefits of these initiatives, in terms of food access as well as jobs. But within the neighborhoods, especially among organizations led by people of color and with more long-term ties to the neighborhood, these initiatives are as much about community control over land and development as they are about food and jobs. DSNI, City Growers, and UFI each has a board and staff leadership who are predominantly people of color with deep ties to the neighborhood. The Food Project, which started in the Boston suburbs and moved to the Dudley neighborhood, has white leadership and has been conscious of diversifying both its staff and board. These racial and class differences—between partners in the Boston Food Solidarity Economy and within organizations—result in ever-present tensions that must be recognized, navigated, and negotiated.

Insufficient attention to these power asymmetries may reinforce inequalities and tensions and fundamentally undermine cooperation across movement actors. For example, City Growers and The Food Project are both looking to access more land, which may put them into competition with one another in city land-disposition processes or even within the Dudley land trust. Without ways to resolve these organizational tensions, rooted in solidarity values, privilege and power based on racial and socioeconomic hierarchies may be exploited. At worst, these divides can set actors working against each other rather than working together.

THE FUTURE: CONSTRAINTS AND POSSIBILITIES

This case study of an emerging Boston Food Solidarity Economy shows both the constraints and possibilities for moving toward food justice and sovereignty. The desires for a food solidarity economy abound, as evidenced by the numerous initiatives and their increasing interconnectedness. Yet this solidarity economy cannot fully articulate itself without addressing the constraints of its existence within both neoliberal ideologies and the governmental policies and economic systems that have shaped it—and that it is transforming. The community push-back against the zoning process in Dorchester was a crucial part of this.

The most immediate constraints faced by local initiatives are economic and political. All the entities in the Boston Food Solidarity Economy face financing challenges. The start-up initiatives for City Growers, Dorchester Food Co-op, and CERO are surmounting this start-up phase by pursuing nonprofit sources, self-financing, and/or equity partners. Garrison-Trotter Farm brought in the TPL for its access to government and foundation funding. Dorchester Food Co-op has a base of dues-paying members, but for its store it is partnering with a larger nonprofit developer to access more conventional community-development financing. CERO was incubated in nonprofits but raised start-up capital through a direct public offering, in which nonvoting equity shares were sold at a minimum investment of $2,500. The more well-established City Fresh Foods recently gained a new equity investor, the Boston Impact Initiative, whose mission is to invest in SE. This move will help City Fresh Foods transition to worker ownership (Tanaka 2015). New partnerships and possibilities are emerging for developing finance that is within SE itself, including partners in public, private for-profit, and nonprofit entities. These financing innovations are crucial for these initiatives to launch themselves at a feasible scale. If successful, the initiatives may grow and need solidarity financing to compete with the conventional food economy.

There are also political constraints due to neoliberal policies biased toward free markets, global trade, and ever-larger corporations. The current agri-industrial food system is the backdrop for the emerging Boston Food Solidarity Economy. But the movement for a food solidarity economy is organizing to shift policies and politics, particularly at a local and a state level. Article 89 removed the legal barrier to commercial farming in the city. CERO is part of the Boston Recycling Coalition, which is working toward zero-waste policies, shifting city contracts toward local businesses like CERO, and raising wages and working conditions within the recycling industry. DSNI has convened the Greater Boston Community Land Trust Network to advocate more city support of land trusts. There is potential for more coalition building between these SE initiatives and the various labor initiatives to organize food service workers,[10] many of whom live in lower-income communities of color. But this organizing and coalition building also requires resources and time. The movement-building aspects of solidarity work deserve more attention and strategy.

Finally, the ideological constraints of neoliberalism continue to be present. A first hurdle has already been overcome by the mere existence of these SE initiatives. They are showing that "another world is possible." They are also succeeding, to some extent, in shifting ideas about the role of government in job creation and support for cooperative businesses. Even if the start-up entities do not succeed in the long term, they have instilled a sense of possibility that goes beyond neoliberalism. There remains the challenge of seeing this emerging economy as more than just a "boutique" alternative that remains marginal to the lives of most residents. Without a sense that this economy can be more than marginal, indeed transformative, there is the danger that these solidarity alternatives might be seen as anomalies that cannot be scaled up or replicated. Also, there is the danger that the entities making up the Boston Food Solidarity Economy will remain fragmented as islands within the dominant economy. This fragmentation may be further fueled by competition for funding and resources between entities.

The fact that this solidarity economy is small now does not mean that it should be dismissed or seen as irrelevant; rather, it should be seen as the beginning of a broader transformation. More work needs to be done to fan the sparks of desire for a solidarity economy as well as to build its political and economic institutions. The partners are working together politically and developing economic business ties, but more can be done to amplify and broadcast the counter-hegemonic aspects of this work.

CONCLUSION

In this chapter, we have used both an urban political ecology lens and an SE framework to begin to understand and analyze the challenges and opportunities inherent in the emerging Boston Food Solidarity Economy. The proliferation of multiple food justice efforts in lower-income communities of color is impressive: cooperatives, land trusts, social enterprises, and more are sprouting, fueling desires for a more democratic, just, and sustainable food system—for food justice and sovereignty. Yet this emergence is occurring within a landscape of deeply embedded social and spatial inequalities and injustices, which were produced by, and are bolstered by, neoliberalism. We have teased out some of the tensions and contradictions that arise from the interface of the Boston Food Solidarity Economy with larger markets in which food and land are commodities. These challenges to growth include the role of nonprofits and of funding, as nonprofits are ever more integrated into a neoliberal logic of privatization, state roll-back, and unfettered markets; as well as racial and class tensions arising from historical disinvestment and neglect, racist banking and housing policies, and the socioeconomic and racialized positionalities of the various organizations involved.

We believe, however, that there is something potentially transformative emerging in the Boston Food Solidarity Economy. Though not centrally coordinated, these individual efforts are finding each other and cooperating both politically and economically. They are organizing and fighting for more supportive policies. They are looking to cooperate with each other in building local supply chains. Perhaps the next step is recognizing that the sum is greater than the parts and that collectively, they may just add up to something truly transformative. But all of this will take more than just good policy and viable businesses. It will take organizing and movement building as well to shift entrenched power relations.

NOTES

1. This section draws on Loh and Shear (2015).
2. This chapter uses *solidarity economy* broadly as a term that embraces a diverse array of movements attempting to build noncapitalist economies, including social economy.
3. Several initiatives are attempting to gather and synthesize SE concepts and practices across the globe, including the Intercontinental Network for the

Promotion of Social Solidarity Economy (RIPESS, http://www.ripess.org/) and the United Nations Research Institute for Social Development's project on Potential and Limits of Social and Solidarity Economy (http://www.unrisd.org/sse).

4. All data in this paragraph are from Boston Redevelopment Authority neighborhood reports using American Community Survey 2007–11 estimates (May 2013).

5. Eminent domain is the power to seize privately owned land for public purposes (paying fair compensation), usually a power held only by government.

6. The classic board of a community land trust consists of equal numbers of people who live on or lease the land, other local community residents, and members representing the broader public interest. This three-part governing body helps balance the varying interests (Davis 2014).

7. Note that while the Food Project is a nonprofit, it also earns revenue by selling to market. The greenhouse grows enough produce for market to pay much of the operating costs, so that they can offer year-round growing space and educational programs for local residents, youths, and organizations.

8. Dorchester Food Co-op is navigating the same challenges as other cooperatives that are based in communities of color, such as those in Philadelphia, Chicago, and Oakland described in chapters 8 and 9 of this volume.

9. CERO was incubated by the Boston Workers Alliance and the Massachusetts Coalition for Occupational Health and Safety.

10. These include UNITE/HERE Local 26 unionizing cafeteria workers; the Restaurant Opportunities Centers United; and Fast Food Workers Alliance.

REFERENCES

Agyeman, Julian, and Allison Alkon. 2014. "'Silence Is Not Consent': Plantation, Poison and the Politics of Planning for Urban Agriculture in Boston." *Just Sustainabilities* (blog), December 20. http://julianagyeman.com/2014/12/silence-not-consent-pesticides-poison-politics-planning-boston/.

Agyeman, Julian, and Jesse McEntee. 2014. "Moving the Field of Food Justice Forward through the Lens of Urban Political Ecology." *Geography Compass* 8: 211–220.

Alkon, Alison Hope, and Julian Agyeman, Eds. 2011. *Cultivating Food Justice: Race, Class, and Sustainability.* Cambridge, MA: MIT Press.

Allard, Jenna, and Julie Matthaei. 2008. Introduction. In *Solidarity Economy: Building Alternatives for People and Planet,* ed. Jenna Allard, Carl Davidson, and Julie Matthaei, 1–18. Papers and Reports from the U.S. Social Forum 2007. Chicago: ChangeMaker.

Allegretto, Sylvia, Marc Doussard, Dave Graham-Squire, Ken Jacobs, Dan Thompson, and Jeremy Thompson. 2013. "Fast Food, Poverty Wages: The Public Cost of Low-Wage Jobs in the Fast-Food Industry." October 15. UC Berkeley Labor

Center and University of Illinois Urbana-Champaign. http://laborcenter
.berkeley.edu/pdf/2013/fast_food_poverty_wages.pdf. Accessed January 7, 2015.

Altuna-Gabilondo, L. 2013. "Solidarity at Work: The Case of Mondragon." United
Nations Research Institute for Social Development blog, July 18. www.unrisd.org
/80256B3C005BE6B5/%28httpNews%29/DA6E37662364DDC8C1257BAC00
4E7032?OpenDocument.

Anderson, Colin R., Lynda Brushett, Thomas Gray, and Henk Renting. 2014.
Working together to build cooperative food systems. *Journal of Agriculture, Food
Systems, and Community Development* 4(3): 3–9.

Boston Neighborhood Network News. 2014. Interview with William Epperson of
the Boston Department of Neighborhood Development, July 11. http://vimeo
.com/100542050. Accessed January 5, 2015.

Brenner, Neil, and Nik Theodore. 2002. "Cities and the Geographies of 'Actually
Existing Neoliberalism.'" *Antipode* 34: 349–379.

Davis, John E. 2014. "Origins and Evolution of the Community Land Trust in the
United States." http://greenfordable.com/clt/archives/1700.

DeFilippis, James, Robert Fisher, and Eric Shragge. 2010. *Contesting Community: The
Limits and Potential of Local Organizing.* Piscataway, NJ: Rutgers University Press.

Gaffin, Adam. 2011. "Zoning Commission Goes with Scientists over City Coun-
cilor; Approves Urban Farm Zone." *Universal Hub.* www.universalhub.com
/2011/zoning-commission-goes-scientists-over-city-counci.

Gibson-Graham, J. K. 1996. *The End of Capitalism (As We Knew It): A Feminist
Critique of Political Economy.* Minneapolis: University of Minnesota Press.

———. 2006. *A Postcapitalist Politics.* Minneapolis: University of Minnesota Press.

Gibson-Graham, J. K., Jenny Cameron, and Stephen Healy. 2013. *Take Back the
Economy.* Minneapolis: University of Minnesota Press.

Gottlieb, Robert, and Anupama Joshi. 2010. *Food Justice.* Cambridge, MA: MIT Press.

Graeber, D. 2010. "On the Moral Grounds of Economic Relations: A Maussian
Approach." *Working Paper Series 6.* Open Anthropology Cooperative Press.
http://openanthcoop.net/press/http:/openanthcoop.net/press/wp-content
/uploads/2010/11/Graeber-On-the-Moral-Grounds-of-Economic-Relations4.pdf.

Gundersen, Craig, Emily Engelhard, Amy Satoh, and Elaine Waxman. 2014. "Map the
Meal Gap 2014: Technical Brief." Chicago: Feeding America. www.feedingamerica
.org/hunger-in-america/our-research/map-the-meal-gap/2012/2012-map-the-
meal-gap-tech-brief.pdf.

Guthman, Julie. 2008. "Neoliberalism and the Making of Food Politics in California." *Geoforum* 39: 1171–1183.

———. 2011. "'If They Only Knew': The Unbearable Whiteness of Alternative
Food." In *Cultivating Food Justice: Race, Class, and Sustainability,* ed. Alison
Hope Alkon and Julian Agyeman, 278–296. Cambridge, MA: MIT Press.

Hachmyer, Caitlin. 2013. "The Institutionalization of Food Movement Projects and
the Role of Land Rights in Social Transformation: Stories from Boston, Detroit
and Philadelphia." Master's thesis, Tufts University, Boston. Available from Proquest database.

Hancock, Matt. 2008. "Competing by Cooperating in Italy: The Cooperative District of Imola." In *Solidarity Economy: Building Alternatives for People and Planet,* ed. Jenna Allard, Carl Davidson, and Julie Matthaei, 228–238. Papers and Reports from the U.S. Social Forum 2007. Chicago: ChangeMaker.

Harvey, David. 2005. *A Brief History of Neoliberalism.* New York: Oxford University Press.

Heynen, Nik, Hilda E. Kurtz, and Amy Trauger. 2012. "Food Justice, Hunger, and the City." *Geography Compass* 6: 304–311.

Holland, Dorothy, Donald M. Nonini, Catherine Lutz, Lesley Bartlett, Marla Frederick-McGlathery, Thaddeus C. Guldbrandsen, and Enrique G. Murillo, Jr. 2007. *Local Democracy under Siege: Activism, Public Interests, and Private Politics.* New York: New York University Press.

Holt-Giménez, Eric. 2011. "Food Security, Food Justice or Food Sovereignty." In *Cultivating Food Justice: Race, Class, and Sustainability,* ed. Alison Hope Alkon and Julian Agyeman. Cambridge, MA: MIT Press.

Kawano, Emily. 2013. "Social Solidarity Economy: Toward Convergence across Continental Divides." United Nations Research Institute for Social Development blog, February 26. www.unrisd.org/80256B3C005BE6B5/search/F1E9214 CF8EA21A8C1257B1E003B4F65?OpenDocument.

Kirkpatrick, L. Owen. 2007. "The Two 'Logics' of Community Development: Neighborhoods, Markets, and Community Development Corporations." *Politics and Society* 35: 329–359.

Laville, Jean-Louis. 2010. "Solidarity economy *(Economie solidaire)."* In *The Human Economy: A Citizen's Guide,* ed. Keith Hart, Jean-Louis Laville, and Antonio D. Cattani, 225–235. Cambridge, UK: Polity Press.

Lewis, Michael, and Patrick Conaty. 2012. *The Resilience Imperative: Cooperative Transitions to a Steady-State Economy.* Gabriola Island, British Columbia: New Society.

Loh, Penn. 2014. "Land, Co-ops, Compost: A Local Food Economy Emerges in Boston's Poorest Neighborhoods." *Yes! Magazine,* November 7. Accessed at www .yesmagazine.org/commonomics/boston-s-emerging-food-economy.

Loh, Penn, and G. Lloyd. 2013. "The Emerging Just and Sustainable Food Economy in Boston." *Practical Visionaries* (blog), December 20. https://pennloh .wordpress.com/2013/12/20/the-emerging-just-and-sustainable-food-economy-in-boston/.

Loh, Penn, and Boone Shear. 2015. "Solidarity Economy and Community Development: Emerging Cases in Three Massachusetts Cities." *Community Development* 46: 244–260.

Loh, Penn, Heidi Stucker, Hannah Sobel, and Jesse Seamon. 2013. "Dudley Resident Gardens: Summer 2013 Survey Results." *Practical Visionaries* (blog), December 20. https://pennloh.wordpress.com/2013/12/20/dudley-resident-gardens-summer-2013-survey-results/.

Mauss, Marcel. 1990 [1924]. *The Gift: The Form of Reason for Exchange in Archaic Societies.* New York: W.W. Norton.

McClintock, Nathan. 2014. "Radical, Reformist, and Garden-Variety Neoliberal: Coming to Terms with Urban Agriculture's Contradictions." *Local Environment: The International Journal of Justice and Sustainability* 19: 147–171.

Medoff, Peter, and Holly Sklar. 1994. *Streets of Hope.* Boston: South End Press.

Mendell, Marguerite. 2009. "The Three Pillars of the Social Economy: The Quebec Experience." In *The Social Economy: International Perspectives on Economic Solidarity,* ed. Ash Amin, 176–207. London: Zed Books.

Miller, Ethan. 2006. "Other Economies Are Possible! Organizing Toward an Economy of Cooperation." *Dollars & Sense* 266 (July–August): 11–15. www.dollarsandsense.org/archives/2006/0706emiller.html.

———. 2010. "Solidarity Economy: Key Concepts and Issues." In *Solidarity Economy I: Building Alternatives for People and Planet: Papers and Reports from the 2009 U.S. Forum on the Solidarity Economy,* ed. Emily Kawano, Tom N. Masterson, and Jonathan Teller-Elsberg. Amherst, MA: Center for Popular Economics.

Morales, Alfonso. 2011. "Growing Food *and* Justice." In *Cultivating Food Justice: Race, Class, and Sustainability,* ed. Alison Hope Alkon and Julian Agyeman, 149–176. Cambridge, MA: MIT Press.

Oorthuys, Valerie. 2015. "Telling the Story of Food Justice: A Case Study of the Urban Farming Institute of Boston." Master's thesis, Tufts University Department of Urban and Environmental Policy and Planning. Available from Proquest database.

Polanyi, Karl. 2001 [1944]. *The Great Transformation: The Political and Economic Origins of Our Time,* new edition. Boston: Beacon Press.

Quiñones, Benjamin R., Jr. 2008. "Facets of Solidarity Economy." In *A Non-Patriarchal Economy Is Possible: Looking at the Solidarity Economy from Different Cultural Facets,* ed. Marcos Arruda, 17–85. Alliance for a Responsible, Plural and Solidarity-based Economy.

Ramírez, Margaret Marietta. 2014. "The Elusive Inclusive: Black Food Geographies and Racialized Food Spaces." *Antipode* 47: 748–769.

Restakis, John. 2010. *Humanizing the Economy.* Gabriola Island, British Columbia: New Society.

Rosenberg, Greg, and Jeffrey Yuen. 2012. "Beyond Housing: Urban Agriculture and Commercial Development by Community Land Trusts." Lincoln Institute of Land Policy. www.lincolninst.edu/pubs/2227_Beyond-Housing.

Stoecker, Randy. 1997. "The CDC Model of Urban Redevelopment: A Critique and an Alternative." *Journal of Urban Affairs* 19: 1–22.

Swyngedouw, Erik, and Nikolas C. Heynen. 2003. "Urban Political Ecology, Justice and the Politics of Scale." *Antipode* 35: 898–918.

Tanaka, Aaron. 2015. Boston Impact Initiative. Personal communication.

Thaden, Emily. 2012. "Results of the 2011 Comprehensive CLT Survey." The Housing Fund, Vanderbilt University, in partnership with National Community Land Trust Network and Lincoln Institute of Land Policy. http://cltnetwork.org/wp-content/uploads/2014/01/2011-Comprehensive-CLT-Survey.pdf.

Walsh, Martin J. 2014. "Housing a Changing City: Boston 2030." Boston Mayor's Office, October. www.cityofboston.gov/dnd/boston2030.asp.

White, Monica M. 2010. "Shouldering Responsibility for the Delivery of Human Rights: A Case Study of the D-Town Farmers of Detroit." *Race/Ethnicity: Multidisciplinary Global Perspectives* 3: 189–211.

Wright, Erik O. 2010. *Envisioning Real Utopias*. London: Verso.

TWELVE

———

Grounding the U.S. Food Movement

BRINGING LAND INTO FOOD JUSTICE

Tanya M. Kerssen and Zoe W. Brent

> No one can live without breathing, eating and drinking. Food can come only from the soil; and Nature has provided earth, air and water for our equal use. Whoever denies our right to use either [sic] of these denies our right to life itself. . . . Those who have no money stand most in need of access to the soil . . . but government also allows those who are fortunate enough to be wealthy, to monopolize and speculate in the soil, and thus place it a vast deal further from the poor. The farther it goes from our reach the more helpless we are.
>
> J. E. THOMPSON,
> "Land Monopoly—Despotism," 1844

INTRODUCTION

Across the United States—the wealthiest country in the world—people are clamoring for healthy, affordable food and for the resources to produce it. Over the past two decades, the U.S. food movement has grown dramatically and has steadily incorporated a broad spectrum of issues, from labor and environmental struggles to calls for food security, food justice, and local, organic, non-GMO, and cruelty-free food. Once concerned primarily with the interests of consumers, the diverse communities and organizations that make up the U.S. food movement are increasingly drilling down to the deeper capitalist foundations and political–economic contradictions of our food system. This has brought many activists—from struggling organic farmers to underserved urban neighborhoods—to the bedrock of the food question: land.[1] Three decades of neoliberal globalization have driven a massive agrarian transition around the globe. The livelihoods of smallholders, farmworkers, fisher-people, communities of color, and Indigenous peoples have been severely eroded by global market forces. A global wave of dispossession and land concentration has shifted agricultural land use toward extractive industries and feed and fuel crops, thereby concentrating land ownership and dramatically reconfiguring landscapes in the Global North and South.

In the face of the momentous neoliberal transformations of the global food system, community-based food movements in the United States have grown tremendously over the past thirty years. These movements consist of diverse issue- and identity-based struggles focused on, among other issues, environmental justice; the rights of food workers and farmworkers; communities of color suffering disproportionately from diet-related diseases; urban food insecurity; and critiques of structural racism. While these movements are beginning to address the land question in various ways, they are mostly disconnected from the profound, if contentious, history of land and resource struggles in the United States—protagonized largely by Native peoples, African Americans, wageworkers, and family farmers.

Other than efforts to conserve agricultural land through trusts and easements, the contemporary U.S. food movement has remained largely detached from land issues. In part, this is because the agrarian question—the role of agriculture in the development of capitalism and the struggle between agrarian capital and peasants—was largely settled in the United States at the turn of the last century in favor of large, corporate, capital-intensive farms. Furthermore, the U.S. food movement—with some radical exceptions[2]— makes few references to global historical trends and movements around land grabbing, land concentration, and land reform. Therefore, we begin by providing some national and global historical context—in the limited way possible within this chapter's space constraints—regarding the centrality of land in U.S. and world history.

In the following sections, we focus on land in an effort to (1) make sense of the crises and rapid transformations underway in our nation's food system, invariably linked to global trends and processes; and (2) highlight land as a potential area of political convergence among the diverse groups that have organized their constituencies and supporters to confront these crises. We argue that understanding the history of land struggle, and placing it more centrally in the contemporary U.S. food justice agenda, can facilitate strategic alliances among movements centered on workers' rights, financial regulation, antiracism, antipatriarchy, the right to water, climate justice, and other concerns, thus strengthening the food movement's transformative potential. Finally, we suggest that the concept of "land justice"—the right of underserved communities and communities of color to access, control, and benefit from land, territory, and resources—provides a useful and inclusive strategic framework to "ground" the food justice movement in material concerns. We begin by situating land struggles in global historical context and proceed to highlight current trends in U.S. efforts for land and food justice. By focusing on the ways that land is intimately connected to a wide variety of food justice concerns, we hope to establish strategic common ground upon which different movements might find a basis for political convergence.

Land and land-based resources are rapidly becoming a central issue for landless workers, peasants, retiring farmers, young and aspiring farmers, urban residents, Indigenous peoples, artisanal and craft food makers, and community-based retailers. Indeed, land is at the nexus of multiple crises presently faced by underserved and vulnerable communities worldwide. Land concentration and barriers to land access lie at the heart of our global capitalist food system. Understanding the importance of land as the foundation of both capitalism and its alternatives is critical for building a stronger movement and advancing meaningful transformation of the food system.

LAND AND GLOBAL CAPITALISM

Land is the foundation of our food system—a source of nourishment and cultural identity, and the basis for life itself. Like food, it is a terrain of struggle, a reflection of power relations, and a potential lever for social transformation. If we are to transform the capitalist food system, it is critical that we understand how capitalism expands by availing itself of the land, its resources, and its occupants—while profoundly transforming our relationship to the earth. The belief that access to land is a fundamental right, and not a mere commodity from which to profit, has driven agrarian resistance since the dawn of capitalism.

For over four centuries, capitalism has expanded by expelling people from the land and turning the "commons"—land and resources collectively managed and used for community benefit—into private property, generally reserved for large landholders. In England in the sixteenth through nineteenth centuries, this process was known as the "enclosures" because it literally fenced off land that was previously accessible to all. The period was also marked by countless rebellions and "enclosure riots" by peasants defending their commons (Meiksins Wood 1998).

The landless masses produced by the enclosures were forced to sell their labor at starvation wages to the emerging manufacturing sector to survive. Indeed, industrial capitalism could not have developed without the coerced and exploited labor of former peasants. And it cannot continue without their exploitation either. For instance, a small farmer in Mexico undertaking the long and risky migration to the United States to work on a commercial farm, in a processing plant, or in a restaurant kitchen must first be "freed" from their land either by coercion or by policies that make it impossible to live from farming. This ongoing process of dispossession and dislocation keeps capitalism supplied with a vast, vulnerable, and underpaid reserve army of labor—now just as it did in sixteenth-century England.

In the United States today, we commonly associate land reform with communism or with countries of the Global South—for instance, China, the Soviet Union, Bolivia, Cuba, Mexico, Nicaragua, Guatemala, India, South Korea, and Zimbabwe, which all implemented some form of state-led land-redistribution program in the last century. Many twentieth-century land-reform projects—and the peasant movements that drove them—were intimately bound up with national liberation movements. The quest for political sovereignty was directly and inescapably linked to the land question and the ability to control and benefit from territorial resources.

Land reform was also a tool in U.S. state-building and counterinsurgency projects around the world after World War II. In the 1970s in Southeast Asia and again in the 1980s in Central America, the U.S. Agency for International Development (USAID) promoted massive, state-sponsored "land-to-the-tiller" programs. In a desperate attempt to keep peasants from supporting revolutionary movements, USAID helped right-wing governments buy land for distribution to poor farmers. In the 1980s and '90s, the International Monetary Fund, World Bank, and USAID began promoting "market-assisted land reform" (MALR) in debt-ridden countries of the Global South. Advocates of MALR frowned upon expropriating land from the rich to give to the poor, instead favoring a neoliberal "willing buyer—willing seller" model (Courville and Patel 2006, 6). The new paradigm was a move away from redistributive reforms toward a focus on "efficient" land markets (ibid.). These so-called market efficiencies usually turned out to be quite regressive, and peasants, vulnerable and burdened with debt, frequently lost their land.

In Honduras, for example, the MALR model supported by the United States—combined with policies that privatized cooperative farms, bringing them onto the global market—reversed the gains of previous land-reform programs of the 1960s and '70s. This led to a reconcentration of the country's richest farmland in the hands of a few wealthy businessmen (Kerssen 2013). Generally, land concentration around the world has remained high, even in countries that experienced land-reform programs earlier in the twentieth century.

Peasants and workers fought back with nonviolent (though often heavily repressed) occupations intended to force the hand of government to support the right to land. The most widely known land occupation movement is undoubtedly Brazil's MST (Movimento dos Trabalhadores Rurais Sem Terra, or Landless Workers Movement), whose one million members—many from desperately poor urban favelas—have succeeded in occupying and set-tling over eight million hectares (nearly twenty million acres) of land for community-based food production (Rosset 2011). The international peasant confederation La Vía Campesina, of which the MST is a member, later emerged in 1993 (now composed of more than two hundred million members on five continents). With its roots in peasant and small farmer organizations of the Global South, La Vía Campesina views land as a key battleground in the struggle against neoliberal globalization and for the creation of food sovereignty: "the right of all people to healthy and culturally appropriate food produced through ecologically sound and sustainable methods, and their right to define their own food and agriculture systems" (La Vía Campesina 2007).

LAND THEFT, CONCENTRATION, AND REFORM IN THE UNITED STATES

Everything in U.S. history is about the land—who oversaw and cultivated it, fished its waters, maintained its wildlife, who invaded and stole it [and] how it became a commodity ("real estate") broken into pieces to be bought and sold on the market.

ROXANNE DUNBAR-ORTÍZ, *An Indigenous Peoples' History of the United States, 2014*

Compared to the peasant movements of the Global South, contemporary U.S. food movements have been slow to address the land question—in spite of a rich history of land-reform advocacy and constant struggles of territorial resistance since the founding of the United States. To be sure, this history is complex and cannot be fairly addressed in this short chapter. In the first instance, it is a history fraught with the conflicts and contradictions of geno-cidal settler colonialism on one hand and the emancipatory aspirations of working-class European immigrants and enslaved Africans/African Americans on the other. The former—advanced by wealthy white men and political elites—advocated the westward occupation of Native American land in the interest of "Manifest Destiny," which claimed the United States had a divine right to rule the North American continent. The latter struggled for freedom, livelihoods, and land access within and beyond the frontiers of the emerging North American empire.

During the turbulent years leading up to the Civil War, industrial capital-ism expanded rapidly in places like New York, Pennsylvania, and Massachusetts. As mining, textiles, flour mills, and iron factories grew, so did abysmal working and living conditions. In the 1840s, a growing urban, working-class "agrarian-ism" flourished into a full-fledged movement demanding "land for workers," organized as the National Reform Association. The Reformists believed that "a more egalitarian distribution of land would diffuse wealth and democratize power, allowing the working classes to shape a more rational world" (Lause 2005, 66).

National Reform's collaboration with the abolitionist movement yielded an ideology of "free labor" and "free soil" that resisted the expansion of slav-ery into northern states and newly colonized territories. An interracial labor solidarity emerged, which condemned both chattel slavery and wage slavery, asserting land reform as the solution to both. George Henry Evans, one of the founders of National Reform, wrote that "not only did the slaves have a natural and moral right to take possession of themselves, but of land enough to live upon" (ibid., 80). This position, advanced by radical Republicans, Black leaders, and abolitionists, predated Union Army General William T. Sherman's (empty) promise of "forty acres and a mule" for former slaves by two decades.

For Native peoples, however, the 1862 Homestead Act—which provided the "free public lands" National Reform had fought for—and the 1863 Emancipation Proclamation, both signed by President Lincoln, were not victories but disasters. The Homestead Act privatized nearly three hundred million acres of Indigenous collective land (i.e., commons), breaking them up into 1.5 million homesteads for landless settlers (Dunbar-Ortíz 2014, 140). As Dunbar-Ortíz notes, this served as an "escape valve, lessening the likeli-hood of class conflict as the industrial revolution accelerated the use of cheap immigrant labor" in the East (ibid., 141). The Emancipation Proclamation, which allowed freed slaves to serve in combat, led to the creation of special military units composed of "Buffalo soldiers" sent to invade the "Wild West"—facing, of course, fierce resistance from Indigenous communities. As Native historian Jace Weaver writes, "The Indian Wars were not fought by the blindingly white American cavalry of John Ford westerns but by African Americans and Irish and German immigrants" (quoted in ibid., 148). Far from redistributive, the U.S. version of "land reform" was expansionist, genocidal, and racially determined.

As a result of U.S. land policies in the late nineteenth century that emphasized widespread, decentralized land ownership, by 1900 roughly 75 percent of (white) adult men in the United States owned land in rural areas (Engerman and Sokolof 2008). By comparison, in Mexico on the eve of the Mexican Revolution in 1910, only 2.4 percent of rural heads of household owned land (ibid.). After the Civil War, Reconstruction and the Freedmen's Bureau helped usher in a period of civic participation and agrarian prosperity among communities of former slaves. Ku Klux Klan violence and the Jim Crow laws, however, disenfranchised African American farmers, forcing many into sharecropping and wage slavery. In spite of this, by 1910, Black family farmers had acquired fifteen million acres "without benefit of the Homestead Act and in the face of great hostility and violence" (Holt-Giménez 2014, 3).

During this time, the U.S. food system was also undergoing technology-driven transformation and expansion, beginning with the introduction of mechanical reapers, combines, and tractors in the mid-1800s. Over the next century, the railroad greatly facilitated their adoption across the Midwest as farm machinery shifted from animal traction to steam and then to gasoline and diesel. The monopoly power of banks, railroads, and agricultural machinery giants helped introduce a new era of mechanized, large-scale, corporate agribusiness.

Following World War II, agricultural production intensified further and the number of large, corporate farm operators increased (Lauck 1996). New technologies such as the row-crop tractor and chemical inputs allowed farmers to work vast tracts of land and reduce labor inputs, thus unleashing a self-propelling cycle of capitalist investment that for much of the country "made it necessary to farm more land to pay for the technology" (Strange 1988, 46). While the modernization of agriculture is often presented as an era of seamlessly productive social and economic progress, it required the dissolution of much of the rural commons and the steady "transition" of farming families out of the countryside and into urban industries.

Meanwhile, corporate consolidation—both in farming itself and in upstream and downstream industries like fertilizers and food processing—prompted a mounting fear among farmers that their interests would again be subordinated to those of agribusiness. Lauck (1996, 204) points out that "fifteen years of mergers between 1950 and 1965 left 80% of value-added food products in oligopolistic industries." Reflecting these concerns, the First National Conference on Land Reform took place in San Francisco in 1973 and was followed by smaller Midwestern land conferences that "decried the onslaught of large corporate farms" (Lauck 2000, 31). Senator Fred Harris (Democrat, Oklahoma) even advocated the "need for land reform" in the U.S. Senate, and the National Farmers Union called for a "Land Reform Program in which the Federal government would buy good land for resale to small family farmers at reduced prices" (ibid.).

Despite these efforts, over the past four decades many farmers' worst fears have come to pass. Increased corporate control of food, farming, land, and water have steadily undermined family farming and eroded democracy in the food system. What's more, the zeal for exploring new mineral and energy resources, warns Dunbar-Ortíz (2014, 210), "could spell a final demise for Indigenous land bases and resources." And new processes such as financialization, gentrification, and climate change are compounding historical inequities. The impacts of these processes have been felt in the cities as well as the countryside: for instance, the foreclosure crisis unleashed in 2010 and the rise of urban agriculture movements have generated new land questions regarding the human right to housing, city land, and the urban commons. Just as rural land is out of reach of many would-be farmers, it is becoming increasingly difficult for underserved urban neighborhoods to access public or private land for community gardens, grocery stores, recreation, and community building. Bringing land into food justice radicalizes the work by addressing race, class, and gender "in relation to dispossession and control in the food system" (Holt-Giménez and Wang 2011, 98).

LAND AS A NEXUS OF CRISIS, RESISTANCE, AND TRANSFORMATION

This section outlines six issues frequently highlighted in the food justice movement—far from an exhaustive list—in which land is critical. As such, we argue that land is an important "nexus" between global crises and social justice struggles in the United States and one that could be seized upon as the basis for more effective movement building. Each of the areas described below is a site of capital expansion, growing crisis, and deepening inequality hinging on land, but each also embodies opportunities for alliances, resistance, and systemic change. While the U.S. food movement is fragmented and stratified, we argue that land—and the concept of "land justice"—can be a unifying issue. A focus on land among different issue- or identity-based segments of the food movement could form the basis of important alliances and become powerful levers for change within the food system. Nevertheless, for this to occur, historical divisions of race, class, and gender—between and within U.S. social movements—will need to be acknowledged and dealt with.

Land and Labor

> Labor and land are no other than the human beings themselves of which every society consists and the natural surroundings in which it exists. To include them in the market mechanism means to subordinate the substance of society itself to the laws of the market.
>
> KARL POLANYI,
> *The Great Transformation*, 1944

Along with capital, land and labor are the basic elements for creating value in the food system. Understanding how the evolving combination of land and labor has shaped the food system—and how the food system exploits them— is the first step in bringing justice to both.

The U.S. food system has always relied on the exploitation of vulnerable groups of workers—beginning with the importation of indentured servants from England in the 1600s to work in the fields and the transatlantic slave trade from the sixteenth to the nineteenth century (National Farmworker Ministry 2014). From the 1860s to the 1930s, as U.S. agriculture rapidly expanded, the United States imported large numbers of Asian immigrants; by 1886, seven out of eight farmworkers were Chinese (ibid.). Mexican peasants kept the U.S. food system running throughout World War II. In 1942, more than four million Mexican farmworkers were brought to the United States under what became the Bracero Program. Mexican labor was cheap, and, because of their foreign citizenship and their contract stipulations, farmworkers were prohibited from organizing or seeking redress against the rampant labor violations that plagued U.S. agriculture (Center for History and News Media 2014). Cheap immigrant labor turned World War II into an agricultural boom and placed the United States in the forefront of the global agricultural export market. Throughout the twentieth century, as large-scale and corporate-controlled agriculture expanded, the reliance on immigrant labor increased in fields and processing plants.

Of course, U.S. farmworkers have a long history of resisting exploitation and organizing for better conditions. In the 1960s, Filipino American grape workers in Delano, California, reached out to Latino labor organizer Cesar Chavez, then leader of the National Farm Workers Association (NFWA), to join their strike against low pay and poor working conditions. Aware of how growers historically pitted different races and ethnic groups against one another to break strikes, the NFWA voted to join the Filipino workers.[3] Drawing support from other unions, churches, students, and civil rights groups, the strike grew and turned into a nationwide consumer grape boycott that "connected middle-class families in big cities with poor farm worker families in the California vineyards [as] millions stopped eating grapes" (United Farm Workers n.d.). By 1970, the Delano Grape Strike and Boycott had succeeded in obtaining union contracts, better pay, benefits, and protections for California grape workers.

Today, most migrant farmworkers in agricultural states like California are farmers themselves—primarily Indigenous farmers from Mexico and Central America—who were forced to leave their land as a result of "free trade" policies such as the North American Free Trade Agreement (NAFTA) that undermined their farming economies back home (Bacon 2008). About five hundred thousand Indigenous farmers from Oaxaca, one of Mexico's poorest states, now live in the United States—three hundred thousand in California alone (ibid.). Unlike market integration treaties in the European Union that guaranteed worker mobility within their trade zones, NAFTA architects hardly took labor into account (Fernández-Kelly and Massey 2007). This led to a "lopsided process of development in which rising capital mobility and growing U.S. investment south of the border coincided with repressive efforts to limit the cross-border movement of Mexicans" (ibid.). In other words, capital could now travel freely, but human beings desperately seeking livelihood opportunities faced an increasingly militarized border region.

Upon arriving in the United States after a long, expensive, and perilous journey, migrant farmworkers tend to be severely underpaid, and they must endure conditions of isolation and fear under the constant threat of deportation (Minkoff-Zern and Getz 2011, VICE News 2014). Women are especially vulnerable, as illustrated by high levels of gender-based violence against female farmworkers (Meng and Human Rights Watch 2012). Unfortunately, labor exploitation is not limited to large-scale corporate farms but can also extend to small- and medium-sized family farms that feel the pressure to compete with larger operations (Gray 2014, Moskowitz 2014).

Farmworkers today are following Chavez's important legacy of nonviolent organizing. The farmworker strike—and allied consumer boycott—against Sakuma Berry Farm in Washington State is emblematic. Organized by the farmworker union Families United for Justice (Familias Unidas por la Justicia) with the support of the nonprofit Community to Community Development (C2C), the ongoing strike protests against sub-minimum wages, racial discrimination, poor living conditions, and workplace intimidation on the family-owned and operated berry farm (Scrivener and Guillén 2013). Additionally, C2C has been promoting women-led cooperatives and community land-ownership models in hopes of establishing local, worker-controlled food production.

Labor's relation to land, as outlined above, begins by generating an exploitable labor force by separating peasants from the land. Those hired back as laborers on large-scale agricultural enterprises will be touted as examples of "job creation." But the low-paid jobs generated by large farms pale in comparison to the livelihoods lost from small-scale farming.

Because roughly half of all farmworkers in the United States are immigrants without legal status—with some estimates of 70 percent or higher (Farmworker Justice 2014)—not only are their wages driven below the poverty line, but the costs for the reproduction of the labor force itself are neatly avoided by U.S. agriculture. The value of these savings is added to the surplus value extracted by the grower–capitalist in the production process, resulting in superprofits. This "superexploitation" of labor actually raises the market value of the land itself. While there are many factors contributing to the unaffordability of agricultural land today, the "subsidy" from the superexploitation of immigrant labor figures prominently in the creation of land value. The dual process of land dispossession and the superexploitation of labor creates profits and the accumulation of value for agrarian capital, but brings ruin to rural societies.

Thus, the value of land is strategically linked to full legal rights for all farmworkers—regardless of their immigration status. If large, industrialized farms were forced to pay living wages and provide decent working conditions, it would eliminate unfair competition with farms that do pay fair wages. It would also deflate the part of agricultural land values captured through the exploitation of labor.

Even with increased mechanization, land can only produce food (and profits) through the application of labor. Consequently, workers occupy a strategic point of leverage—especially when allied with consumers—for transforming the food system. Peasant demands for viable livelihoods and freedom from dispossession in the Global South are also structurally consistent with the demands for land access and labor rights in the United States. If family farms and living wages were prioritized in the United States and in international trade agreements, large-scale corporate agriculture would lose its false "competitive advantage," opening the way to a more equitable distribution of land.

Land and Finance

The rise of the finance sector in the world economy has led to widespread speculation, volatility, and commodity "bubbles" in which vast fortunes are made (and sometimes lost). In this section, we describe how finance affects the availability of rural and urban land for food production and suggest that understanding the destructive role of unregulated finance can help build links between inner-city food justice activists and small-scale and aspiring farmers.

Since the financial crisis of 2007–08, speculative investments in U.S. farmland have skyrocketed. Brian Briggeman, a former economist for the Federal Reserve Bank of Kansas City, estimates that approximately 25 percent of farmland acquisitions are a result of financial speculation and hedging (Food & Water Watch 2011, National Family Farm Coalition 2012). In other words, land is no longer just a productive asset; it has also become a financial asset—a process Fairbairn (2014) calls the "financialization of land." Farmland is drawing attention from high-net-worth individuals like George Soros as well as institutional investors like pension funds, hedge funds, university endowments, private foundations, and sovereign wealth funds (ibid.). The pension fund TIAA-CREF (n.d.), for instance, had an investment portfolio in farmland valued at $2 billion in 2010. University investment funds are also engaging in speculative landgrabs. Harvard, for example, has invested in farmland—from Romania to Chile to California—to bolster its asset portfolio (McDonald 2012).

This disturbing trend is a result of policy changes that paved the way for the institutional ownership of land. These include the deregulation of financial markets in the 1970s;[4] reforms in the U.S. tax code in the 1980s;[5] and declining Federal Reserve interest rates on loans to private banks since the 1980s, which provided more money for borrowing and investing. These financial manipulations are responding to the tremendous concentration of global wealth in corporate hands; the absence of productive investments (due to global recession); and the accumulation of vast amounts of cash—the "Global Pool of Money" (National Public Radio 2008). All this cash needs to be invested in something that will retain or increase value.

Meanwhile, small-scale farmers are finding it increasingly difficult to access the credit they need to keep operations going, and this often causes them to lose their land (Food & Water Watch 2011). According to the 2012 U.S. Census of Agriculture, the average age of farmers in the United States is fifty-six (U.S. Department of Agriculture 2010). As these farmers retire, young and aspiring farmers face high land prices and little or no access to credit (Stone 2014). As noted above, for farmworkers, poverty wages make the transition to farm owner especially challenging. And much of America's next generation is crippled by debt; in 2013, the total of all U.S. student loan debt exceeded $1.2 trillion dollars, the majority of which ($1 trillion) was owed to the U.S. federal government (Denhart 2013).

Faced with competition from institutional investors and burdened by debt and low wages, it is no surprise that aspiring farmers struggle to find land. According to a survey of over a thousand U.S. farmers carried out in 2011 by the National Young Farmers Coalition, the two largest obstacles young farmers confront are access to capital and access to land (Lusher Shute 2011). According to Bob St. Peter, director of Food for Maine's Future and a member of the National Family Farm Coalition,

> Here in the US, 400 million acres of farmland are going to change hands over the next 20 years. Whether those lands will support diversified family farms or multi-national corporations is one of the most important political questions in the US today. (Quoted in La Vía Campesina 2012)

Efforts to "tilt the playing field away from speculators and Big Ag" (St. Peter and Patel 2013) include programs to forgive student debt in exchange for growing food. As St. Peter and Patel argue, "A student loan payment could become a land payment under the right policy" (ibid.).

The trend in the financialization of land also affects cities, and communities of color have been most severely affected. For instance, the securitization of risky ("subprime") mortgages became immensely profitable for banks and investment firms. In the lead-up to the 2007 financial crisis, predatory, subprime lending practices are estimated to have caused a loss of $71–93 billion in asset values among African Americans alone (Harvey 2012, 54). Overall, four million people lost their homes in the U.S. foreclosure crisis, constituting a massive process of dispossession (ibid., 21).

The crash in real estate values—combined with the deregulated financial environment—laid out the welcome mat for investors to purchase land at rock-bottom prices and speculate on their eventual increase in value. The case of Hantz Farms in Detroit illustrates this trend. Under the guise of scaling up urban agriculture and revitalizing the city's blighted land, John Hantz hopes his farm of high-value hardwood trees "will create land scarcity in order to push up property values—property that he will own a lot of" (quoted in Holt-Giménez 2012).

The Detroit Black Community Food Security Network (DBCFSN) has voiced strong opposition to the Hantz project. As DBCFSN cofounder Malik Yakini observed:

> They don't have any sense of using urban agriculture to empower communities. They are driven by the profit motive.... There are major questions around use and ownership of land. And how land serves the common good as opposed to trying to serve the interests of wealthy individuals who are trying to make a profit. (Quoted in Wallace 2011)

Valuing farmland as a real estate commodity rather than for its productive value is a threat to both rural and urban farming and points to the need for alliances between urban food justice organizations like DBCFSN and rural communities and movements. For instance, taking private land out of the market—through agricultural and community trusts and easements—can protect it from financialization: there are nearly thirty million acres in agricultural land trusts in the United States. But unless government and philanthropies foot most of the bill, this is too expensive an option for underserved communities. A dual process of reregulation of the finance sector and viewing public land as a public good—for example, by making empty lots available for cheap, long-term leases—may provide a better avenue of access.

Addressing the impact of financial actors on land access further opens up the potential for convergence with mobilizations for financial regulation, such as factions of the 2011 Occupy Wall Street movement that continue to advocate for regulation and accountability in the financial sector. Opening up new land questions around the right to housing and further possibilities for alliances are groups like Occupy Homes—begun in Minnesota as part of the anti-foreclosure movement, it has helped several homeowners regain their homes even after their properties had been sold by banks (Nelson 2012).

Land and Race

Land is the basis of all independence. Land is the basis of freedom, justice, and equality.

MALCOLM X, 1963

Structural racism—in which people of color are politically, economically, and socially denied their rights—is evident throughout the food system. For instance, people of color are systematically exploited as cheap labor while also facing high rates of food insecurity and diet-related disease. Additionally, they also experience very low rates of land access and ownership. This section suggests that addressing institutional racism in land tenure is a necessary step in addressing the demands for agricultural land that are sweeping the country and in building food justice.

Historically, race has been a key determinant of land access and control in the United States. Military force first paved the way for the concentration of land in the hands of white settlers, displacing Native Americans and subsequently appropriating the land and labor of Mexicans/Mexican Americans, Japanese Americans, and African Americans (Holt-Giménez 2014). Since the abolition of slavery, African Americans faced persistent racism in their efforts to access and hold on to land. White European immigrants came to dominate farm ownership nationwide. According to the 2012 U.S. Census of Agriculture, some 96 percent of all "primary farm operators" in the United States are white and 98 percent of the acreage in privately held farmland is owned by whites (U.S. Department of Agriculture 2012, 13).

Landgrabs provoke more than homelessness and loss of livelihoods—they devastate people culturally and spiritually, wrenching them from the place that defines them. By 1887, Native peoples had lost 97.7 percent of their original land base (Olund 2002). The right to self-determination and management of what land remains under tribal control has been recognized by federal policies like the Indian Reorganization Act of 1934 and the Indian Self-Determination and Educational Assistance Act of 1975. However, the Indian Land Tenure Foundation argues that "federal, state, county and local governments often challenge American Indian sovereignty, especially when there are questions of jurisdictional authority" (Indian Land Tenure Foundation n.d.). Disregard for tribal sovereignty is heightened by the fact that a large portion of Indian reservations are located in the so-called "western energy corridor," sitting atop some of the most mineral-rich regions of the country (LaDuke 2002, 135).

A history of violent dispossession, broken treaties, and "legal" theft of Indigenous land has led to an increasing focus on sovereignty as the central Native American strategy for land reform (Dunbar-Ortíz 1984). Native peoples have used legal strategies to try to maintain control of existing reservation land and lay claim to land outside reservations or to government reparations for stolen land. Organizations like the White Earth Land Recovery Project in northern Minnesota also work to preserve and restore "traditional practices of sound land stewardship, language fluency, community development, and strengthening spiritual and cultural heritage" (White Earth Land Recovery Project 2013).

The steady loss of Black-owned farmland, from its peak of fifteen million acres, is due, in no small part, to the structuralized racism of public agencies like the U.S. Department of Agriculture (USDA) that excluded Black farmers from credit and farming supports offered to white farmers. Because of their heightened vulnerability to volatile market forces, the first farmers to lose their land in the U.S. farm crisis of the late 1970s were African Americans. Later, the crisis spread to white-owned farms, ultimately eliminating half of the U.S. farming population by the end of the decade (Strange 1988). Between 1920 and 2000, the population of Black farmers declined by 98 percent (Wood and Gilbert 2000).

The Federation of Southern Cooperatives/Land Assistance Fund and the Land Loss Prevention Project were founded in 1967 and 1982, respectively, to help African American farmers retain their land amid ongoing discriminatory practices and economic crises. In the 1990s, these organizations and the Farmers' Legal Action Group began investigating and further documenting discriminatory practices (Hinson and Robinson 2008). This led to a class-action lawsuit *(Pigford v. Glickman)* accusing the USDA of denying loans, disaster relief, and other benefits to hundreds of Black farmers. Following

Pigford, similar discrimination cases were brought against the USDA by Native American farmers *(Keepseagle v. Vilsack),* Latino farmers *(García v. Vilsack),* and women farmers *(Love v. Vilsack).* The original *Pigford* lawsuit was settled in 1999; in many of the cases, it took a decade or more for settlement payments to be disbursed.

The racism that facilitated white settlement of the United States and laid the foundation for the current food system reveals deep divides over land. These racial divides further weaken a rural sector that has been politically weakened by its small demographic. To be at all effective in opening up farmland access—for everyone—the food movement will need to build cross-race, cross-class, and consumer–producer alliances for land reform.

Land and Gender

Throughout U.S. history, women's labor—as farmers, slaves, servants, wives, mothers, and workers—has been critical to producing value from the land, reproducing the farm family, and ensuring the survival of land-based livelihoods. And yet women have generally been subordinate within the patriarchal model of both family farming and large-scale, corporate agriculture. In other words, the exploitation of labor as a subsidy to agrarian capital, as described above, is highly gendered, as women's unpaid or underpaid labor— in the field, factory, and home—often goes unrecognized in the creation of value. Paradoxically, women experience higher rates of food insecurity, even in the United States, where 35.1 percent of all female-headed households were food-insecure in 2010 (Patel 2012). The gendered nature of hunger and exploitation in the food system also takes place in class-specific and racialized ways, making an "intersectional" feminist approach—one that views sexism, racism, trans/homo-phobia, and classism as fundamentally inseparable—critical to understanding how patriarchy upholds an unjust system of land control.

Globally, women are the face of food production, but they are also the face of hunger. In most countries of the Global South, women farmers produce 60–80 percent of the food consumed (ActionAid 2010). They also carry out most of the work related to child care, food preparation, and collection of fuel and water (FAO 2013). Neoliberal policies, which spurred a predominantly male out-migration from the countryside and slashed government social services, increased the burden of women's unpaid agricultural and caregiving work (Nobre 2011). Additionally, women increasingly make up the majority of wageworkers in export-oriented agribusiness value chains—in jobs that tend to be temporary, poorly paid, and highly discriminatory.[6] Despite their central role in feeding people and creating value in the global food system, women are highly marginalized when it comes to control over land and resources. Women farmers, for instance, are far less likely to hold legal land titles than their male counterparts; while producing the majority of the world's food, women in the Global South own only 1 percent of the land (Courville and Patel 2006). And since their presence on the land is often invisible in state cadasters and property registries, they are highly vulnerable to land and resource grabs.

The rise of industrial agriculture in the twentieth century reinforced farming as a male-dominated profession, bolstering patriarchal and heteronormative gender identities, "which dictate that women are 'farmwives' and men are 'farmers'" (Trauger 2004, 289). In the Global South, U.S.-promoted industrial agriculture, known as the Green Revolution, systematically ignored women's agroecological knowledge, excluded women from policy decisions, and marginalized women from access to the capital required to participate in resource-intensive farming (Patel 2012). The FAO notes that "if women had the same access to productive resources as men, they could increase yields on their farms by 20–30 percent ... raise total agricultural output in developing countries by 2.5–4 percent [and] reduce the number of hungry people in the world by 12–17 percent" (quoted in ibid., 2).

And yet important changes are afoot. In the United States, typical "women's work"—such as caring for animals and growing food for family consumption, long viewed as marginal to mechanized, input-intensive monocultures—has gained new currency in the movement for local and sustainable food. New niche markets are opening up—for products like pastured poultry, organic eggs, goat's milk, mutton, wool, and organic fruits and vegetables—in which women producers are thriving (Trauger 2004). In Kansas, between 2007 and 2012, the state saw a spike in women farmers producing sheep and goats (87 percent increase), vegetables and melons (35 percent), and fruits and nuts (9 percent) (Kansas Rural Center 2015). According to the USDA's Economic Research Service, the number of women-operated farms more than doubled between 1982 and 2007, to nearly one million (Bader 2013). Women have also been important leaders in urban agriculture movements, developing community farm and garden projects in underserved neighborhoods around the country (Allen and Sachs 2007).

Nonetheless, on average, women's farms tend to be smaller—40 acres compared to 149 acres for male farmers (Karpf 2011). Their incomes also tend to be lower, with 75 percent of women farmers earning less than $25,000 a year (Bader 2013). Women still face large obstacles with respect to accessing land, markets, extension services, credit, and other resources. In response, organizations like the Iowa-based Women, Food, and Agricultural Network (founded in 1997) and the Oklahoma-based National Women in Agriculture Association (founded in 2008) work to amplify the voices of women farmers; advocate better policies, such as subsidies for farmers' markets and local-food promotion; and facilitate access to land, networking, and educational opportunities.

The number of lesbian/gay/bisexual/transgender/queer (LGBTQ) farmers is also on the rise. Beginning in 2014, the USDA, in collaboration with the National Center for Lesbian Rights, hosted the first Rural Pride Campaign focused on visibilizing the LGBTQ experience in farming and rural areas. One of the challenges is the perception of LGBTQ identities as fundamentally urban, a stereotype that identifies the countryside as "a sort of geographic closet that is inherently hostile and inhospitable to queer identity formation" (Brekhus 2011, 39). In fact, "almost 10 percent of all same sex couples in the United States live in rural areas; [they] are twice as likely to live below the poverty line than same-sex couples in cities; [and] they tend to have lower incomes than straight rural couples" (Johnson 2014).

Women farmworkers, food workers, and domestic workers arguably face even steeper challenges than women farmers, earning extremely low wages and subjected to gender-based violence and racism. According to the U.S. Department of Labor, in 2005 women farmworkers earned between $2,500 and $5,000 per year, compared to their male counterparts, who earned between $5,000 and $7,500 (cited in Allen and Sachs 2007, 6). Additionally, many women dislocated from their land in the Global South travel to industrialized countries like the United States to to find jobs as domestic workers. As a result, upper-middle-class women, most of them white, are able to work outside the home while transferring the tasks of household reproduction—procuring and preparing food, child and elder care, and so on—to poor women of color. While privileged women in the Global North have escaped onerous gendered work in the fields and in the home, this has mostly not occurred as a result of greater participation of men in these tasks (i.e., gender equality), but rather through racialized exploitation of other women.

Despite women's central role in food production, household reproduction, the creation of value on the land, and leadership in creating food and agriculture alternatives, the gendered nature of land and resource control in the food system remains sorely understudied. Genuine change in the food system requires recognizing the value of women's work on the land and in reproducing farmer and worker households, which have long served as a de facto subsidy to capital. Further, this must be done in an intersectional way that does not universalize the experience of white, cisgender, upper-middle-class women and that forges broad feminist alliances among women and with men.

Land and Water

Control over water is almost always linked to land. Historically, "water grabs" have often been behind large land acquisitions. Land-based water grabbing threatens communities in two key ways: (1) by appropriating water for irrigation-intensive, monocrop production or speculation (betting that land values will rise as water scarcity increases); or (2) by contaminating water sources that sustain local livelihoods and food production. In these ways, the land–water nexus brings smallholders, fishers, rural communities, and environmentalists into the same arena—though not always the same side—of land and water struggles.

First, access to water greatly affects the value of land. In California, agriculture uses some 80 percent of the state's surface and groundwater resources combined (Philpott 2015). As drought conditions have worsened, some farmers are drilling deeper and deeper for groundwater. In the Central Valley, the heart of California's industrial agriculture sector, aquifers lost twenty cubic kilometers of groundwater between 2003 and 2010—enough to supply household water to New York City for eleven years (ibid.). But global demand is driving the rapid expansion of water-intensive almond orchards throughout the Central Valley. And new financial actors are seizing the opportunity. TIAA-CREF purchased thirty-seven thousand acres of California farmland and now claims to be one of the top five almond producers in the world, rallying investors behind the crop boom and speculating on water scarcity (ibid.). Perversely, water scarcity puts a premium on water-intensive crops, incentivizing their cultivation, the drawdown of aquifers, and land grabbing in the areas where they can be grown.

Second, extractive industries like mining affect the productive and life-giving capacity of nearby waterways and groundwater supplies. According to the Community Water Center, the San Joaquin region of California's Central Valley has the highest levels of water contamination in the state, primarily as a result of "the application of fertilizers and pesticides, large-scale animal feed operations, and mining" (Community Water Center n.d.).

President Obama's "all of the above" energy strategy has expanded extractive industries by pushing for more domestic energy development—from agrofuels to oil to natural gas (Medlock 2014). The development of hydraulic fracturing or "fracking" is an especially fast-expanding sector of energy production in the United States, with serious implications for land and water. As government agencies approve exploration on public land across the country, concern is growing over its impacts—especially on water resources. Besides the intensive water requirements of fracking, the Pennsylvania Department of Environmental Protection, for example, found that drilling and fracking have contaminated 234 private drinking-water wells in the past seven years (CHPNY 2014).

In response, anti-fracking movements are emerging across the country. The 2014 elections saw the passage of four different moratoriums on fracking. Initiatives like the Our Power Campaign are connecting communities that are actively taking control of their own energy production—with projects in Black Mesa, Arizona; Detroit, Michigan; Richmond, California; San Antonio, Texas; Jackson, Mississippi; and eastern Kentucky. As the campaign website describes:

> With a deepening climate crisis, community rights to land, water and food sovereignty are increasingly necessary to both adapt to climate impacts and mitigate the causes of climate change. From Indigenous Peoples' struggles to retain ancestral water rights, to the creation of local seed banks, to burgeoning urban and rural struggles for local land reform—resource rights are an effective solution for a just transition. (Our Power n.d.)

Places like Alaska have also become the targets of new offshore oil drilling and large-scale mining operations. Bristol Bay, Alaska, the largest sustainably managed salmon fishery in the world, is currently threatened by a proposed open-pit copper and gold mine known as Pebble Mine. The mine is projected to produce between 2.5 and 10 billion tons of waste—enough to bury the city of Seattle—and require environmental treatment "in perpetuity" (Save Bristol Bay n.d.). Fearing the disastrous impacts on fishing communities, the Bristol Bay Regional Seafood Development Association has successfully campaigned to block Pebble Mine for nearly a decade. In response, the U.S. Environmental Protection Agency was forced to publicly recognize the disastrous potential impacts of the mine on the surrounding wetlands and fisheries.

Land and water availability and quality are not only fundamental to the livelihoods of farmers and fishers, but to rural and urban communities as well. To the extent that these actors can strategically direct their resistance against the financial, speculative, and extractive interests driving land and water grabs, resistance will be more effective and the movements will be strengthened.

Land and Climate

Climate justice activists and food justice activists are increasingly finding that their struggles are linked because the unsustainable and inequitable land-use practices that drive poverty and hunger are also creating environmental pollution and warming the planet. Land links climate justice and food justice struggles in four critical ways: (1) the greenhouse gas emissions generated by land use (from agriculture to the extraction and burning of fossil fuels); (2) the disproportionate impact of climate change on small farmers and marginalized communities; (3) land speculation related to climate volatility; and (4) "false solutions" to climate change that facilitate the further appropriation of community land and resources.

First, agriculture, livestock, and other related land uses (such as deforestation) are responsible for just under a quarter of global greenhouse gas emissions (Working Group III 2014). Yet not all agriculture systems are created equal. While industrial agriculture represents the majority of emissions from global agriculture, ecologically based practices—used primarily by small-scale farmers—not only contribute fewer emissions, but also sequester more carbon and other greenhouse gases (Lin et al. 2012). Nonetheless, the incentives to double down on large-scale, energy-intensive monocultures far outweigh the incentives to diversify agriculture and conserve natural resources.

Second, crop losses due to the effects of climate change—such as more intense droughts and floods—hit small farmers the hardest, threatening their hold on land. Climate change also affects livestock and fisheries through, for example, reductions in good-quality forage and changes in marine life due to increased water temperatures, respectively (U.S. Environmental Protection Agency 2014). Third, many investors view climate change as an opportunity. With increased climatic instability, land degradation, and water scarcity come the potential for soaring profits. As celebrity investor Jeremy Grantham observes, "Good land, in short supply, will rise in price to the benefit of the landowners" (quoted in Oakland Institute 2014, 4).

Finally, many so-called solutions to climate change also threaten to displace marginalized communities and small food producers from the land. For example, the Center for Food Safety documents the introduction of genetically engineered (GE) tree plantations as a strategy for "climate mitigation" and biofuel production. Fast-growing trees such as GE eucalyptus—approved for experimental planting across seven U.S. southern states—extend the industrial, chemical-intensive model that threatens soils and waterways, biodiversity, and land-based livelihoods.

In another example of pseudo-solutions to climate change, on September 24, 2014, the Global Alliance for Climate Smart Agriculture was launched in New York City, seeking to link agribusiness to expanded carbon offset markets. Despite its name, so-called climate-smart agriculture "incentivizes destructive industrial agricultural practices by tying it to carbon market offsets based on unreliable and non-permanent emissions reduction protocols" (Chappell and Majot 2014). For the international peasant movement La Vía Campesina (2014),

> Climate smart agriculture begins with deception by not making a differentiation between the negative effects of industrialized agriculture and the real solutions offered by traditional sustainable peasant agriculture.... Climate smart agriculture will lead to further consolidation of land ... creating dependency on so-called new technologies through their complete packages that include prescriptions of "climate smart [seed] varieties", inputs, and credit, while ignoring traditional tried and true adaptive farming techniques and stewardship of seed varieties in practice by farmers.

As demonstrated by the People's Climate March in September 2014, the movement for climate justice is fast gaining momentum and linking numerous community-based struggles—many rooted in the defense of land and resources. The burgeoning climate justice movement brings together urban communities of color fighting air pollution (e.g., the struggle of Richmond, California, against oil giant Chevron) and Native American communities fighting extraction on their territories (e.g., Navajo and Hopi resistance to coal mining in the Black Mesa region of Arizona; Our Power 2014). In April 2014, the "Cowboy Indian Alliance" in Washington, D.C., united ranchers, farmers, and Native Americans in opposition to the proposed Keystone XL oil pipeline (Khan 2014). In cities, churches, and college campuses across the country, a movement for "divestment" from fossil fuels is rapidly spreading (Maxmin and StudentNation 2013). Disinvestment necessarily implies a transformation of the model of industrial agriculture and extractive industries that most threatens the ability of people all over the world to live dignified lives on the land.

CONCLUSION: BRINGING LAND INTO FOOD JUSTICE

The food justice movement in the United States finds itself at an interesting moment of convergence and impasse. On one hand, financialization and the neoliberal "privatization of everything" have exacerbated capitalism's long-standing social, environmental, and economic inequities, unleashing multiple crises. This has intensified labor, race, gender, finance, water, and climate issues in general, expanding these sites of resistance within the U.S. food movement. On the other hand, many activists are finding it increasingly difficult to move forward on food justice issues without addressing the ownership, use, value, and distribution of capitalism's building blocks: land, labor, and capital. By focusing on the land question, we seek to link the diverse struggles within the food movement and to sharpen the structural focus of food justice. We chose land as a nexus (rather than labor or capital) because the food movement has largely neglected land as a justice issue, as a potential lever for important policy change, and as the foundation for powerful alliances across various issues in the food movement.

While the efforts to buy back land from the market for community use (e.g., community land trusts) are important examples of how U.S. movements are working to reestablish the public sphere and the commons, the food justice movement will never have enough money to buy all the land needed to tip the scales of the food system in its favor. Reform of the food system will be shallow without land reform. Clearly, this is hazardous— though not uncharted—political ground. It is one thing for women, underserved communities, and people of color to demand equitable access to healthy food, living wages, support for organic farming, farmers' markets, and food stamps. It is another, arguably far more threatening thing for them to demand land.

However, the food justice movement elides the land question at its own peril. While it may be tactically safe to limit social justice demands to the products of the food system rather than its means of production, strategically this is a dead end. Farms, gardens, corner stores, markets, and food hubs do not exist in cyberspace nor as smartphone apps; they are constructed on the land that is foundational to the wealth, politics, and socioeconomic control of community food systems.

Further, privileged communities are accessing land (through agricultural trusts, informal easements, leases, etc.) by using their access to capital, social connections, and financial opportunities even as underserved communities of color are losing their private and common property through gentrification and landgrabs. Unless it addresses the land question, the food justice movement risks being perpetually subordinated to the political agendas of those who have access to and control over land. And unless it addresses the contradictions of race, gender, and class, the food movement will not be able to build the social force needed to create structural transformation.

The six sites of struggle outlined above do not constitute an exhaustive list—nor are they mutually exclusive. Social change does not occur along a single trajectory, but at the messy intersection of race, class, sexuality, gender, and many other sites of power and identity. Nonetheless, the land nexus demonstrates key ways in which diverse movements across the United States are structurally linked through a struggle for land, resources, and territory. Of course, resistance to neoliberal land and resource grabs is not enough; new ways of thinking about property and resource management that reflect and honor the history of local land-users and oppressed communities are required. Movements must conceptualize "property" in ways that resist neoliberalism and open up spaces for justice-oriented, community-based alternatives. They must challenge market-led orthodoxy by insisting that access to productive land should not be restricted to the highest bidder, but rather distributed equitably.

It is difficult to imagine transformative change in the food system without government support—at the local, state, or federal level—for redistributive and restorative land reform. Given the diversity of struggles that converge around land, the challenge is to articulate a clear, pluralistic political platform with inclusive demands that are centered by land. Emerging from analyses of struggles in the Global South, the concept of "land sovereignty" provides a potential rallying point for uniting diverse agrarian struggles (Borras and Franco 2012). Land sovereignty demands access to, use of, and control over land and its benefits for poor and working peoples. It resists the corporate push to enclose the commons by asserting people's human right to land. Land sovereignty goes beyond viewing land reform as the struggle for a parcel of land to also considering land as part of a territory and part of food-system transformation.

What would land sovereignty—a concept that invites diverse and contextually specific interpretations of its meaning—look like for the U.S. food justice movement? Clearly, apart from addressing agrarian demands to reestablish the small and midsize family farm, it must support both rural and urban struggles against gendered and racialized food insecurity and gentrification. It must also support immigrant, women's, LGBTQ, and workers' rights. We suggest that it would, at its core, be a call for land justice. Land justice would ground a just food system, providing communities with both a physical place and political space to dismantle the neoliberal food regime. Land justice would provide the ground upon which communities could reconstruct not only our food system, but also our public sphere. Land justice—in theory and in practice—would require co-construction by a broad coalition of allies with a commitment to food justice.

NOTES

1. This chapter's epigraph is quoted in Lause (2005, 21).

2. Notably the U.S. Food Sovereignty Alliance and its members (http://usfoodsovereigntyalliance.org/).

3. The two unions merged in 1966 to form the now famous United Farm Workers.

4. Like the federal Employee Retirement Income Security Act in 1974 and the Reagan administration's deregulation of antitrust statutes (see Gunnoe 2014).

5. For example, the decrease in the tax rate on capital gains from 40 percent in the late 1970s to 15 percent today—in addition to the Reagan administration's Tax Reform Act of 1986—has had the effect of shifting the tax burden away from the financial sector and onto industry and labor (Gunnoe 2014).

6. For instance, women make up 60 percent of the workers in shrimp processing in Bangladesh, 79 percent of workers in floriculture in Zimbabwe, and 90 percent of poultry workers in Brazil (Mehra and Rojas 2008).

REFERENCES

ActionAid. 2010. "Fertile Ground: How Governments and Donors Can Halve Hunger by Supporting Small Farmers." April. London: ActionAid.

Allen, Patricia, and Carolyn Sachs. 2007. "Women and Food Chains: The Gendered Politics of Food." *International Journal of Sociology of Food and Agriculture* 15: 1–23.

American Farm Bureau Federation. 2015. "Fast Facts about Agriculture." www
.fb.org/index.php?fuseaction=newsroom.fastfacts.

Bacon, David. 2008. *Illegal People: How Globalization Creates Migration and Criminalizes Immigrants.* Boston: Beacon Press.

———. 2013. *The Right to Stay Home: How US Policy Drives Mexican Migration.* Boston: Beacon Press.

Bader, Eleanor J. 2013. "Women Lead the Way in Sustainable and Organic Agriculture." *Truth-Out,* November 17. http://truth-out.org/news/item/20047-women-lead-the-way-in-sustainable-and-organic-agriculture.

Borras, Saturnino M. 2008. "La Vía Campesina and Its Global Campaign for Agrarian Reform." *Journal of Agrarian Change* 8: 258–289.

Borras, Saturnino M., and Jennifer C. Franco. 2012. "A Land Sovereignty Alternative? Towards a Peoples' Counter-Enclosure." July. Transnational Institute. www
.tni.org/paper/land-sovereignty-alternative.

Brekhus, Wayne H. 2011. "*Out in the Country: Youth, Media, and Queer Visibility in Rural America* by Mary L. Gray (Review)." *Contemporary Sociology* 40: 39–41.

Bronstein, Jamie L. 1999. *Land Reform and Working-Class Experience in Britain and the United States, 1800–1862.* Stanford, CA: Stanford University Press.

Carlin, Tina. 2013. "Land Prices and Fracking." August 23. http://placestories.com
/story/142128.

Center for History and News Media. 2014. "Bracero History Archive." http://
braceroarchive.org/.

Chappell, M. Jahi, and Juliette Majot. 2014. "'Climate Smart Agriculture' Isn't. Agroecology Is." *Common Dreams,* October 9. www.commondreams.org/views
/2014/10/09/climate-smart-agriculture-isnt-agroecology.

CHPNY. 2014. "Compendium of Scientific, Medical, and Media Findings Demonstrating Risks and Harms of Fracking (Unconventional Gas and Oil Extraction)." New York: Concerned Health Professionals of NY. http://concernedhealthny
.org/compendium/.

Community Water Center. n.d. "Contamination." www.communitywatercenter
.org/contamination. Accessed December 20, 2014.

Courville, Michael, and Raj Patel. 2006. "The Resurgence of Agrarian Reform in the Twenty-First Century." In *Promised Land: Competing Visions of Agrarian Reform,* ed. Peter Rosset, Raj Patel, and Michael Courville, 3–22. Oakland, CA: Food First Books.

Denhart, Chris. 2013. "How The $1.2 Trillion College Debt Crisis Is Crippling Students, Parents and the Economy." *Forbes,* August 7. www.forbes.com/sites
/specialfeatures/2013/08/07/how-the-college-debt-is-crippling-students-parents-
and-the-economy/.

Dunbar-Ortíz, Roxanne. 1984. "Land Reform and Indian Survival in the United States." In *Land Reform, American Style,* ed. Charles Geisler and Frank Popper. Totowa, NJ: Rowman & Allanheld.

———. 2014. *An Indigenous Peoples' History of the United States.* Boston: Beacon Press.

Engerman, Stanley L., and Kenneth L. Sokolof. 2008. "Once upon a Time in the Americas: Land and Immigration Policies in the New World." In *Understanding Long-Run Economic Growth: Geography, Institutions, and the Knowledge Economy*, ed. Dora L. Costa and Naomi R. Lamoreaux, 13–48. Chicago: University of Chicago Press.

Fairbairn, Madeleine. 2014. "Farmland Meets Finance: Is Land the New Economic Bubble?" *Land & Sovereignty in the Americas Series* 5. Oakland, CA: Food First and Transnational Institute.

FAO. 2013. "International Year of Family Farming 2014 Master Plan (Final Version)." May 30. www.fao.org/fileadmin/user_upload/iyff/docs/Final_Master_Plan_IYFF_2014_30–05.pdf.

Farmworker Justice. 2014. "Selected Statistics on Farmworkers." November 6. www.farmworkerjustice.org/sites/default/files/NAWS%20data%20factsht%201–13–15FINAL.pdf. Accessed January 30, 2016.

Fernández-Kelly, Patricia, and Douglas S. Massey. 2008. "Borders for Whom? The Role of NAFTA in Mexico–U.S. Migration." *Annals of the American Academy of Political and Social Science* 610: 98–118.

Foner, Eric. 1989. *Reconstruction: America's Unfinished Revolution, 1863–1877*. New York: Harper and Row.

Food & Water Watch. 2011. "Don't Bank on It: Farmers Face Significant Barriers to Credit Access during Economic Downturn." March. www.foodandwaterwatch.org/reports/farmers-face-significant-barriers-to-credit-access/.

Fraley, Jim. 2007. "Reparations, Social Reconciliation, and the Significance of Place: A Legal and Philosophical Examination of Indigenous Cases in the United States and Their Global Implications." *Humanity & Society* 31: 108–122.

Gray, Margaret. 2014. *Labor and the Locavore: The Making of a Comprehensive Food Ethic*. Berkeley: University of California Press.

Gunnoe, Andrew. 2014. "The Political Economy of Institutional Landownership: Neorentier Society and the Financialization of Land." *Rural Sociology* 79: 478–504.

Harvey, David. 2012. *Rebel Cities: From the Right to the City to the Urban Revolution*. New York: Verso Books.

———. 2014. *Seventeen Contradictions and the End of Capitalism*. New York: Oxford University Press.

Hinson, Waymon R., and Edward Robinson. 2008. "'We Didn't Get Nothing': The Plight of Black Farmers." *Journal of African American Studies* 12: 283–302.

Holt-Giménez, Eric. 2012. "A Tale of Two ... Farms?" *Huffington Post*, July 10. www.huffingtonpost.com/eric-holt-gimenez/a-tale-of-two-farms_b_1660019.html.

———. 2014. "This Land Is Whose Land?" April 25. Oakland, CA: Food First. https://foodfirst.org/publication/this-land-is-whose-land/.

Holt-Giménez, Eric, and Yi Wang. 2011. "Reform or Transformation? The Pivotal Role of Food Justice in the U.S. Food Movement." *Race/Ethnicity: Multidisciplinary Global Contexts* 5: 83–102.

Indian Land Tenure Foundation. n.d. "Sovereignty & Jurisdiction." www.iltf.org /land-issues/sovereignty-and-jurisdiction.

Johnson, Kristine. 2014. "American Gaythic: LGBT Farmers Gain Visibility." *Civil Eats,* August 19. http://civileats.com/2014/08/19/american-gay-thic-lgbt-farmers-come-out-of-the-shadows/.

Kansas Rural Center. 2015. "Kansas Women Farmers Shift Agriculture and Food Production Trends." January 8. http://kansasruralcenter.org/kansas-women-farmers-shift-agriculture-and-food-production-trends/.

Karpf, Sheila. 2011. "Male-Dominated Big Ag Woos Women with Paternalistic Marketing Blitz." *Grist,* February 25. http://grist.org/factory-farms/2011–02–24-male-dominated-big-ag-woos-women-with-partenalistic-marketing-dr/.

Kerssen, Tanya M. 2013. *Grabbing Power: The New Struggles for Land, Food and Democracy in Northern Honduras.* Oakland, CA: Food First Books.

Khan, Naureen. 2014. "Cowboys and Indians Ride into U.S. Capital to Protest Keystone Pipeline." *Al Jazeera America,* April 22. http://america.aljazeera.com /articles/2014/4/22/keystone-xl-protestcowboysindiansranchers.html.

LaDuke, Winona. 2002. *The Winona LaDuke Reader: A Collection of Essential Writings.* Stillwater, MN: Voyageur Press.

Lauck, Jon. 1996. "American Agriculture and the Problem of Monopoly." *Agricultural History* 70: 196–215.

———. 2000. *American Agriculture and the Problem of Monopoly: The Political Economy of Grain Belt Farming, 1953–1980.* Lincoln: University of Nebraska Press.

Lause, Mark A. 2005. *Young America: Land, Labor, and the Republican Community.* Urbana: University of Illinois Press.

La Vía Campesina. 2007. "Declaration of Nyéléni." February 27. http:// viacampesina.org/en/index.php/main-issues-mainmenu-27/food-sovereignty-and-trade-mainmenu-38/262-declaration-of-nyi.

———. 2012. "Farmers Demand the World Bank and Wall Street Stop Grabbing Their Lands." Press release, April 23. http://viacampesina.org/en/index .php?option=com_content&view=article&id=1219:la-via-campesina-and-the-international-womens-day&catid=20:women&Itemid=39.

———. 2014. "UN-Masking Climate Smart Agriculture." September 23. http:// viacampesina.org/en/index.php/main-issues-mainmenu-27/sustainable-peasants-agriculture-mainmenu-42/1670-un-masking-climate-smart-agriculture.

La Vía Campesina, Sofía Monsalve, Peter Rosset, Saúl Vicente Vázquez, Jill K. Carino, and ROPPA. 2006. "Agrarian Reform in the Context of Food Sovereignty, the Right to Food and Cultural Diversity: 'Land, Territory and Dignity.'" *International Conference on Agrarian Reform and Rural Development Issue Paper* 5. www.nyeleni.org/IMG/pdf/landandfoodsov_paper5.pdf

Lin, Brenda B., M. Jahi Chappell, John Vandermeer, Gerald Smith, Eileen Quintero, Rachel Bezner-Kerr, et al. 2012. "Effects of Industrial Agriculture on Climate Change and the Mitigating Potential of Small-Scale Agro-ecological Farms." *Animal Science Reviews* 2011: 69.

Lusher Shute, Lindsey. 2011. "Building a Future with Farmers: Challenges Faced by Young, American Farmers and a National Strategy to Help Them Succeed." November 20. Hudson, NY: National Young Farmers Coalition.

Maxmin, Chloe, and StudentNation. 2013. "Why Divestment Is Changing the Climate Movement." *The Nation,* January 24. www.thenation.com/blog/172411/why-divestment-changing-climate-movement.

McDonald, Michael. 2012. "Mendillo Returns to Farms as Harvard Vies for Ivy Rebound." *Bloomberg News,* September 18. www.bloomberg.com/news/2012-09-18/mendillo-returns-to-farms-as-harvard-vies-for-ivy-rebound.html.

Medlock, Kenneth B., III. 2014. "The American Energy Renaissance: Who Is to Credit and What Is the Future Direction?" *Forbes,* January 28. www.forbes.com/sites/thebakersinstitute/2014/01/28/the-american-energy-renaissance-who-is-to-credit-and-what-is-the-future-direction/.

Mehra, Rekha, and Mary Hill Rojas. 2008. "A Significant Shift: Women, Food Security and Agriculture in the Global Marketplace." Washington DC: International Center for Research on Women.

Meiksins Wood, Ellen. 1998. "The Agrarian Origins of Capitalism." *Monthly Review* 50 (July–August). http://monthlyreview.org/1998/07/01/the-agrarian-origins-of-capitalism/. Accessed February 1, 2015.

Meng, Grace, and Human Rights Watch. 2012. "Cultivating Fear: The Vulnerability of Immigrant Farmworkers in the US to Sexual Violence and Sexual Harassment." New York: Human Rights Watch.

Minkoff-Zern, Laura-Anne, and Christy Getz. 2011. "Farmworkers—The Basis and Bottom of the Food Chain." *Globalization Comes Home* 18(1). http://reimaginerpe.org/node/6338. Accessed January 29, 2016.

Moskowitz, Peter. 2014. "Small Farms, Big Problems: Labor Crisis Goes Ignored in Idyllic Setting." *Al Jazeera America,* July 29. http://america.aljazeera.com/articles/2014/7/29/small-farms-labor.html Accessed January 30, 2016.

National Family Farm Coalition. 2012. "Institutional Investors and the Great American Farmland Grab." July. www.nffc.net/Issues/Corporate%20Control/TIAA-CREF%20Backgrounder_2.3.13.pdf.

National Farmworker Ministry. 2014. "Timeline of Agricultural Labor." http://nfwm.org/education-center/farm-worker-issues/timeline-of-agricultural-labor/.

National Public Radio. 2008. "Global Pool of Money Got Too Hungry." May 9. www.npr.org/templates/story/story.php?storyId=90327686.

Nelson, Sara. 2012. "Occupy Homes MN: The Anti-foreclosure Movement Builds Solidarity among Debtors." June 28. Antipode Foundation. http://antipodefoundation.org/2012/06/28/occupy-homes-mn-the-anti-foreclosure-movement-builds-solidarity-among-debtors/.

Nobre, Miriam. 2011. "Women's Autonomy and Food Sovereignty." In *Food Movements Unite! Strategies to Transform Our Food Systems,* 293–306. Oakland, CA: Food First Books.

Oakland Institute. 2014. "Down on the Farm—Wall Street: America's New Frontier." www.oaklandinstitute.org/sites/oaklandinstitute.org/files/OI_Report_Down_on_the_Farm.pdf.

Olund, Eric N. 2002. "From Savage Space to Governable Space: The Extension of United States Judicial Sovereignty over Indian Country in the Nineteenth Century." *Cultural Geographies* 9(2).

Our Power. 2014. "Our Power in Full Force." *YouTube,* September 16. www.youtube.com/watch?v=t5PPMoHeoio&feature=youtu.be.

———. n.d. "About the Campaign." www.ourpowercampaign.org/campaign/. Accessed January 7, 2015.

Ozer, Kathy. 2014. "Land Monitor." Rural Digital Advocacy Grant Program. www.ruralxchange.net/wp-content/uploads/2014/01/NFFC-Final-Report-for-posting.pdf.

Patel, Rajeev C. 2012. "Food Sovereignty: Power, Gender, and the Right to Food." *PLoS Medicine* 9(6).

Philpott, Tom. 2015. "Invasion of the Hedge Fund Almonds." *Mother Jones,* January 12. www.motherjones.com/environment/2015/01/california-drought-almonds-water-use.

Polanyi, Karl. 2001 [1944]. *The Great Transformation: The Political and Economic Origins of Our Time,* new edition. Boston: Beacon Press.

Rosset, Peter. 2011. "Food Sovereignty and Alternative Paradigms to Confront Land Grabbing and the Food and Climate Crises." *Development* 54: 21–30.

Save Bristol Bay. n.d. "About Pebble Mine." www.savebristolbay.org/about-the-bay/about-pebble-mine. Accessed November 20, 2014.

Scrivener, Leah, and Rosalinda Guillén. 2013. "It's a Labor Dispute, Not a 'Cultural Misunderstanding': Sakuma Workers Organize." August 25. Oakland, CA: Food First. http://foodfirst.org/its-a-labor-dispute-not-a-cultural-misunderstanding/

Shiva, Vandana. 1999. "Monocultures, Monopolies, Myths and the Masculinization of Agriculture." *Development* 42: 35–38.

Stone, Andrea. 2014. "American Farmers Are Growing Old, with Spiraling Costs Keeping Out Young." *National Geographic,* September 19. http://news.nationalgeographic.com/news/2014/09/140919-aging-american-farmers-agriculture-photos-ngfood/.

St. Peter, Bob, and Raj Patel. 2013. "This Land Is Our Land?" *Civil Eats,* October 18. http://civileats.com/2013/10/18/this-land-is-our-land/#sthash.SxIi1q2l.dpuf.

Strange, Marty. 1988. *Family Farming: A New Economic Vision.* Lincoln: University of Nebraska Press.

TIAA-CREF. n.d. "Brazil Farmland: Emerging Market, Growing Opportunity." www.tiaa-cref.org/public/about/asset-management/innovation-stories/brazil-farmland. Accessed January 5, 2015.

Torrez, Faustino. 2011. "La Via Campesina: Peasant-Led Agrarian Reform and Food Sovereignty." *Development* 54: 49–54.

Trauger, Amy. 2004. "'Because They Can Do the Work': Women Farmers in Sustainable Agriculture in Pennsylvania, USA." *Gender, Place & Culture: A Journal of Feminist Geography* 11: 289–307.

Trauger, Amy, Carolyn Sachs, Mary Barbercheck, Nancy Ellen Kiernan, Kathy Brasier, and Jill Findeis. 2008. "Agricultural Education: Gender Identity and Knowledge Exchange." *Journal of Rural Studies* 24: 432–439.

United Farm Workers. n.d. "The 1965–1970 Delano Grape Strike and Boycott." www.ufw.org/_board.php?mode=view&b_code=cc_his_research&b_no=10482.

U.S. Department of Agriculture. 2010. "2007 Census of Agriculture." *Quick Stats.* http://quickstats.nass.usda.gov/results/1B8E2222-EB1A-3EA7-B99C-39AB8070A164.

———. 2012. "Census of Agriculture Race/Ethnicity/Gender Profile." National Agricultural Statistics Service. http://agcensus.usda.gov/Publications/2007/Online_Highlights/County_Profiles/Vermont/cp50007.pdf.

U.S. Environmental Protection Agency. 2014. "Climate Impacts on Agriculture and Food Supply." www.epa.gov/climatechange/impacts-adaptation/agriculture.html#impactslivestock.

VICE News. 2014. "The Worst Job in New York: Immigrant America." July 23. www.youtube.com/watch?v=QXUdozfL7iM.

Wallace, Hannah. 2011. "Malik Yakini of Detroit's Black Community Food Security Network." *Civil Eats,* December 19. http://civileats.com/2011/12/19/tft-interview-malik-yakini-of-detroits-black-community-food-security-network/#sthash.AvyTLvmV.dpuf.

White Earth Land Recovery Project. 2013. "White Earth Land Recovery Project." http://welrp.org/. Accessed January 5, 2015.

Wood, Spencer, and Jess Gilbert. 2000. "Returning African American Farmers to the Land: Recent Trends and a Policy Rationale." *Review of Black Political Economy* 27(4): 43–64.

Working Group III. 2014. "Climate Change 2014: Mitigation of Climate Change." Contribution to the *IPCC 5th Assessment Report,* April 12. http://report.mitigation2014.org/drafts/final-draft-postplenary/ipcc_wg3_ar5_final-draft_postplenary_chapter11.pdf. Accessed September 25, 2014.

World Bank. "Urban Population (% of Total)." http://data.worldbank.org/indicator/SP.URB.TOTL.IN.ZS.

THIRTEEN

———

Conclusion

A NEW FOOD POLITICS

Alison Hope Alkon and Julie Guthman

IN 2006, WHEN COLLECTING DATA for her book *Black, White, and Green,* Alison spoke with Kirk, a manager at the first entirely organic farmers' market in the United States. Like most of the market's vendors and customers, he was white, college-educated, and politically progressive. Kirk described the farmers' market as a way to advocate for a healthy environment while working around, rather than challenging, an unresponsive state:

> I think that people continue to work on the government, but the government hasn't shown us anything good for an awfully long time. Democrat or Republican, they still don't get it.... With the government, it's like fighting fires with them. Trying to control the spread of GMOs and the release of the new most toxic chemical, like trying to stop the move from methyl bromide to methyl chloride or whatever it is.... We can't even get methyl bromide phased out and that's been worked on for years!... We do not want to see our food supply controlled by corporations. They're blowing it in so many other ways and they already control so much of the food supply! I can know where [my food is] coming from so that I don't have to be a part of that ... so that I can find an alternative to that and feed that.

For Kirk, as for many supporters of alternative food systems, farmers' markets represent an alternative, not only to agribusiness, but to traditional forms of social-movement activity. Alternative food activism maintains a grand vision for social change, one that imagines a safe and secure food system that can nurture healthy bodies, an environment in which biodiversity and a reverence for nature replace toxic chemicals, and a distribution of wealth away from corporate producers and distributors, shared among an array of small growers and entrepreneurs. However, as we and many others have written previously, this vision is limited, failing to see the needs and struggles of the low-income communities and communities of color, including farm and food workers, who are most harmed by the industrial food system (Alkon 2012, Alkon and Agyeman 2011, Allen 2004, Guthman 2011, 2008a, 2008b, Slocum 2007).

This volume has added another layer to our critique of alternative food systems, arguing that they are apolitical and nonstrategic in their pursuit of even this limited vision. There is little effort to build coalitions, pressure regulators, change policy and enforcement, or remake political institutions. Indeed, while food activists widely share Kirk's outrage at corporate control of the food system, farmers' markets do nothing to restrict these harmful actions. Their theory of social change is one of attrition. Individuals will become educated about the harmful practices of corporate food and will gradually abdicate their roles in the industrial food system, leaving it to collapse (Alkon 2012, Guthman 2011). While it's not written about food, this defeatist mentality is perhaps best summed up by the last verse of Lew Welch's "Chicago Poem":

> You can't fix it. You can't make it go away.
>   I don't know what you're going to do about it,
> But I know what I'm going to do about it. I'm just
>   Going to walk away from it. Maybe
> A small part of it will die if I'm not around
>
>   feeding it anymore.

It is a powerful poem, but the political system Welch wailed against is still here, and so is industrial food. The poet eloquently voices a longing to turn away from what is violent and toward what is beautiful. Opting out, however, may leave problems to fester and even grow. Moreover, it's a choice not all can make. Advocates for this kind of secessionist food activism have long failed to imagine, let alone learn about, the reasons why low-income people and people of color have not "walked away" from industrial food systems.

It's been a decade since Kirk conveyed his description of the farmers' market, and it seems, in part, to be a product of the larger political landscape of its time. Until the 2016 election, the George W. Bush presidency—made possible by a single vote in the Supreme Court—had been the high mark of cynicism in the United States, and young people, especially, were thoroughly disenchanted with conventional electoral politics. Moreover, his continuation of neoliberal economic policies—including tax cuts as a solution to any problem he saw—brought the economy to the brink of collapse in 2007, after which a major upward distribution of wealth took place.

Despite the shocking and horrifying election of Donald Trump, today's political landscape looks quite different, as the expectation-dashing Bernie Sanders candidacy also made clear. (Indeed, we would argue that it was only a set of unfortunate circumstances that gave Trump the victory—and that, had the Democratic Party played its cards right, a democratic socialist would have ascended to the White House.) Thanks especially to the new political sensibilities of the millennial generation, the past decade has witnessed something of a revitalization of the Left—and the new forms of food activism we've described in this book are part and parcel of this. To be sure, activists have been working on many of the issues described in this volume for decades. Yet two more recent struggles for economic and racial justice laid the groundwork for the New Food Activism we have described. It is fitting that they parallel the food justice and neoliberalism critiques that lie at the heart of this volume: Occupy and Black Lives Matter.

OCCUPY

In a blog post dated July 13, 2011, the anticonsumerist magazine *Adbusters* issued a call for activists to meet in Lower Manhattan on September 17 and "set up tents, kitchens, peaceful barricades and occupy Wall Street for a few months." When the day came, protesters marched through downtown Manhattan and gathered in Zuccotti Park. A few hundred spent the night singing, dancing, engaging in a general assembly meeting, and eating meals donated by local sympathizers. No demands were made, but, according to one extensive study of Occupy Wall Street, "A wide array of grievances was aired, with goals including a more equitable distribution of wealth, less influence of corporations and especially the finance sector over politics, more and better jobs, an end to foreclosures, bank reform, and various types of debt forgiveness—in sum, a halt to the rising inequality and economic injustice plaguing the country." The protesters' focus on economic inequality is perhaps best summed up by their clarion call that they are "the 99 percent"—in opposition to the 1 percent of elites who both caused and profited from the 2008 economic crisis, and who have long enjoyed disproportionate influence on political processes. This call resonated throughout the country and around the world. Within a week, there were occupations in Chicago, San

Francisco, Los Angeles, Toronto, London, Madrid, Algiers, Tel Aviv, Tokyo, Hong Kong, and Sydney. By early October, multiple occupations were sprouting each day. Videos of harsh police repression, including police spraying mace on nonviolent protesters from New York City to Davis, California, went viral and helped garner public sympathy.

Popular media generally depict Occupy as a failure. The occupations themselves were relatively short lived. Most had been cleared by riot police by mid-November, and repressive tactics and the oncoming winter dissuaded activists from trying again. The media, at first supportive and excited by the protests, turned against them, describing the camps as dirty, disorderly, and dangerous. Protesters themselves were alternatingly depicted as homeless criminals and "trust funders."

And yet Occupy has changed the way we talk, and even the way we think, about inequalities. The term *the 99 percent* and its counterpart *the 1 percent* continue to function as a shorthand for both income inequality and the corrupting force of money in politics. Inequality and the wealth gap are now fundamental aspects of the Democratic party platform, and the salience of these ideas clearly made the Sanders presidential run exceed expectations. The grassroots movement of food workers and other low-wage employees seized on the energy of Occupy to revive their call to raise the minimum wage, and cities throughout the country have raised their minimum hourly wages to as much as $15. Environmental-movement protests opposing the Keystone XL pipeline built on Occupy's energy to launch large protests that were eventually successful. Sixteen states and more than six hundred towns have passed calls to overturn Citizens United, a Supreme Court decision that significantly increases the influence of money in politics. Current demands for student debt reform, pay equity for women, and paid family leave are getting serious attention in a way that, ten years ago, seemed unfathomable.

Neoliberalism, as we described in the Introduction, operates not only at the policy level but also as a set of subjectivities, influencing our imaginings of what is possible. Many recall British Prime Minister Margaret Thatcher's refrain "There is no alternative," canonized as TINA, repeated to instill the idea that only a neoliberal policy framework would do. The food movement has promulgated its own version of TINA thinking in its emphasis on the building of alternatives, and on economic support for those alternatives, as nearly the sole way to create an environmentally and socially just agriculture. In Julie's parlance, neoliberalism had so narrowed the politics of the possible that the kinds of collective campaigns for regulatory reform depicted in this book seemed impossible, as did the reimagining of fundamental aspects of neoliberalism such as individualism and private property. Occupy succeeded in destroying the dominance of this TINA thinking, expanding the politics of the possible to include the kinds of food movements depicted in these pages. Some, like the campaigns to wage raises and improve working conditions depicted by Lo and Koenig, are aimed at practical reforms that will instantly improve the lives of those most harmed by the industrial food system. Others, like the land politics described by Michelle Glowa, are more radical and visionary, seeking longer-term transformations of neoliberal institutions like private property. Both of these projects are impossible within TINA thinking. Their strength is a part of the legacy of Occupy, a wave of social-movement activity aimed at subverting political and economic inequalities.

BLACK LIVES MATTER

In the summer of 2013, upon the acquittal of George Zimmerman for the murder of an unarmed youth named Trayvon Martin, an African American community organizer named Alicia Garza wrote a Facebook post titled "A Love Note to Black People," calling for her community to "get organized" and "get active." The post concluded with the phrase "Our Lives Matter, Black Lives Matter." Together with Patrisse Cullors and Opal Tometi, Garza launched this phrase as a hashtag and then as a movement. They used social media to reach thousands of sympathetic readers—largely marginalized people, including (and these of course overlap) Black people, women, the working poor, and LGBT communities. Their first action was a series of nonviolent protests in Ferguson, Missouri, after the murder of unarmed, eighteen-year-old Michael Brown by a police officer. More than five hundred activists arrived from across the country. Although Black Lives Matter was not the only group initiating this protest, they were among the best organized, and their name emerged as the phrase most clearly capturing the struggles of Black communities to affirm their right to exist in the face of police brutality, racial profiling, and broader racial inequalities. By autumn, the deaths of a number of other African Americans, some captured by cell phone cameras, had spun the hashtag into a mass movement. There are currently more than twenty chapters in the United States, and more in Europe, Africa, and Latin America (see http://www.blackpast.org/perspectives/black-lives-matter-growth-new-social-justice-movement). They have successfully brought attention to disparities in police killings, and to racism within the criminal justice system writ large. Indeed, the movement's 2016 platform, titled a "Vision for Black Lives," makes demands in a number of areas, including food and agriculture. Among these are increased access to healthy food, support for Black agriculture, protection for farmworkers, and an end to the privatization of prison labor and services, including farmwork and food services.

With its focus on racial justice, the Black Lives Matter movement parallels the food justice critique described in this book. While the phrase "food justice" has often been co-opted, a growing number of activists—food and otherwise—are increasingly seeing the intersections between inequalities and a variety of social issues. Alternative organizations rooted in marginalized communities, such as the food hubs depicted in chapter 9, have made racial justice a key component of their food work, tying it to legacies of racism and economic disinvestment in their communities. The Dudley Street land trust combines affordable housing and urban farming, helping create green amenities while alleviating the pressure of Boston's increasingly expensive housing market. Farm and food workers like those depicted in the second part of this book have made tremendous strides, from the success of the Coalition of Immokalee Workers' Campaign for Fair Food to local efforts to raise the minimum wage as high as $15 an hour; the latter have received some of their strongest support from food and restaurant workers. At the same time, collective regulatory campaigns, such as those described in the first part of the book, have at times succeeded in reducing the health and economic risks foisted upon vulnerable populations. In addition to these successes, in which marginalized communities have used food issues to organize for themselves, projects like the co-ops in chapter 8—which began in wealthier neighborhoods—are increasingly aware of and working to address inequalities within and beyond the food system. Many of the activists depicted in this volume recognize not only that Black and Brown lives matter, but that food activism can be a vehicle for improving those lives. This is a far cry from the color-blind food activism that began to receive media, activist, and scholarly attention in the early to mid-2000s. And though color-blindness continues to pervade much food activism, and resources are disproportionately available to whiter and more well-established organizations, the rise of a race-conscious food activism is certainly heartening, especially in a political moment when Black Lives Matter is forcing white America to confront institutional racism in the criminal justice system and beyond.

The old food activism remains alongside the emergence of the new. Apolitical and market-based approaches continue to drive the development of alternative food commodities and spaces of commerce. But increasingly, those working to create alternative food systems in marginalized communities draw upon and add to the food justice critique, fighting for recognition of their farmers, food entrepreneurs, and food traditions. And collective campaigns draw on the rising interest in all things food to bring supporters into their efforts to regulate the corporate food regime, restricting the use of pesticides and GMOs and improving farm and food workers' pay and working conditions. These forms of activism are not new—indeed, they are long-standing tools of the Left that far precede the current rebirth of alternative food systems. And yet what's new is the strategic nature of food activists, their increasing collaboration and coalition building, and the ways they make use of the popularity of ethical consumption to go beyond the building of alternatives and to work toward transformative change.

We began working on this project in 2013. Occupy had long been dormant and Black Lives Matter had not yet emerged. But as we contemplate the activism highlighted here, the parallels are striking. They suggest that what we are witnessing is not only a New Food Activism, but a new activism more generally, in which food politics is one arena among many. And it couldn't come at a better time. We write this before Trump has taken office. Yet through his suggested appointments, it has become eminently clear that he will take aim at virtually all the arenas in which the state has played a somewhat protective role, including worker rights, environmental health and safety, voting rights, and much else. We suspect that much of the public policy that supports food eaters, producers, and workers will come under attack as well: food assistance, pesticide regulation, research funding for sustainable agriculture—not to mention immigrant rights, given his most vocal threats to deport Mexicans and "build a wall." Over the next several years, it will be critical for food activists to join others and double down on efforts to thwart the Trump agenda, to resist the roll-back, and to defend democratic institutions.

This volume seeks to inspire activists and students to continue to see connections and create alliances between food activism and efforts to address inequalities, and to become deliberately strategic in their campaigns and efforts to effect broader and lasting changes for those who have most suffered from the past and current order. Progressive social changes in the food system, and in society more broadly, can only be possible if we continue to show up for one another—in the streets, in the courtroom, and in the halls where policy is crafted. Only by continuing to stand together can we transform our food system into one that nurtures us all. There really is no alternative.

REFERENCES

Alkon, Alison Hope. 2012. *Black, White, and Green: Farmers Markets, Race, and the Green Economy.* Athens: University of Georgia Press.

Alkon, Alison Hope, and Julian Agyeman, Eds. 2011. *Cultivating Food Justice: Race, Class, and Sustainability.* Cambridge, MA: MIT Press.

Allen, Patricia. 2004. *Together at the Table: Sustainability and Sustenance in the American Agrifood System,* new edition. University Park, PA: Penn State University Press.

Guthman, Julie. 2008a. "Bringing Good Food to Others: Investigating the Subjects of Alternative Food Practice." *Cultural Geographies* 15: 431–447.

———. 2008b. "'If They Only Knew': Color Blindness and Universalism in California Alternative Food Institutions." *The Professional Geographer* 60: 387–397.

———. 2011. *Weighing In: Obesity, Food Justice, and the Limits of Capitalism.* Berkeley: University of California Press.

Slocum, Rachel. 2007. "Whiteness, Space, and Alternative Food Practice." *Geoforum* 38: 520–533.

CONTRIBUTORS

JULIAN AGYEMAN is a professor in the Department of Urban and Environmental Policy and Planning at Tufts University. He is the originator of the concept of "just sustainabilities," the full integration of social justice and sustainability. His most recent book is the coauthored *Sharing Cities: A Case for Truly Smart and Sustainable Cities* (2015).

ALISON HOPE ALKON is an associate professor in the Department of Sociology at the University of the Pacific, where she also teaches in the MA program in Food Studies. She is the author of *Black, White, and Green: Farmers Markets, Race, and the Green Economy* (2012) and the coeditor of *Cultivating Food Justice: Race, Class, and Sustainability* (2011).

ZOE W. BRENT is a researcher with the Agrarian and Environmental Justice team at the Transnational Institute and is currently pursuing her PhD at the International Institute of Social Studies in The Hague. She works on issues related to food, land, and water politics. Her recent coauthored publications include "Contextualising Food Sovereignty: The Politics of Convergence among Movements in the USA" (*Third World Quarterly*, 2015) and "Sowing Insecurity: Food and Agriculture in a Time of Climate Crisis" (*In These Times*, 2016).

EMILY EATON is an associate professor in the Department of Geography and Environmental Studies at the University of Regina. She is the author of *Growing Resistance: Canadian Farmers and the Politics of Genetically Modified Wheat* (2013). Her current work is focused on the political economy of oil in Saskatchewan, Canada.

MELEIZA FIGUEROA is a PhD candidate in the Department of Geography at the University of California, Berkeley. Her current research examines the intersection of agroecology and urban sustainability in the Brazilian Amazon's "forest cities."

MICHELLE GLOWA is an assistant professor in Anthropology and Social Change at the California Institute of Integral Studies. Her research interests include critical political ecology, urban social movements, and agrifood studies.

JULIE GUTHMAN is a professor in Social Sciences at the University of California, Santa Cruz, where she teaches several courses in the politics of food and agriculture. Her publications include two multi-award-winning books: *Agrarian Dreams: The Paradox of Organic Farming in California* (2014, second edition) and *Weighing In: Obesity, Food Justice, and the Limits of Capitalism* (2011).

JILL LINDSEY HARRISON is an associate professor in the Department of Sociology at the University of Colorado Boulder. Her research is focused on environmental sociology, sociology of agriculture and food systems, environmental justice, political theories of justice, and immigration politics, with a regional emphasis on the United States. She has used her research on political conflict over agricultural pesticide poisonings in California, recent escalations in immigration enforcement in rural Wisconsin, and government agencies' environmental justice efforts to identify and explain the persistence of environmental inequalities and workplace inequalities in the United States today. She has published numerous articles and chapters and wrote *Pesticide Drift and the Pursuit of Environmental Justice* (2011), which won awards from the Rural Sociological Society and the Association of Humanist Sociology.

TANYA M. KERSSEN writes and teaches on the political economy of food, agriculture, and international development. She is the author of *Grabbing Power: The New Struggles for Land, Food and Democracy in Northern Honduras* (2013) and currently works with the international research and advocacy organization GRAIN.

BIKO KOENIG is a PhD candidate in the Department of Politics at the New School for Social Research, where he also teaches in the Environmental Studies program. His research is focused on labor, social movements, and nonprofit institutions.

JOANN LO is codirector of the Food Chain Workers Alliance, a national coalition of worker organizations throughout the food system. A graduate of Yale University, she has almost twenty years of experience in labor and community organizing.

PENN LOH is a lecturer and the director of the Master of Public Policy Program and Community Practice in the Department of Urban and Environmental Policy and Planning at Tufts University. He partners with various community organizations in the Boston area and with the Right to the City Alliance and the Center for Economic Democracy. From 1996 to 2009, he served in various roles, including executive director, at Alternatives for Community & Environment, a Roxbury-based environmental justice group.

LAURA-ANNE MINKOFF-ZERN is an assistant professor in the Food Studies program at Syracuse University, in the David B. Falk College of Sport and Human Dynamics. She is also affiliated faculty in the Geography and Women's and Gender Studies departments. Her research and teaching broadly explore the interactions between food and racial justice, labor movements, and transnational environmental and agricultural policy.

JOSHUA SBICCA is an assistant professor in the Department of Sociology at Colorado State University, where he teaches courses on social problems, social movements, and food and agriculture. His work is focused on the intersections between the politics of food justice, social movements, and social inequalities. He is also interested in coalition development and how social movements use food to resist and alter various power relationships.

ANDREW ZITCER is an assistant teaching professor at Drexel University in Philadelphia. He researches cooperative practices in social and economic life.

INDEX

Pesticide Action Network (PAN), 44, 80, 100

Pigford v. Glickman, 299–300. *See also* lawsuits

planning, 99, 172, 189, 238, 245, 270–271

policymakers, 2, 10, 233, 259

political ecology, 21, 259, 278

politics of consumption, 1–2, 133, 259

politics of conversion, 2

politics of the possible, 15, 82–83, 99, 261, 319–320

Pollan, Michael, 12, 17, 42

positionality, 71, 76, 78, 278

poverty: among food system workers, 45, 108, 113–123, 148, 159, 167; antipoverty activism, 18; effect on food access, 9, 211 (*see also* access); wages, 112, 296 (*see also* wages)

praxis, 125, 253

private property, 72, 232–253, 270, 273–274, 286, 320

privatization, 10, 233, 245–246, 260, 269, 274, 278, 307, 321. *See also* neoliberalism

privilege, 159, 160, 169, 251, 269, 276. *See also* race; racism

protests: against methyl iodide, 81, 90–92; against GMOs, 84, 90; against Wal-Mart, 111, 116, 150; confrontational tactics, 123–125 (*see also* confrontational politics); Occupy Wall Street, 318–320 (*see also* Occupy Wall Street); protection of street vendors, 119, 130; urban gardens as, 233, 246, 250

public health, 11, 36–38, 42, 49, 77, 83, 87–88, 121, 208

public hearings, 87, 91, 98

public land, 233, 238, 241–246, 252–258, 273, 275, 297, 304

public sphere, 75, 307, 309

race: and food systems, 10, 18, 259, 275, 291–293, 298–300, 308, 321 (*see* inequalities); and cooperatives, 191, 198–201, 207, 215–219; in coalitions, 109, 262

racism: anti-racism, 190; Black Lives Matter (*see* Black Lives Matter); economic development, 241, 259 (*see also* block busting; redlining); food justice, 6–10,

15, 161, 285; in food access, 211; in food systems, 216, 219, 233; in land access, 298–300

real estate, 19, 235, 245–246, 249, 251, 253, 258, 266, 270, 273, 288, 297

redevelopment, 249, 265, 267, 270

redlining, 9, 211, 265. *See also* housing

regulation: environmental, 36, 45; of industrial agriculture, 2, 14; of GMOs (*see* genetically modified organisms); of pesticides (*see* pesticides); of methyl iodide (*see* methyl iodide); of finance, 297–298; voluntary alternatives to, 6, 13, 70

resistance: land-based, 20, 238, 286–291, 305; to herbicides, 56, 68–69; to neoliberalism, 210, 217, 228, 253, 308; to racism, 10; to WalMart, 116. *See also* social movements; protests; contentious politics

Restaurant Opportunity Center, 110, 126, 172

restaurant workers, 3, 111, 113, 136, 171, 321

restaurants, 1, 158, 287

risk assessment, 81, 87, 93, 95, 98–100

Rosenberg, Jay, 249

Roundup Ready Wheat, 55–61, 64–77

Roxbury, MA, 257, 264–266, 273, 326

Roy, Arundhati, 13

rural: farmers, 19, 55, 58, 67, 161–162, 211, 216–217; food justice organizations, 172; land owners, 290–291, 295, 297, 300–305; Latin America, 166; pesticide reform activists, 81; perspectives on GMOs, 75; rural/urban tensions, 173

Safeway, 4, 116, 140, 162

San Francisco Bay Area Planning and Urban Research Association (SPUR), 247

Sanders, Bernie, 318

Saskatchewan Association of Rural Municipalities, 74, 77

Sbicca, Joshua, v, 10, 18–19, 107–132, 326

scientization, 90–95

seeds, 3, 56, 58, 60, 64, 67–69, 72, 75, 77, 182, 228, 247, 250, 304, 306

self-determination, vi, 22, 108, 119, 206–231, 233, 242, 246, 298–299

WalMart, 4, 11, 19, 110–119, 122–126, 133–134, 146–152, 191–192
Weaver's Way Co-op, 182–203
White Earth Land Recovery Project, 299
whiteness in food movements, vii, 1–2, 4–10, 136, 160–161, 187, 199, 207, 215–222, 298–303
Whole Foods, 110, 115, 137, 198, 219, 227
working conditions: for farmworkers, 15, 110, 144–147, 157, 163–165, 293–294 (*see also* farmworkers); for food workers, 19, 107–109, 119, 134, 148, 172 (*see also* food workers)
workplace justice, 134, 137
World Bank, 11, 287
Wright, Jifunza, 212

Yakini, Malik, 297

Zigas, Eli, 247
Zitcer, Andrew, vi, 19, 181–205, 327
zoning, 10, 257, 270, 271, 272, 276

Made in the USA
Middletown, DE
30 September 2020